R. McCoy

ss.

LINCOLN
IN TEXT AND CONTEXT

Collected Essays

LINCOLN
in Text and Context

Collected Essays

DON E. FEHRENBACHER

STANFORD UNIVERSITY PRESS
Stanford, California 1987

Stanford University Press
Stanford, California

Printed in the United States of America

CIP data appear at the end of the book

For two other Lincolns: Bernice and Bob

Preface

The first house that I can remember fronted on the Lincoln Highway, which ran through the middle of my home town. A few blocks away were Lincoln Park and Lincoln School, and the best hotel in town was called the Lincoln Tavern. On one schoolyard corner was a big boulder with a tablet commemorating the speech delivered there by Abraham Lincoln during the political campaign of 1856. In the 1920's the time elapsed since the Civil War was less than a full life span. Remnant members of the Grand Army of the Republic still took part in the annual Fourth of July ceremonies, and my grandmother vivified the war for me with the few known details of her father's death in the Battle of Stones River. No doubt this personal background had something to do with the direction that my historical studies later took. At any rate, the first publication of my professional career was an article on Lincoln appearing in the March 1950 issue of the *Abraham Lincoln Quarterly*. I have continued ever since to be deeply interested in the man and his times—and in the cultural tradition that is bound up with his name.

Most of the nineteen essays that follow are about Lincoln, and all are relevant to the study of Lincoln. Most of them have been previously published as articles, pamphlets, or contributions to books, but in varying degrees many have been revised for this collection. It is not a complete collection. A number of relevant publications are omitted here, principally those articles already substantially incorporated in books of my own.[1]

For the most part, I can only thank, without undertaking to name, all the persons and institutions that have given me help along the way, but I must single out Mark E. Neely, Jr., and Edward A. Weeks for making certain important materials available, and my wife, Virginia Fehrenbacher, for her indispensable assistance at every stage of the enterprise.

D. E. F.

Preface

Contents

PART I

YEARS OF CRISIS

CHAPTER I

The War with Mexico: Antecedent of Disunion

Anyone seeking the origins of the Civil War will be drawn sooner or later into study of the conflict that preceded it. The Mexican War proved to be not only a mid-century culmination of American territorial expansion but also a new and fateful departure in the sectional struggle over slavery. The conquest of New Mexico and California, by reopening the dangerous question of the status of slavery in federal territories, inaugurated the sequence of events running from the introduction of the Wilmot Proviso to the attack on Fort Sumter. The issue of slavery in the territories, persisting despite all efforts to resolve it, eventually opened up the career of an Illinois politician named Abraham Lincoln. His rise to national prominence and wartime leadership was thus, in a sense, made possible by that earlier war, which he had viewed at the time with a curious mixture of conventional patriotism, moral outrage, and partisan belligerence.

The campaigns of the Mexican War were just beginning when Lincoln won election to Congress on August 3, 1846. But sixteen months passed before he took his seat, and by that time the fighting was virtually over. He had supported the war at first, delivering a "warm, thrilling, and effective" speech to that effect at a Springfield rally.[1] But he arrived in Washington with a different outlook, one more in accord with the views of Henry Clay and other Whig leaders.[2] Very early in the session he introduced his "Spot Resolutions" disputing the assertion of President James K. Polk that Mexico had shed American blood on American soil. Soon he voted for a resolution declaring that the war had been "unnecessarily and unconstitutionally begun by the President," and shortly thereafter he delivered a set speech attacking Polk's role in both the initiation and the conduct of the war.[3]

Recent scholarship has discredited the notion, once widely held, that Lincoln's criticism of the Mexican War proved ruinous to his political career. There were other, stronger reasons why he was not renominated in 1848 and why the man nominated in his place went down to defeat.[4] Nevertheless, more than once in later years he found it necessary to explain that criticism and defend his patriotism—especially during the senatorial campaign of 1858, when his famous opponent repeatedly charged him with "taking the side of the common enemy against his own country."[5] Again and again Lincoln replied by drawing a distinction between support for the army in Mexico, which he had never voted to withhold, and endorsement of the "origins and justice of the war," which he had consistently refused to give. In the autobiographical sketch prepared after his nomination for the presidency, he declared: "Mr. L. thought the act of sending an armed force among the Mexicans was *unnecessary*, inasmuch as Mexico was in no way molesting, or menacing the U.S. or the people thereof; and that it was *unconstitutional*, because the power of levying war is vested in Congress, and not in the President."[6] This Whig interpretation of the Mexican War, though heavily freighted with partisanship, was also an expression of widespread uneasiness about the emerging moral character of the American nation. The origins of the Mexican War were then and are now a problem of conscience as well as history.

This essay is a slightly revised version of a paper written for a conference celebrating two hundred years of California history held at Stanford University in February 1970. It was published, along with the other contributions to the conference, in George H. Knoles, ed., *Essays and Assays: California History Reappraised* (San Francisco, 1973). The distinctiveness of the paper at that time, if any could be claimed for it, lay in the attention given to Mexican as well as American interpretations of the conflict.

On February 17, 1962, when observance of the Civil War Centennial was proceeding irrepressibly along its course from Fort Sumter to Appomattox, an earlier conflict suddenly made headlines on the front page of the New York *Times*. Attorney General Robert F. Kennedy, during a visit to Indonesia, encountered considerable hostility among students, one of whom demanded his views on the war between the United States and Mexico. "Some from Texas might disagree," he replied, "but I think we were unjustified. I do not think we can be proud of that episode."[7]

The ensuing storm of protest back home was curiously localized. Kennedy, as the *Times* reported, suddenly found himself "the center of a Texas twister." Governor Price Daniel expressed incredulity. A congressman from Dallas reaffirmed Texan pride in the struggle for liberty symbolized by the Alamo. Senator John Tower declared that the Attorney General had displayed a "glaring ignorance" of history and should apologize for his insult to the state of Texas. A publication of the Republican National Committee suggested that Kennedy might next recommend tearing down the Alamo to make way for urban renewal. To be sure, not every prominent Texan spoke his mind. Vice President Lyndon Johnson remained discreetly silent, following the lead of the White House, from which there came only the words "No comment."

With its customary thoroughness, the *Times* also consulted several historians and found them inclined to regard Kennedy as old-fashioned in his judgment of the Mexican War. "It's one of those questions that will never be settled," said Allan Nevins. "The general view of historians used to be that the war was wrong; more recently they have taken the opposite view. Mr. Kennedy, of course, is quite entitled to his opinion, which is the old, traditional one in Massachusetts."

What may have been most notable about the incident was its utter failure to arouse any interest in 49 states. Even the wrath of Lone Star patriots like Senator Tower resulted largely from their apparent inability to distinguish the Mexican War (1846–48) from the War for Texan Independence (1836).

American memory of the nation's first foreign war is surprisingly dim, considering its momentous consequences and its incredibly gaudy cast of leading characters. James K. Polk, the mousy protagonist of the piece, seems all the mousier surrounded by figures like Winfield Scott, a mountain of flesh, talent, and self-esteem; Thomas Hart Benton and his glory-bent son-in-law, John C. Frémont; Nicholas Trist, the barnyard fowl who suddenly became a gamecock; Gideon J. Pillow, Polk's former law partner and ipso facto a major general, whom William T. Sherman described as a "mass of vanity, conceit, ignorance, ambition, and want of truth"; and on the other side, Antonio López de Santa Anna—or most of him, to be precise, for the lower part of his left leg, sacrificed in an earlier battle, had been ceremoniously buried and marked with a monument by his intermittently grateful countrymen.

Even if the Mexican War were not otherwise memorable, it would deserve remembrance for enriching the American comic tradition with such antics as the fierce epistolary duel between Scott and Trist; Scott's arrest of that presidential favorite, General Pillow, on charges of insubordination; Frémont's quarrel with General Stephen W. Kearny, ending in Frémont's court-martial; and the Bear Flag rhetoric of William B. Ide, self-appointed leader of one of the most undermanned and short-lived republics in history.

The war with Mexico is a minor chapter in the military annals of the United States. Of course the public at the time followed the campaigns with an avid interest prolonged by the lively and sometimes rancorous postwar rehash. For a decade or so, place-names like Buena Vista, Cerro Gordo, Contreras, and Molino del Rey were familiar additions to the national vocabulary.[8] The war put one general in the White House, helped another one to get there, and contributed two more presidential nominees. But it soon fell permanently into the shadow of the much greater conflict that followed. Only thirteen years intervened between the Treaty of Guadalupe Hidalgo and the firing on Fort Sumter.

"Still another reason for our apparent indifference to the Mexican War," says Otis A. Singletary, "lies rooted in the guilt that we as a nation have come to feel about it."[9] Robert Kennedy's response to the Indonesian student is thus a case in point. Yet one suspects that most Americans are neither proud nor ashamed of the war but are simply oblivious to it. In the national consciousness it holds a very small place. There was no commission appointed to direct celebration of the centennial in 1946.

South of the border, it has been a far different matter. For Mexico the conflict was not only a major war but a national disaster, and it remains charged with the emotion and romantic imagery so often generated by lost causes. Including Texas, the land ceded to the United States amounted to about 55 percent of Mexican territory. Mexico today, if it had the boundaries of Mexico in 1835, would rank seventh among the nations of the world in area, and probably ninth or tenth in population.

It was the Mexicans who observed the centennial, honoring as usual the Niños Héroes, those young cadets who chose death rather than surrender at Chapultepec. The Niños receive no mention in many American accounts of the war, but Mexico has made them national symbols of courage and patriotism. A contingent of West Point cadets participated in the four-day ceremonies that began on September 13, 1947. Six months earlier, public planning for the commemoration had been momentarily suspended out of courtesy to a distinguished visitor, the President of the United States. But Harry S Truman, in an unadvertised departure from his official schedule, quietly laid a wreath at the monument to the boy heroes. There were some tears, it is said, on the faces of the honor guard as he did so, and soon Mexico City rang with the cry "Viva Truman!"[10] The outburst of public acclaim, which astonished and delighted American officialdom, was a generous response to a simple gesture of goodwill, but it also revealed the depth of feeling with which Mexicans still read this page of their country's history.

There is, in fact, a substantial body of Mexican writing on the war with the United States, most of it untranslated and generally unknown to Americans.[11] Even a cursory comparison of the two national historiographical traditions tends to put the war in a different perspective and freshen one's interest in the subject.

Both traditions incorporate diverse and changing schools of interpretation, but in one there is a fundamental conflict, in the other an underlying consensus. American historiography, like American public opinion in 1846, has been chronically divided over responsibility for the war and the justice or injustice of waging it. Among Mexican historians that subject has never been a serious issue. In their view, the facts leave no room for argument: Mexico was the victim of an aggressive war, deliberately begun without just cause and aimed at territorial conquest. In the fervid prose of one renowned scholar, Justo Sierra, the American menace on the eve of hostilities was "like a hand gloved in iron clutching the throat of a frail and bloodless nation, like a brutal knee in its belly, like a mouth avid with the desire to bite, to rip, to devour, while prating of humanity, of justice, of law."[12]

Mexican historians therefore have not been especially diligent or original in exploring the causes of the war. Instead, the principal task they have set for themselves is to explain how their country came to be such easy prey. To them, the origins of the war, being largely foreign, are of less interest than the domestic sources of Mexican vulnerability and military failure. The bitterest legacy of the conflict, it often seems, is not regret for the loss of provinces never really under effective control, but rather the memory of so much inept leadership, of so many lost battles, and of Mexico City prostrate under a conqueror's heel. The Niños occupy a lofty place in national legend in part because they appear against a background of almost unrelieved national humiliation. It was these little heroes, says one historian, who saved the honor of Mexico.[13]

This question of the reasons for the Mexican defeat, with all its ramifications, divided successive generations of Mexican historians into various schools of interpretation regarding the war with the United States. Inevitably, their differing views reflected the fundamental political and social cleavages, the dominant public issues, of their own times. For example, the disposition of liberal historians to fix much of the blame on the Catholic hierarchy reached its peak during the anticlerical crusade of the 1920's, but with the slackening of religious tension by the 1940's, the Church won exoneration from the worst charges that had been leveled against it.[14]

The adversary system has its advantages in scholarship as well as in courts of law, and the sharp disagreements among historians over the causes of Mexican failure in 1846–48 undoubtedly stimulated their investigations into the problem. Viewed as a whole, the body of writing that accumulated through the years was consistently nationalistic but often severely self-critical. In Sierra's picture of Mexican society on the eve of conflict, love for his country mingles with anger at its fatal shortcomings: "What was actually of no use was the army, debased into an instrument of cynical ambitions; of no use was the middle class, cowardly, fawning and self-seeking; of no use was the clergy, who considered themselves more important than their country and spent their zeal safeguarding their riches. . . . The only element that was of any use was the people, who were . . . exploited by all the others."[15]

Among scholars in the United States, it is the question of how the war began that has inspired the most interest and controversy. Of course the same could probably be said about the study of every other conflict in American history; the outbreak of war presents a classic problem in historical causation, with numerous forces and motives converging on one definite moment of decision. What may be most distinctive about the historiography of the Mexican War is the extent to which the main lines of interpretation were laid down almost from the beginning. The problem of its origins became a major public issue in the United States while the battles were still being fought. Persisting doubts about the justifiability of the war, rooted in the contemporary debate, have continued to animate the scholarly search for its causes. American historians have tended more or less to agree that the ultimate decision for war, whether justified or not, was made in the United States.

Opposition to the war, more partisan than sectional but strongest in the Northeast, was only partly an expression of antislavery sentiment. For half a century afterwards, however, the prevailing school of interpretation echoed the abolitionist rhetoric of the 1840's. Historians from William Jay to James Ford Rhodes in 1892 portrayed the Mexican War as the sequel to the annexation of Texas in a calculated Southern effort to enlarge the domain of slavery.[16]

This "slave-power conspiracy thesis" began to lose favor early in the twentieth century, by which time the Civil War and its aftermath seemed a closed chapter of American history. The thesis did not square with the facts, and it resulted in part from a disposition to read the struggle over the Wilmot Proviso back into the origins of the war against Mexico. Pro-war feeling in 1846 was probably stronger among Westerners than among Southerners, many of whom saw both national and sectional disadvantages in the acquisition of additional Mexican territory. John C. Calhoun refused to vote on the war resolution itself and then spoke out in vain for a purely defensive military strategy. In one of the most effective rebuttals to the slave-power thesis, historian Chauncey W. Boucher declared that he could find no Southerner "who openly or secretly advocated war with Mexico, before war had actually begun, for the sake of adding more slave states."[17]

The condemnation of the Mexican War along antislavery lines was offset by a number of postwar books that endorsed the official views of the Polk administration and placed the blame for the conflict on Mexico.[18] These works emphasized Mexican excesses in the Texan war, Mexican unreasonableness concerning the independence and subsequent annexation of Texas, Mexican failure to pay several million dollars of acknowledged private claims, and Mexican refusal to negotiate a settlement of its differences with the United States. This interpretation received little reinforcement during the long ascendancy of the slave-power thesis, but the new American expansionism at the end of the century produced a favorable setting for its revival. *The Justice of the Mexican War* was the title of one book published, and in *The Winning of the Far West*, a Princeton professor declared that American expansion to the Pacific was "singularly free from violence and fraud," constituting "an achievement in which every citizen of the Republic may feel an honest pride."[19]

It was in Justin H. Smith, however, that the Polk administration acquired its latter-day court historian. Smith's *The War with Mexico* (1919) is a work of such imposing scholarship that it has never been entirely superseded, but the interpretive passages add up to a consistent and often heavy-handed defense of American policy, as even the page headings reveal: Texas Annexed Justly, The United States Conciliatory, War Desired by Mexico, Polk's Course Pacific, Mexico the Aggressor.[20]

Smith's influence on later historical writing is undeniable. He made it difficult if not impossible for any serious scholar to persist in the reductive fallacy of viewing the war as nothing but a wanton attack on a blameless and peaceable neighbor. This does not mean, however, that his own star-spangled interpretation won general acceptance. Modern American historians have tended to divide the responsibility for the outbreak of hostilities—though not always evenly—between the United States and Mexico, while finding the sources of the war in a combination of Mexican debility and the aggressive energy of the United States. The latter was obviously the dynamic element. In the words of Glyndon G. Van Deusen, "The Mexican War was American expansionism in action."[21] The same epigram, with different emotional connotations, might have been written in Mexico at any time after 1846; it epitomized, in subdued language, the standard Mexican explanation of why the war began. Many Mexican historians also embraced the slave-power thesis, and indeed continued to do so long after it had been repudiated by American scholars.[22] In Mexican hands the thesis amounted to a refinement, not a contradiction, of the traditional Mexican interpretation, which blamed the war on the aggressive nationalism and land hunger that Americans called "Manifest Destiny."

In the United States, the national expansion interpretation was advanced as both a rebuttal and an alternative to the sectional slave-power thesis. Yet it also differed from the earlier and later vindicative history. Writers like Justin Smith tended to regard the acquisition of the Southwest in the Treaty of Guadalupe Hidalgo as the fortunate *consequence* of a war begun for other good reasons, while the expansion school treated the desire for such acquisition as a fundamental *source* of the conflict.

Charles T. Porter in 1849 had attributed the war to a national rather than a sectional passion for territorial aggrandizement, but his book was ahead of its time in this respect. Not until after the imperial adventures of 1898 did it become fashionable to present the Mexican War as a chapter in the general history of American expansion. Then books began to appear with titles like *Westward Ex-*

tension and *A Century of Expansion*. In 1907, Jesse S. Reeves summed up the new outlook when he wrote: "In its essentials the expansion of the United States to the southwest is not radically different from its expansion to the west over the Mississippi Valley, to the northwest into Oregon, and on across the Pacific to Hawaii and the Philippines."[23]

The effect was to normalize the Mexican War as part of a much more comprehensive historical process. Here, the influence of Frederick Jackson Turner becomes apparent; for he persuaded innumerable historians of his own and later time that the expansion of national boundaries—in fact, the whole pattern of national development—had been determined and shaped by the "inexorable" westward movement of the American people. Among the many restatements that could be quoted is one by Ray Allen Billington in the 1950's: "Certainly the relentless advance of the pioneer made expansion inevitable."[24]

The word "inevitable" and its equivalents appear more frequently, I believe, in writing about the Mexican War than in the literature of the Civil War. Used with abandon by Mexican as well as American historians, it is sometimes merely a literary flourish, but in the national expansion interpretation the idea of inevitability has functional significance. It may be that whoever studies Manifest Destiny inhales some of its vapors. Even Edward Channing, no Turner disciple, asserted without a trace of irony that "it was the destiny of the United States to extend to the Pacific."[25] At any rate, the expansionism synthesis tended to deemphasize the argument over the justice of the Mexican War by viewing the conflict as, if not quite inevitable, at least the product of irresistible historical forces. Yet at the same time there was a contradictory trend. The reputation of James K. Polk improved considerably in the twentieth century, especially after publication of his diary in 1910. He rose to the rank of tenth greatest president in the 1948 Schlesinger poll and later moved up to eighth. Far from being a mere chip on the wave of Manifest Destiny, Polk won a sometimes grudging respect from many modern historians as a man who knew what he wanted and got it. His determination, in their view, carried expansion into the Southwest when the opportunity presented itself.

Two scholars, Richard R. Stenberg and Glenn W. Price, went further and charged that Polk, using Commodore Robert F. Stockton as his agent, tried to foment hostilities between Texas and Mexico in the spring of 1845, a year before the war began.[26] Their evidence seems inadequate, however. A more successful thesis, anticipated in the 1940's by certain Mexican historians, was presented in Norman A. Graebner's *Empire on the Pacific.* According to Graebner, in the acquisition of Oregon and California the role of Turner's land-hungry pioneers has been exaggerated. In the Far West, unlike Texas, expansionism was primarily commercial rather than agricultural in origin. The harbors of the West Coast, especially San Francisco Bay, were the principal objectives. California in particular was "an area of vital concern for those relatively few merchants, politicians, travelers, and officials who appreciated its commercial significance." Expansion to the Pacific was achieved, Graebner concluded, "through clearly conceived policies relentlessly pursued."[27] Here, then, were the makings of another conspiracy thesis, with Polk's role changed from tool of the slave power to advance agent for mercantile capitalism.

The expansionism of the 1840's can thus be attributed to personal will or to impersonal forces. In modern historical writing, the emphasis often shifts from page to page, and the reader is sometimes left with the impression that the Mexican War was a deliberately engineered irrepressible conflict.

The difficulty may lie in the connection between Texas and California, different but inseparable parts of one complex transaction. The "relentless advance of the pioneer" had preceded national sovereignty into Texas, but on the Pacific frontier Polk anticipated destiny. "In his vision of an American California," says Charles Sellers, "he was ahead of all but a handful of dreamers among his countrymen."[28] Any assertion of inevitability must therefore be made in the past future perfect tense. Walton Bean, for instance, declares that "overland emigration would undoubtedly have made a change to American sovereignty inevitable in a few years."[29] The problem is to determine the relation between potential and kinetic forces. The road to war led through Texas, but the heart of the matter was California.

The conquest of California takes on different coloring in a Mexican version such as *California: Tierra Perdida*, published in 1958. The Bear Flag rebels become outlaws and filibusterers; Archibald Gillespie, messenger of destiny, becomes "Gillespie the spy"; Frémont's party is an "insolent band of adventurers."[30] For the most part, however, Mexican historians have passed lightly over the American occupation of California, realizing that the fate of the province was decided in other places.

The *occupation* itself required no great expenditure of military effort, and only the details were affected by the activities of Frémont and the Bear Flaggers. The *cession* of the Southwest, on the other hand, resulted from a string of hard-won victories in Mexico. California was acquired by war, and there is little reason to believe that it could have been acquired without war.[31] Efforts at purchase were plainly useless. The potentialities of the Larkin intrigue for peaceful separation have probably been overestimated, and in any case, remembering Texas, one can scarcely believe that Mexico would have submitted tamely to such a maneuver. The Bear Flag revolt was an incident of local history that happened only because war seemed imminent, and it actually took place after the war had begun and made it superfluous.

California was critically important, not as the scene of decisive events, but as the gleam in Polk's eye. One complication for historians is that Polk and many other Americans of his time saw a similar gleam in the eye of John Bull. These apprehensions were genuine, even though it now appears that they were mistaken. California, under tenuous Mexican misrule, seemed like a derelict waiting to be claimed as a prize. It had become easy to believe that the contest for possession was really with Great Britain, not Mexico.[32]

Polk, it has often and truly been said, preferred to obtain California by peaceable means if possible, but the critical question is whether his desire for California made the difference between war and peace. That is, did it shape the manner in which he handled the crisis with Mexico over Texas and other issues? If the record does not compel an affirmative answer, it clearly forbids a negative one, for there is too much consistency between Polk's actions before the war and the course that he followed after it had begun. His ordering of Taylor's army to the Rio Grande; his almost eager expectation of hostilities as a consequence; his decision to prepare a war message without waiting for hostilities to begin; his inflammatory assertion that American blood had been spilled on American soil; his rejection of James Buchanan's proposal to disclaim any intention of territorial aggrandizement; his prompt dispatch of Kearny's force to the Southwest; his authorization of Scott's campaign against Mexico City—all seem to be segments of a continuous line running ultimately to California. Whether or not hostilities with an angry Mexico could have been avoided entirely, the design and magnitude of the war were determined by the Polk administration.

The purposes that animated Polk are only part of the story. Equally important was the degree to which he had control of the situation. The situation itself had been created by many forces and influences, including the past actions of both nations. But no enumeration of general causes is ever wholly sufficient to explain a specific event like the outbreak of war. There is always some play of individual choice, some personal refining of cause into effect. For the Mexican leaders of 1845–46—Herrera, Paredes, and Santa Anna—the limits of discretion were exceedingly narrow. The chronic instability of the political system made them virtually the prisoners of popular feeling, and they had little room for maneuver in relations with the United States. Polk, on the other hand, enjoyed a wide range of options—wide enough, probably, to include the choice between peace and war.[33]

This does not mean that, except for Polk, California would today be part of Mexico. The pressure of American expansionism may indeed have been too strong for Mexico to resist indefinitely. But the timing of the acquisition could have been different, and with it the whole calendar of subsequent American history. If one were disposed to indulge in what Raymond Aron has called "retrospective calculations of probability," it would be interesting to construct a hypothetical alternative based on the assumption that Henry Clay, rather than James K. Polk, won the extremely close presidential election of 1844. Knowing Clay's views and those of his party, one can be certain that the counterfactual model would have diverged swiftly and radically from the actuality of history.

CHAPTER 2

The Galena Speech: A Problem in Historical Method

The following essay is a slightly expanded version of an exercise in documentary criticism that appeared originally in *Civil War History*, 16 (1970). Concerned with problems of both text and context, it illustrates the difficulty (discussed more extensively in Chapter 19) of determining the reliability, the precise substance, and the intent of many utterances attributed to Lincoln.

In the Dred Scott decision of March 6, 1857, the Supreme Court was responding to an invitation extended repeatedly by various political leaders for nearly a decade—an invitation to save the nation by resolving the dangerous issue of slavery in the territories. One constitutional historian includes Abraham Lincoln, Henry Clay, Stephen A. Douglas, Daniel Webster, Franklin Pierce, and James Buchanan among the many statesmen who became "increasingly intrigued with a judicial cure for the nation's illness."[1] Douglas and Lincoln make especially interesting examples because later they supposedly hedged or repudiated their willingness to accept a judicial determination of the question. For instance, the historian of the Supreme Court, Charles Warren, declares:

> Lincoln [in 1856] had publicly expressed himself as willing to leave to the Supreme Court, the constitutionality of the Acts of Congress dealing with slavery in the Territories, and to submit to its decision. In 1858, however, he stated that he declined to abide by the decision when rendered; and his views had a powerful effect upon the country.[2]

Yet there are reasons for doubting that either Lincoln or Douglas was as inconsistent as he might seem.

Douglas, in fact, never quarreled with the Dred Scott decision itself; the Court's denial of congressional power to prohibit slavery in the territories merely added constitutional gloss to the political policy that he had championed so successfully with his Kansas-Nebraska Act. What he rejected was the inference that the decision also demolished popular sovereignty by depriving *territorial legislatures* of the power to prohibit slavery. Having acknowledged on the floor of the Senate in 1856 that this too was a judicial question, he nevertheless insisted—and correctly so—that the powers of a territorial government were not at issue in the Dred Scott case.[3] The constitutionality of popular sovereignty thus remained an open question, since the Supreme Court had not yet passed judgment upon it. Accordingly, the controversial "Freeport doctrine," asserting that no such judgment could ever force slavery upon an unwilling people, applied technically, not to the Dred Scott decision, but rather to a hypothetical decision that might one day be rendered. Furthermore, the doctrine was not even a theoretical rejection of judicial authority, but instead a commentary on the practical limits of judicial power. Believing that in this way he had accommodated his views to the Dred Scott decision, Douglas felt no need to question or analyze the institution of judicial review. For Lincoln, however, it was a different matter.

Historians who include Lincoln with other advocates of a leave-it-to-the-Court policy are actually relying upon a single piece of evidence, one that nicely serves to illustrate two classic modes of the historical method—external criticism (involving the problems of authenticity and accuracy) and internal criticism (involving the problems of meaning and credibility).

During the presidential contest of 1856, Lincoln campaigned vigorously for John C. Frémont, nominee of the new Republican party. Among the many speeches that he made (more than fifty by his own count), was one delivered at Galena, Illinois, on July 23. The only record of what he said on that occasion is a newspaper report published three days later in the Galena *Daily Advertiser*. This article consists largely of five paragraphs enclosed in quotation marks, allegedly reproducing the climax of Lincoln's speech.[4] The passage seized upon by some historians is the following:

> Do you say that such restriction of slavery would be unconstitutional and that some of the States would not submit to its enforcement? I grant you that an unconstitutional act is not a law; but I do not ask, and will not take your construction of the Constitution. The Supreme Court of the United

States is the tribunal to decide such questions, and we will submit to its decisions; and if you do also, there will be an end of the matter. Will you? If not, who are the disunionists, you or we?

Are these the authentic words of Abraham Lincoln? One tends to assume so because they appear in the authoritative *Collected Works*. The historian who uses such a source finds most of the work of external criticism expertly done for him. Authorship of each item is verified, and an exact date is assigned if possible; forgeries and apocrypha are excluded; variant texts are collated; emendations are made; allusions in the text (especially to persons) are explained; relevant circumstantial data are provided. Yet the *Collected Works* do not constitute either complete or unimpeachable Lincoln canon. On the one hand, there are many spoken words more or less credibly attributed to Lincoln that the *Works* do not reproduce, such as those recorded in contemporary diaries and letters.[5] On the other hand, the documents contained in the *Works* are by no means equally reliable just because they passed the standard test for inclusion. An ALS (autograph letter signed), for instance, inspires more confidence than a letter printed in a newspaper, with the original not extant.[6]

The many newspaper reports of Lincoln speeches that appear in the *Collected Works* may be divided into several categories as historical sources. First, there are the speeches probably printed from manuscript copies provided by Lincoln but now no longer extant (such as the eulogy on Henry Clay delivered in 1852). Second, there are the speeches recorded in shorthand by stenographic reporters (such as the Lincoln-Douglas debates). Third, there are the summaries and extracts of speeches written by reporters, usually from notes taken on the spot (such as many of the brief public statements that Lincoln made on the journey to Washington in 1861). The third category is obviously somewhat less reliable than the other two, and the report of the Galena speech is an especially dubious case within that category.

For one thing, the journalist who reproduced Lincoln's remarks did so, according to his acknowledgment, "from memory." That is, he had no manuscript copy, no shorthand transcript, no notes of any kind, and he did not reveal just when, during the three-day interval, he undertook this feat of precise recall. The words in the passage, then, are not Lincoln's but rather those of a reporter doing his best, whatever that may have been, to remember what Lincoln had said.

Furthermore, the two most reliable records of Lincoln's campaign oratory in 1856 are the stenographic report of an address delivered at Kalamazoo, Michigan, and a manuscript of about two thousand words in his own handwriting, which may have been used as the basis of a number of speeches, since it includes their principal themes. In neither of these documents is there any suggestion of submitting the territorial question to the judiciary.[7]

Newspaper accounts of other Lincoln speeches during the campaign indicate that his line of argument remained fairly consistent. Yet nowhere except at Galena was there any report of his mentioning the Supreme Court or discussing the constitutionality of congressional restrictions on the extension of slavery.[8] Instead, his constant insistence that slavery *must* be restricted plainly assumed the power of Congress to do so. Historical precedents, after all, lent full support to such an assumption. The remarks on the subject attributed to Lincoln at Galena are unique in the entire body of the *Collected Works*, and the interpretation placed on those alleged remarks is incompatible with the views that he repeatedly and emphatically enunciated throughout the 1850's.

It is also important to note that Lincoln himself later questioned the accuracy of the newspaper version of his Galena speech. In the autobiography prepared soon after his nomination for the presidency, he wrote:

> In the canvass of 1856, Mr. L. made over fifty speeches, no one of which, so far as he remembers, was put in print. One of them was made at Galena, but Mr. L. has no recollection of any part of it being printed; nor does he remember whether in that speech he said anything about a Supreme court decision. He may have spoken upon that subject; and some of the newspapers may have reported him as saying what is now ascribed to him; but he thinks he could not have expressed himself as represented.[9]

The mildness and candid uncertainty of this statement make the concluding disclaimer all the more credible. Without pretending to remember what he had said on a specific occasion four years earlier, Lincoln was nevertheless sure that his supposed endorsement of a judicial settlement did not ring true. It would have been contrary to the ruling logic and very purpose of his efforts in 1856. Yet the Galena reporter's reconstruction of Lincoln's words can hardly be dismissed out of hand. As an exact transcription deserving to be enclosed in quotation marks, it is clearly suspect, but the reporter, who admired Lincoln, had no intention of misrepresenting him, and his memory after three days was no doubt more reliable than Lincoln's after four years.[10] One must consider it a possibility, at least, that Lincoln, though his phrasing and emphasis may have been different, did say *something* at Galena about the Supreme Court as an arbiter of the territorial question. Is there any way to reconcile this possibility with Lincoln's stated convictions and the general line of his argument in 1856? There is, if one reads the passage in its immediate historical context instead of associating it with the Dred Scott decision, which came more than seven months later.

The Galena *Daily Advertiser*'s heading for the speech was LINCOLN ON DISUNION. Throughout the campaign, Lincoln gave much of his attention to the charge that the Republican party was dangerously sectional and that Frémont's election would mean disruption of the Union. The controversy over the extension of slavery, he maintained, was as much the product of Southern as of Northern sectionalism. The issue would cease to be sectional only if one side yielded, and why should right yield to wrong? As for the Union, no Republican had any intention of dissolving it. Disruption, if it should occur, would be the work of other hands. The Republicans, who were endeavoring only to obtain control of the government by legal means, could scarcely be called disunionists.[11]

Whether persuasive or not, these arguments were the context in which Lincoln mentioned a judicial determination of the territorial issue, if he mentioned it at all. Here is the sentence immediately preceding the Supreme Court passage in his Galena speech: "We, the majority, being able constitutionally to do all that we purpose, would have no desire to dissolve the Union." What followed was certainly not a proposal that the whole problem be dumped in the lap of the federal judiciary. Having asserted the constitutionality of the Republican program, why then reverse himself and call for a court test of its constitutionality? The Supreme Court passage, if it is authentic, can have only one meaning. Lincoln was saying to the South: If you believe that prohibition of slavery in the territories is unconstitutional, you should seek a judicial remedy and accept the decision rendered, rather than disrupt the Union. Republicans, if confronted with the choice, would also submit to such a decision, *rather than disrupt the Union.*

An interesting parallel to the Galena speech is an address delivered by Samuel S. Phelps in the United States Senate on January 23, 1850. Phelps was a Vermont Whig with antislavery convictions but a conciliatory disposition. Unlike most New Englanders, he had voted for the abortive "Clayton compromise" of 1848, which would have encouraged a Supreme Court decision on congressional power over slavery in the territories.[12] Now, in 1850, he again proposed that this constitutional problem be submitted to the Court. "I venture to assert," he said, "that the great mass of the American people will sit down satisfied with the decision of that tribunal upon this question."[13] Here, apparently, is another name for the leave-it-to-the-Court list.

But in their context, the Senator's words have a more limited meaning. Phelps, like the Lincoln of the Galena speech six years later, was addressing himself to Southerners threatening secession if the Wilmot Proviso or its equivalent should be enacted. Such threats were premature, he insisted. "I trust that all parties are willing at the present day, before resorting to measures not sanctioned by the Constitution, to submit the constitutional question, *in the first instance at least*, to the tribunal created for the purpose of deciding it."[14] In short, "let the constitutional modes be exhausted before separate, independent, State action shall be resorted to." After an adverse decision, it would be early enough for the South "to begin to calculate the value of the Union." Thus, contrary to his one gush of optimism, Phelps was far from sanguine about the ultimate effectiveness of any judicial ruling on the territorial issue. What he offered, as in the case of the remarks attributed to Lincoln at Galena, was not so much a "cure for the nation's illness" as an alternative, "in the first instance," to Southern secessionism.

To one problem Phelps gave only passing attention because in the circumstances it seemed remote. What would be the *effect* of a Supreme Court decision against the constitutionality of a federal law excluding slavery from a territory? To what extent, for instance, would it inhibit the subsequent deliberations of Congress? And just how much was implied in a pledge to "accept" or "submit to" such a decision? Since no federal legislation of any importance had ever been invalidated by the Court, the full scope and force of judicial review remained undefined.[15]

Lincoln apparently gave no thought to the operative meaning of judicial review until the Dred Scott decision compelled him to do so. The decision struck at the Republican party's very reason for existence, and yet open defiance of the Court could scarcely be the response of a man who had once urged, "Let reverence for the laws . . . become the *political religion* of the nation."[16] Some Republicans were disposed to avoid the larger constitutional problem by insisting that the Court's invalidation of the Missouri Compromise restriction was obiter dictum and therefore without legal force.[17] Lincoln, however, preferred to go further.

A two-page fragment in Lincoln's handwriting indicates that he began to ponder the scope of judicial review at a time when the Dred Scott decision was impending.[18] But it was at Springfield on June 26, 1857, that he offered his first public comment on the decision and set forth a theory of judicial power. He was replying at this time to a speech made by Douglas two weeks earlier, and the two men argued the question further during their debates in 1858. His later remarks on the subject did not, however, significantly change the substance of this original statement.[19]

To begin with, Lincoln affirmed the finality of the Dred Scott decision as it applied to Dred Scott himself. In this limited respect, Republicans offered no resistance to the Supreme Court. Then, moving on to the larger question, he declared: "We think its decisions on Constitutional questions, when fully settled, should control not only the particular cases decided, but the general policy of the country, subject to be disturbed only by amendments of the Constitution as provided in that instrument itself." The phrase "when fully settled" controls the rest of the sentence, and Lincoln insisted that this condition had not yet been met in the Dred Scott case:

> If this important decision had been made by the unanimous concurrence of the judges, and without any apparent partisan bias, and in accordance with legal public expectation, and with the steady practice of the departments throughout our history, and had been in no part, based on assumed historical facts which are not really true; or, if wanting in some of these, it had been before the court more than once, and had there been affirmed and re-affirmed through a course of years, it then might be, perhaps would be, factious, nay, even revolutionary, to not acquiesce in it as a precedent.
>
> But when, as it is true we find it wanting in all these claims to the public confidence, it is not resistance, it is not factious, it is not even disrespectful, to treat it as not having yet quite established a settled doctrine for the country.

Thus the Dred Scott decision, according to Lincoln, was in an intermediate phase between promulgation and legitimation. Its doctrines were not yet the accepted law of the land. The Republicans, knowing that the Court had more than once overruled its own previous decisions, intended to work for such a reversal in this case. Neither was the Dred Scott decision, at its present stage, absolutely binding on the other two branches of the federal government. Here, Lincoln embraced the Jeffersonian view that the three departments—legislative, executive, and judicial—were coequals in their authority to interpret the Constitution.[20] Fundamentally, however, he was more Jacksonian than Jeffersonian in his theory of judicial power. He seemed less interested in asserting the coordinate authority of Congress and the president than in affirming the ultimate sovereignty of the people as interpreters of the Constitution. "Mere precedent," he quoted Andrew Jackson, "is a dangerous source of authority, and should not be regarded as deciding questions of constitutional power, except where the acquiescence of the people and the States can be considered as well settled." Lincoln, the Whig lawyer, would yield something more to precedent and something less to states' rights, while agreeing that the "acquiescence of the people" was essential.

In 1861, when he took the presidential oath administered by the author of the Dred Scott decision, Lincoln added a passage on judicial review to his Inaugural Address, saying in part:

> I do not forget the position assumed by some, that constitutional questions are to be decided by the Supreme Court; nor do I deny that such decisions must be binding in any case, upon the parties to a suit, as to the object of that suit, while they are also entitled to very high respect and consideration, in all parallel cases, by all other departments of the government. . . . At the same time the candid citizen must confess that if the policy of the government, upon vital questions, affecting the whole people, is to be irrevocably fixed by decisions of the Supreme Court, the instant they are made, in ordinary litigation between parties, in personal actions, the people will have ceased to be their own rulers, having, to that extent, practically resigned their government, into the hands of that eminent tribunal.[21]

Again, one phrase, "the instant they are made," has particular significance. Lincoln rejected the notion that judicial fiat automatically became constitutional law. He persisted in the belief that the issues associated with the Dred Scott decision were still unsettled, and more than once in the years ahead his administration would act on that assumption.[22]

Lincoln, it is obvious, never contemplated a frontal assault on the institution of judicial review. He was even willing to grant the Supreme Court some measure of preeminence as expounder of the Constitution. At the same time, he refused to accept the principle of judicial supremacy that eventually prevailed in the United States. To the remark of Charles Evans Hughes that "the Constitution is what the judges say it is," he would have replied, "Not absolutely and not instantaneously." Especially when a decision was blatantly partisan, seemed erroneous to a large segment of the populace, and contradicted long-established practice, it could not immediately become indisputable constitutional doctrine. Instead, according to Lincoln, such a decision must be legitimated by judicial reiteration and public sanction over a period of time. The people themselves were the ultimate arbiters of constitutional issues.

In political terms, Lincoln was of course trying to justify the platform and very existence of the Republican party without completely repudiating the authority of the Supreme Court. The need to do so dated from the Dred Scott decision, and there can be no doubt that the decision made him more suspicious of judicial power, more unwilling to concede that the Supreme Court is the sole arbiter of constitutional questions. Back in 1839, while defending the constitutionality of a national bank, he had referred to the Court as "that tribunal which the Constitution has itself established to decide Constitutional questions." Yet, even then he had linked the Court with Congress (and especially with the founding fathers in the First Congress) as joint authorities that had long since legitimated the bank.[23] The report of his Galena speech in 1856 is in any case a very flimsy basis for generalizations about his thought on the constitutional aspects of the territorial question. Even if one ventures to assume its accuracy, the leave-it-to-the-Court passage had a narrowly restricted meaning—namely, that either side in a constitutional conflict should be willing to seek and accept a judicial settlement rather than break up the Union. To read more than that from the passage is to wrench a dubious quotation from its authentic context.

CHAPTER 3

Political Uses of the Post Office

Before departing for London in the spring of 1861 to take up his new post as minister to Great Britain, Charles Francis Adams, in the company of Secretary of State William H. Seward, paid a courtesy visit to the White House. He went away mortified—and confirmed in his low opinion of Abraham Lincoln. As Adams later recounted the interview, the President engaged politely but somewhat abstractedly in the verbal amenities, told him that his gratitude should be directed to Seward, who had chosen him, and then, turning to the latter, remarked, "Well, governor, I've this morning decided that Chicago post-office appointment."[1] To Adams the shift from foreign affairs to domestic politics was bound to be disconcerting, but even he probably understood, better than we can today, why the naming of a postmaster for Chicago should have seemed so important to Lincoln.

Patronage was the bonding element of the nineteenth-century party system, and there were more appointments and contracts to be obtained from the Post Office than from all other departments of the federal government combined.[2] But patronage is only part of the story. In every community, the post office was the center of communication, and thus a center of local political power. It was responsible not only for the transmission of letters and other private mail, but also for the circulation of newspapers, periodicals, and government documents—then the principal media of mass information. To an extent now difficult to comprehend, postmasters of that era, even while performing their official duties, served as active agents of party enterprise.

What follows is a brief examination of the post office influence in local Illinois politics during the 1850's. The oldest piece of writing in this book, it is a slightly revised version of an article published in the *Journal of the Illinois State Historical Society*, 46 (1953). Style and content no doubt betray its still earlier origin as part of a doctoral dissertation. Yet I venture to believe that the information in it remains of some interest, and as far as I know, it has not been presented elsewhere.

The United States Post Office had never been completely shielded from the pressures of partisan influence, but the administration of

Andrew Jackson was the first to use it in any significant way as an instrument for the maintenance of political power. Entering the White House in 1829, Jackson persuaded the overly scrupulous postmaster general, John McLean, to accept an appointment to the Supreme Court, and then replaced him with a thoroughgoing politician, William T. Barry of Kentucky. Barry set a pattern of open partisanship in the management of the Post Office that reached its climax during the presidency of James Buchanan in the late 1850's. It was the political and sectional struggle over slavery in Kansas, with the accompanying defections from the Democratic party in the North, that brought a more vigorous and extensive use of federal patronage than ever before. And since Stephen A. Douglas was at the center of the Kansas storm, it is not surprising that the state of Illinois should present a striking picture of postal politics at the local level.[3]

Although nominally chosen by the president or the postmaster general, the postmasters were by this time actually selected by the members of Congress from each state. The congressmen, in turn, usually consulted local leaders, and the people of a community often made their wishes felt by drawing up petitions nominating certain men for the coveted positions. Few of the nearly 1,500 offices in Illinois at the end of the 1850's were of significant monetary value. Only 28 paid more than a thousand dollars a year, and three-fourths paid less than one hundred dollars annually.[4] Even those appointments yielding the top salary of $2,000 were sometimes desired less for the money than for the prestige and power that went with the office. The Springfield postmaster, Isaac R. Diller, told Douglas in 1854 that the job was more trouble than it was worth, and that he kept it only because "it gave me a position to help you and your friends."[5]

In a village or small town, the postmaster was quite often a merchant, station agent, or newspaper editor who ran the post office as a sideline, in much the same way that drugstores today operate postal substations. Often the appointee's literacy was minimal and his sense of responsibility negligible. It was his duty to provide the equipment for the office, and his privilege to choose its location and to fix the hours that it would be open. In 1859, the Mattoon postmaster wrote to Douglas asking his advice in regard to "refitting upp the office & enlarging the same." He was afraid that he might take such a step only to be removed. "If I thought the Administration would retain me as Post Master," he went on, "I should go to considerable expense in fitting upp a good neat & substancial office."[6]

Occasionally the postmaster confused his ownership of the property with ownership of the office. At Decatur, Postmaster Philip B. Shepherd was also editor and publisher of the Decatur *Magnet*, and his assistant on the paper was one John Ryan. In 1859, Shepherd entered into an agreement with his assistant's son, Matthew Ryan, whereby he turned over the post office equipment, resigned his position, and secured the appointment of the elder Ryan in his place, all for the sum of five hundred dollars. When all of this had been accomplished, the Ryans defaulted on their part of the bargain, and Shepherd brought the entire affair out into the open by instituting a suit against Matthew Ryan in the circuit court at Decatur.[7] And in 1856, F. C. Wing of Collinsville reported to Senator Lyman Trumbull that the incumbent postmaster had "sold his property in the place and made over, it is believed, so far as it lay in his power, the good will so to speak, of the post office."[8]

That the part-time nature of the postmastership in smaller communities was often a source of annoyance for the public is suggested by this complaint from Wenona:

> There is a very general *dissatisfaction* with Mr. Van Allen the PM at this place, because he is disobliging & frequently neglects or refuses to let subscribers have their papers, or letters, after coming some distance from the country. The office is in the Passengerhouse, a very unsuitable place and as he is the Station Agent the business of the R. R. Company must be *first* attended to all the time, while those having business at the P.O. must wait often a long time before he is ready to serve them. I myself have gone to the office often & had to wait an hour or more.[9]

Equally productive of friction was the postmaster's power to locate the office wherever he chose. At Sterling, in strongly Republican Whiteside County, the Democratic postmaster in 1858 moved the office from the center of the town to its western edge. When their protests went unheeded, the citizens finally hired a deputy postmaster to get the mail at the new office and distribute it at the old.[10] The location of the post office was also a public issue at Decatur in 1860, with an "Old Square" faction resisting a "New Square" group made up largely of administration (that is, anti-Douglas) Democrats.[11]

Most disconcerting of all, however, was the use of the post office as a weapon in political contests. The postmaster was often the leader for the administration in his locality, and he used his position openly to advance the cause of his party. Through the mails there came regularly from Washington bags of those public documents that members of Congress franked to avid readers among their constituents. Documents supporting the administration were often addressed simply to the postmaster, it being his duty to circulate them in whatever fashion would do the most good. "Every Postmaster in the country," said a Chicago newspaper, "from the incumbent of a metropolitan office to the overseer of a single weekly mail-bag in the remotest 'rural district,' is thus made an active agent of the party, to the detriment if not the entire disregard of the public service."[12]

Toward opposition documents, of course, the postmaster's attitude was likely to be not solicitude but deliberate carelessness. The Chicago post office, distribution center for mail going west, was frequently accused of "detaining" documents opposed to the administration.[13] When Douglas broke with Buchanan in 1858, the full power of the postal system was turned against him, as the following letter indicates:

> I wish to warn you of a practice inaugurated by the Chicago P.M. in reference to *your* documents, which pass thro' his office. They are generally laid aside for a "convenient season," to await distribution, and when the throwers do distribute they handle them so roughly that many packages are broken open, and consequently lost, as many of them are directed to one person or to one office on the outside, while the remainder of the package merely contain the address of the persons and *not* the post office. . . . The above information comes to me thro' the route agents.[14]

With Douglas's onetime friend Isaac Cook in charge, the Chicago office intercepted not only his documents but also his personal mail. Some persons writing to Douglas addressed their letters to his wife or to friends in Washington, in the hope of circumventing this interference.[15]

It was in his control over newspapers that the postmaster wielded the greatest political power. Most of the journals of Illinois in the 1850's were weeklies, and they depended for their very existence on a benevolent postal system. Federal subsidizing of newspaper circulation had a long history. For instance, by a law of 1792 several times renewed, publishers everywhere in the United States could exchange newspapers through the mails free of charge. In the days before telegraphic news service, the network of exchanges served as the country's principal news-gathering system. By the 1840's, some seven million exchange papers were circulating annually. Then, in 1851, Congress added another important benefit by authorizing free delivery of weekly newspapers within the county of publication.[16]

As in the case of government documents, the local postmaster was likely to be much more diligent in delivering those papers that supported his party than those that spoke for the opposition. Until 1854, the selection of postmasters in northern Illinois outside of Chicago was largely the prerogative of Congressman John Wentworth, who made use of his authority to advance the sales of his Chicago *Democrat*.[17] The situation was described by a rival editor:

> Mr. Wentworth has had the appointing of Postmasters hereabouts for a great many years, and he has uniformly used the power so as to increase the circulation of his paper. No man could be Postmaster in his bailiwick who would not perform the drudgery of an active agency for the *Chicago Democrat*, or who would use any exertion to secure subscribers for another Chicago paper.[18]

In addition to acting as a salesman for his party's papers, the postmaster was in an admirable position to discourage the circulation of opposition papers, which could be lost, misdelivered, or delayed until they were stale. The Springfield postmaster was accused of going one step further and canceling subscriptions to papers he did not like, without consulting the subscribers.[19]

The possible influence of the post office on newspaper circulation is suggested in a letter written by a citizen of Kankakee to the postmaster general in 1858. Wishing to praise his local postmaster, he spoke not of efficient mail deliveries but of the fact that "the circulation of *Dem.* papers has been increased more than ten fold within the last eighteen months. While in the same time the repub newspapers have fell off more than one hundred percent. This change, in a great measure, has been brought about by the enterprising perseverance of our P.M."[20]

Thus the post office, used in a partisan fashion, could exercise considerable control over the fortunes of the press. "There is no class in the community so completely at the mercy of government as newspaper publishers," said the Chicago *Democratic-Press*. "The

Post Office Department, if it sets itself against any newspaper establishment, has in its power the means of crippling it very seriously, if not entirely *breaking it down*."[21]

It was this admitted relationship between control of the local post office and the welfare of a newspaper that made the Chicago *Tribune* so anxious to acquire the postmastership for one of its editors in 1861. "We want the office, not wholly for the money there is in it, but as a means of extending and insuring our business and widening the influence of the *Tribune*," Charles H. Ray, one of the editors, wrote to Senator Lyman Trumbull after Lincoln's election. "If Mr. S[cripps] had it the country post masters of the N[orth]west would work to extend our circulation," added Joseph Medill a week later.[22] There was nothing unusual about Lincoln's appointment of John Locke Scripps, a senior *Tribune* editor, as Chicago postmaster in 1861. I have counted more than fifty Illinoisans who were simultaneously postmasters and editors or publishers in the years 1854 to 1861.[23] Doubtless there were also numerous instances of close relationships—of connections through blood, marriage, and friendship—between the two positions.

In addition to its day-to-day functions as part of the political machinery, the post office in emergencies could be used to impose some semblance of discipline upon the party in power. The two important occasions on which the whip was cracked from Washington were in 1854 and 1858. The issue in both cases was Kansas. During the first struggle, Douglas wielded the whip; during the second, he felt its lash. His insistence in 1854 that the Kansas-Nebraska bill be considered a test of party loyalty resulted in heavy defections among postmasters in the northern part of the state. The punishment for their heresy was dismissal. "Senator Douglas is taking off the heads of all the postmasters in the northern part of the State who are not Nebraska men," reported the *Illinois State Journal* in Springfield.[24] It was a tedious process requiring several years to accomplish, but gradually the postmasters turned Republican were weeded out, sometimes as a result of petitions from local Democrats.[25]

The first purge had not yet been completed when another was superimposed upon it. Douglas's outright defiance of the President on the Lecompton issue brought on a veritable reign of terror among Illinois postal officials. "Old Buck has got the guillotine well greased and in full swing," said the Chicago *Democrat*. "From now till election we may expect to hear of Douglas' postmasters' heads falling into the basket as fast as the old machine can be made to work."[26]

As his chief hatchet men against pro-Douglas officials in Illinois, Buchanan chose Isaac Cook and Charles Leib. Cook, a Chicago saloonkeeper and political boss, had been one of Douglas's closest friends until a quarrel over control of the Chicago *Times* made them bitter enemies. He had served a term as Chicago's postmaster, but unsatisfactorily, since he had been unable to account for all the funds. Leib's past was equally questionable and much more varied. Doctor, lawyer, liquor dealer, petty official, he was a political chameleon who had ridden with Jim Lane's "free-state" army in Kansas, edited a Democratic campaign paper in 1856, and become leader of the Buchanan forces in Illinois by 1858.[27]

Though hardly of the highest quality, these men were perhaps the best that could be found, for administration supporters were scarce in Illinois in 1858. Cook was now restored to his old position as postmaster in Chicago, while Leib became the President's special mail agent for the state, traveling about ostensibly in a supervisory capacity, but actually to whip federal employees into line behind the Lecompton constitution for Kansas and against the Douglas forces. As the heads began to roll, some postmasters hurried to Washington in the hope of preserving their jobs, while along the same route sped aspirants for their positions.[28]

Because of a desperate need for newspapers to defend its policies, the administration, through its spokesmen in Illinois, worked strenuously to hold the loyalty of Democratic editors, most of whom leaned toward Douglas. In this struggle for control of the press, federal patronage was used as a threat to editors who were already postmasters, and as a bribe to those who were not.

At Joliet, Postmaster C. Zarley yielded to the pressure and kept his Joliet *Signal* staunchly pro-Buchanan in its editorials,[29] while Charles N. Pine, Princeton postmaster and editor of the *Bureau County Democrat*, was rewarded for his faithfulness to the administration with an appointment as United States marshal.[30] In Peoria, on the other hand, Postmaster Peter Sweat emerged as a cautious supporter of Douglas. Scurrying to Washington in an effort to ward off dismissal, he found that George W. Raney, editor of the Peoria *Democratic-Union*, had arrived there ahead of him. Raney promised to lend editorial support to the administration in exchange for the postmastership, which he received.[31] The editor of the Kankakee *Democrat*, W. N. Bristol, also joined the Buchanan forces in the hope of replacing the local postmaster. "We could buy Bristol back again cheap & would do so if we was satisfied he would stay bought," wrote one of Douglas's regular Kankakee correspondents. Leading anti-administration Democrats in the town, desiring to hold the post office at all costs, advised Postmaster Longfellow to "go down to Springfield and soft soap Cook & Leib." The strategy was apparently successful, for Bristol did not win the appointment, but Longfellow classified himself as a turncoat by his conciliation of the "Buchaneers."[32]

In spite of their hard work and the power behind them, the Buchanan Democrats made a miserable showing in the election of 1858. Their candidates for state offices polled only five thousand votes, about 2 percent of the total cast. There can be little doubt that the nucleus of this small group was officeholders, especially postmasters, who were acting for the most part from the hope of monetary gain rather than from principle.

The use of the Post Office for political purposes, together with generally low standards of delivery service, caused much discontent with the postal system in the 1850's.[33] Post offices, said the Chicago *Democratic-Press*, "constitute, in fact, the perpetual bribery fund of those in power," while the franking privilege, it said, was "one of the most potent engines in the hands of political knaves to carry out their schemes of villainy, that ever was set in operation at the seat of government."[34] There was talk of making the office of postmaster elective, and some persons urged that all or part of the system be placed in the hands of private enterprise.[35]

The great expansion of railroads during the 1850's meant an acceleration of mail deliveries, but it also brought a need for more efficient organization and better-trained personnel, a need difficult to meet because of the partisan uses to which the postal system was put. "It is a notorious fact and a crying sin," complained the Chicago *Journal* in 1856, "that the post offices are made to subserve party ends to the delay and injury of private business."[36]

Republicans were naturally the loudest complainers about Buchanan's use of the Post Office as a political instrument, but on gaining power in 1861, they rivaled their enemies in the energy with which they wielded the patronage. About 80 percent of the "presidential-class" postmasters were replaced during the first year of the Lincoln administration, and within two years some seven thousand lesser postmasters were removed. Furthermore, during the election of 1864, there were Democratic complaints of partisanship in the conduct of Post Office affairs—complaints much like those lodged against the Buchanan administration in 1858.[37] Lincoln, unlike his two immediate predecessors, did not use postal patronage as a means of enforcing party loyalty in Congress. In the unprecedented circumstances of civil war, however, the Post Office was employed to combat subversion by excluding certain inflammatory publications from the mails.[38] After the war, continuing dissatisfaction with the involvement of the postal system in national party politics resulted in many more proposals for election of postmasters,[39] and the dissatisfaction was also an important element in the rise of the civil service movement.

CHAPTER 4

Lincoln and the Mayor of Chicago

Among Lincoln's contemporaries in Illinois politics, there was no more conspicuous figure than the Chicago editor, congressman, and mayor, John Wentworth—a man more feared than admired, but possessed of an enduring popular appeal. His personality and public antics constitute one of the gaudier elements in the early history and folklore of the city. The fact that the great fire of 1871 destroyed most of his letters and other personal documents goes a long way toward explaining why my book *Chicago Giant* was the first biography to be published and remains the only one to date. This essay summarizing Wentworth's relations with Lincoln appeared at about the same time in the *Wisconsin Magazine of History*, 40 (1957).

Even when he straightened up to his full height of six feet and four inches, Abraham Lincoln was not the tallest man among his contemporaries in Illinois politics. That distinction he conceded to "Long John" Wentworth, the first and most prodigious specimen in Chicago's album of political bosses. The two men had little in common besides stature until the slavery controversy drew both of them into the new Republican party. Then their careers began to converge. And in the critical period from 1854 to 1860, when Lincoln was moving into national prominence, Wentworth's huge shadow fell frequently and sometimes ominously across his path.

Chicago had caught its first glimpse of Long John as he came striding into town on an October day in 1836, having covered on foot the last few miles of a journey by stagecoach, railroad, canal boat, and lake steamer from his home in the New Hampshire hills.[1] Newcomers were no novelty in the mushrooming lakeside metropolis, but here was a figure—one hundred and fifty pounds stretched like a string to six and one-half feet—that caused heads to turn for a second look as it passed. The moment was opportune for the arrival of this unseasoned Dartmouth graduate who proclaimed his everlasting devotion to President Andrew Jackson. Democratic leaders in the city desperately needed a new editor for their local newspaper, and Wentworth soon found himself established in the offices of the Chicago *Democrat*, a man of prestige and power at the age of twenty-one.[2]

The experiment proved successful from the beginning. By shrewd management and vigorous editorial tactics, the stripling editor not only avoided the financial disaster that overtook many enterprises in the Panic of 1837, but raised the *Democrat* within a few years to a position of eminence among newspapers of the Northwest. John Wentworth came to typify—indeed, almost to caricature—that boisterous age of American journalism when each newspaper was but an extension of the partisan prejudices and personal mannerisms of its proprietor, and when venom flowed profusely from editorial pens while moderation was scorned as a sign of weakness. Readers opened every issue of the *Democrat* expecting to find a new accusation hurled, another victim impaled, and they were seldom disappointed. Long John displayed such a mastery of vituperative prose that the list of his enemies lengthened almost as fast as the register of subscribers. Hated by the Whigs, feared and distrusted by many leaders of his own party, he nevertheless built a strong following in northern Illinois with his bold and passionate advocacy of Jacksonian doctrines.

It was therefore no surprise to the people of Chicago when this mettlesome youth, after only six years in the editor's chair, began to cast ambitious eyes on a seat in Congress. Democratic rivals branded him a presumptuous upstart, but he won the nomination; Whig editors raked him with their heaviest fire, but he was elected.[3] On December 4, 1843, he took his place in the House of Representatives—the youngest, tallest, greenest addition to it.

Like Stephen A. Douglas, who sat beside him in the Illinois delegation, Wentworth bristled with the rude impatience of the American frontier, and before many weeks of the session had passed he was reading the House a stern lecture on its neglect of Western interests. His theme was the need for river-and-harbor appropriations. Describing the tragic consequences of inadequate navigation aids on the Great Lakes, he argued that the nation's inland waters were as much a federal responsibility as its Atlantic coast. "Too long," he exclaimed, "have the people of nearly half of our Union

. . . been knocking at the doors of Congress, . . . and demanding their unquestionable deserts."[4] Similar harangues followed at frequent intervals, until Long John came to be recognized as the most persistent champion of internal improvements in the entire Congress.

With equal enthusiasm he advocated generous treatment of settlers on the public lands, subsidies for Western railroads, and American expansion to the Pacific. These attitudes were pleasing to the voters of his district, who reelected him in 1844, and again in 1846.[5] Meanwhile, he retained close editorial control of the *Democrat* as his personal organ and through lieutenants in Illinois built up a political machine that seemed almost invincible.

But the outbreak of the Mexican War stirred up the smoldering slavery question and undermined the very foundations of Wentworth's influence. Chicago rivaled the Ohio Western Reserve as a center of free-soil sentiment in the Northwest, and Long John was not only voting his own convictions but reflecting views from home when he supported the Wilmot Proviso.[6] With each passing year thereafter, he found it increasingly difficult to serve both his constituents and his party. Many other men in public life were similarly troubled, for the issue of slavery in the federal territories was bringing division to the Democrats and disaster to the Whigs. A revolution in American politics reached its climax in 1854 when Douglas introduced his famous Kansas-Nebraska bill repealing the Missouri Compromise. In the tempest of opposition that swept through the free states, the Republican party was born.

Wentworth voted against the Kansas measure, and, like other Democrats who thus defied their administration leaders, he suffered abuse and official proscription as a consequence. In addition, the political confusion in his own district forced him to abandon all hope of reelection to Congress.[7] Embittered by this blow to his personal fortunes, yet reluctant to surrender the name "Democrat," he drifted almost against his will into the new party of freedom.

It was at Bloomington in the spring of 1856 that the Republicans of Illinois assembled for their first state convention. In the proceedings, which were suffused with a spirit of moral dedication, both Wentworth and Lincoln played prominent roles. Long John had arrived a day early to take part in the preliminary oratory and was appointed to the committee on nominations. Lincoln brought the excitement of the meeting to its climax with a stirring speech that evoked one final outburst of enthusiasm and completed the fusion of old Whigs, rebel Democrats, abolitionists, and Know-Nothings into a united organization.[8]

During the campaign that followed, both men took the stump for John C. Frémont, the Republican presidential nominee. More than once that summer they shared the same platform. Everywhere their audiences were large and multifarious, for the political mass meeting of the nineteenth century was commonly a family affair, preceded by a community picnic and punctuated by the shouts of children romping about the edges of the throng. At Oregon on August 16, for example, almost the entire population of Ogle County seemed to be present, and while the two tall ex-congressmen sat together on the rostrum they amused themselves by counting the number of babies nursing in their mothers' arms. Lincoln tallied seventy-one; Wentworth, seventy-three. Such people, Long John commented, had no reason to support a "superannuated old bachelor" like James Buchanan. "And if their fathers do their duty," he added, "some of the little fellows will live to see the day when not a slave will curse the American soil."[9]

The election of 1856 ended in a victory for the Democrats and their presidential candidate, but the results in Illinois were less decisive. There, Buchanan's capture of the electoral vote was partially offset by the triumph of the Republican state ticket from governor down. Illinois had clearly become one of those pivotal states that could easily tip the political balance either way in the critical days lying ahead. Republican leaders in the state turned their eyes confidently to the year 1858, when Douglas's term in the Senate would expire. With remarkable unity they quietly agreed that Lincoln, as the recognized leader of the Whig branch of Illinois Republicanism, was the logical man to supplant the "Little Giant." There were whispers that Wentworth also had designs upon the office, but for the moment at least, he had trained his sights upon another target. He wanted to be the next mayor of Chicago.

The voters of Chicago elected their municipal officers every spring, and local Republicans were anxious to win the 1857 contest in order to wipe away the stain of a surprising Democratic victory the year before. To many of them Wentworth was an objectionable candidate, but in a whirlwind tour of street corners and saloons he lined up more than enough support. The Republican convention in

February nominated him by acclamation. "It is rather a bitter pill for some of us to swallow," one delegate admitted, "but on the whole it is the best we can do."[10]

Knowing that he must somehow soothe those Republican tempers ruffled by his candidacy, Long John turned to Lincoln, who happened to be visiting the city for professional reasons, and asked him to take part in a public "ratification" at Metropolitan Hall. Lincoln responded with a speech urging party members to forget their "minor differences and personal prejudices" so that the nation might see Chicago redeemed as a citadel of freedom.[11] The enthusiasm generated at this mass meeting engulfed the Democrats at the polls on March 3. When the returns were all in, Wentworth had defeated his opponent by over a thousand votes to become the city's first Republican mayor.[12]

Jubilant friends and disgusted enemies could agree in the expectation that the reign of "Johannes Elongatus," whether good or bad, would certainly not be dull. Never in all his years as a congressman had Wentworth been given such an opportunity to indulge his taste for authority and display. He presided over council meetings with a despotic gavel, dispensed patronage in cavalier style, and kept a jealous eye upon every detail of municipal government. Having announced that the watchwords of his administration would be "retrenchment and reform," he proceeded to implement the promise in his own unconventional way.

A sharp increase in the tax rate, together with carefully reduced expenditures, enabled him to balance the budget for the first time in several years. And in a bold demonstration of his views on public finance, the new mayor arbitrarily set fire to $96,000 worth of bonds authorized by an earlier city council.[13] With equal zeal and officiousness he directed the activities of the police force, accompanying officers in their raids on gambling dens and brothels, and supervising personally the booking of prisoners at the watch house. When local merchants failed to heed an ordinance forbidding the obstruction of sidewalks, he tore down their overhanging signs and dumped them in a vacant lot.[14] When the wretched and disreputable denizens of the "Sands" refused to vacate their shantytown suburb, he led an expedition that drove many of them out.[15] In the uproar of public response to these highhanded tactics there was a mixture of hearty applause and angry denunciation.

Touring the city regularly, like a medieval baron inspecting his estates, Long John was easily the most familiar figure on the streets. More than a hundred pounds heavier than the gangling youth who had arrived on the scene twenty years before, he was described by a newspaper correspondent as a "shabby, elephantine individual," with a good-natured countenance, who wore a hat turned down all around, a poorly fitted coat, unblacked shoes that seemed three sizes too large, and loose trousers that looked "as if he had jumped too far into them and hadn't time to go back."[16]

Democrats saw the malevolence of Satan in every step that Wentworth took, every word that he uttered, and their chorus of abuse was swelled with many voices from his own party. By the autumn of 1857, the other Republican editors in the city were hounding him unmercifully in their columns. The Chicago *Tribune* warned its readers that he was plotting foul treachery against Lincoln in the hope of winning the prospective Senate seat for himself.[17] But Lincoln feared party disunity more than an ambitious rival. "I do not entirely appreciate what the Republican papers of Chicago are so constantly saying against Long John," he confided to a friend. "I do believe the unrelenting warfare made upon him is injuring our cause."[18]

Whatever aspirations he may have harbored for a time, Wentworth eventually endorsed Lincoln in unequivocal terms, and the *Tribune* discontinued its clamor. But then the Democratic papers revived the rumor and chanted it endlessly. Long John, they predicted, would never allow Lincoln's election to the Senate. Instead, he would pack many county conventions with his own henchmen and try to carry off the prize for himself.[19]

This was unsound prophecy but clever political strategy, for United States senators were chosen by state legislatures, and if the Illinois Democrats could persuade some wavering voters that the senatorial contest was actually between Douglas and the widely disliked Wentworth, they might improve their chances of victory in certain critical districts. The editors of the *Tribune* therefore found it necessary to refute the very story that they themselves had earlier disseminated, and to defend Long John as a "cordial supporter of Abraham Lincoln."[20]

Meanwhile, events at Washington were complicating the political situation in Illinois. Douglas had broken with Buchanan and was leading the fight in Congress against the administration's efforts to admit Kansas as a slave state under the Lecompton constitution. The spectacle of the "Little Giant" in revolt against his own party was so delightful to certain Eastern Republicans like Horace Greeley that they began to recommend his reelection by general bipartisan consent. But Republican leaders in Illinois indignantly rejected the proposal. Desert their own candidate to support Douglas? Never! One act of dubious virtue, they argued, was hardly sufficient atonement for a lifetime of indifference to the evils of slavery. Illinois would make its own decisions without help from "political wet-nurses" in the East.[21]

The delegates who assembled for the Republican state convention at Springfield on June 16, 1858, were therefore determined to make their intentions unmistakably clear. With a wild display of enthusiasm, they unanimously approved a resolution naming Lincoln as their "first and only choice" for the United States Senate.[22] This nomination constituted an unprecedented intrusion on the prerogatives of the legislative caucus and is significant in American political history as one of the first steps toward popular election of senators. Primarily a rebuke to Greeley and other Republicans who had been coquetting with Douglas, it was also aimed—to quote the nominee himself—at "closing down upon this everlasting croaking about Wentworth."[23] Lincoln was obviously referring to the editorials in Democratic newspapers, not, as some historians have erroneously supposed, to an actual conspiracy of Long John and his friends.

Wentworth spent the summer with his family in the East, remote from the memorable contest in Illinois, but the *Democrat* gave Lincoln unfaltering support from beginning to end. "He wears well," it declared while the debates with Douglas were in progress. "He is a standard-bearer every way worthy of the party and its principles—high-toned, chivalric, and honorable."[24] In October, Long John returned to Chicago and threw himself personally into the battle. Almost every evening he lumbered out upon some platform in the city to entertain the crowd with his savage growls, grimaces, and gestures, as he pleaded for a Republican victory.

When the tabulation of votes on election day revealed that Lincoln had suffered defeat by a narrow margin, Wentworth attached no blame to the "noble statesman" himself. The real architect of disaster, he insisted, was the chairman of the state central committee, Norman B. Judd, who had mismanaged the campaign, wasted party funds, and at every turn sacrificed Lincoln's interests to his own swollen ambition.[25] This personal attack upon a prominent Republican was no impulsive outburst, but a calculated maneuver. Long John was firing the first shots in a desperate struggle for control of Chicago.

Judd, a longtime state senator with his eye on the governor's mansion, headed the so-called "*Tribune* Clique," whose hostility had prevented Wentworth's reelection as mayor and threatened to drive him permanently from public life. In his fight for survival against this formidable adversary, Long John wanted the assistance of Lincoln, whom the *Democrat* now labeled "the Great Man of Illinois."[26] More than that, he began to visualize the Springfield lawyer as a possible presidential candidate, with himself as campaign manager. Seward had his Thurlow Weed; why should not Lincoln have his John Wentworth?

The bitterness between Judd and Wentworth became ever more intense as the year 1859 wore on. Each man regarded the other as the most dangerous obstacle in his own path and would give no quarter. On public platforms, in newspaper columns and private correspondence, the quarrel raged, splitting the Republicans of Chicago into angry factions. So fierce were the assaults of the *Democrat* upon Judd's personal character that he was finally driven to legal reprisals. On the first day of December, he brought suit against Wentworth, asking $100,000 in damages.[27]

This was a thrust at Long John's most tender spot, and the tone of his editorials softened immediately. "He is as tame as a punished boy," one man reported. "It is regarded here as almost a miracle that Judd's one blow should have so badly broken the teeth of this dirty dog."[28] The lawsuit dismayed more Republicans than it pleased, however. Two party leaders attacking each other with such ferocity was an alarming spectacle on the eve of a national election. Lincoln, now emerging as a serious contender for the presidential nomination, found himself pressed from all sides to intervene in "the War of the Roses at Chicago."[29] He had little choice but to comply.

Both of the principals in the feud were meanwhile besieging him with importunate letters. Judd demanded and eventually received a statement absolving him of blame for the defeat in 1858.[30] Wentworth's request was more extraordinary. He asked Lincoln to serve as his counsel in the lawsuit![31] Ignoring that brash proposal, Lincoln offered instead to act as mediator. In February of 1860, at a time when he was getting ready for his Cooper Institute speech, he submitted his plan for restoring peace. Wentworth must file with the court a retraction of all charges not strictly political in nature; Judd, in turn, must agree to press his suit no further.[32]

Before the negotiations could be completed, the time for electing municipal officers arrived, and Long John was determined to run for mayor again. The odds against him seemed overwhelming at first. Froth appeared on many Republican lips at the very thought of his return to power. But in spirited primary contests throughout the city he put the Judd forces to rout and carried off the nomination. "This libel suit and other acts of persecution have compelled me to show my strength once more," he boasted to Lincoln.[33]

Judd now faced a painful choice. To support Wentworth would be a humiliating personal surrender; but to bolt the party ticket and help elect a Democratic mayor in the city already designated as the site of the Republican national convention would hardly be discreet conduct for a man who wanted to be governor. After anguished deliberation, he swallowed his pride and went through the motions of advocating Long John's election. The two men even appeared several times together on the same platform, and nothing more was heard of the libel suit. With similar endorsements wrung from other Republican leaders, Wentworth swept to an easy victory at the polls.[34]

Magnanimity had never gained a foothold on Long John's flinty character. He reentered the mayor's office still grimly resolved to prevent Judd's nomination for governor. Nor had he ceased to hope that he might somehow take charge of the Lincoln-for-president movement. In both of these designs he had the support of Judge David Davis, who disliked Judd and admired the "wonderful power of John Wentworth." Davis, a close friend of Lincoln, wrote to the latter urging that Long John be appointed a delegate-at-large to the national convention. "I am satisfied," the Judge told Lincoln, "that he can really do more to advance your interests than any man in Illinois or out of it."[35]

During a Lincoln visit to Chicago early in April, Wentworth broached the subject in a private conference. "Do like Seward does," he bluntly advised, "get some one to *run* you." But Lincoln did not take the hint. Instead, he said something to the effect that a president was made by the course of events, not by the exertions of the candidate. Later, he used this exchange with Wentworth as material for one of his presidential "yarns."[36]

The rebuff failed to shake Long John's hope of participating in the national convention. Surely, he thought, the mayor of the host city would not be relegated to a seat in the gallery! Only a word from Lincoln was needed to make him a delegate, and Judge Davis had virtually promised that the word would be spoken. A prominent role in the convention might then lead to some position of importance in the first Republican administration. Street-corner gossip said that he was aiming at the office of postmaster general.[37]

At the state convention early in May, Wentworth saw all his expectations trampled under foot. Judd, to be sure, was defeated in the contest for the gubernatorial nomination, but this proved to be Long John's only profit from the proceedings. Judd's name, not his, appeared on the list of delegates-at-large. Judd was also retained as chairman of the central committee and awarded the honor of nominating Lincoln for president. The Mayor of Chicago, in sharp contrast, found himself ignored in all appointments and coldly excluded from the inner circle of party authority. His arrogance and vindictiveness had apparently exhausted even Lincoln's monumental patience. "He is today politically ruined," Judd assured Lincoln. "I propose that all of your friends allow Cook County to deal with him."[38]

Wentworth returned home in a mood of sour frustration which was reflected in the editorial columns of the *Democrat*. Without diminishing its routine praise of Lincoln, the paper became increasingly friendly toward Seward, and as the city began to fill up with Republican leaders, Long John was said to be wandering through the crowded hotel lobbies urging the New Yorker's nomination. Bitter reproaches from the Lincoln men followed him everywhere. "I for one think he is a *dog*, and unworthy to be called a member of our party," one of them growled.[39]

Whatever his private feelings, Wentworth received the nomination of Lincoln and Hamlin with outward enthusiasm and pledged full support of the ticket. As the campaign progressed, however, his behavior excited the suspicions of many party leaders. Republican strategy was necessarily aimed at winning the confidence of moderates in the North by dissociating the party from the doctrines of its abolitionist fringe. Yet the editorials in the *Democrat* during the summer of 1860 might almost have been written by William Lloyd Garrison. Its radical pronouncements—including the promise that Lincoln's election would mean "the emancipation of four millions of human beings"—seemed to play directly into the hands of the opposition.[40] Could a man so renowned for his political cunning be unaware of the harm he was doing, or was this the work of a spiteful saboteur? "Beware of traitors!" one Illinois newspaper warned. "There is scarcely any room to doubt that Long John Wentworth, under the guise of friendship for the Republican Party, is laboring to defeat its nominees by attributing to them doctrines which they never held."[41]

Wentworth nevertheless continued to speak in the voice of extremism. He hailed Lincoln's election as a "day of Jubilee" marking the downfall of the slave power in America, and he denounced all efforts to save the Union by compromise with the secessionists. "The irrepressible conflict must go on," said the *Democrat*. "The war of Freedom against Slavery must be waged; the cursed institution must be extirpated."[42]

As for himself, Long John announced that he intended to take a long vacation from politics. Soon after completing his year as mayor, he sold the *Democrat* and turned his attention to the extensive stock farm that had become his greatest joy. Except for one more undistinguished term in Congress during the administration of Andrew Johnson, his stormy public career had come to a premature close at the age of forty-six. But for another quarter of a century he walked the streets of Chicago with proprietary pride, a living reminder to the city of its bygone youth.

And Lincoln, the prairie lawyer suddenly entrusted with the fate of the Republic, found men in Washington who were as eager to "run" him as Wentworth had been. To each one he responded with the same patience and restraint that he had shown in his association with the troublesome Mayor of Chicago.

CHAPTER 5

The Republican Decision at Chicago

Some revisions have been made here and there in this essay, but it is essentially the same as the paper presented at a conference held at Gettysburg College in 1960 and published in Norman A. Graebner, ed., *Politics and the Crisis of 1860* (Urbana, Ill., 1961). Written before the "new political history" reshaped study of the American party system, the essay, I think, remains basically sound as far as it goes, but is now less than adequate as an explanation of how Lincoln came to be nominated for the presidency. In some respects it illustrates the advantages and the limitations of "thick" narrative history—meaning a chronological account that pauses repeatedly to query and reflect and perhaps explain. Such narrative is, in a sense, a compromise between historical reconstruction and historical investigation. It respects the temporal integrity of the past and may to some extent recapture the complexity and subtlety of change over time. But, being chronologically rather than logically systematic, it may leave important questions unsatisfactorily answered or even wholly unnoticed.

Whatever disagreement there may be about the underlying causes of the Civil War, it is clear that the conflict was precipitated in 1860–61 by a series of momentous decisions which began with the election of a Republican president. True, the causal connection between those decisions cannot be regarded as one of necessity. Secession followed closely upon Abraham Lincoln's victory, but reasonable alternatives presented themselves to Southern leaders, the most obvious one being to wait for an overt act of Republican aggression before taking such a drastic step. At the same time, the danger of disunion was unquestionably older than the Republican party and would not have been swept away by a different verdict at the polls in 1860. Nevertheless, as it happened, the election of Lincoln proved to be that particular link between causes and effects that is sometimes called the "occasion." Without it, things would have been different, perhaps even vastly different, depending upon how delicate the balance really was between violence and accommodation.

The choice of Lincoln as his party's nominee had no significant influence upon the Southern decision to secede. Black Republicans all looked alike to the Cotton Kingdom. But in the determination of how secession should be answered, the character of the new president became extremely important, and it made a difference that Lincoln, instead of the more protean William H. Seward, had won the nomination at Chicago. To discover why the Civil War started when it did and in the way that it did, it is necessary to inquire how the Republican party came to be what it was in 1860—namely, a political organization conservative enough to win a presidential election, yet provocative enough to set off a major rebellion. Much of the essence of this early Republicanism is revealed in the elevation of Abraham Lincoln to party leadership.

Robust at birth and swift to achieve power, the Republican party has flourished for so long as one component of a stable two-party system that Americans often forget the precarious uncertainty of its first years and look upon it as a favored child of destiny. It is true that Republicanism gave expression to certain powerful forces and aspirations in American life that were probably irrepressible. The demands of an emerging industrial capitalism and an expanding frontier, and the urgency of humanitarian reform, presumably could not have been stifled by any conceivable means. Yet the precise form that such expression took, as well as the speed and amplitude of its success, resulted in no small part from accident, luck, and free decision.

For one thing, the Republican party made its appearance at a time of extraordinary political turmoil—a condition directly attributable to the furious controversy over the Kansas-Nebraska bill, but also having deeper roots.[1] Apart from the disruptive effects of sectional discord on institutional forms, instability and fragmentation had always been as much the rule as the exception in American politics. The "presidential synthesis" of our history exaggerates the substantialness of national parties before the Civil War and obscures the decentralized, diverse, and mutable character of political association at the state and local levels. There, the party insurgent, the bolted convention, the splinter group, the improvised coalition, and the call for a new party were virtually routine aspects of the political process. These strong centrifugal tendencies in the political heritage and environment of the 1850's were highly conducive to the emergence of new combinations like the Republican party, but prejudicial to their subsequent growth and integration. Why Republicanism was born is perhaps a less important question than how it survived.

Despite the suddenness with which the Republican party entered the scene in 1854, it was in some degree the culmination of a trend toward political sectionalism that had already produced the Free Soil movement of 1848. The causes of this trend have long been a subject of dispute among historians. Opposition to slavery, certainly the most conspicuous factor, once received almost exclusive attention.[2] But then a reaction set in, and it became the scholarly fashion to emphasize economic motives. The agricultural South, according to Charles A. and Mary Beard, was under attack primarily because it stood in the way of tariff protection, internal improvements, and all the other needs of a new, industrial order. The Republican party thus served as the political agency of an economic revolution that eventually freed capitalism from the restraints imposed upon it by the slave power.[3]

One variant of the Beard thesis stressed the clash of the two labor systems, and particularly their competition for Western lands. "The Republican party was not an anti-slavery party," wrote John R. Commons. "It was a homestead party. . . . Only because slavery could not live on one-hundred-and-sixty acre farms did the Republican party come into conflict with slavery."[4] Wilfred E. Binkley, in his history of American political parties, subscribed wholeheartedly to the Commons view, declaring that the slavery issue was "merely incidental" to the Republicans' fundamental purpose of "ensuring the West to free laborers and farmers."[5]

Reinhard H. Luthin summarized another interpretation when he said that the "cohesive force" within the new Republican party was not anti-Southern sentiment at all, but rather hostility to the Democrats—in other words, the "eagerness of the 'outs' to get 'in.' " A large part of the Republican leadership, Luthin asserted, was "amazingly indifferent" to the problem of slavery, but aware of its emotional value as a "vote-getting issue."[6] In this line of reasoning, slavery and economic questions together become merely the manipulative features of a fierce struggle for political power.

According to still another explanation of Republicanism, advanced by Larry Gara and Michael F. Holt, among others, the party was not so much antislavery as anti-Southern. A majority of Republicans, said Holt, "disliked white slaveholders more than black slavery or even slavery extension." They were using antislavery arguments to rescue American liberty and the republican system from domination by the slave power.[7]

Most influential of all in recent years has been the insistence of "ethnocultural" historians that the motive forces of Republicanism are to be found primarily in the values and dynamics of American pietism. The Republicans, according to this interpretation, were essentially latter-day Puritans determined to impose their scheme of right behavior upon the whole of American society. Antislavery was just one manifestation of their broader purpose.[8]

Thus various groups of historians over two generations tried in one way or another to depreciate the significance of slavery in the mid-nineteenth-century party revolution. Beginning in the 1970's, however, there was a strong countertendency to return to the older antislavery emphasis. "There can be no question," wrote Richard H. Sewell, for instance, "that hostility toward slavery lay at the very core of Republican ideology."[9]

Such attempts to isolate the quintessence of Republicanism bring to mind the old story of the blind men trying to describe an elephant, each with his hand on a different part of the creature's body. The burden of proof seems to rest with those who deny that opposition to slavery constituted the emotional core and unifying principle of the early Republican party. The core of a thing is by no means the whole of it, however, and it must be recognized that the word "slavery" acquired many connotative meanings, that a complex set of collateral values, interests, and ambitions attached themselves to the antislavery principle. As a result, various other issues were wrenched from their natural contexts and fused with the problem of Negro servitude. Slavery thus became as much a symbolic as a concrete factor in the sectional conflict, but this does not mean that the attack upon the institution itself was synthetic or incidental. Indeed, the tendency of nearly all public controversy to fall into alignment with the slavery question bespeaks the power with which that question gripped the minds of the American people.

The main features of Republicanism were anticipated in the Free

Soil party of 1848, an alliance of insurgent Whigs and Democrats, together with abolitionists, which was dedicated to the exclusion of slavery from the federal territories. The party platform, significantly, also set forth an economic program embracing river and harbor improvements, free land for settlers, and an adequate revenue tariff.[10] In the presidential election, the Free Soilers ran far behind the two major parties and polled less than 15 percent of the total Northern vote. But this figure, which compares so unfavorably with Frémont's 45 percent in 1856 and Lincoln's 55 percent in 1860, considerably understates the actual Free Soil strength, for many persons in strong sympathy with the movement were unwilling to throw away their votes. And although the party itself went into rapid decline after the territorial question was temporarily settled in 1850, the Free Soil spirit remained a powerful, half-latent force in American politics, ready to erupt at any time through another outlet.

The Kansas-Nebraska bill of 1854 crystallized antislavery feeling once more and at the same time augmented it. Just why this measure should have been so much more devastating in its effect on political structures than the Wilmot Proviso controversy of the 1840's is not easy to explain. One may point, however, to signs of cumulative stress. Grievances, both political and economic, had been piling up, especially in the Northwest, and there was an increasing disposition to regard the "slave power" as the tyrannical source of every affliction and frustration. Furthermore, the constant strain of sectional antagonism had undoubtedly eroded the cohesive strength of the two major parties and brought the Whigs in particular to the verge of disintegration. But the Nebraska matter, while raising the same old question of slavery in the territories, put it in new and explosive terms. The proponents of the Wilmot Proviso had been on the offensive, attempting to bar slavery from all newly conquered land. In resisting the repeal of the Missouri Compromise, however, antislavery forces were fighting a desperate defensive battle to preserve gains long since won and regarded as sacrosanct. The impression that freedom had been thrown on the defensive by an aggressive slave power was reinforced by later events such as the Dred Scott decision, and it accounts in no small degree for the broader appeal of the antislavery cause after 1854.[11]

The violent popular revulsion in the North against the Kansas-

Nebraska Act furnished a basis for the first antislavery party of major proportions, but in the beginning it produced only an extremely loose and tentative coalition. It is true that in some areas a new political organization calling itself "Republican" began to emerge during the summer of 1854. Yet many outspoken critics of the Nebraska policy held aloof at least temporarily from the Republican movement, and a sizable number of them never joined it. For example, nine counties in central and southern Illinois (including Lincoln's own Sangamon) that were anti-Nebraska in 1854 voted Democratic in 1860.[12] The consolidation of seemingly incompatible elements like Whigs and Democrats, nativists and foreigners, radicals and conservatives, into a single party proceeded at varying speeds throughout the free states and was not substantially accomplished for several years. Moreover, with just the single bond of anti-Nebraska sentiment uniting its diverse membership, Republicanism could not at first enunciate a comprehensive political program. This explains the narrowness of the national platform drafted in 1856, which concentrated almost exclusively upon the slavery question. It also helps to explain the presidential nomination of John C. Frémont, a colorful celebrity who was conveniently vague in his politics, except on the subject of slavery.

By confining their attention to a single major issue, the early Republicans were able to achieve numerical strength and some degree of solidarity, but this was a fragile basis upon which to build a permanent organization. What would happen to a party with only one stated purpose if events should strip that purpose of its urgency? The Kansas-Nebraska Act itself, for all the indignation it aroused, did not constitute a durable issue, especially since there was no hope of repealing the measure. Soon, however, the struggle had been transferred to the Western plains. It was the disorder and violence in Kansas that kept the anti-Nebraska coalition alive and helped convert it into a major political party. Yet there remained always the possibility that a sudden and complete pacification of Kansas would deprive Republicanism of its reason for being.

Certain factors in American politics encourage adherence to the two-party system, one being the way in which the nation chooses its presidents. By 1855, there were indications that the simple and familiar two-party arrangement might soon be restored, but exactly what would replace the disappearing Whig party was still far from clear. Republican organizations were strong in some Northern states, weak or half-formed or nonexistent in others. Meanwhile, political nativism was competing for the role of major opposition to the Democracy. Know-Nothingism had become dominant in much of New England; it was powerful enough in New York to win the state election of 1855, and it seemed likely to gain the upper hand in New Jersey and Pennsylvania. Less potent in the Northwest, the Know-Nothings nevertheless held the balance of power in Indiana and Illinois. Furthermore, the movement had the added advantage over Republicanism of appealing to many Southerners, and thus of presenting itself as a national, rather than a sectional, alternative to Democratic misrule. On the other hand, a majority of Northern Know-Nothings were also anti-Nebraskans, and as the turmoil continued in Kansas they became more and more inclined to place slavery ahead of the foreigner on their agenda of public problems. As a result, the American party had hardly organized on a national basis before it began to break apart. When a majority of the "North Americans" decided to support Frémont instead of Millard Fillmore in 1856, the future of Republicanism seemed secure.

The presidential election of 1856, which returned a Democrat, James Buchanan, to the White House, had a decisive influence upon subsequent Republican strategy. First, the election established the Republican party indisputably as the major party of opposition to the Democrats. Although defeated, it had carried eleven of the sixteen free states and was apparently still gathering momentum. Second, the American party, even though it won only a handful of electoral votes, nevertheless had demonstrated impressive strength. Fillmore, while making his best showing in the Southern border states, polled nearly 400,000 votes in the North and unquestionably hurt Frémont more than he did Buchanan. Third, the election had been decided in the states of the lower North, where Frémont carried only Ohio and Iowa, while losing New Jersey, Pennsylvania, Indiana, and Illinois, together with California. Thus the battle areas for 1860 were clearly defined. In order to elect a president, the Republicans would have to hold all of their gains and, in addition, capture several of the five free states lost to Buchanan, including the almost indispensable Pennsylvania.[13] This meant that they had to convert the bulk of the conservative Whig-Americans who had cast some 200,000 votes for Fillmore in those states. How to woo the Fillmore men, how to win the doubtful states, became subjects of frequent discussion among Republican strategists.

One seemingly obvious course was more or less out of the question. Any general appeal to nativist sentiment would alienate the numerous foreign-born Republicans and soil the party's cloak of high idealism. However, since the antislavery foreigners were overwhelmingly Protestant, while the Catholic sons of Ireland tended to remain loyal Democrats, there was some room for exploitation of the religious prejudice in Know-Nothingism. The Chicago *Tribune* stated the case with admirable clarity in 1856 when it declared that the Republican party was just the place for the man who wanted to "repress the political tendencies of a false but arrogant Church, without ostracizing the foreigner whose political and religious sympathies [were] as true and ardent as his own."[14] Anti-Catholicism, although it was never more than one of the fringe themes of Republicanism, entered into denunciations of the Dred Scott decision (Chief Justice Roger B. Taney being a Catholic) and into attacks upon Stephen A. Douglas, who, having taken a Catholic wife, was frequently depicted as a potential tool of the Pope.[15]

The line of action favored by certain Republican leaders was a remodeling of the party to give it broader appeal. A little more flexibility on the subject of slavery would probably bring many Fillmore men, and even some Democrats, into the fold; a stronger emphasis upon economic matters would awaken the interest of persons relatively indifferent to the antislavery crusade. But these were steps to be taken only after careful deliberation because they might lead to serious internal dissension, or to the submergence of Republican identity in a barren and faceless opportunism. Lincoln, for one, was apprehensive about such strategy, and up to the time of his nomination not only opposed any retreat on the slavery issue but also advised against inserting a tariff plank in the platform.[16]

In the end, the election of 1856 had its most significant effect upon Republican thinking when it suggested the kind of presidential candidate needed in 1860. For as the months went by, there was a growing conviction in many quarters that the nominee must be especially attractive to conservative Whig-Americans and able to run well in the doubtful states of the lower North.

Bleeding Kansas had been the main issue of the campaign, its importance enhanced by the civil disorder there, which reached its climax in the late summer of 1856. But then, with the appointment of a new governor, some degree of peace was restored in the territory, and it appeared that the Republicans might at last be running out of battles to fight. Not for long, however. During the first year of the Buchanan administration, one event after another opened up new areas of controversy. "Seldom if ever," wrote Albert J. Beveridge, "has a political party been so favored by fortune as were the Republicans during 1857."[17]

First came the Dred Scott decision, a judicial assault upon the cardinal principle of Republicanism that provoked a storm of protest from the antislavery forces and strengthened their determination to rescue the federal government from its Southern masters. Next, the worst financial panic in twenty years struck the country, bringing bankruptcies, unemployment, and the general gloom of hard times that usually militates against the party in power. The depression, by increasing public discontent with Democratic policies on the tariff, homesteads, and internal improvements, cleared the way for the broader economic program introduced into the Republican platform of 1860. Still another boon to the Republicans was the military expedition of 1857–58 against the Mormons in Utah. Hastily planned and humiliating in some of its consequences, this venture damaged the administration's prestige, made a mockery of popular sovereignty, and dramatized the urgent need for a transcontinental railroad. Then, on top of these developments, the Kansas question flamed up again when the Lecompton constitution, weighted in favor of slavery, was submitted to Congress.

Buchanan's attempt to secure the admission of Kansas as a slave state under the Lecompton instrument caused a popular outburst in the North not unlike that of 1854, and once again the political situation became exceedingly confused and fluid. The most spectacular aspect of the Lecompton affair was Douglas's bold revolt against the administration and the resulting split in the Democratic party. But the controversy had some unsettling effects upon the Republicans too, even though they stood to profit immensely from it. By early 1858, in fact, the party was approaching a major crossroads in its short history, and there was considerable disagreement over the direction next to be taken.

The anti-Lecompton battle in Congress, waged by a coalition of Republicans, Americans, and Douglas Democrats, inspired thoughts of a new grand alliance against the slave power. Douglas himself was so open and enthusiastic in his cooperation with Republican leaders that a number of them became optimistic about the possibility of a merger. That erratic genius of the newspaper world, Horace Greeley, showered praise upon the Little Giant and urged that Republicans join in reelecting him to the Senate.[18] Similar views issued from several other party journals in the East, including the New York *Times*, Thurlow Weed's Albany *Evening Journal*, and the Springfield *Republican*, which declared: "So powerful an instrumentality as Mr. Douglas should not, must not be paralyzed at the very moment when he commences to be of service to the interests of free labor . . . let him not be supplanted by an inferior."[19]

Along with this new-found Republican respect for Douglas went increased tolerance for his "great principle." The progress of events in Kansas seemed to indicate that popular sovereignty, when honestly applied, was enough to win the territories for freedom. Seward very nearly conceded as much on the Senate floor.[20] It appeared that the principle of the Wilmot Proviso was losing some of its relevance, that the final struggle would be between those who demanded and those who opposed federal protection of slavery in the territories. If so, the anti-Lecompton coalition, with its Sewards and Douglases, might well become permanent, replacing or transforming the Republican organization.

Greeley, who loved to play the role of political strategist, saw more than one advantage accruing from the policy he recommended. His extravagant praise of Douglas was intended to strengthen the ties between Republicans and anti-Lecompton Democrats while widening the breach in the Democratic party. In addition, Greeley wanted to gather in the Whig-Americans, and he proposed to quiet their fears of Republican radicalism with a display of generosity toward everyone who had opposed the Lecompton constitution. Douglas, returned in triumph to the Senate, would symbolize the new, conservative phase of the antislavery effort.

These half-developed plans to build a more inclusive opposition party, whatever their chance of success might otherwise have been, ran into angry and adamant resistance from a pivotal group. The Republicans of Illinois, spurning the suggestion that they support Douglas, and denouncing the presumptuous interference of "outsiders," proclaimed their determination to elect no man but Abraham Lincoln. Any lingering uncertainty was removed on June 16, 1858, when the Republican state convention boisterously approved a resolution designating Lincoln as its "first and only" choice for senator.[21] The memorable contest between Lincoln and Douglas then followed, and the latter's brief flirtation with Republicanism came to an end.

It is therefore possible that events in Illinois prevented the emergence of a new political coalition which, because of its conservatism, might have blunted the secession movement and guided the nation past the danger of civil war. In the circumstances, however, the decision of the Illinois Republicans was almost inevitable. Their animosity toward Douglas was too deep and personal to be set aside at anyone's bidding. "I am not willing," declared one man, "that we republicans of Illinois who have received so much abuse at his hands should now turn round and endorse his traitorous cause by giving him the highest office in our hands." The Chicago *Tribune* protested that "if the Republicans of Illinois should . . . re-elect Mr. Douglas, their party would be so disintegrated that the State would be lost to freedom in 1860." But it was Lincoln, as usual, who contributed the most trenchant comment. "My judgment is," he wrote, "that we must never sell old friends to buy old enemies."[22]

Lincoln's views were shaped only in part by personal ambition, for he was utterly convinced that collaboration with Douglas would destroy the Republican party and with it all hope of achieving an early settlement of the slavery issue. The question, he told Lyman Trumbull shortly after the debates of 1858, was whether the Republican organization would "maintain its identity, or be broken up to form the tail of Douglas' new kite."[23] There was consequently a practical purpose as well as deep conviction in his emphasis upon the moral aspect of the slavery problem. That purpose was to differentiate sharply between the basic assumptions and ultimate objectives of Republicanism on the one hand and of Douglasism on the other.

The Republicans, according to Lincoln, believed that slavery was wrong and proposed to treat it as a wrong within the limits of the Constitution, while hoping for its eventual extinction by some peaceful means. Douglas, having little moral objection to the institution, was willing to let it compete as an equal with freedom and saw no reason why the nation should not survive forever, half slave and half free. But in the end, Lincoln maintained, one principle or the other must conquer. A house divided against itself could not stand. And Douglas, whether intentionally or not, Lincoln believed, was serving as "miner and sapper" for the proslavery forces, because his doctrine of calculated indifference was helping to prepare the public mind for the nationalization of slavery.[24]

Thus Lincoln stood opposed to any lowering of the Republican platform for the purpose of accommodating Northern conservatives. Instead, he would accentuate the gulf between those who believed and those who did not believe that slavery was wrong, and then try to persuade all members of the first group that they belonged in the Republican ranks.

Yet if Lincoln's inflexibility on the territorial question was motivated in some degree by concern for the welfare of his party, it also stemmed from conviction, and particularly from his recognition of the question's symbolic importance. To him the restriction of slavery was not only a practical objective in itself, but also an instrument for settling a far more fundamental issue—the very moral status of slavery in a nation dedicated to human liberty. "Never forget," he told a Chicago audience in 1859, "that we have before us this whole matter of the right or wrong of slavery in this Union, though the immediate question is as to its spreading out into new Territories and States."[25] For Lincoln, in other words, slavery restriction was necessary most of all as a commitment to freedom, as an orientation toward that distant goal he had labeled "ultimate extinction."

The year 1860 found the youthful Republican party well organized and resolute, but still comparatively plastic, still awaiting the final molding of its character. Election victories in 1858 and 1859, especially those in Pennsylvania, and the continuing division of the Democrats inspired a general feeling of optimism. On the other hand, the John Brown raid threw Republican leaders temporarily on the defensive, and the preliminary organization of the Constitutional Union party in February darkened prospects of absorbing the Whig-Americans. Everywhere the need was felt to present Republicanism as safely conservative, worthy to exercise power. Lincoln's Cooper Union address of February 27, while yielding nothing in the matter of principle, was soberly phrased, devoid of the more provocative themes in his House Divided speech, and designed to demonstrate historically that the Republicans were the true intellectual heirs of the Founding Fathers.[26] Seward, delivering a major Senate speech two days later, was almost frantically conservative in his plea for reconciliation between what he euphemistically termed the "capital" states of the South and the "labor" states of the North.[27] Some antislavery radicals entered bitter protests against any retreat from aggressive Republicanism, but many others were willing to make at least limited concessions in order to accomplish the overthrow of the slave power. As the date of their national convention approached, Republicans became increasingly nervous about the decisions they must make. The question debated over and over was whether the party had enough strength to elect its most representative leader or needed to seek out its most available one. And so at Chicago in the third week of May, the Republican party, pulled this way and that by men, events, and the calculations of strategy, at last achieved some measure of self-definition.

The Republican platform of 1860 was drafted by a subcommittee comprised primarily of Westerners, although a Pennsylvanian acted as chairman. In general, the document was broader in its appeal and slightly more conservative in tone (though scarcely so in substance), than the platform of 1856. The subcommittee deleted the offensive reference to "those twin relics of barbarism—polygamy and slavery," and it added a section which in effect condemned the John Brown raid. Furthermore, instead of insisting upon "positive legislation" prohibiting slavery in every territory, the party promised to enact such legislation whenever it should become "necessary." This might appear to have been a partial acceptance of Douglas's doctrine of popular sovereignty, but not so. Later passages specifically denied the power of a territorial legislature to "give legal existence to slavery" and denounced popular sovereignty as a "deception and fraud." The net effect was to offer a territory the choice of excluding slavery itself or having it done by Congress. Other sections of the platform censured illegal trade in African slaves, called for the immediate admission of Kansas, and repudiated the Dred Scott decision without actually naming it. In addition, threats of disunion were sharply denounced as "an avowal of contemplated treason," which it was "the imperative duty of an indignant people sternly to rebuke and forever silence."

Of the last five planks in the platform, one took a forthright antinativist stand against changes in naturalization laws and the abridgment of citizenship rights "hitherto accorded to immigrants from foreign lands." The others, endorsing a Pacific railroad, river and harbor improvements, a homestead law, and some degree of tariff protection, constituted the economic portion of the Republican program. The first two of these items carried over from 1856; the homestead and tariff sections were new, although both subjects had been dealt with in the Free Soil platform of 1848. All four represented concessions to specific sectional and economic interests, but the Pacific railroad was more or less noncontroversial, since both wings of the Democratic party were also pledged to its construction. The other three amounted to flank attacks upon the Southern position, and the homestead proposal in particular may be regarded as the Northern answer to slavery expansion. The tariff plank, a matter of peripheral interest except to Pennsylvania and New Jersey, was mild enough to disarm all but the most extreme opponents of protection.[28]

It is sometimes said that the economic spirit of Whiggery triumphed in the Republican platform of 1860, but unless one defines Whiggery in terms so broad that they become almost meaningless, this interpretation has only limited validity and ignores the dynamics of history. The Whigs were certainly identified with protective tariffs and internal improvements, but the latter had increasingly become a sectional rather than a partisan issue, and the tariff in 1860 was more important to Pennsylvania Democrats than to comparatively indifferent former Whigs in other states. Moreover, the vital homestead plank was definitely not out of the Whig tradition. Insofar as Republicanism contemplated somewhat more governmental intervention in the economic life of the nation, it may perhaps be loosely associated with the spirit of Henry Clay, but the platform of 1860, like the party itself, was actually an amalgam of many things, including strong elements of Jacksonianism as well as Whiggery.

On the convention floor, one major flurry of excitement over the platform occurred when old Joshua Giddings called for reinsertion of a quotation from the Declaration of Independence that had appeared in the 1856 document. What followed was not really a struggle between radicals and conservatives, but rather a debate over how much rhetorical padding should be included in a statement of party principles. The Giddings proposal, though first rejected, was eventually sustained in a burst of glowing oratory, and the amended platform then received a unanimous vote of approval.[29] At this point—about six o'clock in the evening of May 17, the second day of the convention—the delegates decided to adjourn until the next morning instead of proceeding immediately with the business of nominating a presidential candidate. This proved to be a crucial decision because it gave the miscellaneous opponents of Seward extra time in which to negotiate with one another.

What happened in the Wigwam the next day was a drama in two parts: the rejection of Seward and the nomination of Lincoln. Seward's name had dominated preconvention discussion. A tested veteran of many battles against slavery and a political leader of acknowledged skill, he was the logical choice for the presidential nomination. Of course he had acquired numerous enemies in his rise to preeminence, but in the end his fate was sealed by a pivotal group of delegates who, without pronounced personal animus, concluded that he would be a dangerously vulnerable candidate. A reputation for radicalism, not entirely deserved, was the first count against the New York Senator. At heart a man of moderate temperament and considerable flexibility, he could not escape the consequences of his phrase-making talent and was remembered best as the prophet of "higher law" and "irrepressible conflict." Equally important, Seward's open record of opposition to Know-Nothingism and his long feud with the Fillmore wing of New York Whiggery promised to alienate much of the desperately needed American vote. At the same time, his close association with Thurlow Weed repelled many party idealists who regarded machine politics as a synonym for corruption. The conduct of the large New York contingent that came to vote and shout for Seward at Chicago deepened the suspicion that his supporters were not altogether respectable. "They can drink as much whiskey," wrote Murat Halstead, "swear as loud and long, sing as bad songs, and 'get up and howl' as ferociously as any crowd of Democrats you ever heard, or heard of."[30]

So the cry was raised that the nomination of Seward would spell defeat, that he could not carry the doubtful states of the lower North. Among the prominent members of this chorus, significantly, were the gubernatorial candidates for Pennsylvania and Indiana.[31] Worried talk about "availability" had been stimulated by Democratic gains in certain New England spring elections and, more recently, by the entry of John Bell and Edward Everett in the presidential race as nominees of the newly organized Constitutional Union party. As for the spectacular events at Charleston early in May, their total effect was not entirely clear. In itself, the disruption of the opposition brightened Republican prospects and therefore strengthened the case for Seward. But the expected nomination of Douglas by Northern Democrats when they reassembled at Baltimore would bring a powerful figure, freed of association with the slaveholders, into competition for the moderate vote in the free states. With Seward running against the Little Giant, it was argued, the contest might well end in the House of Representatives, where a Republican victory seemed doubtful.

The opposition to Seward gathered strength during the first two days of the Republican convention, and yet it showed little sign of uniting on a single candidate. Just before midnight on May 17, a disconsolate Greeley, supporting Edward Bates of Missouri, sent a telegram to his New York *Tribune* predicting that Seward would be nominated.[32] Even as he did so, however, a discernible trend toward Lincoln was beginning to emerge from the confusion. The skillful work of Lincoln's managers at this juncture undoubtedly contributed much to his success, but certain favorable circumstances made their achievement something less than miraculous.

In the first place, Lincoln became Seward's chief rival because the other candidates for that position were exceptionally weak. Salmon P. Chase, the only man approaching Seward's stature as an antislavery leader, was considered more radical than the New Yorker and never had a chance. Some Ohio delegates hoped to drop Chase and start a boom for their uncouth senator, Benjamin F. Wade, but the Chase men blocked the scheme. Pennsylvania, with its immense influence, could offer nothing better than Simon Cameron, a political turncoat, reputedly corrupt, and once closely allied with the Know-Nothings. Edward Bates appealed to many conservatives and to strategists like Greeley who wanted to remove the stigma of radicalism and sectionalism from the Republican party. But he was a rather colorless man in his late sixties, a halfhearted Republican who had supported Fillmore in 1856. His nomination, in addition to offending foreign-born voters and the more dedicated opponents of slavery, would have amounted to a retreat and a misrepresentation. The lesser candidates in the field, like William L. Dayton and John McLean, had little hope unless the leaders should falter and the convention become deadlocked.

And then there was Lincoln, a newcomer to prominence in national politics who nevertheless possessed several important advantages, not the least of which was the luster of his dramatic encounters with Douglas. He seemed more moderate than Seward, largely because of his less conspicuous role in the struggle against slavery; he had never taken a public stand for or against nativism and was therefore unobjectionable to foreigners and Know-Nothings alike; he was the favorite son of a critically important state; and his frontier background would be a great campaign asset. These were the major elements in Lincoln's much-discussed "availability." Yet at the same time, and equally important, this product of the Western prairies was firm and forthright in his position on slavery—a thoroughgoing and thoroughly representative Republican as well as an available one. His nomination would involve no sacrifice of the party's principles, no dilution of its will.

Lincoln's candidacy was built upon a foundation of united support from his own state, the Illinois delegation having been instructed to vote for him as a unit. But it was Indiana that made him a major contender. The Hoosiers, without a candidate of their own, and convinced that Seward could not be elected, gave some thought to Bates but then decided to cast all 26 of their votes for Lincoln on the first ballot. This sizable gain helped soften up the Pennsylvania delegates, most of whom now agreed to make Lincoln their second choice. The views of Pennsylvania in turn exercised a profound influence upon the rest of the convention.[33] Accordingly, when the hour arrived for placing names in nomination, a two-man race had already begun to take shape, with Seward in the lead, but Lincoln possessing the greater momentum.

On the first ballot, Seward received 173½ votes to Lincoln's 102, with ten other candidates trailing far behind. Needing only 60 more votes to win, Seward had little chance of getting them. The sectional nature of his weakness was manifest in the fact that the states of the lower North, stretching from New Jersey to Iowa, gave him only 3½ votes out of 170. In the succeeding stages of the contest, he made only slight gains within that critical area. The second ballot followed immediately, and, with Pennsylvania leading the way, a shift to Lincoln brought him almost even with Seward, 184½ to 181. The trend was now plain, and to no one's surprise, Lincoln's total on the third ballot surged to 231½, just 1½ votes short of victory. Four delegates from Ohio quickly switched to Lincoln, and the battle was over. Outside, the city of Chicago began its wild celebration, and the name "Lincoln" flashed along telegraph wires across the country. The Seward men were stunned not only by defeat but by the swiftness with which it had come. They walked, Halstead said, "from the slaughterhouse, more ashamed than embittered."[34]

A great deal has been written about the clever tactics of Lincoln's managers and about the lavish promises of patronage with which they lured delegates to their side. Yet it should be remembered that the Seward forces had just as many offices to peddle and more money at their disposal. Neither should the influence of the pro-Lincoln galleries be overestimated. In the vice-presidential contest, after all, the crowd shouted for Cassius M. Clay, but the prize went to Hannibal Hamlin.[35] The convention was neither bought nor stampeded. The very pattern of voting reveals a realistic decision that the leading candidate could not win in the general election and must give way to someone who could. Yet in nominating the more "available" Lincoln, the Republicans did not compromise themselves or their objectives. And without knowing it, they had made the most memorable choice in all the history of the presidency.

Back in 1854, the men calling themselves Republicans had constituted the radical wing of the anti-Nebraska coalition. Then a more moderate element had entered the picture and directed the work of effective organization. By 1858, some of its leaders were disposed to broaden the base of the party and reconstruct it along more conservative lines. If Republicanism had retained its pristine character, it probably would not have come to power. If, on the other hand, the party had followed the course marked out by Greeley, secession just might have been prevented, or at least postponed. But in choosing the middle way, in nominating an Abraham Lincoln, the Republicans made themselves both invincible in the North and unacceptable in the deep South.

Southern apprehensions, although fed by hysteria, were to some extent rooted in reality. For there was an unmistakable ambivalence at the core of Republicanism, well exemplified in Lincoln's contemplation of "ultimate extinction" while offering to guarantee the security of slavery where it already existed. Furthermore, dimly visible behind this aggressive new political machine were the mobilizing forces of an economic order that likewise seemed inimical to the Southern way of life. The Republican party in 1860, although posing no great immediate threat to the slaveholding society of the South, nevertheless carried within it an implication of that society's doom. In their eventual decision to withdraw from the emerging newer nation symbolized by Lincoln, Southerners were in effect attempting to hold back a future that appeared to have no place for them.

CHAPTER 6

The Election of Lincoln as a Crucial Event

The election of 1860 was certainly "crucial" and probably also "critical." These two words might seem to be more or less synonymous, but the latter has come to have a restricted, technical meaning in the study of American politics, owing to the sustained influence of an article published in 1955 by V. O. Key, Jr. Key was concerned with voting behavior, and he defined a critical election as one entailing a sharp and lasting realignment of party loyalties.[1] On the other hand, "crucial," as applied to elections, has retained its more general meaning of decisive—consequential—supremely important. That was how it was understood by the four historians who participated in a symposium at the American Philosophical Society in 1972, and whose papers were subsequently published, under the supervision of Arthur S. Link, as *Crucial American Elections* (Philadelphia, Pa., 1973). My contribution, which is here presented with some minor revisions, evinces more than a little fascination with the problem of defining cruciality.

In 1860, the presidential race should have been a close one between Stephen A. Douglas of Illinois and William H. Seward of New York, with some lesser competition from the remnants of the Whig and American parties. If Douglas had won, there probably would have been no secession; if Seward had won, there probably would have been no firing on Fort Sumter. Instead, a majority of Republicans in convention rejected Seward and nominated Abraham Lincoln, while a large minority of Democrats, most Southerners, rejected Douglas and split their party. Lincoln, less handicapped than Seward by the stigma of radicalism, won an election that the New Yorker might have lost. The Deep South, to whom all Republicans looked alike, rejected Lincoln as president and seceded from the Union. Lincoln and other Republican leaders rejected compromise while also refusing to acquiesce in peaceable separation. And the war came.

Of all American presidential elections, that of 1860 is the one that most obviously qualifies as "crucial." Indeed, it might well be regarded as a model of crucial elections, except that in some ways and especially in its aftermath, the election of 1860 was unique. If a crucial election is a contest that leads directly to disunion and civil war, there has been only one such phenomenon in American history—a phenomenon full of its own special drama and meaning, but not lending itself readily to analogy or comparative analysis. So perhaps it would be more useful to say that this was one of a number of elections that may be labeled *crucial* but the only one that proved to be *catastrophic*. The distinction is important because it is one thing to study the election of 1860 as an example of a crucial election and something else again to study it as the immediate cause of the Civil War. But if we begin by identifying the elements of cruciality that it shares with certain other presidential campaigns, we may then more easily recognize the influences uniquely linking this election with catastrophe.

Of course the meaning and importance of an election may vary considerably according to the angle of observation. For American Catholics, the presidential campaigns of 1928 and 1960 had special significance. For American Negroes, the famous contests of 1800 and 1828 were virtually meaningless, whereas the election of 1868 was perhaps crucial. The fundamental distinction, however, is between the contemporary view and the retrospective one. To participants, a crucial election is one that offers a relatively clear choice on matters of great importance; to historians, it is one that had notable consequences or marked a sharp turn in the course of events. These do not necessarily amount to the same thing. For example, voters in 1932 had more of a choice, and voters in 1964 had less of a choice, than they realized at the time. But concerning the election of 1860 there appears to be no doubt. From almost every point of view it was a crucial election, recognized as such by contemporaries and confirmed as such by successive generations of historians. The angle of observation may affect its meaning but cannot diminish its importance.

If the election of 1932 seemed crucial at the time, it was because of the historical context rather than the range of choice apparently offered by the contestants. Not until four years later did the electorate have an opportunity to pass judgment on the New Deal. An election held in critical times is to some extent a crucial one ipso facto, no matter who the candidates may be, for a crisis can magnify the effect of minor differences. For example, the campaign of 1848 took place during a four-year sectional crisis over slavery in the newly acquired territories of the Far West, but the two major candidates offered voters such a blurred choice that they divided both the North and the South rather equally between them.[2] By 1850, however, the difference between Zachary Taylor and Lewis Cass was enough to have perhaps precipitated the Civil War ten years ahead of time, if Taylor's death had not intervened.[3]

In the case of 1860, to be sure, crisis is equated with the secession movement that followed the election. There is not enough recognition of the extent to which the entire contest was conducted in an atmosphere of crisis. John Brown's grave was still new when the national conventions assembled in the spring, and rumors of incipient slave uprisings, supposedly plotted by itinerant abolitionist agents, continued to ripple through the Southern states. Fear that a Lincoln victory might inspire reenactment of "the horrors of St. Domingo" was expressed privately on the eve of the election by no less a personage than the Chief Justice of the United States.[4]

A slave-revolt panic had also struck the South four years earlier,[5] and in several other ways the elections of 1856 and 1860 were remarkably similar. Voters in each instance had a relatively clear and decisive choice on the same paramount issue. Party alignments were much alike, except for Democratic unity in 1856 and division in 1860. Civil war in Kansas provided a background of crisis in 1856, and fear of a Republican victory inspired the Southern threats of secession that were to be heard again in 1860. The outcome, of course, was different in 1856. Instead of escalating the sectional crisis, it evoked the loudest sighs of relief since the success of compromise in 1850. But does the different outcome exclude the campaign of 1856 from the category of crucial elections? Was it any less critical than the campaign of 1860? There is a parallel in the elections of 1796 and 1800, which presented similar issues and the same presidential candidates but had different results. The choices, potentialities, and hazards were much the same on both occasions; yet only the victory of Jefferson over Adams is ordinarily labeled "crucial."

Obviously, we have come up against the definitional problem already mentioned. Does cruciality inhere primarily in choices offered or in decisions taken, in the alternatives or the results? And further, is a decision to embrace change or initiate action more "crucial" than a decision to reject change or refrain from acting? The standard attitude of American historians seems well illustrated in their treatment of these two pairs of elections, 1796 vs. 1800 and 1856 vs. 1860. Apparently, the decision is what counts, but a negative decision does not count very much.

If so, however, then what about the election of 1896? Here, as in 1796 and 1856, the alternatives overshadow the outcome, and who lost seems more important than who won. Yet historians commonly regard the McKinley-Bryan contest as "crucial." In some significant way, it must resemble the elections of 1800 and 1860, but how? Let us imagine that a suicidal young man named John Doe goes to a tenth-floor window, climbs out on the ledge, thinks about it, and climbs back inside. Later, he goes to the same window, climbs out on the ledge, and jumps. Which was the more crucial decision? Before replying, you should of course ask, "How *much* later?" If it was an hour, a month, or even a year, the right answer is no doubt "the decision to jump." But what if the interval was thirty or forty years, during which time Mr. Doe became a famous author, a millionaire, and a two-handicap golfer with a beautiful, passionate wife and six gifted, nonrebellious children? The effective duration of a decision may largely determine just how crucial it was. The elections of 1796 and 1856 were both reversed four years later. The election of 1896, on the other hand, produced a decision that lasted. Like the campaigns of 1800 and 1860, it ushered in an identifiable historical period of some duration.

In addition, the McKinley-Bryan contest is one of the presidential campaigns that have acquired transcendent meaning as embodiments of the elemental and everlasting clash between democracy and privilege. Bryan, the "great commoner," became a major figure in America's democratic mythology, along with Jefferson, Jackson, Wilson, and Franklin Roosevelt. But the election of 1860 was no classic confrontation of classes, and the victor differed from those five leaders in his party allegiance. There is no reason why the greatest human symbol of democracy should have been a Whig-turned-Republican or why he should have emerged in the year 1860—no reason, that is, save the unique personality and genius of Abraham Lincoln. Still, symbolic heroes and crucial elections seem to go together, perhaps because historians put them together, and the election of 1860 is no exception.

There *is* a conspicuous exception, however, that poses another terminological question. The heroic figure of George Washington is not associated with a "crucial" election. Yet the office of the presidency was virtually tailored to fit this man, and in certain respects no other election was as important—indeed, as *necessary*—as his in 1789. But of course it was also a foregone conclusion. No one else received any electoral votes in 1789 or 1792. The question is, how *close* must an election be to qualify as "crucial"? Can a mismatch such as that of 1936 (Roosevelt, 532 electoral votes; Landon, 8) be called "crucial," even taking into account the false expectations aroused by the *Literary Digest*?[6] A lopsided score does not necessarily make a contest less critical—not, for instance, in the seventh game of a World Series. Yet, in popular thought at least, a crucial election must be in some way a historical forking-point. This means that in retrospect it probably must be a contest that might easily have had a different outcome, such as the elections of 1876 and 1884. The conception of what is "crucial" usually includes some elements of contingency and choice, even of horseshoe-nail causality. It is extremely difficult to associate cruciality with inevitability.

Since hope springs eternal, an election more often seems close in prospect than in retrospect. It is not customary to acknowledge even the possibility of defeat, and only once in American history has the outcome of a relatively close election been openly predicted months ahead of time, not only by the winners but by many of the losers. Lincoln won the presidency in 1860 by converting a mere 39 percent of the popular vote into 59 percent of the electoral vote. Some modest changes in a few strategic places would have produced a different result.[7] Yet by midsummer numerous Americans were echoing John D. Ashmore of South Carolina in his assertion that Lincoln's election was "almost certain."[8]

There were several influences contributing to this anomaly. First, the division of the opposition meant that no other candidate could possibly win in the electoral college. The only real alternative to a Lincoln victory was an election thrown into the House of Representatives, where the Republicans might have had some trouble piecing out a majority. Thus the choice offered voters was simply "yes" or "no" on Lincoln, without any assurance that a "no" vote would stick.[9] Furthermore, the sectional commitments were so firmly set in most parts of the country that the decision actually rested with a trio of pivotal states—Pennsylvania, Indiana, and Illinois—all of which had recorded strong shifts toward Republicanism.[10] And finally, Southern fire-eaters loudly predicted a Lincoln victory in order to encourage preparations for secession.

Thus, in spite of all the oratory and pageantry, the election of 1860 was not in itself a suspenseful contest. The tension mounting day by day resulted much less from uncertainty about the outcome than from anxiety about the expected sequel. Any lingering doubt was dissolved in October when Republican candidates won the state elections in Pennsylvania and Indiana. Even Stephen A. Douglas acknowledged defeat at this point. "Mr. Lincoln is the next President," he declared. "We must try to save the Union."[11] This, mind you, was a month before the presidential election. We tend to think of a crucial campaign as one in which there is considerable doubt about the outcome, but here there was an unusual degree of certitude about the outcome long before the votes were counted, and this certitude may have turned a crisis into a catastrophe.

The presidential election of 1860 was by no means the only one to precipitate a crisis. The years 1800 and 1876 immediately spring to mind. However, both of those crises were caused by the abnormal inconclusiveness of the election results—in sharp contrast to the grim certainty of Lincoln's victory. Neither was the campaign of 1860 unique in reflecting a sectional cleavage in national politics, for as far back as 1796 the election of John Adams had constituted a triumph of North over South. Only in 1860, however, did a large bloc of states fail to give the winning candidate a single popular vote.[12] And although the two-party system has certainly broken down at other times, only in 1860 do we find the oddity of virtually two separate presidential races (Lincoln vs. Douglas in the North and Bell vs. Breckinridge in the South), one of which was more or less inconsequential. Furthermore, Lincoln was not the first president-elect to be regarded as in league with the Devil, but whereas in 1801, for instance, certain New England ladies allegedly feared that Thomas Jefferson would confiscate their Bibles, in 1860 many

Southerners feared that Lincoln would subvert their slaves and thus put their very lives in danger.

Of course these and other peculiar characteristics setting the election of 1860 apart from other presidential campaigns were to some extent merely symptoms of the sectional conflict. Indeed, it is difficult to put aside an impression that the voters in 1860 were essentially acting out a decision already firmly made. One leading dictionary defines "crucial" as "involving a final and supreme decision," but in historical causation as in the functioning of a bureaucracy, the final decision may not be the truly effective one. In the drama called "The Coming of the Civil War," the election of 1860 often seems to be more a part of the denouement than a part of the climax. So many options had already been closed off by the late 1850's that there may have been no forking-point left with a path leading directly away from disaster. A Republican failure to capture the presidency in 1860 would probably have meant skirting the precipice for another four years. In contrast, the campaign of 1844 can be viewed as a real turning-point; for the nomination of Van Buren instead of Polk or the election of Clay instead of Polk would have changed the whole timetable of history by preventing or at least delaying the territorial expansion that revived the sectional quarrel over slavery.

If alternatives were limited in 1860 because of decisions reached in earlier elections, they were even more profoundly affected by decisions made less formally and more gradually outside the electoral process. I refer especially to the development of the Southern conviction that slavery must be protected at all costs, to the diverging sectional beliefs about the value and sanctity of the Union, and to the hardening opinion of a Northern majority that slavery was incompatible with the destinies of the Republic. These were the fundamental decisions acted out in the election of 1860 and in its aftermath of secession and civil war.

The election itself may be viewed as a terminal symptom, the study of which only scratches the surface of the problem of war causation that has so fascinated historians. Yet the election also proved to be that point of conversion where general attitudes and beliefs are translated into specific actions. One suspects that cataclysmic events sometimes fail to occur, even in the presence of adequate causes, simply because no adequate point of conversion ever materializes.

The record of sectional confrontations dating back to the 1790's made it abundantly clear that no common interest—not even the defense of slavery—could induce the South to act as a unit. Fire-eaters lived with the memory of the cold reception given the Virginia and Kentucky Resolutions in other Southern states, of South Carolina out on its lonely limb in 1833, of Southern congressmen refusing to sign Calhoun's "Southern Address" in 1849, of the abortive efforts to launch a secession movement in 1851. But then, complete unity was not necessary, for if a respectable number of states were to act in concert, the rest of the South would probably follow. The problem of secessionists in these first-line states, stretching around the coast from the Carolinas to Texas, was not so much to arouse sentiment as to crystallize initiative.

In the past, Southern disaffection had usually been inspired by proceedings of Congress, such as the enactment of a tariff measure in 1832 and the introduction of the Wilmot Proviso in 1846. But Congress was a place where half-loaves were common fare, and in each instance the crisis had been defused by compromise or something resembling compromise. This had happened as recently as 1858, when the so-called "English bill" put an end to a fierce controversy over the proposed admission of Kansas with a pro-slavery constitution.[13] Two years earlier, however, the presidential election had for the first time become a potential signal for disunion, and by 1860 it was evident that a Lincoln victory would have a more explosive effect than any legislative proposals likely to receive serious attention from Congress in the immediate future. The Buchanan administration had in fact managed to sweep the dangerous territorial issue somewhat messily under the rug, but, ironically, it had done so in a manner that enhanced Republican chances of capturing the presidency. This meant that control had shifted from the professional politician to the ordinary voter, particularly the Northern voter. And the impact of an election, unlike that of a bill before Congress, cannot be moderated by postponement or last-minute compromise.

For the fundamental causes of the Civil War we should have to look much deeper into American history, but if we are just trying to understand why the final crisis came about when it did and took the form that it did, then the campaign of 1860 and the electoral process as a whole deserve close attention. Consider, for instance, the effect of Lincoln's nomination instead of Seward's, which may well have made the difference between victory and defeat for the Republicans; or the influence of the general-ticket system in the choice of electors, which enabled a man to become president against the wishes of three-fifths of the voters.

Especially important were the conditions and arrangements that made the presidential election a long-expected, clear-cut signal for rebellion and allowed secession to proceed so far without resistance. They include the four-month interval between election day and inauguration day (a constitutional relic foolishly retained in the era of the railroad and telegraph); those October state elections that confirmed Southern apprehensions a month ahead of time; and all the peculiar circumstances that caused a relatively close election to be regarded far in advance as virtually a foregone conclusion. For a moment, imagine Lincoln winning instead an election that was in doubt all the way—better still, an election thrown into the House of Representatives. Would Southerners, hopeful to the last, have been able then to launch such a successful disunion movement? It seems unlikely. The pall of inevitability hanging over the campaign (which sets it apart from other crucial elections in American history) had the effect of providing additional time for plotting to mature and for the idea of secession to become domesticated in Southern minds.

As for the question of why the mere election of a Republican president should have provided sufficient impulse for disunion, let it be remembered that, along with all the Southern fears of what might happen after Lincoln took office, there was the fear in some quarters that nothing very dramatic would happen at all—that Republican subversion of the slaveholding system would proceed so gradually and insidiously as to attenuate Southern resistance. The four months preceding the inauguration of the *first* Republican president constituted a unique span of time when the threat to the South was unlimited as a potential but untested as a reality. Thus the election of Lincoln was a more compelling signal for concerted Southern action than any that had ever been sounded before or was ever likely to be sounded again.

CHAPTER 7

The New Political History and the Coming of the Civil War

Any serious student of Abraham Lincoln's career must come to grips sooner or later with the question of what brought about the Civil War; for the biographer's understanding of the causes of the conflict is likely to have a significant effect on how he views Lincoln. Indeed, the Lincoln image changes noticeably with the historiographical climate. Over the past century, interpretation of Civil War causation has passed through a number of fairly distinct phases, such as the Beardian emphasis upon economic factors and the "revisionist" perception of a war that could and should have been avoided. In recent years, treatment of the subject has been strongly affected by the quantitative methods of the "new political history" as applied to the study of antebellum politics. The following examination of that effect was presented at the University of Washington in August 1984 as my presidential address to the Pacific Coast Branch of the American Historical Association. It was published in the May 1985 issue of the *Pacific Historical Review*.

In the year 1900, Edward Eggleston's presidential address to the American Historical Association was titled "The New History." By that phrase he meant historical study of the common people and how they had lived, with much less emphasis, accordingly, on the politics, statecraft, diplomacy, and warfare that had long been the staples of schoolbook history and historical scholarship.[1] Eggleston did not invent the phrase, and the need for a newer, better kind of history had often been proclaimed—by Henry Thomas Buckle and Herbert Spencer some forty years earlier, for instance, and by Voltaire a century before them.[2]

It was James Harvey Robinson of Columbia University who appropriated the phrase as the title of a book and made it the battle cry of an informal, high-spirited movement among certain academic historians for reform of historical scholarship. *The New History*, published in 1912, the year also of Woodrow Wilson's New Freedom and Theodore Roosevelt's New Nationalism, reflected its Progressive context in maintaining that study of the past should be undertaken primarily in order to make the present more understandable and thus facilitate progress toward a better future. To fulfill this utilitarian purpose, said Robinson, history must extend its reach to the totality of human experience and must concentrate on "the normal and long enduring rather than the transient and exceptional." Freeing itself from the "trammels" of the literary tradition, history must embrace and synthesize all the other disciplines dedicated to the systematic study of human society. "The sciences relating to mankind will hereafter dominate the work of the historian," he predicted.[3]

Thus amalgamation with the social sciences, though perhaps not the central theme of the "new history," was a significant part of its credo. Not until more than half a century later, however, did it begin to appear that Robinson's prediction might prove to be accurate. For a time, despite the preaching and practice of a few prophets like the indefatigable Harry Elmer Barnes,[4] history and the social sciences tended, if anything, to drift further apart in the United States. This tendency was especially pronounced in the case of political science, which moved steadily away from its historical outlook and reliance on the genetic method toward an analytic and presumably more scientific mode heavily dependent on behavioral psychology.[5] It is true that the two most influential explanations of the American past came from two early advocates of the "new history" and that the work of both men had interdisciplinary implications. Yet neither Frederick Jackson Turner's frontier hypothesis nor Charles A. Beard's economic interpretation of politics, for all the argument and scholarship that each inspired, drew the practice of historians appreciably closer to that of the social sciences.

Of course, the isolation of history as a discipline never approached totality. One way or another, many historians kept at least sporadically in touch with work being done in other fields. Some even borrowed concepts and terminology from the social sciences to enrich their own scholarship. But very few endeavored to actually *become* social scientists in pursuing their study of the past.[6] The barriers against doing so included professional inertia and academic departmentalization, but perhaps most important was a widespread conviction that the practice of history differed fundamentally from that of the social sciences, being concerned with the particularities of human experience in all their rich and subtle variety, rather than with the regularities and universals that can be abstracted from such experience.

This "idiographic" character of history was generally affirmed in 1946 by the group of distinguished historians who, as the committee on historiography of the Social Science Research Council, produced Bulletin 54, *Theory and Practice in Historical Study*. According to one of the basic "propositions" presented in their report: "The ideal which controls the historian in search of the utmost knowledge of the past is to achieve the most informed understanding of *occurrences* and *personalities* that available sources and discriminating imagination will permit."[7] To be sure, the committee also paid its brief respects to the principle of interdisciplinary scholarship, but it gave much more attention to the problem of causality, and the longest chapter in the book was a case study of historical writing about the causes of the Civil War.[8]

Thomas C. Cochran, probably the strongest advocate of social science methodology on the committee, declared in 1948, "Fifty years of rapid growth in the social sciences have had surprisingly little effect on the general content and synthesis of American history."[9] Yet the very article in which he made this complaint proved to be one of the early manifestoes of a new "new history" that would have a striking effect on American historical scholarship. In 1954, a reconstituted SSRC committee on historiography, with Cochran now its chairman, presented another report, Bulletin 64, and devoted the whole of it to *The Social Sciences in Historical Study*. The most striking recent change in the study of history, the committee declared, was "the growing emphasis on fraternization or amalgamation with other disciplines."[10]

The shape of the new "new history" was at first but dimly apprehended. At a conference sponsored by the SSRC in 1953, fifteen leading historians freely acknowledged the value of interdisciplinary scholarship. "Nevertheless," says a report of the discussion, "the sense of the meeting was that historians should not consciously attempt to remake history in the social-science image and should not attempt to restore communication with the social sciences simply by adopting social science methods as their own."[11] Richard Hofstadter, writing in 1956, suggested that the formal methods of the social sciences, useful though they might be, were less significant than the "substantive findings" of those disciplines and the "speculative richness" that their perspectives added to the study of history.[12] It is especially worth noting that Bulletin 64 devoted only one of its 171 pages to discussion of "quantitative method."[13] And as late as 1960, a member of the faculty of the New School for Social Research could assert: "The trend in the social sciences toward the quantitative methods and techniques of the natural sciences . . . has no counterpart in historiography."[14]

Yet in 1960 the quantification revolution was well under way. V. O. Key's "A Theory of Critical Elections," which was to have such profound influence on the analysis of American voting behavior, had appeared a few years earlier. Alfred H. Conrad and John R. Meyer had published their essay on the profitability of slavery, often cited as the first significant product of modern cliometric scholarship. Merle Curti had produced *The Making of an American Community*, a critique of the Turner thesis, in which he made extensive statistical use of manuscript census returns and other quantifiable data. Lee Benson, already launched on his crusade for a more systematic historical scholarship, had just completed his seminal work, *The Concept of Jacksonian Democracy*. And Robert William Fogel was presumably viewing with pride his first book, a financial study of the Union Pacific Railroad, in which he used formal economic theory to analyze historical data and arrive at characteristically revisionist conclusions.[15]

There was resistance, of course, to what Carl Bridenbaugh called "that Bitch-goddess, Quantification," enough so that Fogel in 1979 characterized the relationship between "scientific" and "traditional" historians as one of "cultural warfare."[16] Resistance would have been obscurantist if it had been directed merely at efforts to introduce greater statistical precision into study of the past. In fact, few American historians stood openly opposed to such efforts, though many were avowedly skeptical about their potential value. But the word "quantification" came to signify much more than sophisticated measurement. It connoted the whole theoretical structure and operational strategy of the social sciences, including especially the building and testing of explicit models of human behavior. The nature of the struggle between the "scientifics" and the "traditionals" has been obscured by confusion of the narrow and broad meanings of "quantification," as well as by the disposition of some of the more amiable quantifiers to portray their work as simply an enrichment of traditional historical methods, rather than a repudiation of them. But the question ultimately at issue was whether the discipline of history should be radically restructured in the image of the social sciences.[17]

The new "new history" that had emerged into full view by the end of the 1960's was actually a cluster of movements associated with different behavioral science disciplines. So it became customary to speak of the new economic history, the new social history, the new political history, and (a breed somewhat apart) the new psychological history, or psychohistory. The term "new political history," as Allan Bogue has suggested, might well have been used to characterize the work of scholars like Hofstadter, Bernard Bailyn, and Eric Foner, who were "exploring the significance of political ideas, symbols, and ideologies."[18] Instead, the label was appropriated (no doubt by analogy with the flourishing "new economic history") to designate the growing fellowship of political historians committed particularly to the use of quantification and more generally to the research methods and theory of the behavioral sciences.

The richness of quantifiable data encouraged practitioners of the new political history to concentrate heavily on voting behavior—that is, upon popular elections and legislative roll calls. Their two most important conceptual achievements have been the stability-realignment model of national elections, formulated principally by political scientists, and the ethnocultural (or ethnoreligious) interpretation of voter motivation, which is largely the work of historians. Beginning with Benson's work on the Jacksonian period, the ethnocultural model has substantially replaced the older Progressive interpretation of American political alignments as reflecting primarily economic and class divisions.

Religion and ethnic identity, and the social attitudes derived from them—these, according to the ethnoculturalists, have been the major determinants of voting choice. In its most reductive version, as set forth by Ronald P. Formisano, Paul Kleppner, and others, the ethnocultural thesis presents an American electorate divided between pietist and anti-pietist subcultures: the one fervently puritan, the other coolly ritualistic; the one determined to impose rules of right behavior on the community, the other setting faith apart from conduct and resisting efforts at moralistic control; the one supporting Whigs and Republicans, the other faithfully Democratic.[19] In *Iolanthe*, a lonely sentry muses on the fact that "every boy and every gal born into the world alive is either a little Liberal or else a little Conservative." Perhaps if W. S. Gilbert had chosen to comment on politics in the United States, he would have written something like this:

> Every American live birth,
> Whether natural or surgical,
> Means one more little pietist
> Or else one more liturgical.

Although the statistical methods and theoretical constructs of the ethnoculturalists have been called into question,[20] the general substance of their interpretation has won much acceptance and remains to date the most conspicuous finding of the new political history.

For a century and more, the most common complaint lodged against books of history had been that they were crammed with the details of specific *events* that were seldom worth the trouble of remembering. The French *Annalistes* Lucien Febvre and Fernand Braudel echoed Herbert Spencer and James Harvey Robinson in depreciating *l'histoire événementielle*, and they in turn were echoed by advocates of the new social science history in the United States. For instance, Samuel Hays maintained that the conceptual frameworks of historical scholarship "should be oriented toward *structure* rather than *event*." Fascination with sensational events, he said, tended to limit the historian's imagination and make history virtually structureless, except for "the accidental juxtaposition of those events in a time sequence."[21]

But events come in many sizes, and a super-event like the French Revolution or the American Civil War, because it plays havoc with structure and continuity, is both a nuisance and a challenge for scholars viewing the past from a social science perspective. To Frederick Jackson Turner, for instance, the Civil War was of marginal interest. He subordinated the sectional struggle between North and South to the process of westward expansion and declared in his most famous essay that when American history came to be viewed properly, the slavery issue would appear merely as "an incident."[22]

Charles A. Beard likewise belittled the moral conflict over slavery but made the Civil War itself a social cataclysm of prime importance in his economic interpretation of American history.[23]

In the 1940's and 1950's, when a good many founders of the "new political history" were entering the professional scene, Civil War causation was the most intensively discussed problem in American historiography—the principal matter at issue being the validity of the "revisionist" or "needless war" interpretation. In one eight-year interval, major works on the subject were published by Avery Craven, Roy F. Nichols, David M. Potter, Kenneth M. Stampp, and Allan Nevins (whose contribution ran to four volumes), and these were but a fraction of the total output during the period. Lee Benson later ventured the guess that "more scholarly man years have probably been devoted to 'the coming of the Civil War' than to any other past event, American or non-American."[24]

Benson himself contributed several times to the discussion, but, with a few exceptions, the "new political history" tended to deemphasize the sectional conflict. Cochran had predicted such a tendency,[25] and Joel H. Silbey vehemently rationalized it in 1964. His article, "The Civil War Synthesis in American Political History," was an indictment of all those historians whose primitive research methods, "inaccuracies," "oversimplifications," and "naïveté about the political process" had produced a false impression that the antebellum years were predominantly a period of increasing sectional antagonism. On the contrary, said Silbey, recent scholarship raised "serious doubts about the importance of sectional differences as far as most Americans were concerned," and even as late as the election of 1860, "many nonsectional issues were apparently more immediately important to the groups involved than any imminent concern with Northern-Southern differences." The Civil War, Silbey lamented, has accordingly had a "pernicious influence" on the study of antebellum politics because it has "distorted the reality of political behavior" in that era.

All was not lost, however. He, Silbey, and certain other scholars were already engaged in deflating the "myth" of a "universal preoccupation" with sectionalism. Instead of depending upon the dubious evidence available in contemporary letters, newspapers, and other documentary sources, they were acquiring a much better understanding of public attitudes through statistical analysis of elections and legislative voting. "Historians," Silbey admonished, "must become more aware of the complexities of human behavior," and must recognize that "single-factor explanations" are not likely to work.[26]

Of course the scholars whom Silbey criticized had not been as simpleminded as he portrayed them. For instance, when he assured his readers that "sectional matters were not the only problems confronting congressmen" in the antebellum period, he was denying what no historian had ever affirmed. His essay relied heavily upon use of such straw-man tactics. Furthermore, although it is true that our perceptions of the antebellum era are profoundly affected, and no doubt distorted, by our knowledge of what came next, that can scarcely be viewed as a peculiarity of Civil War historiography. Intervening events and developments affect the perception of any historical period and largely determine how it shall be studied. That retrospective influence constitutes one of the historian's occupational hazards. Hindsight is not an unmixed blessing; we can only try to maximize its advantages and minimize its disadvantages.

As it happened, scholarly interest in the sectional conflict was already subsiding when Silbey's article appeared. The civil rights revolution shifted attention to the problem of race, and thus to the study of slavery, emancipation, and reconstruction. Beyond that, young historians were being drawn toward other periods, fresher themes—indeed, into virtually whole new fields, such as women's history. And the progress of quantification had a transforming effect on the choice and design of many research projects. As the years passed, Silbey could presumably rejoice in the fact that the "pernicious influence" of the Civil War on the study of antebellum politics was declining. Yet by 1982, when he published another article on the subject, he had succumbed to the fascination of Civil War causality. He declared that the problem remained "open and alive to additional historical exploration," and that it "must be considered yet again if we are to understand it fully and accurately."[27]

At the same time, Silbey found new reason to be vexed with "traditional" historians. Their recent writings about the sectional conflict, he complained, had not taken the findings of the "new political history" properly into account. And "unfortunately," he added, "few of the new political historians themselves have tried to deal directly with the coming of the Civil War." His essay, to which I shall return later, was undertaken as a step toward repairing that deficiency and toward "integrating the factors unearthed by students of the new political history into our understanding of the breakup of the Union."[28]

One member of the "new political history" school who had previously displayed a persistent interest in the coming of the Civil War was Lee Benson, most notably, perhaps, in an essay titled "Explanations of American Civil War Causation: A Critical Assessment and a Modest Proposal to Reorient and Reorganize the Social Sciences." Exasperated with the American "historiographic system" for its failure to reach scientific agreement on the causes of the Civil War, Benson elected to deal with the subject by assimilating it to the more general problem of "internal war" and the still more general problem of violence. He proposed creation of an institute for research on violence, funded with one billion dollars over a twenty-year period. In the meantime, he offered his own "tentative explanation of Civil War causation," simply as an illustration of how theory could be used to "generate hypotheses about a specific internal war." According to Benson's own summary, "a small group of Southern Nationalists" brought about secession and thus, "much more than any other group," pushed the nation into civil war. They succeeded in doing so largely because the American political system, particularly the presidency as it was shaped by Andrew Jackson, proved "favorable to their cause."[29] This verdict, which combined an unusual institutional interpretation with an old-fashioned conspiracy thesis, did not prove to be a major breakthrough in Civil War historiography.

The coming of the Civil War was an event of such magnitude and complexity that it may be useful at this point to divide the subject somewhat arbitrarily into three overlapping categories as follows: first, the structural background of the war, which embraces all the social and psychological conditions and all the institutional arrangements impinging on it, such as the Revolutionary tradition, the constitutional order, the slaveholding system, the staple-crop economy, revivalistic religion, the progress of public education, mass immigration and nativism, republican ideology, literary romanticism, racial attitudes, and the process of westward expansion; second, the critical background of the war, which refers to the progressive intrusion of the slavery question into American public life from the founding of the nation to the showdown in 1860; third, the immediate background of the war, including the election of 1860, the secession movement, and the precipitation of hostilities.

The structural background of the Civil War is obviously a subject too complex and unbounded for treatment merely in the narrative manner. Its investigation requires theoretical moorings, analytical modes, and conceptual frameworks other than, or in addition to, chronological ones. In short, the task seems well suited for scholars using the methods of social science. Although most of the accumulated writing on the subject has come from "traditional" historians, an impressive example of what the new "new history" can accomplish is the extensive work of cliometricians on the slaveholding economy. As for practitioners of the "new political history," their scholarship has begun to illuminate both the structural and the critical background of the war, but to simplify matters, I shall treat it primarily in the latter category.

One good example of the structural approach, however, is a thoughtful essay by Thomas B. Alexander titled "The Civil War as Institutional Fulfillment." In some respects following the lead of Benson, Alexander maintained that certain features of the American political system "directly facilitated the onset of the Civil War." For instance, the symbolic importance of the presidency, which proved so crucial in 1860, would have been considerably reduced if the Constitutional Convention had created a plural rather than a unitary executive, as some of its members proposed.[30] Similarly, the manner of electing presidents, the haphazard erection of states, and the voters' cultivated fidelity to party—all paved the way to disunion.[31]

Alexander's argument was persuasive as far as it went, but he looked at only one side of the ledger. The institutional arrangements of which he spoke were at least partly offset by others that tended to postpone the day of reckoning between North and South. If a unicameral national legislature had been established as the Virginia plan proposed, if representation in Congress and in the Electoral College had been based upon free population alone as Northern delegates desired, if amendment of the Constitution had been made easier, then a critical number of Southerners might well have been driven much earlier to the conviction that the slaveholding system was no longer safe within the Union.

The critical background of the Civil War—that is, the process by which the slavery issue became a disruptive force in national politics—is more limitable in both scope and time than the structural background of the war. Attention centers mainly on the political universe, primarily in the period 1819–60 and even more intensively in the years 1846–60. Election results and various other records provide rich data for quantitative investigation, while the problems of how political behavior was motivated and how it was related to the rest of the culture invite the application of social science theory and methods. Yet sequential connections were also important, and there is a need for narrative as well as analysis—not story-telling narrative but "thick" narrative, which examines the complex tissues of change as it proceeds along a chronological course.

Among the first works of the "new political history" directly affecting interpretation of the coming of the Civil War were two studies of congressional voting behavior published in 1967. Joel H. Silbey's *Shrine of Party* covered both houses for the years 1841–52, while Thomas B. Alexander's *Sectional Stress and Party Strength* extended from 1836 to 1860 but covered only the House of Representatives. Silbey struggled to give his book a revisionist cast by emphasizing the persistent strength of partisanship in contrast with the more episodic intrusions of sectionalism. But his conclusion that party loyalty predominated in the 1840's, *except* on slavery issues and *except* in intervals of crisis such as 1849–50, amounted to little more than insisting that the bottle was half-empty instead of half-full. As many reviewers noted, both the Silbey and Alexander volumes actually tended to confirm statistically the traditional picture of a sturdy party system increasingly battered and weakened by sectional antagonism.[32]

In any case, to treat sectionalism and partisanship strictly as competing loyalties, with one or the other necessarily predominant, is to overlook their progressive interpenetration and the resulting decline in the number of congressmen (principally Southern Whigs and Northern Democrats) who had to choose between them. Consider, for instance, Silbey's assertion that the voting on the Kansas-Nebraska bill in 1854 revealed "a degree of party unity within both parties despite the intense sectional rhetoric in Congress."[33] Thus we have party "unity" contrasted with sectional "rhetoric." But the fact is that the division on the measure was even more sectional than partisan. The measure received 72 percent of the Democratic votes in both houses and 27 percent of the Whig votes. It received 89 percent of the Southern votes and 36 percent of the Northern votes. What these figures reveal is the extent to which the parties themselves, by 1854, had taken on sectional colorings.

In their analyses, Alexander relied partly, and Silbey wholly, upon Guttman scaling, a technique for measuring intensity of attitudes, positive and negative, on a particular issue or cluster of related issues. Although devised for another purpose, the technique has proved usable and useful in roll-call studies, but it is not automatically scientific. The procedure involves certain qualitative and arbitrary decisions which, if misguided, can lead to bizarre results. For example, Silbey's scalograms on the "compromise issue" in 1850 are simply out of touch with reality. They indicate, among other things, that there were "pro-compromise" majorities in both houses and that only 31 percent of the members of Congress were "anti-compromise"; that Southerners were far more "pro-compromise" than Northerners (86 percent to 21 percent in the Senate and 63 percent to 44 percent in the House); that only one out of eighteen Southern Democratic senators was "anti-compromise"; that John Wales of Delaware, one of only four men to vote for passage of all six compromise measures in the Senate, was nevertheless "anti-compromise"; and that of the twenty senators from the future Confederate states appearing on the scalogram, every single one was more "pro-compromise" than Stephen A. Douglas. Nineteen of those twenty, incidentally, appear on a scalogram of "sectionalism" for the same session of Congress and score an average of 17.2 on a scale of 18, with the 18 representing the pro-Southern extreme; yet all nineteen turn up as "pro-compromise" on the "compromise" scalogram.[34] They include such men as Andrew P. Butler, Jefferson Davis, Robert M. T. Hunter, James M. Mason, and Pierre Soulé, all of whom were actually enemies of the Compromise from beginning to end.[35]

It is in fact very clear from the voting record that only about one-quarter of the members of Congress can be classified as "pro-compromise" in the sense of lending some measure of support to both Northern and Southern portions of the compromise package; and that only about one-quarter of those true compromisers were Southerners—most of them from the border states. Southerners in

Congress voted overwhelmingly for the pro-Southern measures in the Compromise of 1850 and overwhelmingly against the pro-Northern measures. That scarcely adds up to a pro-compromise posture. By joining forces with the sectional supporters of each bill as it came up separately for consideration, the little band of compromisers in each chamber assembled the votes necessary for passage. The result, as David M. Potter has suggested, was more of an "armistice" than a compromise.[36]

Quantification went astray in this instance partly because the question of compromise was not suited to Guttman scaling; for, while the strongest proponents of compromise favored all the compromise measures, the fiercest opponents of compromise favored some of those same measures, very often even a majority of them. But in addition, the roll calls that Silbey used in his scalograms on the compromise issue were not well chosen, and often the votes that he identified as "pro-compromise" were actually pro-Southern.[37] The principal consequence of these misjudgments was great exaggeration of the support for compromise among members of Congress in general and among Southern members in particular.

Nothing in the critical background of the Civil War is more crucial than the political revolution in which the Whig party disappeared and was replaced by an entirely sectional Republican organization. This transition from the second to the third American party system extended over a number of years, though the focal event was the Kansas-Nebraska Act of 1854. The transition figures prominently in the "critical realignment" synthesis of voting behavior, but that model contributes little except the principle of periodicity to explaining why such a revolution should have occurred. The brief explanations offered now and then by Walter Dean Burnham, the leading realignment scholar, seem to have been derived from the current historical scholarship. By the 1970's, significantly, Burnham had embraced the ethnocultural thesis in its reductive, pietist vs. ritualist version.[38]

The ethnocultural interpretation introduced by Lee Benson in his study of Jacksonian politics was offered as a rebuttal and an alternative to the economic explanation of political behavior that had been associated especially with Charles A. Beard. But when the ethnoculturalists applied the thesis to the 1850's, they were disposed to join hands with Beard in depreciating the significance of the slavery controversy as a political determinant. The struggle over the Kansas-Nebraska Act, they maintained, was of less importance in bringing about the disruption of the second party system than ethnic and religious conflicts at the local level over such issues as prohibition, sabbatarianism, and Know-Nothingism.[39]

This might be called the observational or analytic version of the ethnocultural interpretation. Based upon perceptions gained from intensive studies at state and local levels, it stressed the complexity and mutability of American politics in the early 1850's, while at the same time discounting as oversimplification the antislavery explanation of the rise of the Republican party. But when certain ethnocultural historians undertook to synthesize—to impose conceptual order on the observed diversity—they themselves carried oversimplification about as far as it could go.

According to Richard J. Jensen, for instance, "When Americans became converted to religion in the nineteenth century (in 1800 few were churchgoers), those people who were psychologically more modern chose pietistic denominations, while the traditionalists favored the liturgical churches." To this remarkable account of how American church membership originated, Jensen added the flat assertion, "Pietists voted mostly Republican and liturgicals Democratic, that much is certain."[40] Which meant that the character of Republicanism was largely determined by the pietistic urge to regenerate society. Reading Jensen convinced Burnham that "pietistic revivalism provided both the absolutism and the moral energy required to bring about the realignments of the 1850's and, hence, the war against secession and slavery."[41] Thus, while the observational version of the ethnocultural interpretation minimized the emotional and moral appeal of the slavery issue among Republicans and Democrats alike, the reductive version portrayed the new Republican party as a body of fervid, self-righteous crusaders for a better world, including a world without slavery.

Two questions arise at this point, one about the general validity of the ethnocultural thesis, the other regarding its relevance to the coming of the Civil War. On the first question, scholarly opinion is mixed. Various critics have exposed the methodological and conceptual weaknesses of the thesis. For instance, church membership, itself difficult to quantify accurately, is of doubtful reliabilty as an indicator of the religious attitudes and "belief systems" that supposedly governed political behavior. Also, large segments of the population proved difficult or impossible to incorporate in the ethnocultural model—specifically, (1) Southerners, who were more often than not both pietistic *and* Democratic; (2) Methodists, the largest Protestant denomination, who appear sometimes in the pietist column and sometimes in the anti-pietist column; and (3) the many people who were hostile or indifferent to religion.[42] Nevertheless, as the perception of a general tendency frequently discernible, the ethnocultural interpretation must be taken into account, whether it is fully accepted or not. The pervasiveness of religious and ethnic influences in American politics has been amply demonstrated. What remains hypothetical is the assertion that those influences were consistently the prime determinants of voting behavior.

As for the second question (relevance to the coming of the Civil War), the observational version of the ethnocultural interpretation enriched scholarly understanding of the political realignment of the 1850's, but in the process, and especially in depreciating the slavery issue, it made the emergence of the Republican party more perplexing than before. Michael F. Holt, who had joined other ethnoculturalists in minimizing the slavery issue, became dissatisfied with what remained as an explanation of the realignment and accordingly developed a provocative new interpretation based largely upon two questionable propositions: that the second party system broke up because it ran out of issues, and that the real concern of the 1850's was not slavery but the preservation of those American values associated with the word "republicanism."[43]

The observational version also did little to explain why the anti-Nebraska coalition soon overshadowed nativism as a political force and grew so swiftly to become the North's majority party. Such explanation, to be sure, was not the purpose of the ethnoculturalists, who were concerned primarily with mass behavior at the polls. But what this illustrates is that social science history, with its highly directional, problem-solving purposes, tends to trade comprehensive grasp for penetrative power.

The reductive version of the ethnocultural thesis, aligning aggressive, culturally imperialistic pietists against defensive, pluralistic ritualists, had the advantage of boldness and clarity, but not of sufficient credibility. A stereotypic characterization of Republicanism that would surely have pleased Jefferson Davis was its principal contribution to the literature of the sectional conflict.

Of course the Republican party was actually a congeries of unusually heterogeneous elements. If one attempts to apply the ethnocultural stereotype even to the members of Lincoln's cabinet, the results are hilarious. William H. Seward, despite his Whig background, was a member of the liturgical Episcopalian church and behaviorally an anti-pietist. Salmon P. Chase would seem to have been the ideal pietist in the cabinet, but his religiosity was largely derived from his uncle and guardian, an Episcopal bishop. Montgomery Blair, probably the most puritanical cabinet member in his personal conduct, was a Presbyterian all right, but also a former Jacksonian Democrat who returned to the Democratic fold after the war. Gideon Welles regarded himself, perhaps not with entire accuracy, as a Jeffersonian freethinker. And no one is likely to classify Simon Cameron as a pietist. Are we nevertheless to believe, simply on the basis of correlations between voting and church membership, that the nearly two million men who voted for Lincoln in 1860 fitted the stereotype far better than this handful of advisers?

The secession crisis of 1860–61, though in a sense part of the critical background of the Civil War, invites separate consideration because it was during that climactic interval that the background blended into the foreground and the causes of the war began to produce their chain of effects. Until the attack on Fort Sumter, various kinds of voting constituted much of the important action in the crisis—voting at the national party conventions, in the presidential election, in the secession elections and conventions, in the congressional efforts at compromise, and at the Washington Peace Conference. Consequently, there is rich material and good reason for quantitative analysis of both mass and elite political behavior. But at the same time, one must pay close attention to the sequence, interaction, and reverberation of events, as well as to the play of contingency and individual personality upon the alternative possibilities that clustered along the path from election to civil war.

Secession was a very formal action, hard to set in motion and only partly successful when it did get under way. It is difficult to conceive of any other reasonably likely event besides the election of a Republican president that could have provoked a secession crisis in 1860 or in the years immediately following. For the student of Civil War causation, then, the key question about Lincoln's election is this: How did the Republicans, after losing in 1856, manage to capture the presidency in 1860? What made the difference? More specifically, was it a continuing growth of antislavery and anti-Southern sentiment in the North as a result of such events as the Lecompton controversy and the Dred Scott decision? Was it the broadening of the Republican appeal to include other issues besides antislavery? Was it Republican success in absorbing much of the Northern nativist vote by 1860? Did the split in the Democratic party, which shifted Stephen A. Douglas somewhat toward the antislavery side, work to the advantage or disadvantage of the Republicans? Did the nomination of Lincoln instead of Seward (openly anti-nativist and considered the more radical) secure victory where there would otherwise have been defeat? Practitioners of the "new political history" have seldom addressed these questions directly. They have concentrated on who voted for whom in 1860 and especially on whether the various ethnic groups supported or opposed the Republican cause.[44] Their studies have thus far only begun to penetrate the reasons for the surge of Republican power between 1856 and 1860.[45]

In any case, the heart of the matter is Southern secession; for it was the most extraordinary action in the sectional crisis—the one requiring the greatest amount of initiative. Quantitative studies have already produced much new information, particularly with respect to who voted for and against secession. In 1960, Seymour Martin Lipset offered statistical evidence that lesser Southern folk supported John Breckinridge as a matter of Democratic party loyalty but then opposed secession as a matter of class interest, while large slaveholders made the same switch in reverse, voting with partisan loyalty for the more moderate John Bell but then allowing class feelings to dictate their support of secession.[46] Later writing on the subject rejected or severely revised the Lipset formulation. Especially impressive was a study of three Gulf states by Peyton McCrary, Clark Miller, and Dale Baum, which lent some support to Lipset's finding of realignment but little to his class-interest explanation. The study revealed significant differences from state to state, with the largest amount of realignment occurring in Alabama and the least in Louisiana.[47]

Yet what Joel Silbey found sadly lacking in the literature on the coming of the Civil War was an application of the ethnocultural thesis to the explanation of secession. So in his 1982 essay he set out to repair that omission. Acknowledging that the thesis did not directly fit Southern politics, he asserted that what counted most was the Southern perception of Northern politics. The antislavery aspect of Republicanism did not constitute enough in itself to account for secession, Silbey maintained. What the secessionists truly feared, being principally Democrats, was the same thing that Northern Democrats feared—the cultural imperialism of the Republicans, whose rule "would lead to an unacceptably restrictive society with a dominant, snooping, interfering government forcing conformity to a narrow set of behavioral norms." Thus Southern defense of the peculiar institution was just part of the defense of all those pluralistic values that Democrats everywhere held so dear. With Lincoln's election, the secessionists took decisive action because they realized, said Silbey, that "the same power used to defeat drunken Irish Catholics could be used to destroy slavery."[48]

Perhaps the first thing to be noted about this contribution to the Civil War synthesis is that Silbey did not build his argument on a foundation of quantitative analysis. Instead, he relied entirely on the kind of evidence that he had denigrated in his 1964 essay—namely, letters, speeches, and editorials. Furthermore, only about one-third of the primary sources that he cited were associated with the seceding states. He justified quoting indiscriminately from Northern and Southern Democratic newspapers on the ground that they all had similar "sentiments" where ethnocultural matters were concerned.[49] That, however, was not an established fact to be assumed, but rather an assertion to be proved. Furthermore, a sentiment allegedly so common in both North and South seems of limited value as an explanation of sectional conflict and civil war.

Methodology aside, there are also substantive weaknesses in this ingenious argument equating secessionism with Southern Democrats, and Southern Democrats with anti-pietism. The first part of the equation is accurate only as a general tendency, with some notable exceptions. In Alabama, for example, it appears that a majority of Democrats opposed secession, while the Bell supporters, if they voted at all, favored it.[50] The second part of the equation is not accurate even as a tendency. Even assuming that the reductive distinction between pietism and anti-pietism has merit, Southerners were predominantly members of pietistic rather than liturgical churches. The South had its own brand of puritanism, its own sabbatarian and temperance crusades, its own extensive networks of social control. Indeed, because of security considerations, the slaveholders' South was the most regulated society in the country and the one in which freedom of expression was most at hazard. Neither Silbey nor anyone else has produced evidence that the secessionist Democrats were peculiarly libertarian and permissive in their social attitudes, or peculiarly sympathetic toward ethnic minorities and nonconformists. Furthermore, the alleged threat of cultural imperialism that Northern Democrats were supposedly resisting came from Republican control of state and local governments, but there was no possibility of such control in the South and thus no Republican threat to any part of the Southern social order, except slavery.

Of course, Southerners did sometimes denounce Northerners, and especially New Englanders, as puritan zealots, but that was part of the rhetoric of controversy. They also denounced the North as a land of deviants and libertines, of "Socialists, . . . revolutionists, rioters, anti-renters, Infidels, Mormons, Shakers, Greeleyites, Fusionists, Owenites, Free Lovers," and of "disgusting experiments in new forms of society."[51] For what little it might be worth, one could easily put together a string of quotations showing antebellum Southerners to have been moralistic bigots rather than freedom-loving pluralists in their view of Northern society. It should be added that when Confederate propagandists vilified Lincoln, they portrayed him, not as a puritan fanatic, but rather as a blasphemous, lecherous, pornographic drunkard. That was a puritanical vision of the ultimately evil man.

Explaining the course of events from secession to the firing on Fort Sumter constitutes a different kind of historical problem. What happened did not flow wholly out of accumulated, irresistible social forces; it was also shaped by random influences, contingent circumstances, personal impulses, and deliberate choices. The important decision-making was concentrated in the hands of a relatively few people, who cannot easily be unitized and treated as statistics. In studying the outbreak of hostilities, one is impressed again with the irregularity of the past, with the uniqueness of each moment, with the individuality and unpredictability of human behavior.

Consider, as one small example, the ambiguity of motive and the irony of consequence in Major Robert Anderson's decision to move his troops from Fort Moultrie to Fort Sumter on December 26, 1860. Anderson, a professional soldier and a Southerner, wanted to avoid surrendering his command, but he also wanted to avoid armed conflict. His removal to the more defensible Sumter, unauthorized by his superiors, was a pacificatory effort at disengagement. But Moultrie in December had nothing like the enormous symbolic meaning attached to Sumter by the following April, when the guns of a proud new republic opened fire on the fort. Thus, by postponing the day of reckoning in Charleston harbor, Anderson greatly increased its impact. He alone determined the place and nature of the confrontation that erupted into civil war. I can see no way to quantify the many ramifications of his action and no better way to handle such a subject than by employing the traditional skills of the historian.

From the *Annaliste* point of view, a single event of this kind amounts to just a surface bubble on the vast stream of the *longue durée*. But who is to say that against the background of the ages a critical moment counts for less than a stagnant century? Before we accept the invidious distinction between structure and event, let us at least be clear about which is the more fundamental. Social structure is a pattern of regularity perceived in human behavior, and regular behavior is essentially the continuing repetition of common events. Therefore, events are, in a sense, the building blocks of social structure. Of course the biggest structure of any kind is the physical universe, and it originated, according to current cosmological theory, in that primordial event called the "big bang." It seems to me, with the historiography of the Civil War very much in mind, (1) that the distinction between structure and event may be misleading because the difference between them is so far from absolute; (2) that one must, after all, know events in order to perceive structures and consider structures in order to understand events; and (3) that while a structureless history would have little meaning, an eventless history would have little interest.

Also, I do not find in the recent historiography of the Civil War anything approaching "cultural conflict" between traditional and scientific historians.[52] For one thing, the latter are hybrids, not pure scientists. The members of the ethnocultural school, for instance, rely heavily upon traditional sources and methods as well as upon quantification and social science theory. Their data may be more systematically gathered, but their inferences from the data are not more scientifically drawn than those of traditional historians. At the same time, the new history has been welcomed rather than rejected by the great majority of historians, who have made serious efforts to incorporate its findings in their teaching and scholarship.[53] It is true that the new methods have penetrated rather slowly into graduate history programs, but we have reached the day when it can be said with some assurance that any young person who enters the vocation without extensive training in social science theory and methods does so at considerable risk to his or her professional future.

Still, history, if it is to remain history, should submit only to being improved, and not to being dominated, by social science methodology. More would be lost than gained in the complete transformation that one ethnocultural historian was envisioning when he declared that the "proper objective of historical practice" is the development of social theory.[54] This pronouncement runs contrary to the whole spirit of history, which is inclusive, rather than exclusive, and pluralistic in purpose. Surely, no improvement in method would be worth losing touch with the contextual richness of the past and the individuality of human experience. Those are the special qualities of history in its classic mode, the study of which promises, not social solutions, but personal enrichment of the life of the mind.

PART II

THE WAR YEARS

CHAPTER 8

Only His Stepchildren

The two most successful biographies of Lincoln published in the second half of the twentieth century have been those by Benjamin P. Thomas (1952) and Stephen B. Oates (1977).[1] One of the notable differences between the two books—a difference reflecting profound changes in American society during the twenty-five-year interval—is the greater attention that Oates gives to the subject of race. "Only His Stepchildren" was written four years before the appearance of the Oates biography, at a time of deepening historical interest in American racial attitudes as already manifested in such works as Winthrop D. Jordan's *White over Black* (1968) and George M. Fredrickson's *The Black Image in the White Mind* (1971). Presented as the annual Robert Fortenbaugh Memorial Lecture at Gettysburg College in November 1973, it was published a year later in Volume 20 of *Civil War History* and subsequently reprinted in George M. Fredrickson, ed., *A Nation Divided: Problems and Issues of the Civil War and Reconstruction* (Minneapolis, Minn., 1975). Much has been written since then about Lincoln and race, but in preparing this essay for republication, I have let the original interpretation stand, making only a few stylistic and bibliographical changes. The newer literature on the subject, such as LaWanda Cox's important book *Lincoln and Black Freedom* (1981), is given some attention in later chapters.[2]

If the United States had a patron saint it would no doubt be Abraham Lincoln; and if one undertook to explain Lincoln's extraordinary hold on the national consciousness, it would be difficult to find a better starting point than these lines from an undistinguished poem written in 1865:

> One of the people! Born to be
> Their curious epitome;
> To share yet rise above
> Their shifting hate and love.[3]

A man of the people and yet something much more, sharing popular passions and yet rising above them here was the very ideal of a democratic leader, who in his person could somehow mute the natural antagonism between strong leadership and vigorous democracy. Amy Lowell, picking up the same theme half a century later, called Lincoln "an embodiment of the highest form of the typical American."[4] This paradox of the uncommon common man, splendidly heroic and at the same time appealingly representative, was by no means easy to sustain. The Lincoln tradition, as a consequence, came to embrace two distinct and seemingly incompatible legends—the awkward, amiable, robust, rail-splitting, storytelling, frontier folklore hero, *and* the towering figure of the Great Emancipator and Savior of the Union, a man of sorrows, Christlike in his character and fate.

Biographers have struggled earnestly with this conspicuous dualism, but even when the excesses of reminiscence and myth are trimmed away, Lincoln remains a puzzling mixture of often conflicting qualities—drollness and melancholy, warmth and reserve, skepticism and piety, humbleness and self-assurance. Furthermore, he is doubly hard to get at because he did not readily reveal his inner self. He left us no diary or memoirs, and his closest friends called him "secretive" and "shut-mouthed." Billy Herndon in one of his modest moods declared, "Lincoln is unknown and possibly always will be."[5] Plainly, there is good reason for scholarly caution in any effort to take the measure of such a man.

No less plain is the intimate connection between the Lincoln legend and the myth of America. The ambiguities in his popular image and the whisper of enigma in his portraits have probably broadened the appeal of this homespun Westerner, self-made man, essential democrat, and national martyr. Almost anyone can find a way to identify with Lincoln, perhaps because "like Shakespeare . . . he seemed to run through the whole gamut of human nature."[6] Whatever the complex of reasons, successive generations of his countrymen have accepted Abraham Lincoln as the consummate American—the representative genius of the nation. One consequence is that he tends to serve as a mirror for Americans, who, when they write about him, frequently divulge a good deal about themselves.

Of course the recurring election of Lincoln as Representative American has never been unanimous. There was vehement dissent at first from many unreconstructed rebels and later from iconoclasts like Edgar Lee Masters and cavaliers of the Lost Cause like Lyon

Gardiner Tyler.[7] In the mainstream of national life, however, it became increasingly fashionable for individuals and organizations to square themselves with Lincoln and enlist him in their enterprises. Often this required misquotation or misrepresentation or outright invention; but however it could be arranged, lobbyists and legislators, industrialists and labor leaders, reformers and bosses, Populists, Progressives, Prohibitionists, and Presidents all wanted him on their side. New Deal Democrats tried to steal him from the Republicans, and the American Communist party bracketed him with Lenin. Lincoln, in the words of David Donald, had come to be "everybody's grandfather."[8]

Most remarkable of all was the growing recognition of Lincoln's greatness in the eleven formerly Confederate states, ten of which had never given him a single vote for president. This may have been a necessary symbolic aspect of sectional reconciliation. Returning to the Union meant coming to terms with the man who had saved the Union. No one took the step more unequivocally than Henry W. Grady, prophet of the New South, who told a New York audience in 1866 that Lincoln had been "the first typical American, the first who comprehended within himself all the strength and gentleness, all the majesty and grace of this Republic."[9] When Southerners talked to Southerners about it, they were usually more restrained. Nevertheless, by the early twentieth century, the Lincoln tradition was becoming a blend of blue and gray, as illustrated in *The Perfect Tribute*, a story from the pen of an Alabama woman about a dying Confederate soldier's admiration for the Gettysburg Address.[10]

Bonds of sympathy between Lincoln and the South had not been difficult to find. He was, after all, a native Southerner—implacable as an enemy, but magnanimous in victory and compassionate by nature. In his hands, nearly everyone agreed, the ordeal of Reconstruction would have been less severe. Even Jefferson Davis concluded that his death had been "a great misfortune to the South."[11]

In addition, Lincoln seemed to pass the supreme test. He could be assimilated to the racial doctrines and institutional arrangements associated with the era of segregation. The historical record, though not entirely consistent, indicated that his opposition to slavery had never included advocacy of racial equality. With a little editing here and some extra emphasis there, Lincoln came out "right" on the Negro question. This was a judgment more often understood than elaborated in Southern writing and oratory, but certain self-appointed guardians of white supremacy were sometimes painfully explicit in claiming Lincoln as one of their own. He had been willing, they said, to guarantee slavery forever in the states where it already existed. He had issued the Emancipation Proclamation with great reluctance. He had opposed the extension of slavery only in order to reserve the Western territories exclusively for white men. He had denied favoring political and social equality for Negroes, had endorsed separation of the races, and had persistently recommended colonization of Negroes abroad. This was the Lincoln eulogized by James K. Vardaman of Mississippi, perhaps the most notorious political racist in American history, and by the sensational Negrophobic novelist Thomas Dixon. In his most famous work, *The Clansman*, Dixon had Lincoln as president parody himself during a discussion of colonization: "We can never attain the ideal Union our fathers dreamed, with millions of an alien, inferior race among us, whose assimilation is neither possible nor desirable. The Nation cannot now exist half white and half black, any more than it could exist half slave and half free."[12]

When one remembers that all this time millions of black Americans were still paying homage to the Great Emancipator, dualism seems all the more characteristic of the Lincoln tradition. Racist elements, to be sure, were never very successful in promoting the image of Lincoln as a dedicated white supremacist, but support from an unlikely quarter would eventually give the idea not only new life but respectability in the centers of professional scholarship.

During the first half of the twentieth century, Lincoln studies became a functional part of the literature of the Civil War, in which the problem of race was present but not paramount. Titles of the 1940's indicate the general bent of interest: *Lincoln and His Party in the Secession Crisis*; *Lincoln and the Patronage*; *Lincoln's War Cabinet*; *Lincoln and the Radicals*; *Lincoln and the War Governors*; *Lincoln and the South*. There was, it should be observed, no *Lincoln and the Negro*. That would come, appropriately, in the 1960's.

The sweep of the modern civil rights movement, beginning with the Supreme Court's antisegregation decision in 1954, inspired a new departure in American historical writing. Never has the psychological need for a usable past been more evident. Black history flourished and so did abolitionist history, but the most prestigious field of endeavor for a time was white-over-black history. Attention shifted, for example, from slavery as a cause of the Civil War to slavery as one major form of racial oppression. With this change of emphasis, the antebellum years began to look different. A number of monographs appearing in the 1960's, such as Leon F. Litwack's *North of Slavery*, demonstrated the nationwide prevalence of white-superiority doctrines and white-supremacy practices. Many Republicans and even some abolitionists, when they talked about the Negro, had sounded curiously like the slaveholders whom they were so fiercely denouncing. In fact, it appeared that the North and the South, while bitterly at odds on the issue of slavery, were relatively close to one another in their attitudes toward race. And Lincoln, according to Litwack, "accurately and consistently reflected the thoughts and prejudices of most Americans."[13]

The racial consensus of the Civil War era made it easy enough to understand why black Americans failed to win the equality implicit in emancipation, but certain other historical problems became more difficult as a consequence. For instance, if most Northerners in 1860 were indeed racists who viewed the Negro with repugnance as an inferior order of creation, then why did so many of them have such strong feelings about slavery? And why did racist Southerners fear and distrust racist Republicans with an intensity sufficient to destroy the Union? And does not the achievement of emancipation by a people so morally crippled with racism seem almost miraculous—like a one-armed man swimming the English Channel? No amount of talk about overwrought emotions or ulterior purposes or unintended consequences will fully account for what appears to be a major historical paradox, with Lincoln as the central figure.

When the civil rights struggle got under way in the 1950's, both sides tried to enlist Lincoln's support, but the primary tendency at first was to regard desegregation as a belated resumption of the good work begun with the Emancipation Proclamation. Many leading historians agreed that during the presidential years there had been a "steady evolution of Lincoln's attitude toward Negro rights."[14] The changes carried him a long way from the narrow environmental influences of his youth and made him, in the words of Richard N. Current, more relevant and inspiring than ever "as a symbol of man's ability to outgrow his prejudices."[15]

This was the liberal interpretation of Lincoln's record on racial matters. It came under attack from several directions, but especially from the ranks of intellectual radicalism and black militancy, both academic and otherwise. New Left historians, many of them activists in the battle for racial justice, could find little to admire in Abraham Lincoln. Compared with abolitionists like William Lloyd Garrison and Wendell Phillips, he seemed unheroic, opportunistic, and somewhat insensitive to the suffering of black people in bondage. He was "the prototype of the political man in power, with views so moderate as to require the pressure of radicals to stimulate action."[16] His prewar opposition to slavery, embracing the Republican policy of nonextension and the hope of ultimate extinction, reflected a "comfortable belief in the benevolence of history." It amounted to a "formula which promised in time to do everything while for the present risking nothing."[17]

Election to the presidency, in the radical view, produced no great transformation of his character. "Lincoln grew during the war—but he didn't grow much," wrote Lerone Bennett, Jr., a senior editor of *Ebony*. "On every issue relating to the black man . . . he was the very essence of the white supremacist with good intentions."[18] He moved but slowly and reluctantly toward abolishing slavery, and his famous Proclamation not only lacked "moral grandeur," but had been drafted "in such a way that it freed few, if any, slaves."[19] His reputation as the Great Emancipator is therefore "pure myth."[20] Most important of all, Lincoln probably believed in the inferiority of the Negro and certainly favored separation of the races. He was, in Bennett's words, "a tragically flawed figure who shared the racial prejudices of most of his white contemporaries."[21]

This, then, was the radical interpretation of Lincoln's record on racial matters, and what strikes one immediately is its similarity to the views of professional racists like Vardaman and Dixon. The portrait of A. Lincoln, Great White Supremacist, has been the work, it seems, of a strange collaboration.[22]

No less interesting is the amount of animus directed at a man who died more than a hundred years ago. In the case of black militants, hostility to Lincoln was no doubt part of the process of cutting loose from white America. Thus there is little history but much purpose in the statement of Malcolm X: "He probably did more to trick Negroes than any other man in history."[23]

For white radicals too, rejection of Lincoln signified repudiation of the whole American cultural tradition, from the first massacre of Indians to the Vietnam War. In what might be called the "malign consensus" school of United States history, Lincoln remained the Representative American, but the America that he represented was a dark, ugly country, stained with injustice and cruelty. Plainly, there is much more at stake here than the reputation of a single historical figure.

James K. Vardaman, it is said, used to carry with him one particular Lincoln quotation that he would whip out and read at the slightest opportunity. This excerpt from the debate with Douglas in 1858 at Charleston, Illinois, is fast becoming the most quoted passage in all of Lincoln's writings, outstripping even the Gettysburg Address and the Second Inaugural. Pick up any recent historical study of American race relations and somewhere in its pages you are likely to find the following words:

> I will say then that I am not, nor ever have been in favor of bringing about in any way the social and political equality of the white and black races,—that I am not nor ever have been in favor of making voters or jurors of negroes, nor of qualifying them to hold office, nor to intermarry with white people; and I will say in addition to this that there is a physical difference between the white and black races which I believe will for ever forbid the two races living together on terms of social and political equality. And inasmuch as they cannot so live, while they do remain together there must be the position of superior and inferior, and I as much as any other man am in favor of having the superior position assigned to the white race.[24]

The quotation seemed especially relevant in the 1960's and 1970's, when problems that had once preoccupied Lincoln's biographers, such as his part in bringing on the Civil War and the quality of his wartime leadership, were more or less pushed aside by a question of greater urgency. It was well phrased in the preface to a collection of documents titled *Lincoln on Black and White*: "Was Lincoln a racist? More important, how did Lincoln's racial views affect the course of our history?"[25]

Anyone who sets out conscientiously to answer such a query will soon find himself deep in complexity and confronting some of the fundamental problems of historical investigation. In one category are various questions about the historian's relation to the past: Is his task properly one of careful reconstruction, or are there more important purposes to be served? Does his responsibility include rendering moral judgments? If so, using what standards—those of his own time or those of the period under study? Then there are all the complications encountered in any effort to read the mind of a man, especially a politician, from the surviving record of his words and actions. For instance, what he openly affirmed as a youth may have been silently discarded in maturity; what he believed on a certain subject may be less significant than the intensity of his belief; and what he said on a certain occasion may have been largely determined by the immediate historical context, including the composition of his audience.

Terminological difficulties may also arise in the study of history, and such is the case with the word "racist," which serves us badly as a concept because of its denunciatory tone and indiscriminate use.[26] Conducive neither to objectivity nor to precision, the word has been employed so broadly as to invite much subdividing. Thus we have been asked to distinguish between ideological racism and institutional racism,[27] between scientific racism and folk racism,[28] between active racism and inactive racism,[29] between racism and racial prejudice,[30] betweeen racism and racialism,[31] between hierarchical racism and romantic racialism.[32]

In its strictest sense, racism is a doctrine, but by extension it has also come to signify an attitude, a mode of behavior, and a social system. The *doctrine*, a work of intellectuals, is a rationalized theory of inherent racial inferiority. In a given person, however, it can be anything from a casual belief to a philosophy of life. As an *attitude*, racism is virtually synonymous with prejudice—an habitual feeling of repugnance, and perhaps of enmity, toward members of another race. It can be anything from a mild tendency to a fierce obsession. Racism as a *mode of behavior* is prejudice activated in some way—a display of racial hostility that can be anything from mere avoidance of the other race to participation in a lynching. Racism as a *social system* means that law and custom combine to hold one race in subordination to another through institutional arrangements like slavery, segregation, discrimination, and disfranchisement. Individuals can help support such a system with anything from tacit acquiescence to strenuous public service in its defense. These multiple and graduated meanings of the word "racism" are important to remember in exploring the historical convergence of Abraham Lincoln and the American Negro.

"One must see him first," says Bennett, "against the background of his times. Born into a poor white family in the slave state of Kentucky and raised in the anti-black environments of southern Indiana and Illinois, Lincoln was exposed from the very beginning to racism."[33] This is a familiar line of reasoning and credible enough on the surface. Any racial views encountered during his youth were likely to be unfavorable to the Negro. But more important is the question of how *often* he encountered such views and how *thoroughly* he absorbed them. Besides, the assumption that his racial attitudes were shaped more or less permanently by his early social environment does not take into account the fact that youth may rebel against established opinion. Lincoln did in a sense reject his father's world, leaving it behind him forever soon after reaching the age of twenty-one. Certainly his personal knowledge of black people was very limited. After catching a few glimpses of slavery as a small boy in Kentucky, he had little contact with Negroes while growing up in backwoods Indiana or as a young man in New Salem, Illinois. Those first twenty-eight years of his life take up just three pages in Benjamin Quarles's book *Lincoln and the Negro*.[34]

If Lincoln entered manhood with strong feelings about race already implanted in his breast, one might expect to find indications of it in his earlier letters and speeches. For instance, on a steamboat carrying him home from a visit to Kentucky in 1841, there were a dozen slaves in chains. They had been sold down the river to a new master, and yet they seemed the most cheerful persons on board. Here was inspiration for some racist remarks in the "Sambo" vein, but Lincoln, describing the scene to a friend, chose instead to philosophize about the dubious effect of "condition upon human happiness."[35] That is, he pictured blacks behaving, as George M. Fredrickson puts it, "in a way that could be understood in terms of a common humanity and not as the result of peculiar racial characteristics."[36] Although one scholar may insist that Lincoln's racial beliefs were "matters of deep conviction,"[37] and another may talk about "the deeply rooted attitudes and ideas of a lifetime,"[38] there is scarcely any record of his thoughts on race until he was past forty years of age. Long before then, of course, he had taken a stand against slavery, and it was the struggle over slavery that eventually compelled him to consider publicly the problem of race.

There is no escape from the dilemma that "relevance" makes the past worth studying and at the same time distorts it. We tend to see antebellum race and slavery in the wrong perspective. Race itself was not then the critical public issue that it has become for us. Only widespread emancipation could make it so, and until the outbreak of the Civil War, that contingency seemed extremely remote. Our own preoccupation with race probably leads us to overestimate the importance of racial feeling in the antislavery movement.[39] In fact, there is a current disposition to assume that if a Republican did not have strong pro-Negro motives, he must have acted for strong anti-Negro reasons, such as a desire to keep the Western territories lily-white.[40]

Actually, much of the motivation for antislavery agitation was only indirectly connected with the Negro. For example, the prime target often seemed to be not so much slavery as the "slave power," arrogant, belligerent, and overrepresented in all branches of the federal government.[41] In Lincoln's case, no one can doubt his profound, though perhaps intermittent, sympathy for the slave. Yet he also hated slavery in a more abstract way as an evil principle and as a stain on the national honor, incompatible with the mission of America.[42]

It is a mistake to assume that Lincoln's actions in relation to the Negro were determined or even strongly influenced by his racial outlook. He based his antislavery philosophy squarely upon perception of the slave as a person, not as a Negro. According to the Declaration of Independence, he said, all men, including black men, are created equal, at least to the extent that none has a right to enslave another. This became a point at issue in the famous debates with Stephen A. Douglas, who vehemently denied that the Declaration had anything to do with the African race. Lincoln, in turn, accused his rival of trying to "dehumanize" the Negro. But he had constructed an argument against slavery which, carried to its logical conclusion, seemed to spell complete racial equality. So Douglas insisted, at any rate, while Lincoln protested: "I do not understand that because I do not want a negro woman for a slave I must necessarily want her for a wife."[43]

Opponents of slavery everywhere had to contend with the charge that they advocated Negro equality. In the Democratic press, Republicans became "Black Republicans," and political survival more often than not appeared to depend upon repudiation of the epithet.

Thus the race question was most prominent in the antebellum period as a rhetorical and largely spurious feature of the slavery controversy.

Lincoln's first general remarks about racial equality on record were made in 1854, when the repeal of the Missouri Compromise restriction drew him back to the center of Illinois politics. What to do, ideally, with Southern slaves, he pondered in a speech at Peoria. "Free them, and make them politically and socially our equals? My own feelings will not admit of this; and if mine would, we well know that those of the great mass of white people will not."[44] More often that year, however, he talked about the humanity of the Negro in denouncing the extension of slavery. Then came the election of 1856 and Frémont's defeat, which Lincoln analyzed with some bitterness: "We were constantly charged with seeking an amalgamation of the white and black races; and thousands turned from us, not believing the charge . . . but *fearing* to face it themselves."[45] It was at this point, significantly, that he became more aggressive and explicit in disavowing racial equality. He began using census figures to show that miscegenation was a by-product of slavery. He spoke of the "natural disgust" with which most white people viewed "the idea of an indiscriminate amalgamation of the white and black races." And, under heavy pounding from Douglas during the senatorial campaign of 1858, he responded again and again in the manner of the notorious Charleston passage quoted above.[46] Indeed, his strongest feeling about race appears to have been his vexation with those who kept bringing the subject up. "Negro equality! Fudge!!" he scribbled on a piece of paper. "How long, in the government of a God, great enough to make and maintain this Universe, shall there continue knaves to vend, and fools to gulp, so low a piece of demagoguism as this."[47]

Most of Lincoln's recorded generalizations about race were public statements made in the late 1850's as part of his running oratorical battle with Douglas.[48] Furthermore, nearly all of those statements were essentially disclaimers rather than affirmations. They indicated, for political reasons, the *maximum* that he was willing to deny the Negro and the *minimum* that he claimed for the Negro. They were concessions on points not at issue, designed to fortify him on the point that *was* at issue—namely, the extension of slavery. If he had responded differently at Charleston and elsewhere, the

Lincoln of history simply would not exist. Words uttered in a context of such pressure may be less than reliable as indications of a man's lifetime attitude.

At least it seems possible that Lincoln's remarks in middle age on the subject of race were shaped more by his political realism than by impressions stamped on his mind in childhood. The principal intellectual influence, as Fredrickson has demonstrated, was Henry Clay, Lincoln's political hero, whom he studied anew for a eulogy delivered in 1852. Clay, in his attitude toward slavery, represented a link with the Founding Fathers. A slaveholder himself who nevertheless believed that the institution was a "curse," he began and ended his career working for a program of gradual emancipation in Kentucky. He helped found and steadily supported the American Colonization Society. In his racial views, moreover, Clay emphasized the Negro's humanity and reserved judgment on the question of innate black inferiority. Lincoln not only adopted Clay's tentative, moderate outlook but extensively paraphrased and sometimes parroted his words.[49]

Considering, then, the peculiar context of his most significant remarks on the subject of race, and considering also his dependence on Clay, it seems unwise to assert flatly, as some scholars do, that Lincoln embraced the doctrine of racism. Not that it would be astonishing to find that he did so. The assumption of inherent white superiority was almost universal and rested upon observation as well as prejudice. Comparison of European civilization and African "savagery" made it extremely difficult to believe in the natural equality of white and black races. Yet Lincoln's strongest statements, even if taken at face value and out of context, prove to be tentative and equivocal. He conceded that the Negro *might not* be his equal, or he said that the Negro *was not* his equal *in certain respects*. As an example, he named *color*, which can be viewed as having a biological implication. But we cannot be certain that he was not merely expressing an aesthetic judgment or noting the social disadvantages of being black. He never used the word "inherent," or any of its equivalents, in discussing the alleged inferiority of the Negro, and it is not unlikely that he regarded such inferiority as resulting primarily from social oppression. In 1862, he compared blacks whose minds had been "clouded by slavery" with free Negroes "capable of thinking as white men." His last recorded disclaimer appears in a letter written as president-elect to a New York editor. He did not, it declared, "hold the black man to be the equal of the white, unqualifiedly." The final word throws away most of the declaration and scarcely suits a true ideological racist. Here there is a doubleness in the man as in the legend. It appears that he may have both absorbed and doubted, both shared and risen above, the racial doctrines of his time.[50]

Lincoln, who had four sons and no other children, was presumably never asked the ultimate racist question: "Would you want your daughter to marry a Negro?" He did indicate a disinclination to take a Negro woman for his wife, thereby agreeing with most of his white contemporaries in their aversion to miscegenation. Otherwise, there is little evidence of racism as an attitude or racism as a mode of behavior in his relations with blacks. Frederick Douglass, sometimes a severe critic of his policies, said emphatically: "In all my interviews with Mr. Lincoln I was impressed with his entire freedom from popular prejudice against the colored race."[51] During the war years in Washington, the social status of Negroes underwent a minor revolution, exemplified in the arrival of a black diplomat from the newly recognized republic of Haiti. Lincoln opened the White House to black visitors in a way that set aside all precedent.[52] Douglass and others appreciated not only his friendliness but his restraint. There was no effusiveness, no condescension. "He treated Negroes," says Quarles, "as they wanted to be treated—as human beings."[53]

On the other hand, Lincoln in the 1850's did plainly endorse the existing system of white supremacy, except for slavery. He defended it, however, on grounds of expediency rather than principle, and on grounds of the incompatibility rather than the inequality of the races. Assuming that one race or the other must be on top, he admitted preferring that the superior position be *assigned* to the white race. There was little association of institutional racism with ideological racism in his thinking. Although he was by no means insensitive to the deprivation suffered by free Negroes,[54] he saw little hope of improving their condition and in any case regarded slavery as a far greater wrong. Moreover, it appeared that any serious attack on institutional racism would raise the cry of "Negro equality," and thereby damage the antislavery cause.

But then, if he hated slavery so much, why did Lincoln not become an abolitionist? There are several obvious reasons: fear for the safety of the Union, political prudence, constitutional scruples, a personal distaste for extremism, and perplexity over what to do with freed slaves.[55] In addition, it must be emphasized that Lincoln, as Lord Charnwood observed, "accepted the institutions to which he was born, and he enjoyed them."[56] Social reformers were a relatively new and not very numerous breed in antebellum America. Lincoln cannot be counted among them. This author of the greatest reform in American history was simply not a reformer by nature. He even acquiesced in the retention of slavery, provided that it should not be allowed to expand. For him, the paramount importance of the Republican anti-extension program lay in its symbolic meaning as a commitment to the principle of ultimate extinction. Some later generation, he thought, would then convert the principle into practice. What this amounted to, in a sense, was antislavery tokenism, but it also proved to be a formula for the achievement of political power, and with it, the opportunity to issue a proclamation of emancipation.

Of course, it has been said that Lincoln deserves little credit for emancipation—that he came to it tardily and reluctantly, under radical duress. "Blacks have no reason to feel grateful to Abraham Lincoln," writes Julius Lester. "How come it took him two whole years to free the slaves? His pen was sitting on his desk the whole time. All he had to do was get up one morning and say, 'Doggonit! I think I'm gon' free the slaves today.'"[57] But *which* morning? That turned out to be the real question.

Lincoln, it should be remembered, was under strong pressure from *both* sides on the issue of emancipation, and so the radical clamor alone will not explain his ultimate decision. Nevertheless, when the war began, many Americans quickly realized that the fate of slavery might be in the balance. Veteran abolitionists rejoiced that history was at last marching to their beat, and Lincoln did not fail to read what he called "the signs of the times." Emancipation itself, as he virtually acknowledged, came out of the logic of events, not his personal volition, but the time and manner of its coming were largely his choice.

There had been enough Republicans to win the presidential election, but there were not enough to win the war. They needed help from Northern Democrats and border-state loyalists, who were willing to fight for the Union, but not for abolition. A premature effort at emancipation might alienate enough support to make victory impossible. It would then be self-defeating, because there could be no emancipation without victory. Lincoln's remarkable achievement, whether he fully intended it or not, was to proclaim emancipation in such a way as to minimize disaffection. He did so by allowing enough time for the prospect to become familiar in the public mind, and by adhering scrupulously to the fiction that this momentous step was strictly a military measure. Much of the confusion about the Emancipation Proclamation results from taking too seriously Lincoln's verbal bowings and scrapings to the conservatives while all the time he was backing steadily away from them.[58]

The best illustration is his famous reply of August 22, 1862, to the harsh criticism of Horace Greeley, in which he said that his "paramount object" was to save the Union. "What I do about slavery, and the colored race," he declared, "I do because I believe it helps to save the Union; and what I forbear, I forbear because I do *not* believe it would help to save the Union."[59] The most striking thing about the entire document is its dissimulation. Although Lincoln gave the impression that options were still open, he had in fact already made up his mind, had committed himself to a number of persons, had drafted the Proclamation. Why, then, write such a letter? Because it was not a statement of policy but instead a brilliant piece of propaganda in which Lincoln, as Benjamin P. Thomas says, "used Greeley's outburst to prepare the people for what was coming."[60]

There were constitutional as well as political reasons, of course, for casting the Proclamation in military language and also for limiting its scope to those states and parts of states still in rebellion. In a sense, as historians fond of paradox are forever pointing out, it did not immediately liberate any slaves at all. And the Declaration of Independence, it might be added, did not immediately liberate a single colony from British rule. The people of Lincoln's time apparently had little doubt about the significance of the Proclamation. Jefferson Davis did not regard it as a mere scrap of paper, and neither did that most famous of former slaves, Frederick Douglass. He called it "the greatest event of our nation's history."[61]

In the long sweep of that history, emancipation had come on, not sluggishly, but with a rush and a roar—over a period of scarcely eighteen months. Given more time to reflect on its racial implications, white America might have recoiled from the act. Lincoln himself had never been anything but a pessimist about the consequences of emancipation. Knowing full well the prejudices of his countrymen, he doubted that blacks and whites could ever live together amicably and on terms of equality.

With stark realism, Lincoln told a delegation of free Negroes in August 1862: "On this broad continent, not a single man of your race is made the equal of a single man of ours. Go where you are treated the best, and the ban is still upon you." And while blacks suffered from discrimination, whites suffered from the discord caused by the presence of blacks. "It is better for us both, therefore, to be separated," he said.[62] But Lincoln apparently never visualized a segregated America. For him, separation meant colonization, which, as a disciple of Henry Clay, he had been advocating at least since 1852. Perhaps the strangest feature of Lincoln's presidential career was the zeal with which he tried to promote voluntary emigration of free Negroes to Africa or Latin America. He recommended it in his first two annual messages, urged it upon Washington's black leadership, and endorsed it in his preliminary Emancipation Proclamation. He had foreign capitals canvassed in a search for likely places of settlement. Furthermore, with funds supplied by Congress, he launched colonization enterprises in Haiti and Panama, both of which proved abortive.[63]

What surprises one the most about these activities is their petty scale. Lincoln implored the delegation of Washington Negroes to find him a hundred, or fifty, or even twenty-five families willing to emigrate. The Haitian project, if completely successful, would have accommodated just five thousand persons—about the number of Negroes born every two weeks in the United States. Back in 1854, Lincoln had admitted the impracticability of colonization as anything but a long-range program.[64] Why, then, was he in such feverish haste to make a token beginning in 1862?

One interesting answer emerges from the chronology. Most of the colonization flurry took place during the second half of 1862. After that, Lincoln's interest waned, although according to the dubious testimony of Benjamin F. Butler, it revived near the end of the war.[65] After issuing the Emancipation Proclamation on January 1, 1863, Lincoln, by all logic, should have pressed harder than ever for colonization, but he never made another public appeal on the subject. It appears that his spirited activity in the preceding six months may have been part of the process of conditioning the public mind for the day of jubilee. The promise of colonization had always been in part a means of quieting fears about the racial consequences of manumission. Offered as the ultimate solution to the problem of the black population, it could also serve as a psychological safety valve for the problem of white racism. This combination of purposes had inspired a number of Republican leaders to take up the cause of colonization in the late 1850's. As one of them put it, the movement would "ward off the attacks made upon us about Negro equality."[66]

In his second annual message of December 1, 1862, Lincoln said, "I cannot make it better known than it already is, that I strongly favor colonization." Then he continued in a passage that has received far less attention: "And yet I wish to say there is an objection urged against free colored persons remaining in the country, which is largely imaginary, if not sometimes malicious." He went on to discuss and minimize the fear that freedmen would displace white laborers, after which he wrote:

> But it is dreaded that the freed people will swarm forth, and cover the whole land? Are they not already in the land? Will liberation make them any more numerous? Equally distributed among the whites of the whole country, and there would be but one colored to seven whites. Could the one, in any way, greatly disturb the seven? There are many communities now, having more than one free colored person, to seven whites; and this, without any apparent consciousness of evil from it.[67]

Here, along with his last public endorsement of colonization, was an eloquent plea for racial accommodation at home. The one might remain his ideal ultimate solution, but the other, he knew, offered the only hope in the immediate future.

Yet, if his plans for reconstruction are an accurate indication, Lincoln at the time of his death had given too little consideration to the problem of racial adjustment and to the needs of four million freedmen. How much that would have changed if he had not been killed has been the subject of lively controversy.[68] Certainly his policies by 1865 no longer reflected all the views expressed in 1858, when he had repudiated both Negro citizenship and Negro suffrage. Now, by fiat of his administration in defiance of the Dred Scott decision, blacks were citizens of the United States, and he had begun in a gentle way to press for limited black enfranchisement. He had overcome his initial doubts about enlisting Negroes as fighting soldiers, was impressed by their overall performance, and thought they had earned the right to vote.

Lincoln once told Charles Sumner that on the issue of emancipation they were no more than six weeks apart.[69] The relative earliness of his first favorable remarks about Negro enfranchisement suggests that he had again read the "signs of the times." It is not difficult to believe that after the war he would have continued closer to the Sumners than to the conservatives, whom he had placated but never followed for long. And one can scarcely doubt that his postwar administration would have been more responsive to Negro aspirations than Andrew Johnson's proved to be.

But for several reasons Lincoln's role was likely to be more subdued than we might expect from the Great Emancipator. First, during peacetime, with his powers and responsibilities as commander in chief greatly reduced, he probably would have yielded more leadership to Congress in the old Whig tradition. Second, at the time of his death, he still regarded race relations as primarily a local matter, just as he had maintained during the debates with Douglas: "I do not understand there is any place where an alteration of the social and political relations of the negro and the white man can be made except in the State Legislature."[70] Third, Negroes as Negroes were nearly always connotative in Lincoln's thinking. Their welfare, though by no means a matter of indifference to him, had never been, and was not likely to become, his "paramount object." They were, in the words of Frederick Douglass, "only his stepchildren."[71]

Finally, in his attitude toward the wrongs of the free Negro, Lincoln had none of the moral conviction that inspired his opposition to slavery. He never seems to have suspected that systematic racial discrimination might be, like slavery, a stain on the national honor and a crime against mankind. Whether that is the measure of his greatness must be left to personal judgment. Of Copernicus we might say: What a genius! He revolutionized our conception of the solar system. Or: What an ignoramus! He did not understand the rest of the universe at all.

CHAPTER 9

Lincoln and the Constitution

One of the more disturbing anomalies in American historical literature is the widespread tendency to regard Lincoln as the greatest of presidents and at the same time as the one who went further than any other in setting aside constitutional restraints. This examination of Lincoln's outlook and conduct with respect to the Constitution, though it will stand by itself, is to some extent a continuation of discussion begun in Chapter 2 and an introduction to matters treated more fully in Chapter 10. Written for a conference on "Lincoln's Thought and the Present" held at Sangamon State University in June 1976, it was published in *The Public and the Private Lincoln* (Carbondale, Ill., 1979), edited by Cullom Davis and others.

The secret of great government, Victor Hugo once remarked, consists in knowing precisely how much of the future can be introduced into the present. By this measure, as well as by numerous others, the Constitution of the United States is one of the supreme achievements in the history of government. Its strength and utility after nearly two centuries testify to the wisdom of the men who framed it, and in some degree to their capacity for introducing the future into the present.

Nevertheless, any reading of *The Federalist Papers*, which were in part an effort to predict how the Constitution would work in practice, will disclose evidence that the Founding Fathers did not always penetrate the distant future in construing their handiwork. James Madison, for instance, assured the people that state governments would in every respect "have the advantage of the federal government," because they would possess more power, command more popular support, and collectively employ many more persons. He also said that in a republican government, the legislative branch was bound to predominate, and therefore constituted the principal threat of usurpation. Alexander Hamilton agreed, explaining that the primary reason for creation of the veto power was not to improve the quality of legislation but rather to provide the president with a means of defending himself against legislative encroachments on his authority. It was Madison who predicted that the House of Representatives would be more powerful than the Senate; and it was Hamilton who characterized the judiciary as "beyond comparison the weakest of the three departments of power," having "no direction either of the strength or of the wealth of the society," and able to take "no active resolution whatever." But the passage that inspired some bitter smiles in the 1970's was the one in which Hamilton discussed the kind of person who would occupy the presidency:

> This process affords a moral certainty that the office of President will seldom fall to the lot of any man who is not in an eminent degree endowed with the requisite qualifications. Talents for low intrigue, and the little arts of popularity, may alone suffice to elevate a man to the first honors in a single State; but it will require other talents, and a different kind of merit, to establish him in the esteem and confidence of the whole Union. . . . It will not be too strong to say that there will be a constant probability of seeing the station filled by characters pre-eminent for ability and virtue.[1]

If Madison, Hamilton, and the other framers could be reconvened to inspect the modern version of the constitutional system created in 1787, they would find it reassuringly familiar on paper but fearfully different in operation. Of all the changes catching their bewildered attention, three would be especially conspicuous—the extraordinary shift of responsibility and authority from the states to the central government; the vast increase in the power of the presidency and in the range of executive functions; and the astonishingly active, even aggressive role now assumed by the judiciary in the determination of public policy. All three of these revolutionary changes in the structure of the American republic took place over long periods of time and can be attributed to no single event, not even an event as momentous as the Civil War. Yet one may appropriately ask the extent to which the process of change in each case was accelerated or retarded by the Civil War and in what manner that process was affected by the character, purposes, and conduct of Abraham Lincoln.

According to the set of answers long standard in American historical writing, the Civil War greatly stimulated the progress of national consolidation and the growth of presidential power, but it further eroded the prestige and authority of a Supreme Court already weakened by the "self-inflicted wound" of the Dred Scott decision. To say that these generalizations are inadequate and therefore misleading is not the same as declaring that they are wrong. Since historical truth is usually complex, and half-truth may sometimes be more harmful than outright error, the historian's most delicate task, and perhaps his most important responsibility, is the work of refining and qualifying generalizations, including his own.

The Civil War did confirm the indestructibility of the American Union, and it did fix the primary locus of sovereignty in the nation, rather than in the several states. Secession, like slavery, was buried at Appomattox, together with the discredited constitutional doctrines of John C. Calhoun. Nationalism thus triumphed in the outcome of the conflict, but long before that day arrived, the conduct of the war had necessitated a great expansion in the responsibilities and authority of the federal government. One case in point is the raising of troops, which at first was managed almost entirely by the state governments but gradually came under federal control, with the states reduced to serving virtually as administrative units in the maintenance of a national army. Similarly, the financial necessities of war compelled the creation of a national banking system to supplement and partly replace the jumble of state banks with their multitudinous currencies. Secession facilitated this and other important legislation by removing from Congress the very elements that had always been most hostile to the expansion of federal power. Meanwhile, the mobilizing armies had become "enormous forcing rooms for the quick flowering of nationalistic feeling,"[2] and civilians were not far behind soldiers in realizing how much more closely the war had bound their lives and hopes to the nation.

Abraham Lincoln presided over this movement toward national consolidation without displaying any serious misgivings about it. His outlook, unlike his background, had never been parochial. His one passion, Walt Whitman observed, was for the federal Union. He paid due respect to the principle of states' rights but insisted that no state except Texas during its decade of independence had ever been a sovereignty. His most emphatic pronouncement on the subject was made as president-elect in the form of a rhetorical question put to an Indiana audience: "If a State, in one instance, and a county in another, should be equal in extent of territory, and equal in the number of people, wherein is that State any better than the county?"[3] And on that memorable day at Gettysburg in November 1863, he said nothing about the states but spoke only of the *nation*—the *nation* conceived in liberty and dedicated to the principle that men are born equal, the *nation* undergoing the supreme test of civil war, the *nation* destined to have a new birth of freedom. It is scarcely surprising that Lincoln, the Great Emancipator, should also have been widely regarded as the great symbol of democratic nationalism, and therefore as an opponent of the particularism and strict constructionalism usually associated with states' rights. He headed a political party, said Alexander H. Stephens shortly after Appomattox, that "virtually hoisted the banner of Consolidation" in a war fought primarily, not against slavery, but against the principle of federalism. Echoing this judgment nearly a hundred years later, the Civil War scholar William B. Hesseltine declared that Lincoln was a revolutionary leader who deliberately "destroyed the rights and powers of the states" in order to erect "a sovereign and centralized nation."[4]

Yet, on closer scrutiny, one is struck by the limited and, in many respects, temporary character of this alleged revolution, and by the tenacity with which federalism survived the war and its aftermath. The North fought for the purpose of canceling secession and blotting the Southern Confederacy out of existence. It would have been logical to obliterate also the agencies that had enacted secession and created the Confederacy. But except for the partition of Virginia, a very special case, the integrity of the rebellious states was never seriously threatened. Proposals for reducing them to the status of federal territories, although seriously discussed, got nowhere in Congress. The slaves of the Confederacy were emancipated; much of the private property there was confiscated or destroyed; Confederate leaders were disfranchised and otherwise punished; but the Confederate states retained their identities and became in time the principal agencies for preserving and elaborating the legend of the Lost Cause.

Lincoln's tentative, experimental program of reconstruction was designed to restore the seceded states quickly and easily to their former places in the Union. Often praised for its magnanimity, it nevertheless largely neglected the problems and needs of four million liberated slaves, whose best hope lay in the continued exertion of federal power for their aid and protection. Lincoln's policy, as it had developed to the moment of his death, would have put the freedman promptly where he was destined to end up eventually—that is, under the domination of white Southerners who held firm control of their state and local governments—but with the important difference that there would have been no Fourteenth and Fifteenth Amendments to carry the promise of a better future.

Historians have offered various explanations of Lincoln's attitude toward reconstruction. For one thing, vindictiveness was simply alien to his nature, and in any case he believed that generous treatment of the defeated South would be sound policy, promoting the spirit of reconciliation necessary for true reunion. Perhaps he also intended that his strategy should lay the foundation for an effective Republican party in the South. Furthermore, he feared eruptions of anarchy and violence when the Confederacy was overthrown and thought that an early restoration of normal civil government would be the best preventive. According to some critics, the lack of sufficient concern for the freedman in his program reflected the common racist assumption that America was a white man's country. It has also been suggested that an uneasy sense of personal responsibility for starting the war made him especially anxious for a speedy restoration of the Union on lenient terms. In addition, Lincoln's disposition to treat the Southern states as though they had never left the Union followed consistently the official Lincolnian theory on the nature of the war, which held that secession was illegal, the Confederacy a fiction, and the Federal Union accordingly still intact.

To these explanations, whatever their value may be, at least one more should be added, and that is Lincoln's essentially traditional conception of the Republic he was trying to save. The Civil War may have had revolutionary effects, but it was begun and prosecuted for conservative purposes—to preserve the Union on one side, to protect slavery on the other. Emancipation, for example, was the revolutionary purpose of only a small abolitionist minority; for most Americans it emerged as a revolutionary consequence of disunion and war. Lincoln and other Northerners, out of their own experience, could nevertheless readily envision a Union restored without slavery, and Southern people, too, realized long before Appomattox that emancipation would be one of the penalties exacted if the Confederacy should fail. But nowhere in either North or South was there reason to expect, or even the capacity to visualize, a Union reconstructed on any basis except the old system of federalism, with its familiar distribution of responsibilities and powers.

Under that system, most of the governmental activity affecting the daily lives of ordinary citizens (not less than 90 percent, according to one contemporary estimate) was carried on by the states and their subdivisions.[5] Thus when Lincoln, during the senatorial campaign with Douglas in 1858, found himself persistently accused of favoring racial equality, he made this reply: "I do not understand there is any place where an alteration of the social and political relations of the negro and the white man can be made except in the State Legislature—not in the Congress of the United States."[6] Seven years later, in the closing days of the war, his outlook on race relations continued to be guided and restricted by his traditional view of federal relations. For instance, he had already come to favor and recommend some measure of Negro suffrage, but he was unwilling to have it imposed on the Southern states as a condition of their restoration. It appears, then, that in spite of his cavalier reference on one occasion to the states as little better than oversized counties, Lincoln's policy-making reflected the orthodox conception of the United States as a relatively decentralized federation in which the state governments played the most active and versatile part.

During the period of Radical Reconstruction that began in the late 1860's, the federal government did, of course, use its civil and military power to compel enfranchisement of the freedman and to lend him certain other kinds of protection. That effort, however, remained vigorous for no more than a decade. By the 1890's, it had come to an end completely, with the Southern Negro secure once again in the iron grip of white supremacy. The overthrow of Radical Reconstruction used to be explained as a popular reaction against partisan, vindictive policies that had become increasingly corrupt in operation. More recently, it has been interpreted as a failure of justice, made more or less inevitable by the racism that infected most white Americans, in the North as well as in the South. Still more recently, some historians have argued that constitutional inhibitions may have been the critical factor. That is, the amount of federal intervention needed to sustain Radical Reconstruction simply could not be squared with the traditional American conception of the structure of the Republic. "Respect for federalism," says one of these scholars, was "the most potent institutional obstacle to the Negroes' hope for protected liberty."[7]

When one turns from Reconstruction itself to other governmental activity of the same period, the centralizing influence of the Civil War becomes no easier to assess. The scope of national legislation expanded considerably, but so too did the scope of state legislation, and any shift in the balance of federalism was a modest one at most. The federal government increased its control over banking and currency after the war, but relinquished its wartime authority over the railroads. Railroad legislation, although badly needed, remained in the hands of the states until a Supreme Court decision virtually compelled passage of the Interstate Commerce Act in 1887. That statute marked the beginning of a new era in which federal power was used extensively for regulatory and police purposes. Populist-Progressive reform may have drawn some general inspiration from the Civil War precedent of vigorous federal action, but otherwise there was not much continuity between those two surges of national effort. On the whole, then, the amount of permanent consolidation produced by the war seems neither small enough to be called unimportant nor large enough to be called revolutionary. The principal achievement for American nationalism under Lincoln's leadership was the negative one of arresting a drift toward decentralization that had become a plunge into disintegration.

The expansion of federal power during the Civil War was closely associated with an expansion of executive power within the federal government. On this latter subject, it appears easy to speak unequivocally, for most historians agree with the statement of Clinton Rossiter that Lincoln "pushed the powers of the Presidency to a new plateau high above any conception of executive authority hitherto imagined in this country."[8] In fact, serious scholars have applied the word "dictator" more often to Lincoln than to any other president. The list of his presidential actions inspiring such judgments is a rather long one. With Congress by his own arrangement not in session, he responded to the attack on Fort Sumter by enlarging the army, proclaiming a blockade of Southern ports, suspending the writ of habeas corpus in certain areas, authorizing arbitrary arrests and imprisonments on a large scale, and spending public funds without legal warrant. He never yielded the initiative seized at this time, and, in later bold assertions of executive authority, he introduced conscription, proclaimed emancipation, and inaugurated a program of reconstruction.

But David Herbert Donald has reminded us that Lincoln was also in some ways a passive president, one who displayed little legislative leadership and exercised surprisingly little control over his department heads; who vetoed only one major piece of legislation and deferred humbly to members of Congress in making his appointments. The explanation, according to Donald, is that Lincoln played almost to perfection the role of a "Whig in the White House."[9]

The American Whigs, taking their name from opponents of the royal prerogative in England, had originated as the party of resistance to the "executive tyranny" of Andrew Jackson, whom they sometimes called "King Andrew the First." Thus, without denying the need for vigorous executive leadership in the prosecution of a war, the Whigs maintained that Congress was the proper source of governmental initiative, and that the president should play no part in the lawmaking process except to implement the legislative will. Lincoln, as president-elect, reaffirmed his adherence to this principle:

> By the constitution, the executive may recommend measures which he may think proper; and he may veto those he thinks improper; and it is supposed he may add to these, certain indirect influences to affect the action of congress. My political education strongly inclines me against a very free use of any of these means, by the Executive, to control the legislation of the country. As a rule, I think it better that congress should originate, as well as perfect its measures, without external bias.[10]

No doubt this political philosophy had considerable influence on Lincoln's performance in office. Of course it could be argued that his presidential style was shaped less by a devotion to Whig theory than by a single-minded determination to win the war. But whatever the reason for it, a curious dualism does run through his use of executive authority. The record suggests that if he had served at a more normal time, his performance in the White House might have been relatively subdued. As it was, he set a precedent for immense expansion of presidential power—presumably applicable, however, only in a state of extreme emergency.

Lincoln believed that the power needed to meet the secession crisis had been provided by the Constitution and vested primarily in the president. He cited the commander-in-chief clause, the clause requiring him to "take care that the laws be faithfully executed," and his presidential oath ("registered in heaven," as he put it) to "preserve, protect and defend the Constitution of the United States." Quite obviously, this emergency power had to be sufficient for the occasion or else it would be useless. Thus the extent of the power depended on the character and magnitude of the emergency, which in turn, because of the nature of presidential responsibility, could be determined only by the president himself.

Not even a universal acceptance of this remarkable argument would have been conclusive, however; for every federal action must pass *two* constitutional tests. The first is whether the Constitution authorizes it; the second is whether the Constitution forbids it. Certain practices of the Lincoln administration plainly conflicted with some of the most cherished clauses in the Bill of Rights. To be sure, the perilous circumstances called for extraordinary measures, and the intent of even the most repressive actions was preventive rather than punitive. Nevertheless, the secret police, paid informers, midnight arrests, crowded prisons, and suppressed newspapers were alien to the American experience, and Lincoln, the most abused of American presidents, suffered his worst abuse as the alleged assassin of his country's freedom.

Lincoln's eloquent defense of his conduct proceeded from the assumption that individual freedom is secure only in a self-governing society. To him, it was a matter of temporarily diminishing the rights of some persons in order to preserve an entire structure of freedom. That structure included not only the Constitution but also the functioning federal republic that made the Constitution a reality and embodied the principle of self-government. All of this was at stake in the war. It would be folly, Lincoln maintained, to sacrifice the structure as a whole while jealously guarding some part of it. "Are all the laws, *but one*, to go unexecuted," he asked, "and the government itself go to pieces, lest that one be violated?"[11]

With such argument Lincoln justified emergency executive power, which he was the first American president to employ on a significant and sustained basis. The concept has roots in the practices of the Roman republic and is embraced by political philosophers as far apart in their points of view as Machiavelli and Thomas Jefferson. The highest duty of a public officer, Jefferson once said, was not strict observance of the written laws but preservation of the country; and there were "extreme cases," he acknowledged, "where the universal resource is a dictator, or martial law."[12] The only recognition of such extremity by the Constitution is the clause permitting the privilege of the writ of habeas corpus to be suspended "when in cases of rebellion or invasion the public safety may require it." But if the clause does furnish some legitimation for the concept of national emergency, it also defines the phenomenon in exceedingly narrow terms—only a state of invasion and a state of rebellion. There have been only two such emergencies since the Constitution was written, and none since 1865.

Yet the greatest growth of emergency executive power has occurred during the twentieth century. Among the notable examples of its exercise are Franklin Roosevelt's order for the virtual imprisonment of some 112,000 Japanese-Americans in 1942, and Harry Truman's order for seizure of the nation's steel mills in 1952. That this concept of extraordinary action in response to desperate necessity has been normalized and even trivialized to the point of becoming a menace, not only to the American public but to the presidency itself, became apparent in the conduct and downfall of Richard Nixon.

It is a long way from the splendor of Emancipation to the shame of Watergate, and yet a line of historical influence runs between them. Makers of the modern "imperial presidency" have drawn heavily on the example and immortal fame of Abraham Lincoln for vindication of their actions, conveniently ignoring the extent to which precedents taken from the Civil War are rendered invalid by its uniqueness. It is accordingly possible to conclude that Lincoln's use of executive power was wise and appropriate in its context, but not an unmixed blessing as a presidential tradition.

right

As Lincoln began to extend the grasp of executive authority after the attack on Fort Sumter, the question arose whether his course of action would be impeded in any serious degree by judicial intervention. The first answer came within a matter of six weeks from the Chief Justice of the United States. Roger B. Taney, now eighty-four years old, went out of his way to challenge the presidential policy of military arrest. At a time when the fate of Maryland seemed to hang in the balance and pro-Confederate rioting in Baltimore threatened to isolate Washington from the rest of the country, he issued a writ of habeas corpus for one John Merryman, a leading Maryland secessionist accused of sabotage and other treasonable activities. The commanding general refused to honor the writ on the grounds that the privilege had been suspended by presidential authority. Taney promptly ordered the general's arrest for contempt of court, but the federal marshal was barred from entering Fort McHenry to carry it out. Taney then acknowledged that he could do nothing more in Merryman's behalf. He nevertheless called upon the President to "perform his constitutional duty" by enforcing the judicial process. Within a week, he added a written opinion declaring that military arrest of civilians and presidential suspension of the writ of habeas corpus were both in violation of the Constitution.[13] Lincoln made no reply to Taney except indirectly by defending his policy in a message to Congress and by continuing to follow it as though the Chief Justice had never spoken.

Ex parte Merryman, says one scholar, "struck the first mighty blow in federal court history on behalf of individual liberties."[14] Yet it is unlikely that Taney had any greater love for personal freedom than did Lincoln, and as for the handling of public disorder, he had once expressed the view that rioters should be fired upon when they cast their first stone.[15] He was actually less interested in protecting civil liberties than in defending the precincts of judicial power against military intrusion. But the biggest difference between the two men in 1861 came to this—the President thought that the Union was worth saving at almost any cost, whereas the Chief Justice did not think that it was worth saving at all. Taney's sympathies were with the Confederacy. He favored peaceable separation, considered the war a descent into madness, detested Republicans as a class, and regarded the Lincoln administration as a hateful despotism. By no recorded public or private utterance did he ever lend encouragement to the cause of the Union. It is testimony, perhaps, to the stability of the American constitutional system that he should have continued in office, without any serious threat of removal, until his death late in 1864.

"From the Civil War down to our own day," writes the constitutional scholar Bernard Schwartz, "the consensus of learned opinion has been that, on the legal issue involved in *Merryman*, Taney was right and Lincoln was wrong."[16] As early as 1866 in *Ex parte Milligan*, with Lincoln's friend David Davis delivering the opinion, the

Supreme Court went part way toward saying the same thing. This merely signified, however, that with the war over, it was better for the public safety to repudiate much of what had so recently been considered vitally necessary. In the overwhelming "now" of 1861, Taney may have been just as wrong as Lincoln had become by 1866. Nearly a century later, Justice Robert H. Jackson pondered the paradox: "Had Mr. Lincoln scrupulously observed the Taney policy," he said, "I do not know whether we would have had any liberty, and had the Chief Justice adopted Mr. Lincoln's philosophy as the philosophy of the law, I again do not know whether we would have had any liberty."[17]

Lincoln's cool disregard of the Merryman opinion has sometimes been taken as an indication of his attitude toward the judiciary in general, and also as exemplifying the sunken prestige of the Supreme Court during the Civil War era. Neither of these impressions is substantially accurate, but there may be some advantage in examining each of them.

Republican denunciation of the Merryman opinion was all the more vehement, of course, because it had been written by the author of the Dred Scott decision. The odium of the Dred Scott case was attached primarily to individual justices, however. The extent to which it undermined the Supreme Court as an institution has been considerably exaggerated. Too much attention has been given to the noisy but unavailing demands of a few antislavery radicals for reorganization of the Court and severe restrictions on its power. Republicans might indulge in fervid oratory about not bowing down to this "judicial Vatican," but for the most part they wanted to change only the membership of the Court, not its structure and functions.

There had been six justices forming the majority that declared the Missouri Compromise unconstitutional in the Dred Scott case. Only four of them continued to serve on the Court during the Civil War, and three of those four (including two Southerners) soon proved themselves to be strong Unionists. Taney alone remained unrepentant and unredeemed, as it were, and Taney alone was responsible for *Ex parte Merryman*, a proceedings at chambers with which the rest of the Court had nothing to do. The often venomous hostility of many radical Republicans followed the Chief Justice into his grave, but one should not make the mistake of assuming that it was directed at the Supreme Court as a whole.

After the war began, the Republicans virtually nullified the two main parts of the Dred Scott decision; for Congress abolished slavery in the territories, and Lincoln's attorney general ruled that, for certain purposes at least, free blacks were citizens. No such attack was launched against the Supreme Court, however. A reorganization act, passed at Lincoln's urging in 1862, was eminently moderate and designed primarily to bring the circuit court system into adjustment with recent population changes. The Court, although it had few opportunities to review wartime legislation and executive orders, generally upheld administration policies, or at least acquiesced in them. At one point, it refused on technical grounds to hear a case that presented issues similar to those in *Ex parte Merryman*. Furthermore, Lincoln's appointees to the Court made it increasingly respectable in Republican eyes, the climax coming when Salmon P. Chase succeeded Taney as chief justice in December 1864. On the whole, then, if one remembers that Taney was an exceptional case, and if one takes into account the fact that the Supreme Court has always tended to play a somewhat subdued role in wartime, it appears that the Civil War Court, far from suffering a decline in prestige, actually gained back some of the prestige sacrificed in the Dred Scott decision.

Lincoln is usually listed among presidential critics of the Supreme Court, along with Jefferson, Jackson, and Franklin Roosevelt, but the nature and limits of his criticism should be understood with some precision. The practice of law had been his career for a quarter of a century, and he had once said that reverence for the law should become "the political religion of the nation." There is accordingly no doubt of his great respect for the judicial process, but he did not believe that public policy should be made in the courtroom. It would be "much safer for all," he maintained, if bad laws were obeyed and swiftly repealed rather than being violated in the hope of having them declared unconstitutional.[18]

This does not mean that Lincoln condemned the institution of judicial review. He did, however, reject the doctrine of judicial supremacy. That is, he acknowledged the power of the Supreme Court to refuse enforcement of a statute on the grounds that it was contrary to the Constitution, but he denied that the rationale of such a decision instantaneously and automatically became constitutional law, binding even upon the legislative and executive branches of the federal government. Instead, the rationale of the decision must be legitimated over a period of time by judicial reiteration, legislative acquiescence, and public sanction. Thus, in 1858, Lincoln announced his refusal to obey the Dred Scott decision as a "political rule," adding more specifically: "If I were in Congress, and a vote should come up on a question whether slavery should be prohibited in a new territory, in spite of that Dred Scott decision, I would vote that it should."[19]

Running like a golden thread across the entire fabric of Lincoln's constitutional thought is the theme of government by the people. He insisted that the war for the Union was a crucial test of the viability of popular government, and more precisely, a test of "whether any government, not *too* strong for the liberties of its people, can be strong *enough* to maintain its own existence, in great emergencies."[20] At the same time, his reconstruction program was inspired in considerable part by an excessive eagerness to restore self-government in the South. And he found the idea of judicial supremacy repugnant because judge-made law is paternalistic rather than democratic; indeed, he took the extreme view that the ultimate power to interpret the Constitution rests with the people themselves, who authorized it and ratified it in the first place.

One of the paradoxes of freedom is that it means both sharing authority and exemption from authority. To Lincoln, the Constitution was essentially an arrangement for the sharing of authority—that is, a structure of self-government. In practice, this meant majority rule, limited by certain guarantees of individual rights, in a system of representative government. During ordinary times, the primary instrument of majoritarian representative democracy was the legislature, which could best reflect and respond to the diverse attitudes and interests of the people. Only an extreme emergency in which the single purpose of national self-preservation overrode all other considerations could justify his own assumption of extraordinary executive powers, and even then he remained responsible to the people. "Their will, constitutionally expressed," he declared, "is the ultimate law for all. If they should deliberately resolve to have immediate peace even at the loss of their country, and their liberty, I know not the power or the right to resist them. It is their own business, and they must do as they please with their own."[21]

Lincoln spoke these words shortly before the election of 1864, when it appeared that a war-weary nation might decide to write off the Union and three years of sacrifice by turning him out of office. Responding to talk of a coup d'état and other wild rumors, he promised categorically that his opponent, if elected, would be duly installed as president on the day appointed by law. Thus he placed the principle of self-government above even his passion for the Union. More than that, he affirmed his adherence to the most critical and most fragile principle in the democratic process—namely, the requirement of minority submission to majority will.

This principle, Lincoln believed, was the one most clearly at stake in the war. "If the minority will not acquiesce," he said, "the majority must, or the government must cease. There is no other alternative; for continuing the government, is acquiescence on one side or the other." He rejected the argument that the people of the Confederacy were fighting for their own version of self-government. Southern independence had never in itself been the goal of more than a small minority. The purpose of secession, first as a threat and then as a reality, was the protection of slavery, an institution by nature incompatible with the ideal of self-government. Secession was the act of a coercive minority attempting to impose its will upon the majority, an act that had no sanction either in the Constitution or in the right of revolution. "If, by the mere force of numbers," he acknowledged in his First Inaugural, "a majority should deprive a minority of any clearly written constitutional right, it might, in a moral point of view, justify revolution. . . . But such is not our case. All the vital rights of minorities, and of individuals, are so plainly assured to them . . . in the Constitution, that controversies never arise concerning them."[22]

The complacency of this pronouncement on the state of civil liberties in his time suggests that Lincoln may have given more thought to the meaning of government *by* the people than to the implications of government *for* the people. His emphasis on majoritarian democracy as the institutional basis for personal freedom seems inadequate and almost irrelevant in our modern society, preoccupied to the verge of obsession with defining the rights of proliferating minorities. Majority rule, as embodied especially in legislative assemblies, appears more and more to constitute democratic inertia in a world of accelerating social change. It is the anvil on which powerful and sometimes coercive minorities hammer out decisions affecting the whole people.

Perhaps we need to remind ourselves from time to time that although there can be majority rule without minority rights, it is unlikely that minority rights could survive very long if majority rule were allowed to disintegrate. "The ultimate power of the majority," says Bertrand Russell, "is very important to minimize the harshness inevitably involved in great changes, and to prevent a rapidity of transformation which causes a revulsion of feeling."[23] Here Russell has suggested a mediative theory of majority rule that may be more realistic than Lincoln's conception of majorities as the principal initiators of social action. The two dynamic elements in any effort at major social change are usually two intensely hostile minorities, one supporting the change and the other resisting it. The function of the majority, however passive it may seem, is to restrain, delay, moderate, and finally absorb the dynamic force of change and then bring it to bear, gradually but insistently, on the dynamic force of resistance. This was not Lincoln's model of majority rule. Yet there were times when he used Congress and the American public in precisely this way, as a massive mediative force between two hostile minorities (notably the radical Republicans and the War Democrats) whose help he needed in the struggle for the Union. By such presidential strategy, Lincoln, more than he intended or realized, was anticipating the future and incorporating it in the present.

CHAPTER 10

The Paradoxes of Freedom

In a civil war, liberty is fearfully at risk. The difficulty of sorting out friends and enemies makes it virtually impossible to suppress the opposition without engaging in some repression of individual freedom. It is a matter of record that the Lincoln administration, in struggling to preserve the Union, resorted to a number of repressive practices. No doubt the crucial question is whether those practices were, in the circumstances, necessary and reasonable or gratuitous and excessive. Beyond any such "situational" evaluation, there arises also the problem of subsequent influence; for an action may be justifiable, even wise, in its immediate context and yet unfortunate as a precedent. This essay takes up the question of how Lincoln fits into the history of freedom. Presented originally as a Bicentennial lecture at Swarthmore College and Gettysburg College in December 1975, under the auspices of Pennsylvania State University, it was published in Norman A. Graebner, ed., *Freedom in America: A 200-Year Perspective* (University Park, Pa., 1977).

key

On April 18, 1864, Abraham Lincoln boarded a train for Baltimore to participate in the opening of the Maryland Sanitary Commission Fair, a fund-raising project for the Civil War equivalent of the Red Cross. This was the city through which Lincoln as president-elect had passed surreptitiously late at night in order to thwart a reported assassination plot—the city in which arbitrary arrest and imprisonment of Confederate sympathizers had been exceedingly common, and in which Chief Justice Roger B. Taney had issued a stern rebuke to the Lincoln administration for its suspension of the writ of habeas corpus. It is therefore not surprising that in Baltimore the President's thoughts should have turned to the nature of liberty. In his short speech during the opening ceremonies he said:

> The world has never had a good definition of the word liberty, and the American people, just now, are much in want of one. We all declare for liberty; but in using the same *word* we do not mean *the same thing*. . . . The

shepherd drives the wolf from the sheep's throat, for which the sheep thanks the shepherd as a *liberator*, while the wolf denounces him for the same act as the destroyer of liberty.[1]

The shepherd in this little parable was obviously Lincoln himself. The sheep was black and one of a great many that the shepherd had rescued. The wolf, not yet on anyone's list of endangered species, represented the slaveholding South. There is no mistaking the hero, the victim, and the villain here, for Lincoln was making no pretense of impartiality. He did acknowledge, however, that the parable embodied a disturbing paradox: any act of liberation may also be, for someone, an act of oppression. The emancipation of four million slaves was a confiscation of property on an enormous scale, to the amount of several billions of dollars. And the famous proclamation with which it began was viewed by the people of the Confederacy as a monstrous, bloodthirsty effort to incite servile insurrection.[2]

For Southerners, emancipation was the culmination of tyranny already well advanced. They had been calling Lincoln a despot ever since the onset of hostilities. He was their George III, implacably denying them the very right of self-government for which Americans of 1776 had risked their lives, fortunes, and sacred honor. A powerful sense of being engaged in reenacting the heroic roles of the Founding Fathers lent the Confederacy much of its élan during the early months of the conflict. Yet Lincoln, from the beginning of the war, had insisted that it was the defenders of the Union who were fighting for the principle of self-government. Long before his thoughts turned seriously to emancipation, he characterized the struggle as one for human freedom generally. It was, he believed, the last great test in the American experiment of popular government and thus a kind of sequel to the Revolution. To members of Congress assembling on the Fourth of July he declared: "Surely each man has as strong a motive *now*, to *preserve* our liberties, as each had *then* to *establish* them."[3]

It is scarcely surprising, to be sure, that Northerners and Southerners should have disagreed about which side was fighting for freedom. The real paradox in Lincoln's case is that so many Northerners likewise called him despot and that so many historians have at least partly confirmed their judgment. Late in 1862, the distinguished Benjamin R. Curtis of Massachusetts, one of the dissenting justices in the Dred Scott case, published a pamphlet virtually accusing Lincoln of assuming dictatorial power.[4] Shortly thereafter, the Democratic governor of New York publicly attributed to the Lincoln administration "a theory which exalts the military power of the President above his civil and constitutional rights. It asserts that he may in his discretion declare war, and then extinguish the State and National Constitutions by drawing the pall of martial law over our vast country."[5] The London *Times*, in denouncing what it called the "gigantic wickedness" of the Emancipation Proclamation, referred to the "absolute despotism of the present Government at Washington."[6] And on the eve of the Battle of Gettysburg, a group of New York Democrats, while pledging their continued support of the war effort, at the same time accused the President of "pretensions to more than regal authority," and of claiming to have found "within the Constitution, a principle or germ of arbitrary power, which in time of war expands at once into an absolute sovereignty, wielded by one man; so that liberty perishes, or is dependent on his will, his discretion or his caprice."[7]

A generation later, Lord Bryce, in his classic study, *The American Commonwealth*, compared Lincoln's powers to those of a Roman dictator and said that he wielded more authority than any Englishman since Cromwell.[8] The historian James Ford Rhodes, a great admirer of Lincoln, acknowledged that in the months following the fall of Fort Sumter, the acts of the President were those "of a Tudor rather than those of a constitutional ruler." "The country attorney of Illinois," Rhodes added, "had assumed the power of a dictator."[9] Samuel Eliot Morison agreed, declaring: "Contemporary accusations against him of tyranny and despotism are strange reading to those who know his character, but not to students of his administration. If Lincoln was the ideal tyrant of whom Plato dreamed, he was none the less a dictator from the standpoint of American constitutional law."[10] Other scholars wrote in similar vein of the presidential decrees, arbitrary arrests, military trials, and various other bold employments of executive power that contributed so much to the emergence of that astonishing modern phenomenon that Arthur M. Schlesinger, Jr., called "the imperial presidency."[11]

In the history of freedom, then, Abraham Lincoln is a somewhat ambiguous figure. He liberated slaves but suppressed the movement for Southern independence. He epitomized democracy but assumed a considerable measure of autocratic power. He preserved the structure of American popular government but in the process impaired some of the substance of American liberty.

The ambiguity, beyond any doubt, inheres partly in the character of Abraham Lincoln himself. He was a complex man and, in some respects, a remote one, seldom indulging in self-revelation. There were profound depths in him and strange contrasts of light and shadow that have made him elusive and puzzling for his biographers, as he was for even his closest friends. It appears that he had no strong appetite for power; yet he was at times almost arrogant in his readiness to grasp and exercise power. His tenderheartedness—no mere legend—is visible in numerous acts of kindness and clemency, but not in the grim determination with which he supported Grant's bloody progress toward Richmond. The transcendent humaneness of the man lent the Civil War much of its luster, but it was his inveterate toughness that helped determine the outcome. The terrible human cost of the conflict nevertheless wore him down and perhaps made him less sympathetic to the complaints of dissidents who suffered only some temporary abridgment of their liberties. Commenting on the most notorious political arrest of the war, he asked: "Must I shoot a simple-minded soldier boy who deserts, while I must not touch a hair of a wiley agitator who induces him to desert?"[12]

If, however, the ambiguity of Lincoln's record in the history of freedom reflects certain characteristics of the man, it also reflects the anomalous character of civil war. The paramount purpose in any war is to defeat the enemy, but the first major task in a civil war is to distinguish enemies from friends. A nation breaking apart seldom does so cleanly; the fracture is usually jagged, ugly, and, in places, indistinct. The outcome of the struggle may depend upon which side can persuade or coerce uncommitted intermediate elements to its support. Thus in every civil war a certain amount of repression may be one of the unavoidable costs of victory.

The state of the nation on March 4, 1861, is difficult to recapture subjectively because it was an alien experience, unique in American history. Within a period of three months, seven states had held special elections, assembled conventions, seceded from the Union, established a new federal republic, drafted its constitution, and elected its first president and vice president. The movement proceeded with such efficiency and speed because Southerners had often rehearsed it in their minds, with the example of the Founding Fathers serving virtually as a script. In the North, meanwhile, there was confusion, discord, and irresolution. Disunion had been predicted often enough, but no one was rehearsed in procedures for dealing with the emergency when it came. The retiring President, a strict constitutionalist, turned the problem over to Congress, which tried to meet a new kind of crisis by imitating the compromisers of 1850.

Some Southerners in Congress and in the Buchanan cabinet acted virtually as Confederate intelligence agents while continuing to draw their federal salaries. A Texas senator remained in his seat long after Texas had seceded, carrying on a program of military recruitment for the Confederacy from an office in Baltimore.[13] The Southerner commanding the Department of Texas first surrendered to state officials all military posts and federal property within his control, *then* resigned from the Army of the United States and accepted a Confederate commission.[14] The Chief Justice of the United States, who detested the incoming Republican party and gave all of his sympathy to the Southern cause, nevertheless clung to the office until his death in 1864—the highest-placed copperhead in the wartime Union government.[15]

Many Northern Democrats insisted that the federal government had no constitutional authority to use force against the seceding states; some abolitionists and Republicans favored peaceable separation as a policy of good riddance to slavery; and it was obvious that any military movement against the Confederacy would set off another round of secession activity in the still uncommitted upper South. In any case, all the talk about "coercion" was for the time being academic, given the smallness of the regular army and the divided loyalties of its officer corps.[16]

Northern confusion and disunity did not end on March 4. The policy of drifting inaction continued, as Lincoln and his cabinet devoted much of their attention to filling offices and to the other managerial tasks facing a new administration. Then time ran out for the garrison at Fort Sumter, and after it surrendered under fire, Lincoln, in a series of decisive actions, gave authoritative definition to a crisis that had not yet been defined. By these actions—which included declaring that an insurrection was in progress, calling for volunteers, increasing the size of the regular army and navy, proclaiming a blockade of Southern ports, and suspending the writ of habeas corpus in certain areas—he also defined the role that he expected to play in meeting the crisis.

Ordinarily, the Thirty-seventh Congress would not have assembled until December 1861. Immediately after the fall of Fort Sumter in April, however, Lincoln summoned it to meet in special session on July 4. This was five months early, but still some two months later than what might seem to have been appropriate in the circumstances. Without any disposition to establish a dictatorship, he nevertheless wanted a breathing spell and a free hand before legislative activity began—an interval in which to assert presidential leadership and set the course of national policy. The initiative seized with this strategy was never lost. In subsequent years, for example, Lincoln on his own authority introduced conscription, proclaimed emancipation, and inaugurated a program of reconstruction.

The Lincoln administration also dealt vigorously and sometimes melodramatically with the problem of disloyalty inside Northern lines. In the process, it infringed upon the authority of Congress, the federal judiciary, and various state governments. Antiwar behavior verging on treason was nothing new in American history, but it posed an especially dangerous threat in 1861, when allegiances were still being sorted out. The secession of Virginia and three more states of the upper South in April and May put intense pressures on Maryland, Kentucky, and Missouri. The struggle for this "great border" was fought in a variety of ways, including movement of troops, political intrigue, mob action, guerrilla raids, and military arrests. Maryland was a particularly critical area at first because a violent upsurge of pro-Confederate sentiment in Baltimore blocked off the most direct access to Washington, which for a time seemed extremely vulnerable to capture.

In the circumstances, it probably was unrealistic to insist, as Chief Justice Taney did in *Ex parte Merryman*, that the administration should rely upon the normal processes of government to deal with rioting, sabotage, and other echoes of rebellion north of the national capital.[17] Units of Maryland militia and Baltimore police participated in the burning of bridges, destruction of railroad track, and cutting of telegraph wires. The police marshal of Baltimore, a secessionist sympathizer, himself directed some of these activities.[18] Even if offenders had been arrested by civil authorities, it was unlikely that any Maryland jury would have convicted them. Lincoln, accordingly, took a step unprecedented in American history. He authorized military commanders to suspend the privilege of the writ of habeas corpus if such action should appear necessary for protection of troop movements or for suppression of legislative efforts to align Maryland on the side of the rebellion.[19] Later he extended these orders geographically, and in 1862 he made them nationwide for specified offenses tending to impede prosecution of the war.[20]

Such suspension made it possible to throw thousands of persons into prison and keep them there for months at a time. Lincoln and his generals also imposed martial law in certain critical areas, caused civilians to be tried before military commissions, and temporarily suppressed a number of newspapers. But the principal weapon against disloyalty continued to be arbitrary arrest (often for reasons that would not have stood up in court), followed eventually in most cases by release without trial.

It is true, as Lincoln himself asserted, that the purpose of these summary detentions was not punitive but preventive, and that the effect was in some respects more humane than trial and conviction would have been. It is also true that the worst excesses were committed by subordinates without presidential approval, and that Lincoln never contemplated a systematic effort to suppress dissent. In fact, he suffered more abuse than any other president, despite having more power to stifle abuse than any other president.

Nevertheless, the security system established by his authority, with its secret police, paid informers, agents provocateurs, midnight arrests, and dank prisons, had an ominous, alien ring for most Democrats, and even for some Republicans. It was Illinois Republican Senator Lyman Trumbull who denounced arrests away from the war zone as "the very essence of despotism."[21] A Democratic pamphlet published in 1863 pictured Lincoln standing trial before great Americans of the past, with George Washington presenting the list of charges. After extensive argument, the Spirit of the Constitution passes judgment: "You were born in the freest country under the sun, but you have converted it into a despotism. . . . I now leave you, with the brand of 'TYRANT' upon your brow."[22]

The President vigorously defended his course of action. He had a sworn obligation to protect the Constitution of the United States, and that in turn meant preserving, *by all necessary means*, the government and nation for which the document had been written as organic law. The Constitution, he argued, plainly authorized the use of extraordinary justice in specified circumstances, but even if this were not the case, must "all the laws *but one* . . . go unexecuted, and the government itself go to pieces, lest that one be violated"? His answer to the question was eventually cast in Lincolnian metaphor: "By general law," he wrote, "life *and* limb must be protected; yet often a limb must be amputated to save a life; but a life is never wisely given to save a limb."[23]

Lincoln's conviction was not shaken by the acknowledged fact that an indeterminate number of innocent persons had suffered arrest and imprisonment at his hands. He seems to have regarded such mistakes as more or less equivalent to battle casualties—both being part of the total human cost of the war. Lincoln, indeed, was rejecting one of the oldest and most honored maxims of jurisprudence: *fiat justitia ruat coelum*—"let justice be done though the heavens fall." He believed that as chief magistrate his first duty was to keep the heavens from falling, if possible.

All of this might seem to place Lincoln on the side of authority against liberty, but he certainly thought otherwise. For him, it was a matter of temporarily diminishing the rights of some individuals so that an entire structure of freedom might be preserved. Thus, while critics persisted in calling him despot, he persisted in describing the Civil War as a struggle for human liberty, affecting not only his own generation but the "vast future."[24] The contradictions, as I have already suggested, reflect the character of the man and the nature of civil war as a social phenomenon, but one must add that they also derive from the exceedingly complex nature of freedom itself.

The proliferated meanings of this familiar word have been studied most exhaustively by Mortimer J. Adler in a work of some fourteen hundred pages titled *The Idea of Freedom*. It is a word that readily inspires paradox, such as the Shavian complaint, "Our liberties destroy all freedom," and the gloomy cynicism, "Men rattle their chains to show that they are free." Adler points out that according to one school of thought, freedom means *exemption* from legal restraint, while to another school it consists in *obedience* to law. The appearance of disagreement is deceptive, however, for the two groups are talking about two fundamentally different categories of freedom.[25] Thus debate on the subject can easily become the mere repetition of variant definitions.

Perhaps the primary distinction to be made is between freedom as the condition of an individual and freedom as the ruling principle of a society. And no doubt the most elemental definition of individual freedom is exemption from physical coercion and forcible restraint. The prisoner sitting in his cell has a fairly clear and simple conception of freedom, but it is one that will prove inadequate as soon as he is released. For people who possess a considerable measure of freedom, the word is likely to have a more complex and extensive meaning, with the emphasis tending to shift from avoidance of restraint to enjoyment of opportunity, from a state of personal independence to a process of self-realization. John Dewey, for instance, defined liberty as power—the "power to act in accordance with choice."[26] Lincoln stressed this positive version of individual freedom when he talked to soldiers about the purpose of the war. The struggle must continue, he told one group, "in order that each of you may have through this free government which we have enjoyed, an open field and a fair chance for your industry, enterprise and intelligence."[27]

The central paradox of freedom is the extent to which it originates in social control. Samuel Johnson once said to Boswell, "Every man has a right to utter what he thinks truth, and every other man has a right to knock him down for it."[28] Now this scarcely summarizes true freedom of speech, which means not only that government will refrain from interfering with a speaker, but that it will intervene, if necessary, to prevent others from interfering. Even when conceived of strictly as the absence of restraint and coercion, liberty, in the words of Edmund Burke, "must be limited in order to be possessed."[29] And liberty conceived of as opportunity for self-realization is even more completely a function of organized social effort. In short, except for the limited negative freedom that a few persons can still acquire through isolation, individual liberties in the modern Western world are essentially the output of free society, and the prime input of such a society is power, properly conferred, organized, and applied.

There are two principal measures of a free society. One is the extent to which it optimizes individual liberty of all kinds. The other is the extent to which its decision-making processes are controlled ultimately by the people; for freedom held at the will of others is too precarious to provide a full sense of being free. Self-government, in Lincoln's view, is the foundation of freedom. The Civil War, he insisted again and again, was being fought to save the world's best example of a free society and to vindicate the very principle of self-government. It was a fiery test of "whether any government, not *too* strong for the liberties of its people, can be strong *enough* to maintain its own existence, in great emergencies."[30]

One can therefore readily perceive that Lincoln and his libertarian critics were looking at freedom from opposite directions and in some degree talking past each other. The critics gave priority to individual liberty in its classic form of immunity from arbitrary restraint and coercion. Lincoln gave priority to maintaining the institutional structure of a free society within which individual liberty had flourished. The two commitments were far from being essentially incompatible, but the pressures of national crisis brought them frequently into conflict.

For example, the former congressman Clement Vallandigham was arrested in 1863 and swiftly convicted by a military commission for making an antiwar speech. Lincoln regretted the action but was reluctant to overrule the general in command. Ohio Democrats soon made things more embarrassing by nominating Vallandigham for governor. But Lincoln, using a light touch and unorthodox tactics, succeeded not only in overcoming the difficulty but in trivializing it. He changed the sentence from imprisonment for the duration of the war to banishment behind Confederate lines. A large delegation of Ohio Democratic leaders called on Lincoln at the White House to demand that Vallandigham be restored to his home and freedom. In the course of their written presentation they asked:

> If a man . . . believes that from the inherent nature of the federal compact, the war . . . cannot be used as a means of restoring the Union . . . but would inevitably result in the final destruction of both the constitution and the Union, is he not to be allowed the right . . . to appeal to the judgment of the people, for a change of policy, by the constitutional remedy of the ballot box?

Lincoln's answer, written on June 29, with Lee's invading army well north of Washington in the vicinity of Gettysburg, was, in effect, *no*, not when that man's speeches had the effect and probably the intent of encouraging military desertion, resistance to conscription, and violent interference with prosecution of the war.[31] In practice, Lincoln's views prevailed, but ideologically there was deadlock.

To the argument of some critics that constitutional liberties remained ever exactly the same in peace and in war, Lincoln replied that the Constitution itself plainly indicated otherwise by permitting the privilege of the writ of habeas corpus to be suspended "when in cases of rebellion or invasion the public safety does require it."[32] To the argument of certain Albany Democrats that his policies were in any case setting a dangerous precedent, he responded with another of his analogies:

> Nor am I able to appreciate the danger, apprehended by the meeting, that the American people will, by means of military arrests during the rebellion, lose the right of public discussion, the liberty of speech and the press, the law of evidence, trial by jury, and Habeas corpus, throughout the indefinite peaceful future . . . any more than I am able to believe that a man could contract so strong an appetite for emetics during temporary illness, as to persist in feeding upon them through the remainder of his healthful life.[33]

Although Lincoln, in a general sense, proved to be right, the history of the United States in the twentieth century suggests that he brushed aside too lightly the problem of the example that he might be setting for future presidents. The concept of emergency executive power is firmly, if somewhat obscurely, fixed in the Lockean political tradition, and even such a confirmed libertarian as John Stuart Mill acknowledged that an "extreme exigency" might require that constitutional government give way to temporary dictatorship.[34]

The limits of such emergency power (if it exists) must be determined by the nature of the emergency itself and are therefore undefinable in specific terms. But what kind of "exigency" is extreme enough to justify suspending constitutional forms? Here, the Founding Fathers offered some guidance by designating rebellion and invasion as the two circumstances in which the privilege of the writ of habeas corpus might be suspended. Not *war* of any kind, it should be noted; not economic depression, or famine, or plague, or flood, or presidential election. Just rebellion and invasion. Lincoln assumed enormous emergency powers and perhaps went beyond necessity, but at least he was acting within the limited definition of national emergency that had been provided by the framers of the Constitution. Furthermore, he made it plain that he regarded his extraordinary authority as temporary. In December 1864, with the conflict grinding to its close, he said to Congress, "The Executive power itself would be greatly diminished by the cessation of actual war."[35]

The modern imperial presidency was built to a considerable extent upon the concept of emergency power, which Lincoln was the first to use on a significant scale, and this in spite of the fact that there has been no real instance of rebellion or invasion since 1865. Franklin Roosevelt in 1941 declared an "unlimited national emergency" more than six months before the attack on Pearl Harbor brought the United States into a war fought far from home. Under the authority of his Executive Order 9066, issued in February 1942, some 112,000 Japanese-Americans were removed from their homes and virtually imprisoned, although they, unlike most persons suffering arbitrary arrest during the Civil War, had done nothing to justify a charge of impeding the war effort. At the hands of various twentieth-century presidents, the meaning of "emergency" and "national security" expanded greatly, and the use of the terms to explain extraordinary executive action became so frequent as to be almost routine. Finally there came the Watergate affair as a sick parody of presidential power responding to grave crisis. It is possible to conclude that Lincoln's judgment was eminently sound in the unique context of the Civil War, and yet not entirely fortunate as an example to be cited by other men acting in different circumstances.

At the same time, there is good reason to remember Lincoln's warning that in moments of crisis an excessive perfectionism may be as dangerous as an excessive use of power. "No small matter should divert us from our great purpose," he said to an Ohio regiment in 1864. "There may be some irregularities in the practical application of our system. It is fair that each man shall pay taxes in exact proportion to the value of his property; but if we should wait before collecting a tax to adjust the taxes upon each man in exact proportion with every other man, we should never collect any tax at all." And to a similar audience a few weeks later he declared: "In no administration can there be perfect equality of action and uniform satisfaction rendered by all. But this government must be preserved in spite of the acts of any man or set of men. It is worthy of your every effort."[36]

How valid was Lincoln's contention that the Civil War, from its beginning, constituted a struggle for freedom having universal significance? Surely, one might argue, a smaller United States could have continued to function as a free society made even freer by disengagement from the states most heavily committed to slavery. Perhaps so, and yet such an alternative may never really have existed. For one thing, Fort Sumter was by no means the last barrier to peaceable separation. The corrosive problem of fugitive slaves would have remained; ownership of the Western territories would have been difficult to settle without violence; and the people of the upper Mississippi Valley were belligerently opposed to surrendering control of the mouth of that great river. Moreover, division of the United States into two independent nations would have meant the intrusion of European balance-of-power politics into North America, and further divisions in one or both republics might even have balkanized the continent. The old free security behind ocean ramparts would have come prematurely to an end, and with it the special environment in which freedom had flourished.

The heart of the matter for Lincoln, however, was the threat that secession posed to democratic government and its core principle, majority rule. He believed that few Southerners really wanted to secede, and that the primary purpose of secessionism had always been to extort concessions from the North and thus enhance Southern power *within* the Union. The critical issue, accordingly, was not whether a state possessed the constitutional right to secede, but how a constitutional majority should respond to the coercive action of a minority. Put in those terms, the problem sounds very familiar to the modern ear, for we live in an age of proliferating coercive minorities—some legal, such as transportation workers on strike; some mildly illegal, such as demonstrators staging a "sit-in"; and some criminal, such as terrorists threatening to kill a hostage unless their demands are met. In many of these situations there is overwhelming pressure on persons in authority to yield or compromise in order to save life, protect property, or maintain public order. But Lincoln in his crisis stood firm, well aware that a historic example was being set. "No compromise, by public servants, could, in this case, be a cure," he told Congress; "not that compromises are not often proper, but that no popular government can long survive a marked precedent, that those who carry an election, can only save the government from immediate destruction, by giving up the main point, upon which the people gave the election."[37] In other words, coercion of government by a minority is incompatible with the principle of majority rule and thus, ultimately, with the preservation of individual freedom.

We today tend to associate minority rights with liberty and majority rule with the bureaucratic establishment that stifles liberty. This is a reflection, perhaps, of the modern consumer mentality, for one ordinarily visualizes rights as in the process of being *exercised* by individuals and minority groups. The only right possessed by a majority, as such, is the right to rule. One can scarcely disagree with the statement of an English historian, Lord Acton, that "the most certain test by which we judge whether a country is really free is the amount of security enjoyed by minorities."[38] What he failed to add, however, is that the provision of such security requires the exercise of sovereign power; and the quality, extent, and durability of such security will depend very much upon who holds that sovereign power and on what terms. Majority rule and minority rights, as Lincoln perceived, are interlocking parts of one structure of freedom.

In his famous utilitarian defense of liberty, John Stuart Mill argued that the ultimate justification for toleration of dissent lies not in the minority's right to speak but in the majority's need to be challenged.[39] In a sense, Lincoln's words and acts during the crisis of civil war offer testimony to the validity of an obverse proposition: The ultimate reason for acquiescence in the decision of a majority lies not in the majority's right to rule but in the minority's need to be secure. For, as Lincoln wrote in the first draft of his First Inaugural, "A constitutional majority is the only true sovereign of a free people."[40]

CHAPTER II

From War to Reconstruction in Arkansas

Historians examining Lincoln's role in the launching of Reconstruction have given primary attention to the course of events in Louisiana, where an administration program began to emerge after the Federal capture of New Orleans in the spring of 1862. Reconstruction got a later start in Arkansas, but what happened there likewise provides some indications of presidential strategy and purpose. And nothing better illustrates the difficulty of combining civil restoration with continued prosecution of the war than the career of General Frederick W. Steele in Arkansas. A considerable part of the following essay originated as a lecture delivered at Stanford University in 1971 on the occasion of an exhibit of Steele Papers given to the University Library.

Written history tends to run in deepening grooves, and the grooves of conventional American history seldom touch Arkansas. Its name does not enter some textbook narratives until they reach the year 1957, when Governor Orval Faubus attempted to block school desegregation in Little Rock. Hernando de Soto is well remembered for "discovering" the Mississippi River in 1541, but few persons know that he also explored Arkansas and its great river, losing along the way a drove of swine from which, according to legend, there descended that symbol of the wild and woolly Southwestern frontier, the Arkansas razorback. The Missouri crisis and compromise of 1819–21 are famous, but not many persons are aware that at the same time there was a bitter struggle over the creation of Arkansas Territory in which valiant efforts to exclude slavery from the region were beaten back in the House of Representatives by margins so narrow that at one point Speaker Henry Clay broke a tie with his vote for slavery. Similarly, many a professor lecturing on the Civil

War has gotten through the whole story without mentioning Arkansas.

To be sure, the outcome of the war was determined elsewhere. Nevertheless, the opposing sides fought fiercely for the soil of Arkansas and made it the scene of more military engagements than were fought in any other state except Virginia and Tennessee. Arkansas, where South blended into West, was the Union shield for Missouri, the Confederate shield for Texas, and of prime importance in the great struggle for control of the Mississippi River. Tenth in population among the eleven Confederate states, Arkansas produced more cotton than Tennessee or South Carolina and almost as much as Texas. It was also a significant source of foodstuffs, the value of its livestock amounting to about half that of Texas.

Arkansas, like Virginia and Tennessee, did not secede until after the firing on Fort Sumter, and like those same two states, it was regionally divided by the sectional conflict. Disunion had its strongest support in the river bottom and prairie areas of the east and south. The plateau and mountain regions of the north and west were more lukewarm in their acceptance of secession. These mixed feelings, together with Confederate reverses in the region, eventually produced much disenchantment with the Southern cause and made Arkansas one of the partly conquered states in which the Lincoln administration experimented with efforts to form a civil government loyal to the United States.

As early as July of 1862, Lincoln appointed John S. Phelps military governor of Arkansas, just as, three months earlier, he had named Andrew Johnson military governor of Tennessee. Phelps, a Democratic congressman from Missouri, was given broad discretionary authority, but he accomplished little, and his appointment was quietly revoked a year later.[1] What Lincoln really wanted, in any case, was not military government but the restoration of civil government in the Confederate states as soon as they were reconquered or partly reconquered. And so, in December 1863, he initiated the "presidential" phase of Reconstruction by issuing his "Proclamation of Amnesty and Reconstruction." It included his famous ten-percent plan, whereby a small minority of qualified voters who had taken an oath of allegiance to the United States could reestablish a state government, provided that the abolition of slavery was acknowledged.[2]

Lincoln's intense desire for a swift return of the rebel states to their normal places within the Union may have had deep psychological roots in his sense of personal responsibility for a war that had been precipitated by his election and hastened by his refusal to endorse measures of compromise.[3] No doubt he also saw an urgent need to encourage Unionist elements in the Confederate states and give them something to fight for. Furthermore, Lincoln's reconstruction policy was in many ways just an extension of strategy that had already been used with considerable success in the border states of Maryland, Kentucky, and Missouri—that is, the use of military power to raise up and protect local pro-Union leadership in the operation of a loyal state government. But quasi-puppet regimes trying to function in areas still experiencing civil conflict tend to attract the services of too many turncoats, opportunists, and timeseekers. Lincoln's program of reconstruction was beset by many difficulties, not the least of which, as the Arkansas experience would demonstrate, was quality of local personnel.

The military struggle for Arkansas had begun in March 1862 with the Union victory at Pea Ridge in the northwest corner of the state. At about the same time, the Union drive for control of the Mississippi was getting under way. Memphis and Helena were taken in the summer, and farther south, Arkansas Post fell to an assault in January 1863. Grant's capture of Vicksburg in July 1863 not only cleared the Mississippi but released troops for service elsewhere. One of the first moves was an advance westward from Helena into the heart of Arkansas for the double purpose of taking Little Rock and preventing Confederate troops in the region from participating in operations east of the Mississippi. After a campaign of some forty days, with numerous minor engagements but no major battles, a campaign in which the Northern general systematically outmaneuvered his Confederate opponent, the Union forces entered Little Rock on September 10, 1863.[4]

The victorious commander of this expedition (whose performance, according to Civil War historian Kenneth P. Williams, displayed a "brilliance and boldness" worthy of Stonewall Jackson) was Frederick W. Steele, Major General, U.S. Volunteers.[5] Steele may well qualify as one of the forgotten commanders of the Civil War. His role was often significant, and in ability he ranked well above the average; yet no biography of him has ever been published, whereas there are three biographies of the Confederate general who opposed him, Sterling Price.[6] A New Yorker and a regular army man, Steele had graduated from West Point in 1843, ranking thirtieth in a class of thirty-nine that included George B. McClellan (second) and Ulysses S. Grant (twenty-first). He served with Winfield Scott in Mexico, winning two brevets for gallantry, then, like so many other Army regulars, spent the decade of the 1850's at various frontier posts. An infantry captain at the outbreak of war in 1861, he rose rapidly in rank to command a regiment, then a brigade, then a division. He had served in the Vicksburg campaign before leading the Little Rock expedition in the late summer of 1863. He reached the peak of his career in January 1864 with appointment to the command of the newly created Seventh Corps and the newly created Department of Arkansas. A corps was an operational military unit; a department was the basic territorial organization. Thus Steele, like most department commanders, had two different kinds of responsibility, and in Arkansas this was to make things especially difficult.

A slight figure of a man, weighing only about 125 to 130 pounds, including his robust beard, Steele was efficient, good-natured, and convivial—a bachelor, a horse-fancier, and apparently something of a dandy. One of his nieces, writing to relatives in California, reported that she had received a letter from Uncle Fred. "He says he is living in Little Rock, like a 'fighting cock,' has six fast horses, and a Rebel sweetheart. I think the 'little General' is getting rather fast."[7] But on the battlefield, Steele was, in the words of a Price biographer, "tough, determined, and clever."[8]

As commander of the Department of Arkansas, Steele's task was to fortify Little Rock and consolidate his hold on the center of the state, encourage a resurgence of Unionism, protect Unionists from Confederate reprisals, and recruit enlistments, both for the Federal army and for the home guard. In short, he commanded an army of occupation and thus had the role of de facto military governor, with its many diverse problems and petty details.[9] This meant a considerable dispersal of his forces, while he himself became something of a desk general, having office hours from eight to four and hearing the advice, requests, and complaints of numerous visitors.

At the same time Steele was an operational corps commander in a still active theater of the war. Confederate troops to the south and west under General Edmund Kirby-Smith remained a constant threat, and Steele had to be ready to concentrate his troops against a major attack from that quarter. Confederates still controlled much of the southern part of Arkansas, and a Confederate state government still functioned at the town of Washington in one of the southwestern counties. In addition, Union commanders in other regions cast covetous eyes on Steele's divisions. William T. Sherman asked for one of them during the Chattanooga campaign in October 1863. Steele refused to comply without "positive orders," saying that to do so would leave his force so weak that "the Union men of Arkansas would lose their confidence in my ability to protect them."[10]

In the end, Steele found himself faced with two contradictory sets of demands upon him. His military superiors ordered him to launch an offensive into southwestern Arkansas toward Shreveport as part of the projected Red River campaign, while at the same time the President wanted him to cooperate with and supervise the establishment of a reconstruction government in Arkansas. It is scarcely surprising that Steele failed to perform either task to everyone's satisfaction.

Pressure for the organization of a loyal civil government in Arkansas came from within the state and from the White House. The occupation of Little Rock and Lincoln's Proclamation of Amnesty and Reconstruction had already brought many Arkansans into the Union fold. Some were old Unionists who had been submerged in 1861. Others had been neutralists or lukewarm in their adherence to the Confederacy. Still others were weather vanes changing their allegiance to fit the main chance. There was Edward W. Gantt, for instance, who had briefly held a general's commission in the Confederate Army, and William M. Fishback, a personal acquaintance of Lincoln who had voted for secession in the state convention of 1861.[11]

The sight of men like Gantt and Fishback playing prominent roles in the reconstruction movement caused bitter feelings among original Unionists and contributed to the destructive factionalism of early reconstruction politics in Arkansas. Thus, C. V. Meador, a Douglas Democrat and Unionist who had returned with Steele's occupation of Little Rock to publish the *National Democrat*, at first supported the movement for a state government but then turned cool toward it as he became convinced that it was being used by turncoat rebels to their own advantage. His criticism of the Gantt-Fishback faction grew increasingly vituperative, and they replied just as vehemently in the columns of their own newspaper, the *Unconditional Union*. The latter, for example, spoke of Meador and his allies as "treason and murder-stained, brazen-headed reptiles," to which Meador responded with "loathsome creatures, full of venom, abuse, greed and ignorance."[12] Each side insisted that the other was pro-Confederate.

Nevertheless, various Union mass meetings issued calls for a constitutional convention, and its irregularly elected delegates began to assemble in Little Rock on January 4, 1864. The convention drafted a constitution not radically different from the old one, except that slavery was abolished. It appointed a provisional government and designated March 14 as the day for submission of the constitution and election of state officers.[13] This was all remarkably fast work, considering the fact that Little Rock had been in Union hands for only four months. In Louisiana, by way of contrast, two years elapsed between the occupation of New Orleans and the framing of a free-state constitution.

Lincoln, in the meantime, had been laying his own plans for Arkansas, which included requiring modification of the state constitution to abolish slavery and scheduling the election of a governor.[14] When he learned about the convention, however, he wrote to Steele instructing him to give it full support and make all necessary arrangements for the election on March 14. "Take hold with an honest heart and a strong hand," the President urged. "Do not let any questionable man control or influence you." And in another letter: "Of all things, avoid if possible, a dividing into cliques among the friends of the common object. Be firm and resolute against such as you can perceive would make confusion and division."[15] As the election day drew near, he telegraphed to Arkansas political leaders: "Do your best to get out the largest vote possible; and, of course, as much of it as possible on the right side."[16]

Steele considered it his duty as a soldier to carry out the directives of the administration without question.[17] He publicly praised the work of the constitutional convention and promised full military protection at the forthcoming election.[18] But as March 14 approached, he was faced with the imminent necessity of converting an army of occupation into an expeditionary force for the biggest field operation of his career.

The Red River campaign had been under consideration for a long time, and there were complex purposes behind it, including the desire to clear Arkansas and Louisiana of Confederate forces, the desire to capture large stores of cotton in the region, and the desire to invade Texas, not only as an encouragement to Unionist elements there but as a diplomatic gesture against France, which was in the process of occupying Mexico and setting up Maximilian as emperor. In retrospect, it appears to have been a move in the wrong direction at the wrong time. Grant, commanding the forces in the West, would have preferred to strike at Mobile. Sherman in Tennessee was already planning his spring operation in Georgia. Not even the general in command of the operation, Nathaniel P. Banks, was enthusiastic about it.[19] Nevertheless, at the insistence of General-in-Chief Henry W. Halleck, preparations went forward and were virtually completed by the end of February. The plan called for Banks, reinforced with 10,000 additional troops on loan from Sherman and accompanied by a fleet of gunboats, to proceed swiftly up the Red River. Steele would strike southwestward at the same time, and the two forces would converge on Shreveport. The timing was crucial. Sherman had insisted that his troops must be returned to him in Tennessee by mid-April, and the naval force would be safe on the upper Red only during early spring high water.[20]

Steele, although apprised of the plans, persisted in believing that he would not be expected to set forth until after the March 14 election, and then perhaps only to make a demonstration southward for the purpose of drawing off some of the Confederate forces.[21] Sherman, after a conference with Banks, sent an urgent letter to Steele on March 4. Banks was about ready to leave, he reported, with the clear implication that Steele should be starting at the same time. After destroying the rebels on the Red River, Steele could then perhaps send 5,000 to 8,000 men to Tennessee. "As a friend and brother officer," Sherman wrote, "I advise you to move with great rapidity and not stand too much on preliminary preparation."[22]

But on March 7, Steele was writing to Banks that there had been "no material change in the situation of affairs" at Little Rock. "If you should start on your expedition as indicated," he politely added, "please communicate with me as often as possible." In addition to some cavalry, he would "endeavor" to send a column of infantry and some light guns on the road southward. Notice, he said "send," not "lead," and he made no mention of getting anywhere near Shreveport. To both Banks and Sherman, Steele explained that many of his veteran troops were on furlough, the roads were impassable, and forage was scarce. Besides, the President wanted the election of March 14 to be a success, and there were rumors that Confederate guerrillas would attempt to disrupt the election. Troops were needed to protect the voters, distribute the poll books, and administer the oath of allegiance.[23] Sherman had no patience with the intrusion of politics into the conduct of war. "If we have to modify military plans for civil elections we had better go home," he snorted.[24]

The election came off as scheduled, having been extended, for greater convenience, over a three-day period, March 13–15. The constitution was overwhelmingly approved, with 12,177 voting for it and 226 against. This was double the number of votes necessary under Lincoln's ten-percent plan. A governor, other state officers, a legislature, and congressmen were also elected. Unquestionably there had been a good deal of irregularity in the polling, especially in counties still more or less under Confederate control. Many of these were virtually vest-pocket districts. It is said that one legislator was elected with two votes, one his own, and that both ballots were cast on the streets of Little Rock.[25] Nevertheless, Arkansas now had an official loyal government, though plainly a flimsy one. Steele promptly telegraphed the good news to the President, adding, "I believe every man elected will support your administration."[26] The New York *Times* hailed Arkansas as the first Confederate state to reconstitute itself as a free state. "The President's method of reconstruction," said the *Times*, "may now be considered to be 'in the full tide' of successful experiment. It is progressing with every promise of complete success."[27]

By election time, Steele had reluctantly begun getting ready for his advance toward the Red River. The move, he thought, was unwise because it would expose Arkansas to Confederate raiding, and it was unnecessary because Banks, with reinforcements from Sherman, already had enough troops "to drive Kirby Smith's whole command into the Gulf."[28] On March 12, Steele expressed his misgivings directly to Halleck. "Sherman insists upon my moving upon

Shreveport," he telegraphed. "I have prepared to do so, against my own judgment and that of the best-informed people here." The roads were "impracticable"; the country to be traversed was "destitute of provision." He had proposed instead to "threaten the enemy's flank and rear" with cavalry and "make a feint with infantry on the Washington road." But he had "yielded to Sherman and Banks" and would be on the march in a day or two. "Please give me your opinion immediately," he requested.[29]

At this point, however, Grant replaced Halleck as general in chief. Informing Steele that Sherman was now in command of the Military Division of the Mississippi, he added: "You will therefore treat his request in regard to your co-operation with Maj. Gen. N. P. Banks accordingly." A day later, he made his order explicit: "Move your force in full co-operation with General N. P. Banks' attack on Shreveport. A mere demonstration will not be sufficient."[30] Sherman followed on March 20 with a letter that amounted to a reprimand,[31] but by that time Steele was already hastily completing his arrangements for departure. On March 23 and 24, his column marched southward out of Little Rock. Counting reinforcements expected to join him en route, it was an army of about 11,000 men.[32]

But Steele had been unable to make adequate logistical arrangements, and the problem of supplies handicapped him throughout the campaign.[33] The muddy ground and swollen streams slowed his advance, and he met persistent Confederate opposition. Engaged almost continuously in heavy skirmishing, Steele, with his usual competence in the field, moved steadily forward, passing through Arkadelphia and apparently headed for the Confederate capital at Washington. He still had fewer than 8,000 men, however, and was delayed for at least a week awaiting the arrival of troops from Fort Smith. Finally, on April 12, he resumed his advance and again outmaneuvered the Confederate commander, Sterling Price. After a clever feint toward Washington, he turned southeastward and occupied the important town of Camden, intending to use it as his advance base of operations.[34]

At Camden, Steele received bad news from the south. Banks had not reached Shreveport and was never going to get there. Repulsed with heavy losses in a battle near Mansfield, Louisiana, he had decided to withdraw. Steele, who could not have been expected to continue advancing on Shreveport alone, now suspected that his own position was precarious, and he was right. Kirby-Smith, the supreme Confederate commander in the Southwest, determined to destroy Steele's force. He detached three divisions from the Red River campaign to reinforce Price and eventually took personal command in Arkansas. Steele's situation became more desperate when the Confederate forces captured two big wagon trains, inflicting heavy losses on the escorts.[35]

April 26 and 27, Steele began his retreat from Camden. Through steadily falling rain, the Confederate forces pursued and finally caught up with him at Jenkins Ferry on the Saline. Steele, brought to bay, established a defense perimeter with 4,000 troops and fought off the enemy while the wagons and the rest of the force were crossing on a pontoon bridge. He thus managed to extricate himself and destroyed the bridge, leaving the frustrated Confederates stranded on the far side of the stream. It was a narrow escape, skillfully wrought, but as Steele's exhausted and depleted force staggered back into Little Rock there appeared to be little other reason for congratulation.[36] April had now given way to May. With Banks still retreating in Louisiana, the Red River campaign had ended almost on schedule, but not in the manner envisioned.

Blame for the failure of the Red River campaign fell largely on Banks, but Steele's reputation likewise suffered. In early April, Grant had decided to remove Banks and put Steele in charge of all military operations west of the Mississippi from Arkansas to the Gulf.[37] A month later, after Steele's retreat from Camden, the appointment went instead to General Edward R. S. Canby, with Steele remaining in command of the Department of Arkansas.[38] Then, in September of 1864, Sterling Price led a large force across the Arkansas River west of Little Rock and began an extensive raid into Missouri. Steele was criticized for allowing him to do so virtually unmolested.[39] Grant, who had previously regarded Steele as one of his best generals, lost patience and in November caused him to be relieved from the Arkansas command.[40] This was a military decision that had political implications.

As the administrator of Lincoln's reconstruction program in Arkansas, Steele could not avoid becoming a political figure, and for a number of reasons he was viewed with deepening suspicion and hostility by some of the more radical elements in the Republican party. "The newspaper correspondents are lying about you fearfully," Steele's brother John reported from Washington in May of 1864. Most of the attacks, he added, came from "that class of radicals who abuse everybody."[41] John B. Steele was in fact part of the problem, for he occupied a Democratic seat in Congress, faithfully supporting the war, but staunchly opposing the radicals. Furthermore, in Arkansas, General Steele quickly earned a reputation for leniency in dealing with former Confederates. He openly labeled his policy "conciliatory," and it did him no good to be praised for his conduct by the copperheadish Chicago *Times*.[42] Isaac Murphy, governor of Arkansas under the new constitution, complained to Lincoln that the military did not provide adequate protection for loyal citizens. Rebels, he said, were "basking in the favor of Federal power and occupying places of profit and trust."[43] Horace Greeley came to regard Steele as virtually disloyal, declaring that he "never struck one hearty blow at the Rebellion where he could . . . avoid it," and that he was "identified in principle and sympathy with the enemy on every point but that of Disunion."[44] One must note also that in April 1864, when Grant proposed to place Steele in command of the Arkansas and Gulf departments combined, Halleck demurred, saying there were so many "political objections" that "it would be useless to ask the President to do it."[45] No doubt Steele's removal did tend to please radical Republicans and displease conservative Unionists.[46] Yet there is no evidence that it had a political purpose or that it marked a change in Lincoln's policy.[47] Steele had, in fact, been a diligent agent of presidential reconstruction in Arkansas, and Lincoln never found any fault with the conciliatory course he followed. For that matter, Lincoln's personal intervention in Arkansas was on the whole more limited in time and scope than his supervision of reconstruction in Louisiana. That difference deserves some attention.

The once orthodox view of Lincoln as a conservative reconstructionist, committed primarily to achieving sectional reconciliation rather than racial equality, has been effectively challenged in recent years, most notably in a book by LaWanda Cox. It is her contention that Lincoln, in his outlook and purposes, was much closer to the radicals than to the conservatives, and that at the time of his death he was leading the way toward the achievement of suffrage and other basic rights for emancipated slaves.[48] As far as specific reconstruction programs are concerned, her evidence is limited almost entirely to what happened in Louisiana.

Efforts at restoring Louisiana to the Union had begun late in 1862 with the election of two congressmen, both of whom were permitted for a brief interval to take their seats in the House of Representatives. The establishment of civil government proceeded very slowly, despite repeated urging by Lincoln. State officers were not elected until February 1864, after which a constitutional convention labored at its task from early April until late July. Long before that time, Lincoln had told General Banks that the new constitution should provide for the education of young blacks, and it appears that during 1863 he endorsed the inclusion of freeborn Louisiana Negroes in the registry of voters.[49] Then, in March 1864, he wrote to Michael Hahn, the newly elected governor of Louisiana, suggesting that the constitutional convention bestow the right to vote upon "some of the colored people . . . as, for instance, the very intelligent, and especially those who have fought gallantly in our ranks."[50] The members of the convention ignored the hint and awarded suffrage to white men only. Under pressure from Banks, they did authorize legislative expansion of the franchise and with equal reluctance included a requirement for tax-supported education of blacks as well as whites.[51] There matters rested when the war came to an end. In his last public address on April 11, 1865, Lincoln defended his Louisiana policy and affirmed his desire for limited black enfranchisement in that state. Cox maintains that he fully intended to force concessions along those lines from the Louisiana legislature.[52]

Against this pattern of continuing presidential intervention in Louisiana, one must set the fact that Lincoln communicated scarcely at all with Steele and Governor Murphy in Arkansas after the spring of 1864. From Arkansas, moreover, he asked nothing more than a loyal government and the abolition of slavery. He made no effort to control the racial policies of the state.[53] He offered no objections to the Arkansas constitution of 1864 and never urged that it be changed, even though the document excluded all blacks from suffrage and officeholding, withheld from them the right to bear arms, made no provision for their education, and authorized a limited system of indentured servitude.[54] Furthermore, he never publicly defended the reconstruction government of Arkansas as he did that of Louisiana. This striking contrast in his treatment of the two states can be explained in two ways: either Lincoln concentrated most of his attention upon Louisiana because he had determined to make it his prime model of reconstruction;[55] or else his racial policy in Louisiana was not representative of a general plan but rather a special recognition of "the exceedingly unusual social, economic, and educational accomplishments of Louisiana's middle-class Negroes."[56] The evidence, including Lincoln's own testimony, lends support to either interpretation. Thus, in the last speech of his life, he declared: "What has been said of Louisiana will apply generally to other States." Presumably that included his endorsement of suffrage for certain blacks. But then he went on to insist, as he had before, that the "peculiarities" of each state required diversity rather than uniformity in the planning of reconstruction, and there too he must have had racial policies in mind.[57]

Of course Lincoln's reconstruction policies in Louisiana and elsewhere were mixed responses to pressures from without and inspiration from within. They reflected not only his perception of what was desirable but also his estimate of what was possible. His personal values and beliefs were almost always immersed in political strategy. It is therefore difficult to separate Lincoln the leader from Lincoln the acquiescer and confirmer—difficult to determine, for instance, whether he or Banks was the chief architect of presidential reconstruction in Louisiana.[58] Not untypically, his letter to Governor Michael Hahn suggesting limited Negro suffrage, although it no doubt expressed private conviction, was prompted by a petition from New Orleans blacks presented to him on the preceding day.[59]

Lincoln's program of reconstruction can perhaps be understood best as the product of reactive leadership—that is, as a series of calculated responses to changing military and political conditions. In the beginning, it was a wartime program, intended primarily to facilitate military victory and the progress of emancipation. Lincoln wanted to detach Southerners from their Confederate allegiance and to set in motion a process of abolition by state action. And fearing that the fundamental purposes of the war were at risk in the approaching presidential election, he also had his eye on the additional electoral votes that would undoubtedly come to him from any Confederate states fully restored to the Union. During the early stages of the program, it should be noted, Lincoln plainly conceived of reconstruction as a task for white Southerners working in cooperation with army commanders. Such was the import of his ten-percent plan, announced in December 1863, and his subsequent letter to Hahn raising the question of black suffrage in Louisiana was more of an exception than a new departure.

A year later, the circumstances were much changed. With the election won and the end of the war at last in sight, reconstruction would now have to be dealt with as an end in itself and as a postwar enterprise. Congress had refused to recognize the functioning Lincoln governments and at the same time had failed to install its own reconstruction program.[60] Just how much control Lincoln would continue to exercise was far from clear. He still hoped for a quick restoration of the seceded states and wanted especially to salvage the existing structure of government in Louisiana, if at all possible. He continued to insist that reconstruction should be allowed to vary in its details from state to state. As for black suffrage, he publicly endorsed a limited version of it in his final speech, but there is no evidence that he was yet ready to advocate universal manhood suffrage for the mass of freed slaves.[61] His thoughts on these subjects were, like the circumstances, in flux. What was most striking about his view of reconstruction at the time of his death was its combination of flexibility and goodwill. Those were the qualities that the nation would soon miss the most.

Frederick Steele, after his departure from Arkansas, returned to active field duty on the Gulf Coast and was one of the principal commanders in the successful assault on Mobile in April 1865. Remaining in the regular army after the war at the rank of colonel, he died suddenly in San Mateo, California, on January 12, 1868, two days before his forty-ninth birthday. At that very time in Arkansas, under the supervision of another Civil War general, another convention was drafting another state constitution—one that fully embodied the principle of racial equality. But of course its work too was to last for only a brief interval.

CHAPTER 12

The Weight of Responsibility

The central argument of this short essay was originally set forth during the course of a public lecture at Stanford University in the 1960's. Condensed and substantially rewritten, the lecture became the paper that I read at a symposium on Lincoln at Springfield, Illinois, in February 1974. The paper was published the following year in Volume 68 of the *Journal of the Illinois State Historical Society*, and that version is presented here, except for some stylistic changes.

On the evening of March 13, 1863, Abraham Lincoln slipped unobtrusively into the presidential box at the Washington Theatre to see James Henry Hackett in his celebrated role of Falstaff. Soon thereafter, Hackett sent the President a copy of his new book, *Notes and Comments upon Certain Plays and Actors of Shakespeare*. In a belated letter of acknowledgment, Lincoln wrote:

> Some of Shakspeare's plays I have never read; while others I have gone over perhaps as frequently as any unprofessional reader. Among the latter are Lear, Richard Third, Henry Eighth, Hamlet, and especially Macbeth. It is wonderful. Unlike you gentlemen of the profession, I think the soliloquy in Hamlet commencing "O, my offence is rank" surpasses that commencing "To be, or not to be." But pardon this small attempt at criticism. I should like to hear you pronounce the opening speech of Richard the Third.[1]

Hackett proudly issued the letter in a broadside printing, supposedly "for private distribution only" among his personal friends, but it quickly found its way into the newspapers. "Mr. Lincoln's genius," said the New York *Herald*, "is wonderfully versatile. No department of human knowledge seems to be unexplored by him. . . . It only remained for him to cap the climax of popular astonishment and admiration by showing himself to be a dramatic critic of the first order, and the greatest and most profound of the army of Shaksperean commentators."[2]

Hackett expressed some concern about the buzz of reaction to the letter. Lincoln replied in good humor. "Give yourself no uneasiness," he wrote (yet carefully marking this second letter "Private"). "My note to you I certainly did not expect to see in print; yet I have not been much shocked by the newspaper comments upon it. Those comments constitute a fair specimen of what has occurred to me through life. I have endured a great deal of ridicule without much malice; and have received a great deal of kindness, not quite free from ridicule. I am used to it."[3] Some weeks later, Lincoln entertained Hackett at the White House and then went three nights out of four to see him play Falstaff in *King Henry IV* and in *The Merry Wives of Windsor*.[4]

Lincoln's love for Shakespeare dated back to his youth but was intensified during the presidential years; for then his new circumstances lent new personal meaning to certain plays and passages. And although he enjoyed seeing Edwin Booth as Hamlet or Edwin Forrest as King Lear, what he liked best of all was to corner an acquaintance or one of his secretaries and read some of his favorite lines aloud. The artist Francis B. Carpenter, for example, once heard him recite the opening soliloquy from *Richard III* "with a degree of force and power that made it seem like a new creation."[5] Of course the very sound of Shakespearean language had its strong appeal for a man who was still chastening and perfecting his own literary style, but there was more than aesthetic appreciation in Lincoln's devotion. Carpenter quotes him as saying on one occasion: "It matters not to me whether Shakespeare be well or ill acted; with him the thought suffices."[6] To some indeterminable extent and in some intuitive way, Lincoln seems to have assimilated the substance of the plays into his own experience and deepening sense of tragedy.[7]

That he should have done so is scarcely surprising. For in most of his favorite plays, power and politics are the central theme. Even the miseries of Lear begin with a foolish misuse of power, indulged in because he has "for a long time been raised by his royal state so far above humanity that he has lost touch with reality." The central figure in these plays is usually a king—that is, a head of state like Lincoln—whose court is a place of tension and intrigue, and who spends much of his time hearing requests for favors, conferring with advisers, planning military campaigns, and devising counterplots against treason. "To Shakespeare," says Rebecca West, in words that would have had special meaning for Lincoln, "a king was a man who had been appointed by fate, by a force half within him and half outside him, to be the custodian of an idea, and to exercise this function in the midst of a mob of barons who were rarely if ever entirely loyal to him or the idea."[8]

A king like Lear or Richard II represents legitimate power that may be put to wrongful use, but legitimacy in turn faces the constant threat of usurpation, or power acquired illegitimately. In some cases, as in *Hamlet*, the usurper has already made himself king before the play begins; in others, as in *Macbeth* and *Richard III*, he does so on stage. Although usurpation may be invited by circumstances, it nevertheless springs from ambition and lust for power. The usurper is usually a man of superior ability and sometimes, in Lincoln's own words, a "towering genius."

In the most notable speech of his youth, Lincoln had warned that the possible emergence of such a man, driven by a burning thirst for glory, constituted the chief potential threat to American liberties.[9] But the effect of the warning, according to Edmund Wilson, is "somewhat ambiguous." Lincoln, Wilson asserted, in a now well-known critical conceit, "projected himself into the role" he was describing "with a fire that seemed to derive as much from admiration as from apprehension."[10] There is much better evidence that Lincoln was able to project himself histrionically, with a mixture of repugnance and sympathy, into the role of that most ambitious and villainous of usurpers, Shakespeare's Richard III. Perhaps Richard's talk about his own "rudely stamped" features, and his figure so "unfashionable" that dogs barked at it, struck a responsive chord in the awkward, homely man from Illinois, who grew a beard at the age of fifty-two in order to look a little more like a president.[11] Or it may have been Richard's sardonic detachment, his capacity for self-mockery, that Lincoln most appreciated.

Ambition Lincoln could readily understand because he had had the taste of it in his mouth for a long time. But the exercise of presidential authority seems to have given him little personal pleasure. He had no "love affair with power" in the White House, such as Richard E. Neustadt attributes to Franklin D. Roosevelt.[12] Instead, throughout the whole of his presidency he felt an enormous burden of responsibility for the conduct of a war that chewed up human lives at a frightful rate. Gradually the burden pressed him down, and, as Richard Hofstadter phrased it, "a deathly weariness settled over him."[13] Like so many of Shakespeare's kings, Lincoln found no savor in the fulfillment of his ambition and only a hollow crown. What he needed at times was not a "cheering up" but rather companionship in melancholy, and this may explain his fascination with darker passages in Shakespeare, such as the outburst of Richard II beginning:

> . . . of comfort no man speak.
> Let's talk of graves, of worms and epitaphs;
> Make dust our paper and with rainy eyes
> Write sorrow on the bosom of the earth.[14]

But in Lincoln's view, no other play could rival *Macbeth*, and he was drawn especially to the scene following the murder of Duncan. Six days before his own death, while steaming back up the Potomac after a visit to captured Richmond, he read and reread this passage to his companions, pausing to expatiate on Shakespeare's discerning portrayal of the murderer's mind.[15] More unusual was his strong affinity for the self-examination undertaken by Claudius, Hamlet's uncle and the usurper of the throne of Denmark, in the lines beginning, "O, my offence is rank." According to Carpenter, Lincoln called this soliloquy "the choicest part of the play" and "one of the finest touches of nature in the world."[16] Macbeth and Claudius are regicides, and in both of these passages the theme is unexpiated guilt. Claudius wants to pray for forgiveness, but how can he expect pardon while retaining the benefits from his crime? In the end, as George Lyman Kittredge says, Claudius "only succeeds in reasoning himself, with pitiless logic and intellectual honesty . . . into assurance of his own damnation."[17] Macbeth does not engage in such extensive meditation, but there are some striking parallels of feeling and imagery:

> *Claudius* What if this cursed hand
> Were thicker than itself with brother's blood.
> Is there not rain enough in the sweet heavens
> To wash it white as snow?
>
> *Macbeth* Will all great Neptune's ocean wash this blood
> Clean from my hand?
>
> *Claudius* [after trying in vain to pray]
> My words fly up, my thoughts remain below.
> Words without thoughts never to Heaven go.

Macbeth [after trying in vain to say "Amen" in response to the "God bless us" of a half-awakened chamberlain]

But wherefore could not I pronounce "Amen"?
I had most need of blessing, and "Amen"
Stuck in my throat.

There is no substantial evidence that Lincoln suffered from a sustained sense of guilt, either real or neurotic. Yet at times his responsibilities as president must have weighed as heavily as the guilt of any assassin, and the latest casualty lists may have seemed like accusations. It is not altogether unlikely that in the gloom of some sleepless night he too beheld blood upon his hands or found a prayer faltering on his lips.

Like Claudius, Lincoln wrestled with the problem of what prayer means, and, with a pitiless logic of his own, he reasoned himself into the position of being unable to pray for what he most intensely desired—military victory over the Confederacy. As the Civil War continued, he became convinced that God could not be summoned exclusively to the aid of one side or the other—certainly not to the side of slavery, and, from the evidence of the battlefields, not to the Northern side either:

> In great contests each party claims to act in accordance with the will of God. Both *may* be, and one *must* be wrong. God can not be *for*, and *against* the same thing at the same time. In the present civil war it is quite possible that God's purpose is something different from the purpose of either party—and yet the human instrumentalities, working just as they do, are of the best adaptation to effect His purpose. I am almost ready to say this is probably true—that God wills this contest, and wills that it shall not end yet.[18]

It was in the will of God that Lincoln found the only adequate counterweight for a burden of responsibility too heavy to carry alone. A large part of that burden consisted in living with the consequences of decisions that had gone wrong. For example, the elevation of General John Pope to command of the Army of Virginia was followed two months later by a crushing defeat at Bull Run. After the results of the battle were known, Lincoln told his cabinet that he felt "almost ready to hang himself."[19]

No less painful were the doubts that must have assailed Lincoln from time to time about his part in bringing on the war. Had he been wrong to oppose those last efforts at compromise in the winter of 1860–61? Could the effusion of blood have been avoided by giving up a few square yards of ground in Charleston Harbor? According to more than one Civil War scholar, these questions may have haunted Lincoln throughout his presidency. Perhaps a sense of personal responsibility, as well as his compassionate nature, impelled him to be so generous in the issuance of pardons. And perhaps his program of reconstruction, with its hasty restoration of civil government and magnanimous attitude toward the defeated South, reflected, in part, a "desire for personal absolution."[20]

Viewed in such light, some of Lincoln's most familiar words take on additional meaning. "I claim not to have controlled events," he wrote in April 1864, "but confess plainly that events have controlled me."[21] Without denying that the statement is an honest expression of humility, one can nevertheless read the words also as an effort to disclaim responsibility, or at least lighten its intolerable weight. Yet at other times he had spoken differently. "We—even *we here*—hold the power, and bear the responsibility," he told the members of Congress in December 1862.[22] Believing in both the prevailing will of God and the freedom of man, Lincoln, as he pondered the origins of the Civil War, found himself needing two explanations, one stressing human conduct and the other stressing divine agency.

Both explanations, as he perfected them, appear within the text of the Second Inaugural. First comes the secular, official formulation: "Both parties deprecated war; but one of them would *make* war rather than let the nation survive; and the other would *accept* war rather than let it perish. And the war came." But this is not the ultimate explanation, for the willful actors in the drama of conflict are to some undetermined extent the instrumentalities of another will:

> The Almighty has His own purposes. "Woe unto the world because of offences! for it must needs be that offences come; but woe to that man by whom the offence cometh!" If we shall suppose that American Slavery is one of those offences which, in the providence of God, must needs come, but which, having continued through His appointed time, He now wills to remove, and that He gives to both North and South, this terrible war, as the woe due to those by whom the offence came, shall we discern therein any departure from those divine attributes which the believers in a Living God always ascribe to Him?[23]

Here was a cruel doctrine, offered to explain a cruel war. Yet the argument provided a logical basis for the principle of "malice toward none," because it absolved the South as well as the North from ultimate responsibility. And, by presenting himself in each moment of decision as an instrument of the Almighty, the argument likewise absolved Abraham Lincoln. But no matter how well this theological construct satisfied his need for an impersonal explanation of the war, there were apparently intervals when it did not carry conviction, and then, with no counterweight at work, the full burden of responsibility crushed his spirit. It was in those dark hours, perhaps, that he felt himself in communion with the most wretched and unredeemed of Shakespeare's monarchs. Sometimes the anguish of renewed awareness overtook him even in the midst of laughter. "All of a sudden," wrote the Marquis de Chambrun, "he would retire within himself; then he would close his eyes, and all his features would at once bespeak a kind of sadness as indescribable as it was deep. After a while, as though it were by an effort of his will, he would shake off this mysterious weight under which he seemed bowed; his generous and open disposition would again reappear."[24]

Lincoln is the supremely tragic figure of a tragic war, and not only because of the way his life ended. He rose to the presidency from deeper obscurity than any of his predecessors, only to find himself in the grip of a deadly historical irony. That is, his own unexpected and dazzling personal triumph in 1860 had signalized—indeed, to some degree had caused—the onset of national calamity. For a man sensitive enough to perceive the irony and its bloody implications, there was bound to be, always, sorrow on the bosom of the earth.[25]

CHAPTER 13

The Death of Lincoln

Most biographers of Lincoln have given scant attention to his death, leaving that subject to amateur investigators fascinated by the mystery enveloping the assassination. Only recently have professional scholars begun to examine the event in detail and ponder its various meanings and consequences. This effort at putting the death of Lincoln into a broad historical context was presented as an address on February 12, 1983, at the Lincoln Memorial Shrine in Redlands, California. It was subsequently published in pamphlet form by that institution. I have made some revisions, such as taking note of the important book by William Hanchett, which appeared later the same year.

Abraham Lincoln was shot in Ford's Theatre by the well-known actor John Wilkes Booth at approximately 10:15 in the evening of Good Friday, April 14, 1865. He died about nine hours later at 7:22 A.M. Ten days before, he had walked the streets of Richmond, the Confederate capital, shortly after its evacuation by Lee's army, only to return and be killed in his own capital city. The shock of that crime was as instantaneous as a major earthquake, but its full historical meaning became visible only with the passage of time, and it is still being assessed.

There are five aspects of the death of Lincoln that especially deserve to be studied and reflected upon: (1) Lincoln's own personal attitude toward death and its possible influence on his career; (2) the assassination, including its background and aftermath, as one of the greatest real-life murder mysteries of all time; (3) the historical consequences of the event, particularly in relation to the course of Reconstruction and the racial sequel to emancipation; (4) the prominent place of Lincoln's death in the whole history of assassination as a social phenomenon; (5) the contribution of the assassination to the Lincoln legend, and thus to the structure and substance of the American mythology.

For Lincoln in childhood, youth, and maturity, there were close, grievous encounters with death—his mother, struck down by something called the "milk sickness" when he was nine; his only sister, Sarah, dying in childbirth when he was eighteen; Ann Rutledge, whose death he mourned when he was twenty-six; and his two sons, Eddie and Willie, who died when he was forty-one and fifty-three. There is abundant evidence that much of Lincoln's recurring melancholy was associated with reflections on the swiftness of time, the evanescence of youth, and the certainty of death. His favorite poem, "Mortality," begins by comparing human life to "a swift-fleeting meteor, a fast-flying cloud," and ends on the same note:

> 'Tis the twink of an eye, 'tis the draught of a breath
> From the blossom of health to the paleness of death,
> From the gilded salon to the bier and the shroud—
> Oh, why should the spirit of mortal be proud![1]

And in a poem of his own, inspired by a return to his Indiana home after fifteen years' absence, Lincoln wrote:

> The friends I left that parting day—
> How changed, as time has sped!
> Young childhood grown, strong manhood grey,
> And half of all are dead.
>
> I hear the lone survivors tell
> How nought from death could save,
> Till every sound appears a knell,
> And every spot a grave.[2]

There are indications that Lincoln gave more than occasional thought to his own death and that as president he had some premonitions of an untimely end. Among the various scraps of evidence on this subject, none is more dramatic than Lincoln's report to several cabinet members on the last day of his life that he had once again dreamed of being aboard a strange vessel "moving with great rapidity towards an indefinite shore."[3]

Historians have recently given considerable attention to death as a social institution, and it is not surprising that their work should inspire some new conjectures about the effect of private anxieties upon Lincoln's public career. Robert V. Bruce, for instance, has presented the following well-reasoned argument: Lincoln's chronic melancholy and frequent bouts of depression were manifestations of a lifelong inner struggle to cope with the transience of individual existence, the inescapable mortality of human consciousness. At the same time, unlike most of his contemporaries, he could not take comfort from expectations of a better world to come; for he apparently had no firm faith in life after death. His antidote for despair, says Bruce, was "the concept of immortality through remembrance, eternal consciousness by proxy in the mind of posterity." And furthermore, his desperate determination to achieve this quasi-immortality of lasting renown was "a powerful force in his uncommonly absorbing ambition."[4]

Dwight G. Anderson develops the same theme in a more extreme fashion. Lincoln was "a man hounded by a death anxiety," Anderson declares. "He not only feared death but wished for it; he saw death not only as an enemy but as an ally." This obsession became transformed into a quest for the symbolic immortality of everlasting fame, which Lincoln pursued by assuming the role of revolutionary tyrant when the outbreak of civil war presented him with the opportunity.[5]

One can easily see some merit in the theory that Lincoln's concern about death affected his private life and public career, but its plausibility should not blind us to the fact that the supporting evidence is rather thin and on the whole suggestive rather than conclusive. There remains reason to doubt that Lincoln's attitude toward death was sufficiently different from those of his contemporaries to account in any substantial way for his unique role in history. Personal encounters with death and anxiety about afterlife were common experiences in Lincoln's time, as they have been throughout history, and the idea of survival through remembrance was a familiar theme, popularized most notably in Nathaniel Hawthorne's story "The Ambitious Guest."

Furthermore, many of Lincoln's contemporaries were at least as ambitious as he—think of Stephen A. Douglas and Salmon P. Chase, for example. Did their ambition likewise stem from concern about death? If so, then we have no distinctive explanation of Lincoln's character and achievement; if not, then something else must have motivated them, and perhaps that something else would suffice to explain Lincoln's ambition also. It might well be argued from the evidence that he was a person of rather ordinary attitudes, anxieties, and aspirations, but one of extraordinary ability and strength whose peculiar combination of qualities happened to fit the peculiar circumstances of the sectional crisis. Of course no simple formulation can satisfactorily explain the complex linkages between motivation, purpose, social context, and achievement. I am disposed to believe, however, that Lincoln's career was shaped more by his zest for life than by his occasionally morbid concern about death.

The assassination of Lincoln has never ceased to fascinate the American people, and it continues to receive both popular and professional attention. A remarkable variety of writing on the subject has appeared just in the past decade. There is no more respectable work, for example, than Thomas Reed Turner's *Beware the People Weeping*, a careful, scholarly study, completed originally as a doctoral dissertation.[6] At the other extreme is an absurd but apparently profitable venture in sensationalism called *The Lincoln Conspiracy*.[7] One can also read a highly entertaining novel on the subject by G. J. A. O'Toole, an expert examination of the technical evidence by a noted physician, John K. Lattimer, and a masterly critique by William Hanchett of the "many theories, hypotheses, and speculations put forward since 1865."[8]

An interesting sidelight on the medical evidence is the theory of a Southern California physician that the diabolic heroics of John Wilkes Booth were probably unnecessary. For Lincoln, according to Dr. Harold Schwartz, suffered from a genetic disorder called Marfan's syndrome and was already in the later stages of congestive heart failure at the time of his assassination. Thus far, Dr. Schwartz seems to have won more attention than credence from professionals in medicine and history. But of course there is no way of proving him right or wrong.[9]

Booth, after shooting Lincoln, broke his leg in a dramatic leap from the presidential box to the stage of Ford's Theatre. He nevertheless managed to mount a horse and flee southward out of Washington, escaping capture for eleven days after the death of the President. Federal troops at last surrounded him and a companion as they lay sleeping in a Virginia tobacco barn, and when Booth refused to surrender, he was shot and killed. Nine other persons were implicated in the assassination. Eight of them were brought to trial before a military commission and convicted. Four were executed, and of the four sent to prison, one died there. The other three were pardoned several years later by President Andrew Johnson. John H. Surratt, Jr., the ninth person implicated, fled to Canada, then to Europe, and was finally captured in Egypt more than a year and a half after the assassination. Brought back to the United States and placed on trial in a civil court, he escaped conviction because of a hung jury.

Booth's original purpose, formed perhaps as early as the summer of 1864, had been to kidnap the President. The decision to commit murder instead was apparently not made until April 13 or 14. Final plans called for the simultaneous killing of Lincoln, Vice President Johnson, and Secretary of State William H. Seward. The attack upon Johnson never materialized, but Lewis Thornton Powell (alias Payne) made his way into Seward's home and wounded him severely, though not fatally. At least six of the nine persons later brought to trial were certainly involved with Booth in the kidnapping plot; at least three were certainly involved with him in the plan for multiple assassination. Thus there was, undoubtedly, a *conspiracy*, defined by the *Oxford English Dictionary* as "a combination of persons for an evil or unlawful purpose." But the critical question is, how far did the conspiracy reach? What persons were involved? As a murder mystery, the assassination of Lincoln is not a "whodunit," but rather a "whoalldunit."

In their shock and anger, Northerners were disposed to believe that Booth and his accomplices had acted under orders from Confederate headquarters in Richmond. The theory of a great Southern conspiracy received official endorsement from the new President, Andrew Johnson. He issued a proclamation declaring that the assassination had been "incited, concerted and procured" by Jefferson Davis and certain other rebel leaders.[10] The evidence supporting this charge proved to be unreliable, however, and Davis, though held in prison for two years, was never brought to trial. By 1867, certain radical leaders were carrying their political quarrel with President Johnson to the point of trying to implicate him in the assassination, but that accusation likewise failed to carry conviction. The idea of an extensive plot involving important historical figures went out of fashion. Historians of the late nineteenth and early twentieth centuries generally portrayed the conspirators as a small group of social misfits drawn to their erratic, intemperate leader by the force of his personality and by their common devotion to the Confederate cause.

Then, in 1937, Otto Eisenschiml, a chemist and businessman turned amateur historian, revived the suspicion of a great conspiracy, giving it a new twist. Since that time the idea has flourished astonishingly, even though professional historians have generally treated it with disdain. Eisenschiml presented Secretary of War Edwin M. Stanton as the treacherous villain who engineered the assassination, his purpose being to clear away the main obstacle to radical reconstruction of the defeated South.[11] Although certain puzzling features of Stanton's behavior served as a point of departure, Eisenschiml acknowledged that his case against the Secretary consisted almost entirely of inference and conjecture. Stanton, in fact, appears to have been more concerned about Lincoln's safety than any other public official in Washington. Yet the public dearly loves a grand conspiracy. The Eisenschiml thesis, elaborated and expanded by other writers, was promoted by the newspapers, network television, the Book-of-the-Month Club, and *Reader's Digest*. Moreover, it was reinforced by some new though questionable evidence that came largely from a single source.[12]

Thus the assassination of Lincoln was turned into a kind of national fantasy, taken seriously by some people and enjoyed tongue-in-cheek by others. In this world of gossamer fact and vivid imagination, one can even find Seward joining Stanton as co-leader of the great plot, and Booth is often pictured as eluding his would-be captors, who kill and bury another man in his place.[13] Most extravagant of all is the contention in *The Lincoln Conspiracy* that four separate groups of public officials and businessmen conspired simultaneously to remove Lincoln from the scene and made use of Booth as an agent of their designs. The list of alleged plotters reads like a *Who's Who* of the Civil War era. It includes Confederate President Jefferson Davis and Confederate Vice President Alexander H. Stephens, financier Jay Cooke, journalist Thurlow Weed, Senator Benjamin F. Wade, and of course Edwin M. Stanton.[14] The success of *The Lincoln Conspiracy* (over one million copies already printed) only serves to demonstrate that many Americans find junk history as appealing as junk food.

It is possible, to be sure, that the plot against Lincoln did extend beyond the circle of those persons brought to trial, and certain anomalies and mysteries in the assassination story do encourage speculation about a grand conspiracy. But the evidence of such a conspiracy remains unsubstantial. In words once used by Lincoln, it is "as thin as the . . . soup that was made by boiling the shadow of a pigeon that had starved to death."[15]

For historians, the most important question to be asked with regard to the assassination is not how it came about, but rather how it affected the course of American history—and more specifically, the course of Reconstruction after the Civil War. One immediate consequence was a change in the Northern mood, an overlay of grief and anger on the celebration of victory and, accordingly, a resurgence of hostility toward the defeated South. The assassination undoubtedly helped set the emotional tone for a harsher reconstruction policy. Beyond that, however, is the question of how much difference it made to have Andrew Johnson, rather than Abraham Lincoln, in the White House from April 1865 to March 1869.

The answer once widely accepted by scholars ran somewhat like this: Lincoln at the time of his death had developed a sensible, generous plan for restoring the Union. Johnson tried to follow the plan but lacked the necessary political skill and political standing. He fought a long, brave, losing battle with the radical Republicans in Congress, who imposed their own vindictive system of military reconstruction upon the South. The result was a legacy of sectional bitterness that might have been avoided if Lincoln had survived.

Some historians came to the conclusion that not even Lincoln could have stemmed the radical tide. T. Harry Williams, for instance, maintained that the radicals already held the upper hand at the time of the assassination. "They had conquered Lincoln, they would conquer Johnson," he wrote. "With a grim confidence, they entered the savage years of the tragic era."[16] One finds a similar view in a little fantasy by Oscar Lewis titled *The Lost Years*. Lincoln, as Lewis imagines it, survives the wound inflicted by Booth and serves until the end of his term on March 3, 1869. The radicals have long since gained control of Congress and put their program in force. Lincoln retires a beaten and unpopular man. He takes a trip to California via the newly completed transcontinental railroad and spends the summer with an old friend in the gold-country town of Auburn. There he makes a public gesture in behalf of a girl who has met hostility and discrimination from town officials because of her father's Confederate service. The gesture captures attention throughout the country and helps set public policy on a course toward the sectional reconciliation that Lincoln as president failed to achieve.[17]

Such, then, was the standard interpretation that prevailed in the first half of the twentieth century, with Lincoln and Johnson portrayed as unsuccessful champions of a generous reconstruction policy that would have avoided the sectional bitterness subsequently provoked by the radical program. By the 1960's, however, Lincoln's plans for restoration of the Union were being reconsidered and found wanting in the light of the modern civil rights movement. It now appeared that his much-acclaimed leniency toward the defeated white South had meant inadequate protection for the liberated black South. "The Reconstruction advocated by Lincoln and Johnson," wrote Kenneth M. Stampp and Leon F. Litwack, "envisioned 'loyal' state governments with full jurisdiction over local matters, including the right to determine the Negro's place in their society."[18] A black writer phrased it more pungently. "Reconstruction, Lincoln style," he wrote, "was going to be a Reconstruction of the white people, by the white people, and for the white people."[19] In other words, the radical Republicans had been right in their insistence upon sterner measures of control and right, above all, in their enactment of the Fourteenth and Fifteenth amendments.

Thus Lincoln's name continued to be linked with Johnson's in Reconstruction history, but the policies attributed to them jointly were no longer viewed with approval. Any defense of Lincoln in the civil rights context would obviously require separating him from Johnson and moving him closer to the radicals. And that is precisely the line of argument followed in recent years by a number of historians. That Booth and his pocket pistol did decisively alter the course of Reconstruction is the judgment of both Peyton McCrary and LaWanda Cox in their two studies of Lincoln's policies in Louisiana. "Given the differences in principle and prejudice between Lincoln and Johnson," Cox declares, "Reconstruction history would have followed a different path both at the nation's capital and in the secession states of the South had Lincoln lived out his second term of office. Of that there can be no doubt."[20] Biographer Stephen B. Oates agrees, declaring that Lincoln, at the time of his death, "seemed on the verge of a new phase of reconstruction, a tougher phase that would call for some form of Negro suffrage, more stringent voting qualifications for ex-Confederates, . . . and perhaps an army of occupation for the postwar South. . . . In other words, the President was already considering in 1865 what Congress would later adopt in the days of 'Radical Reconstruction.'"[21]

Oates has perhaps gone too far in assimilating Lincoln to the radicals, but his conjectures are not incompatible with the drift of the evidence and the character of the man, whom he rightly views in dynamic rather than in static perspective. For myself, I see no reason to change a conjecture that I offered in 1963: "If Lincoln had survived, the battle [with Congress] that Johnson lost might never have been fought. Possessing both greater wisdom and greater political strength, Lincoln was more capable of arranging a sound compromise that would have combined the better features of the Radical program of reconstruction with his own magnanimity and humane understanding."[22]

The word "assassination" is derived from medieval Arabic, but the deed itself has a much longer ancestry. Regicide, tyrannicide, and other varieties of public murder date back to Julius Caesar, back to Philip, the father of Alexander the Great, and even further into the past. In American history, however, the phenomenon was almost unknown until the death of Lincoln. Before that fatal evening in Ford's Theatre, there had been no assassination of a major public figure, and only one significant attempt, in almost nine decades of national independence.

Not that political *violence* was uncommon in those years. Every now and then, a heated debate in Congress turned into an exchange of blows and sometimes into a general brawl. The attack on Senator Charles Sumner, antislavery orator from Massachusetts, by a South Carolina congressman is one of the landmarks in the coming of the Civil War. And the practice of dueling took the lives of several prominent men, including Alexander Hamilton and Senator David Broderick of California.

Even in the White House there were incidents. Secretary of the Treasury William H. Crawford once flew into a temper and brandished his cane at President James Monroe, who offered to defend himself with fireplace tongs.[23] John Quincy Adams recorded in his *Memoirs* a half-dozen interviews with a man who had threatened to murder him. This pest, a court-martialed army surgeon named

George P. Todson, called repeatedly at the White House demanding reinstatement. When queried about the threat of assassination, he said that he had given up the idea. On one occasion, he asked the President for money to pay for his lodgings and return fare to New Orleans. Adams finally arranged to have him appointed surgeon on a naval vessel headed for Africa, but that brought only a temporary respite. What is most amazing, of course, is that Adams continued to see Todson every time he put in an appearance.[24]

It was upon Andrew Jackson, easily the most violent person ever to occupy the White House, that the first attempt at presidential assassination was made. Two pistols misfired at close range, and Jackson miraculously escaped martyrdom. His close call did not result in any increase of presidential security, for the assassin proved to be insane and the whole affair was generally regarded as a freakish accident. Lincoln's secret nighttime passage through hostile Baltimore as president-elect seems to have been the first instance in which serious precautions were taken.

Until the Civil War, assassination was simply not a thing to be reckoned with in the United States. After the war, however, it soon became familiar in American experience. Along with numerous attacks upon lesser officials, the following milestones were passed: in 1868, the first assassination of a member of Congress; in 1873, the first attempt on the life of a state governor; in 1881, the second assassination of a president; in 1889, the first attack upon a member of the Supreme Court (his assailant being shot to death); in 1893, the first assassination of a city mayor; in 1900, the first assassination of a governor; and in 1901, the third assassination of a president.[25]

No doubt there was more than one influence contributing to this surge of political violence in the United States. It may be viewed as a malignant legacy of the Civil War, as a manifestation of the increasing importance attached to government in American expectations, and as a consequence of the social and psychological dislocations produced by the modern industrial order. But in addition, man is an imitative animal, and it seems likely that after the death of Lincoln, assassination came much more readily to mind as a possible course of action.

Since the death of Lincoln, three presidents and one presidential candidate have been assassinated; one president and one former president (who was also a presidential candidate) have been wounded by gunfire; and there have been four additional attempts to assassinate a president or president-elect. In five of those ten events, other persons were killed or wounded. In only two was no one hurt at all.[26]

The climax of national tragedy in the deaths of John F. Kennedy, Martin Luther King, and Robert F. Kennedy within a five-year period of the 1960's inspired a great deal of research into the social and psychological causes of assassination. A study issued by a public task force in 1970 concluded that presidential assassination was typically anomic—that is, undertaken primarily for private rather than political reasons. Indeed, the report declared flatly that most presidential assassins (including John Wilkes Booth) have been "mentally disturbed persons who did not kill to advance any rational political plan."[27]

This simplistic explanation of assassination as typically pathological has been challenged in a book by James W. Clarke, a political scientist. Clarke maintains that some presidential assassins, Booth among them, were rational men, though extremists, who acted primarily for political reasons. Booth's motives, he says, have been misunderstood by writers who ignore the political context of his deed and assume that "only a deranged person could have killed so noble a human being" as Abraham Lincoln. Actually, throughout the South and among many Northerners, Lincoln was regarded as a cruel despot and even a monster. In the circumstances, then, Booth could rationally view himself as a patriot. His motives, says Clarke, were "akin to those of the German officers who conspired and attempted to kill Hitler."[28]

The death of Lincoln was unique among presidential assassinations (successful and abortive) in the amount of public hatred concentrated and expressed in the act of the assassin. It was also very nearly unique in being clearly the achievement of a conspiratorial group. Suspicion of conspiracy has attached to several other assassinations, notably that of President Kennedy, but the only other verified instance of collaboration is that of Oscar Collazo and Griselio Torresola, the two Puerto Rican nationalists who tried to storm Blair House and kill Harry S Truman. Moreover, Booth was different from other presidential assassins in being already a famous man—one of the leading actors of his day—rather than just a face out of the crowd. And as an actor he knew how to turn his crime into a dramatic performance, with that leap from the presidential box to the stage and that cry of "*Sic semper tyrannis*!" In one respect, however, Booth was like all presidential assassins except one. He did his killing with a handgun.

There remains for consideration the mythologizing effect of the assassination. While sustaining the hatred of Confederates, copperheads, and certain radical members of his own party, Lincoln was also perceived by many of his supporters as something less than a success in the presidency. Richard Henry Dana wrote in 1863 that the most striking thing about Washington politics was the absence of personal loyalty to the President. "He does not act, or talk, or feel like the ruler of a great empire in a great crisis," Dana complained. "He likes rather to talk and tell stories with all sorts of persons . . . than to give his mind to the noble and manly duties of his great post. It is not difficult to detect that this is the feeling of his cabinet. He has a kind of shrewdness and common sense, mother wit, and slipshod, low levelled honesty, that made him a good western jury lawyer. But he is an unutterable calamity to us where he is."[29] Even taking into account all of those contemporaries who did recognize greatness in Lincoln, one finds a remarkable contrast between his reputation while still alive and his subsequent historical stature. Did assassination make the difference? And if so, why are James A. Garfield and William McKinley so dimly remembered?

Lincoln did not have to die in a certain way to be ranked high among American presidents. After all, he presided over the United States during its greatest domestic ordeal. As commander in chief he led the way through disappointment and defeat to total victory. In the midst of war he inaugurated the nation's greatest social reform. And all the while he was mobilizing the American language with such skill as to set a new standard of eloquence in public discourse. He is, consequently, a significant figure in American literature as well as in American history. Posterity surely would have honored him, whatever the time and manner of his death, but whether it would have elevated him to preeminence among American heroes is another question.

A cultural hero may or may not be a figure of history, but he is always in some degree a figure of legend, and legend (or myth) is essentially a complex of images charged with cultural meaning and responsive to certain cultural needs. The assassination rounded out the partly formed Lincoln legend, giving it perfect shape and profound emotional appeal. Death took the man at the very climax of his career and left him no disillusioning aftermath, no downward slope into retirement and old age. The timing of the event on Good Friday, the outpouring of funeral sermons on Easter Sunday, the fact that he too could be called a "savior" and a "redeemer"—this was the very stuff of apotheosis.

Yet, more important than such extravagant analogy was the sudden realization, with Lincoln's death, that in his life and character there had been something eloquently expressive of America. No one better described that realization than a writer for the New York *Herald* soon after the assassination:

> Whatever judgment may have been formed by those who were opposed to him as to the calibre of our deceased Chief Magistrate, or the place he is destined to occupy in history, all men of undisturbed observation must have recognized in Mr. Lincoln a quaintness, originality, courage, honesty, magnanimity and popular force of character such as have never heretofore, in the annals of the human family, had the advantage of so eminent a stage for their display. He was essentially a mixed product of the agricultural, forensic and frontier life of this continent—as indigenous to our soil as a cranberry crop, and as American in his fibre as the granite foundations of the Appalachian range. He may not have been, and perhaps was not, our most perfect product in any one branch of mental or moral education; but, taking him for all in all, the very noblest impulses, peculiarities and aspirations of our whole people—what may be called our continental idiosyncrasies—were more collectively and vividly reproduced in his genial and yet unswerving nature than in that of any other public man of whom our chronicles bear record.[30]

Here one can see legend enriching history in response to the emotional needs of the culture. The United States, as a young nation cut off by revolution from its cultural heritage, could not draw upon a dim, distant past for its folk heroes and had to shape them instead from contemporary materials. Washington and the other great leaders of the Revolutionary era were heroes indeed, but none of them quite suited the nineteenth-century need for a heroic *common* man—a representative not only of American nationality but of American democracy. Lincoln fitted the role perfectly—fitted it in his background, in his outlook, in his appearance, in his style, and in the very structure of his life.

Furthermore, his personal legend profoundly altered that of the nation. The national myth had for the most part celebrated *achievement*, such as the winning of independence and the conquest of the wilderness. To that national tradition the Lincoln legend now added the element of high tragedy. In Lincoln's tragic death, as in the lines of sadness etched on his face, there was epitomized all the pain and sorrow of a nation's descent into the self-destructive violence of civil war. But to that dark perception one should add the reminder that the function of tragedy is to purge the emotions and thus uplift the spirit.

PART III

IMAGES OF LINCOLN

CHAPTER 14

The Changing Image of Lincoln in American Historiography

David M. Potter's inaugural lecture as Harmsworth Professor of American History at Oxford University in 1947 was titled "The Lincoln Theme in American National Historiography." Twenty years later, I offered a supplement to the Potter study as my own Harmsworth inaugural lecture.[1] Much more has been published about Lincoln since that time—too much to incorporate in this revised version of my lecture, which has been allowed to stand substantively as a view of Lincoln literature from the vantage point of the late 1960's. Some of the more recent writings about Lincoln are discussed elsewhere in this book, most notably in Chapters 15 and 16.

When Lyndon B. Johnson, on February 12, 1968, drew a parallel between his wartime ordeal and that of Abraham Lincoln, he was striking one of the most familiar poses in American politics. Herbert Hoover, in the gloom of the Great Depression, comforted himself with the same kind of analogy and with the remembrance that Lincoln had survived an enormous amount of abuse and won reelection. Harry Truman repeatedly compared his problems to those of the Civil War President, who, he insisted, would have despised the modern Republican party. John F. Kennedy, as president-elect one hundred years after Lincoln, consciously imitated the latter in delivering a farewell to the people of his state. And indeed it appears that in the whole gamut of American politics, no reactionary is so blind, no revolutionary so militant, no misfit so freakish that he cannot find a place in Abraham's bosom.[2]

Why Lincoln has become the central figure of a national mythology is not easy to explain. One can begin with the appealing character of the man himself, the strangely moving quality of his prose, the dramatic perfection of a career rising from deep obscurity to exalted tragedy, the unique claims of the Civil War on American historical consciousness and of the Negro on America's collective conscience. Yet Lincoln's symbolic importance transcends his own life and time. He has been abstracted from history to serve as the representative American, and as a consequence, much of the nation's self-image is visible in the image of Abraham Lincoln that successive generations have fashioned.

Lincoln biography, now well into its second century of accumulation, can be divided into several distinctive, though somewhat imprecise, historical periods. From the 1860's until about 1900, the field was dominated by men who had known Lincoln more or less intimately and who drew upon their own memories as well as the available records. They were followed by a group of amateur biographers, some highly talented and all a generation removed from the experience of the Civil War. During this second phase, which lasted approximately thirty years, the major contributions came from a journalist, a clergyman, a poet, and two politicians. The third period, extending from the 1920's into the 1950's, was a time of professionalization and rising critical standards, as academic historians entered the field in force. Those years were so rich in achievement that they could be labeled the "golden age" of Lincoln scholarship. In some respects the third period continues, but a fourth phase is now readily discernible. Its most striking characteristic is the change of perspective in Lincoln studies resulting from the civil rights revolution and the transformation of American racial relations.

The two outstanding works by men close to Lincoln appeared almost simultaneously about a quarter of a century after his death. Strikingly dissimilar, they represented divergent streams of interpretation and conflicting views of the biographer's task.

John G. Nicolay and John Hay, Lincoln's private secretaries in the White House, produced a superior example of the conventional Victorian "life-and-times." Their ten volumes were comprehensive in scope but concentrated heavily on the public man and the presidential years. Detailed military history sometimes pushed Lincoln himself aside for chapters at a time. This was the "official" biography in the sense that its authors alone before 1947 had access to Lincoln's personal papers, treasure guarded by a dragon named Robert Todd Lincoln. Nicolay and Hay set a high standard of thoroughness and accuracy, but their interpretation now seems uncritically laudatory, and because of its great bulk, the work has undoubtedly been more often mined than read.[3]

Much briefer and more personal was the biography by William H. Herndon and his collaborator, Jesse W. Weik, which focused mainly on the pre-presidential years. Herndon had long resolved to rescue his law partner from idolators who were turning him into an unbelievable national saint and, as he explained in his own galloping prose, to portray Lincoln "*just* as he lived, breathed—ate and laughed," with all his "passions—appetites—and affections—perceptions—memories—judgment—understanding—will." The book written to achieve this purpose inevitably scandalized many readers with its gossipy discussion of Lincoln's private life and blunt descriptions of the crude pioneer society that shaped him.[4] Yet no other biography of the man has been nearly so influential. Our Lincoln of popular remembrance is in considerable degree Herndon's Lincoln, the rollicking backwoods youth with a curious strain of melancholy, the prairie lawyer with a mark of genius. Because of its appealing vitality, the portrait has survived increasing doubts about its level of accuracy. Herndon's work was based largely upon reminiscence, the least reliable of all primary source materials. To his own recollections, leavened by a lively imagination, he added those of many other persons, which he gathered in interviews and correspondence after Lincoln's death. This "Herndon-Weik Collection," now in the Library of Congress, is too valuable to ignore but extremely difficult to verify. Herndon used the material indiscriminately, and according to *his* biographer, he is important partly because of the "errors that he spread."[5]

Conventional historians helped create one image of Lincoln; Herndon and Weik were preeminent in evoking another. Against the towering Emancipator and Savior of the Union, they set the virile, earthy son of the frontier West. Demigod and folk hero, both legends are founded on historical fact, and scholars have struggled with the problem of reconciling the two. A common solution has been to present Lincoln as the frontier hero down to 1860 and as the national saint after that, along with some vague observations about his remarkable "growth" in the presidency.

In Lincoln literature, the years from 1865 to the end of the century are now important primarily as the period of reminiscences.[6] The accumulation of this material enriched the sources available to later scholars, but it also tested their ability to separate fact from fiction. A case in point is the so-called "lost speech," unrecorded when Lincoln delivered it at Bloomington in 1856, but "reconstructed" some forty years later by Henry C. Whitney from notes allegedly taken on the scene. Whitney's handiwork was challenged when it first appeared in *McClure's Magazine* and today commands no respect whatever. Yet this clumsy fabrication won considerable acceptance for more than a generation. One can find it quoted extensively in several of the best biographies and included in one major edition of Lincoln's writings.[7]

Whitney's venture in ghostwriting had been gullibly sponsored by a young woman just entering the circle of Lincoln biographers. Ida M. Tarbell, though rather easily deceived in spite of her journalistic experience, nevertheless uncovered much new material, corrected many errors, displayed a rare open-mindedness, and graciously encouraged other writers in the field such as Carl Sandburg. Her biography of Lincoln combined respectable scholarship with great popular appeal. Its publication in 1900 serves to mark the beginning of a new period in Lincoln literature. Miss Tarbell tended to idealize Lincoln and the pioneer environment from which he sprang, perhaps reflecting the mood of the 1890's, when agrarianism flowered in the Populist movement and Frederick Jackson Turner introduced his famous frontier hypothesis.[8]

The next major contribution came during World War I from an English peer. Lord Charnwood's *Abraham Lincoln* was, in the words of David M. Potter, "the first genuinely contemplative biography."[9] Written with literary grace and critical acumen, it summed up fifty years of scholarship and gave Lincoln's career a meaning that transcended the boundaries and history of the American nation. Here was no demigod, but a great statesman in spite of his faults and mistakes—one who fully realized the universal significance of the Civil War as a crucial test of self-government. Charnwood's work provided deeper understanding rather than additional information. Subsequent research has diminished its value by exposing the limitations of his sources, and yet few other books on the subject so well deserve to be labeled "classic."[10]

Far different from Charnwood was William E. Barton, pastor of a Congregational church in Illinois who published his first Lincoln book in 1920 at the age of fifty-nine. There followed ten years of astonishing productivity during which Barton earned the reputation of being a "bloodhound after facts."[11] He pursued his quarry deep into local records and took fierce delight in eviscerating errors and myths encountered along the way. In one book, for example, Barton examined the many rumors that Lincoln was illegitimate. He tracked down seven putative fathers, including John C. Calhoun, and then destroyed the case for each one, leaving Thomas Lincoln secure in his moment of glory.[12] On the other hand, a similar investigation led him to agreement with Herndon that Lincoln's mother, Nancy Hanks, had indeed been born out of wedlock.[13] Publication of Barton's two-volume *Life of Abraham Lincoln* in 1925 revealed his deficiencies as a biographer. He had little talent for interpretive synthesis and but a superficial understanding of history. His passion for smaller truths made him primarily a "great historical detective."[14]

Meanwhile, an Illinois poet and a former senator from Indiana were working away at biographies of Lincoln, each projected on a grand scale. Carl Sandburg lived to complete his masterpiece; Albert J. Beveridge did not.

Abraham Lincoln: The Prairie Years appeared in 1926 and won immediate acclaim as a unique artistic achievement, despite some criticism of its inaccuracies and fictional passages. With uncommon sensibility and in evocative, often lyrical prose, Sandburg recaptured the sights, sounds, and feelings of the several worlds in which Lincoln grew up to manhood and then to greatness. In *The War Years*, his monumental sequel published near the end of the next decade, he curbed his poetic imagination to the extent of following more closely the rules of historical scholarship. But his method remained essentially the same—recreating an age in vast panorama and multitudinous detail as the background for a heroic figure shaped with the novelist's technique of cumulative impression and suggestion. To read Sandburg is to walk with Lincoln in an experience more emotional than intellectual. For this reason and others, Sandburg's influence on Lincoln scholarship has never matched the popularity of his work.[15]

Beveridge, who turned to the study of Lincoln after having written a long and distinguished biography of Chief Justice John Marshall, was in many respects a combination of Charnwood and Barton at their best. His own experience in public life gave him an expert's understanding of past politics. By determined effort he had made himself both a historian and a literary artist, supremely capable of integrating biography with the flow of national development. Never satisfied until he had seen every bit of evidence, he did an enormous amount of research and far surpassed all of his predecessors in the use of certain kinds of materials, such as newspapers and legislative journals. Beveridge's worst failing was that he often put too much faith in dubious sources. He accepted Whitney's version of the "lost speech" at face value, for instance, and in his delight at gaining access to the Herndon-Weik papers, he used them with uncritical abandon. Here, for instance, is a passage that he wrote on Lincoln the omnivorous reader:

> In his reading and study Lincoln was a very miser of time, never wasting a moment. . . .When going to his meals a few steps distant, or walking through the dust or mud of New Salem's street, or strolling out into the country, always an open book was in his hand or closed beneath his arm, while he murmured to himself what he had just read. Even when he chanced to be with women and girls, whom he would try to amuse, Lincoln would take a book with him and read between jokes. When passing from one group of men to another, he would read as he walked, closing the volume as he joined the company.[16]

One suspects that the people of a pioneer community would have sent such a fellow to some place other than the state legislature.

Beveridge's young Lincoln therefore has a folklore cast until his entry into politics, when he becomes real but not especially admirable. Having been himself a progressive Republican and a strong supporter of national expansion, Beveridge was displeased by Lincoln's political opportunism and by his opposition to the Mexican War. As the biographer carried his narrative into the 1850's, Stephen A. Douglas became its virtual hero and remained so to the end of an uncompleted work. Beveridge died in 1928, having advanced only as far as the Lincoln-Douglas debates. Two large volumes were published posthumously. They ran to more than 1,300 pages and were so lavishly annotated that the reader often had to follow "a rivulet of text . . . through a meadow of footnotes."[17]

With his amateur status and professional skill, Beveridge well represented a decade of significant transition in the study of Lincoln. Such study had previously been an enterprise more or less separate from historical scholarship, but the two were now converging in the 1920's. And even while gifted amateurs continued to publish the major works, Lincoln biography was being turned into thoroughly professional channels.

Although the change occurred gradually and quietly for the most part, it was dramatized during 1928–29 in a spectacular controversy over the authenticity of certain Lincoln documents appearing in the *Atlantic Monthly*. The documents, though accepted as genuine by Sandburg and Tarbell, were thoroughly discredited by a group of experts whose leading spokesman was Paul M. Angle, youthful secretary of the rather inconspicuous Lincoln Centennial Association in Springfield, Illinois.[18] The swiftness of the exposure contrasted sharply with the long life of Whitney's "lost speech" and made it plain that more rigorous standards were producing a new kind of Lincoln scholarship.

In 1924, the Lincoln Centennial Association (eventually renamed the Abraham Lincoln Association) had been converted from a ceremonial organization to a research and publication center by its president, Logan Hay, a grandson of Lincoln's second law partner. Beginning with Angle, a succession of executive secretaries made the study of Lincoln a full-time professional enterprise. They unearthed new source materials, produced a number of valuable monographs, edited a quarterly journal, and lent expert assistance to other scholars. The climax of the Association's enterprise came with the publication in 1953–55 of *The Collected Works of Abraham Lincoln*, a notable contribution to historical literature.[19]

Another trend toward professionalism set in during the 1920's but developed more slowly. This was the movement of academic historians into the Lincoln field. Nathaniel W. Stephenson led the way in 1922 with an unusual biography that had much merit in spite of its intermittent Freudian interpretation.[20] More significant was the publication four years later of James G. Randall's *Constitutional Problems Under Lincoln*.[21] Randall went on to become the foremost Lincoln scholar, and this specialized study, primarily history rather than biography, was typical of the work that would come from the universities. Since Stephenson's work, academic historians have published many books about Lincoln, but only two of them have been full-length biographies.[22]

The professors made their entry in modest fashion, chiefly by means of scholarly articles with titles like "Lincoln in the Campaign of 1856" and "Indiana Republicans and the Re-election of Abraham Lincoln." Two important books based on doctoral dissertations were published in the 1930's: a literary study of the Lincoln tradition by Roy P. Basler and a detailed treatment by William E. Baringer of Lincoln's rise to national prominence in the years 1858 to 1860.[23] Not until the 1940's, however, did the professorial output of books become impressive. In one of the first volumes to appear during that decade, T. Harry Williams examined the wartime struggle within the Republican organization and concluded that the radicals eventually gained the upper hand over Lincoln and the moderate wing of the party.[24] David M. Potter chose to concentrate on the secession crisis of 1860–61. His book showed that Lincoln misread popular feeling in the Southern states, and it explained how the complex circumstances and a conflict of purposes narrowly limited the choices open to the incoming President.[25] Another revealing monograph, by Harry J. Carman and Reinhard H. Luthin, detailed Lincoln's skillful use of patronage to strengthen his political position.[26]

Meanwhile, Randall had set to work on a larger scale and in 1945 published the first two volumes of *Lincoln the President*. Displaying masterful knowledge while achieving a judicious blend of sympathetic understanding and critical detachment, he wrote investigatively and reflectively, often pausing in his narrative to examine problems faced by Lincoln and by a Lincoln biographer. This was professional scholarship of a high order, though it left too many questions open to be called definitive.[27]

Soon there followed David Donald's illuminating biography of Herndon, and new monographs continued to appear. In a study of wartime executive relationships, William B. Hesseltine concluded that Lincoln won mastery over Northern state governors and thereby brought about a shift toward centralism amounting to constitutional revolution.[28] Kenneth M. Stampp contributed another close examination of the secession crisis in which he gave particular attention to the question of why the North rejected the one available alternative to war—that is, peaceable separation.[29] Williams, turning to military history in his second book, described Lincoln as a "great natural strategist" who did more to win the war than any of his generals.[30]

Two other developments were profoundly influencing Lincoln

studies during these years. One was the enrichment of historical background by a great burst of scholarship on the Civil War era. For example, Allan Nevins published the first four imposing volumes of his *Ordeal of the Union* series, and Bruce Catton moved to the military forefront with a vivid trilogy on the Army of the Potomac.[31] The second important change was in the accessibility of source materials. Lincoln's own files of correspondence were opened at last in 1947 and quickly microfilmed.[32] Rapid progress in microfilming put many other sources within easier reach, and scholars also profited immensely from publication of the *Collected Works* in 1953–55.

At about the same time, Benjamin P. Thomas contributed his one-volume biography, which like Lord Charnwood's book some thirty-five years earlier, provided an admirable new synthesis of foregoing work in the field.[33] Simultaneously, Randall added a third volume to *Lincoln the President*, but then death interrupted his work. The fourth and concluding volume, finished by Richard N. Current, appeared in 1955.[34] That year, being also the one in which publication of the *Collected Works* was completed, serves as a convenient demarcation closing the third and most fruitful period of Lincoln scholarship.

The rise of professionalism, while it sometimes seemed to devitalize Lincoln, resulted in greater knowledge, finer accuracy, and keener critical judgments. More than that, it caused a radical shift of emphasis. The academic scholars were primarily historians rather than biographers. They had little interest in Lincoln's genealogy or the minor details of his private life. Instead, they wanted to investigate the kind of problems that Charnwood had pondered. What part did Lincoln play in the antislavery movement and the formation of the Republican party? Was he essentially a political opportunist? Did his rejection of compromise make the difference between reconciliation and civil war? How decisive was his leadership in the conflict that followed? Did he lag behind or march ahead of Northern sentiment in his progress toward emancipation? To what extent and in what ways was he the representative American of his age? Beginning with Charnwood, Stephenson, and Beveridge, the study of Lincoln had been drawn into the mainstream of American history. Indeed, it became increasingly difficult to separate Lincoln bibliography from the whole body of historical scholarship dealing with the era of the Civil War.

Interpretation of the Civil War had passed through several phases since 1865. First, there was a generation of partisan writers, many of whom had been prominent participants in the conflict. Each stoutly defended his own cause and conduct while fixing the blame for the war upon the other side.[35] In the 1890's, however, a different attitude began to prevail. Wartime passions had cooled, and sectional reconciliation had been substantially achieved with Northern acquiescence in white "redemption" of the reconstructed South. New public issues, such as the mounting struggle between capital and labor, were replacing the old quarrels over the Negro; new national aspirations, such as overseas expansion, were strengthening the bonds of reunion. And at this same time, history was becoming a professional discipline, with objectivity as one of its stated principles. All of these influences encouraged greater detachment in writing about the Civil War.

The new historians of the 1890's—like James Ford Rhodes, John W. Burgess, and Woodrow Wilson—viewed the Civil War as an irrepressible conflict over the issue of slavery, in which both sides acted honorably and courageously. Of course the North, in their judgment, had been fundamentally right to desire the abolition of slavery and to fight for preservation of the Union. The outcome of the war was therefore entirely fortunate, but not so the ensuing period of Radical Reconstruction, which prolonged sectional bitterness by subjecting the prostrate South to Negro-carpetbagger rule. Thus the interpretation of Rhodes and his contemporaries was pro-Northern up to Appomattox but somewhat pro-Southern thereafter. Such were the principal tendencies of what has been called the "nationalist tradition" in Civil War history.[36]

The distinctively Lincolnian cast of this tradition is readily apparent. Lincoln had declared that a house divided against itself could not stand, and in the presidency he developed an almost fatalistic view of the war. He had always thought slavery to be morally wrong, and he asserted more than once that disagreement over the institution was the sole cause of sectional conflict. He never wavered in his determination to save the Union at any cost but remained relatively free of hatred and vindictiveness toward the enemy. His reconstruction program, insofar as he had adopted one by 1865, was much more lenient than that subsequently installed by Congress. There could scarcely be a more favorable historical setting for biography than an interpretive design that largely recapitulated the subject's own outlook.

The nationalist tradition, with Lincoln as its representative figure, dominated Civil War scholarship for more than a generation and is still widely accepted as the orthodox version. But in the 1920's and 1930's, it came under increasing attack from several quarters.

A group of able Southern historians published books and articles that tended to vindicate the antebellum South. They softened the image of slavery, argued that the institution was already on its way to peaceable extinction in 1860, and blamed the war on Northern fanaticism. One of their number, Charles W. Ramsdell, charged that Lincoln deliberately "maneuvered" the Confederates into firing on Fort Sumter so that they, rather than he, would appear guilty of beginning hostilities.[37]

Meanwhile, Charles A. and Mary R. Beard and Vernon Louis Parrington were advancing an economic interpretation of the Civil War. Belittling the causal significance of slavery, they pictured an irrepressible conflict between the old agricultural order and the new forces of industrial capitalism—a conflict that ended with Southern planters driven from power and the way cleared for the onward march of business enterprise. In such an explanation, Lincoln and other Northern politicians became the more or less witting agents of Northern industrialists and financiers.[38]

Lincoln studies were most directly affected, however, by "revisionism," a third variety of dissent from the nationalist tradition. In many respects, the revisionists seemed to share the sympathies of the Southern vindicators, but their outlook was essentially national rather than sectional. Like the Beardians, they denied the sufficiency of the slavery controversy as a cause for civil war; unlike the Beardians, they found no other compelling reason why the conflict should have been irrepressible. The Civil War, according to the revisionists, was a tragic mistake, produced by the unnecessary agitation of an "artificial" issue—that is, whether slavery should be nominally permitted in the Western territories, where conditions were generally inimical to its establishment. Responsibility for the "needless war" rested with blundering politicians and with extremists in both sections who inflamed public feeling to a point beyond rational control. But in thus distributing blame, the revisionists were not entirely evenhanded. They tended to be most emphatic in their condemnation of Northern abolitionists and radical Republicans.

Emerging gradually during the 1920's and 1930's, when Americans were also experiencing disillusionment about their participation in World War I, revisionism reached its peak shortly after 1940. Albert J. Beveridge must be regarded as one of the early revisionists, but the two acknowledged leaders of the movement were Avery Craven and James G. Randall.[39] And at this point, the outline of a striking paradox becomes visible. During the very years of the greatest achievements in Lincoln studies, general interpretation of the Civil War was taking an anti-Republican and therefore anti-Lincolnian direction. Furthermore, several of the most important Lincoln scholars were in the vanguard of revisionist historians.

To Randall, not only the Civil War but modern war in general was irrational, unjustifiable, abhorrent. His sympathies were with political leaders like Douglas who worked the hardest to avert sectional conflict, and yet he retained a deep admiration for Lincoln. Randall adjusted to this difficulty by emphasizing Lincoln's Southern background, overstating his conservatism, and exaggerating the distance between him and the antislavery radicals. On racial issues, especially, he placed Lincoln closer to Douglas and Southern leaders than to the abolitionists. In his treatment of the presidential years, it often appears that Lincoln's worst enemies were neither Confederates nor copperheads but vindictive and unscrupulous radical Republicans, than whom "a more unlovely knot of politicians would be hard to find." Characteristically, Randall disapproved of the provocative House Divided speech, but he defended Lincoln against the charge of having deliberately provoked hostilities at Fort Sumter. His estimate of Lincoln, though judicious in itself, rested on a pronounced interpretive bias.[40]

Among the other Lincoln scholars of the period, revisionism won some wholehearted support, together with a larger measure of partial acceptance that varied in degree and emphasis. The range of its influence extended well beyond the circle of outright converts, and the most noticeable effect was a tendency toward harsher judgment of Lincoln's pre-presidential career. Essentially, this judgment reflected the revisionist disposition to see more politics than principle in Republican agitation of the slavery question. At the hands of certain writers, there emerged a portrait of a shrewd and devious man who usually put expediency first. According to Richard Hofstadter, Lincoln was "thoroughly and completely the politician." His arguments against the extension of slavery were part of a finely calculated strategy for pleasing both "Negrophobes and abolitionists."[41] Donald W. Riddle could see nothing but self-interest and opportunism in his opposition to the repeal of the Missouri Compromise. "Lincoln," Riddle asserted, "was not fighting for a cause. He was using the slavery issue . . . to advance his own political standing."[42] Similar views were expressed by Reinhard H. Luthin. He found little evidence of greatness in Lincoln's Illinois career and "no record of achievement, except the quest for office."[43]

Few of the revisionists were as openly cynical as Riddle and Luthin, however. Most of them came to terms with the Lincoln legend in one way or another—often by stressing his pragmatic wisdom and moral growth in the presidency. By 1960, when Luthin's biography appeared, revisionism as an interpretive synthesis had gone out of fashion, though the color of its influence was still visible in Civil War scholarship. World War II suddenly put American history in new perspective and created an uncongenial setting for the belief that compromise was inherently better than conflict. A counterattack on revisionism began to take shape during the late 1940's. One of its leaders, Arthur M. Schlesinger, Jr., drew a parallel between opposition to slavery and resistance to Nazism. "To say that the Civil War was fought over the 'unreal' issue of slavery in the territories," he wrote, "is like saying that the Second World War was fought over the 'unreal' issue of the invasion of Poland. . . . The extension of slavery, like the extension of fascism, was an act of aggression which made a moral choice inescapable." Thus Schlesinger not only restored slavery to its central position but came close to saying that the Civil War was unavoidable. "Nothing exists in history," he warned, "to assure us that the great moral dilemmas can be resolved without pain."[44] Clearly, this line of argument was in many ways a return to the nationalist tradition and a justification of Lincoln's conduct.

Within Lincoln literature, the most ambitious assault upon revisionism came from a political scientist, Harry V. Jaffa, who, in *Crisis of the House Divided* (1959), keenly analyzed and compared the political ideas of Douglas and Lincoln, to the latter's advantage.

Among other things, Jaffa rejected the view that slavery had reached its natural limits by 1860 and would have fared no better under a policy of popular sovereignty than under one of legal restriction.[45] My *Prelude to Greatness* (1962), a study of Lincoln's rise to the presidency, was likewise in some respects a critique of the revisionist synthesis.[46]

Revisionism became especially difficult to defend after the Supreme Court's desegregation decisions of the mid-fifties inaugurated a revolution in American racial relations. A new wind rose in American historical writing about the Civil War era, and its direction was pro-abolitionist and pro-Negro. Lincoln, whom diehard revisionists were still comparing unfavorably with Douglas and Crittenden, would now be measured against William Lloyd Garrison and Charles Sumner. By placing him in this crossfire of criticism, scholars unintentionally reproduced the conditions of his presidential career.

As celebration of the Civil War Centennial got under way in 1960, one could note a sharp decline of scholarly interest in the causes of the war—the problem that had so preoccupied the revisionists. Attention was shifting to those aspects of the American past that seemed most relevant to the growing struggle for racial equality. The work of Kenneth M. Stampp, for example, reflected this change of emphasis. In his early writings, Stampp had dealt with antebellum politics and the secession crisis. He had even been classified, perhaps mistakenly, as a revisionist.[47] But then he published an imposing study of slavery, which stressed the harshness of the institution.[48] After that, he turned to Reconstruction and, in a brief survey, summed up the new views of the subject that were gaining ascendancy among professional scholars. The radical Republicans, stigmatized by several generations of historians, now appeared in a more favorable light. They, after all, had fought the first battle for racial equality and had succeeded at least in laying the legal foundations for its renewal in the 1950's. Stampp's concluding sentence epitomized a reversal of judgment: "If it was worth four years of civil war to save the Union, it was worth a few years of radical reconstruction to give the American Negro the ultimate promise of equal civil and political rights."[49]

The general surge of interest in race, racism, and slavery was especially strong among the younger scholars who were most earnestly enlisted in the struggle for racial equality and who breathed deeply the atmosphere of revolt on American campuses. The analogies could scarcely have been more obvious: the evil of slavery and the evil of discrimination; the bold abolitionist and the bold freedom rider; the temporizing politician, Abraham Lincoln, and the temporizing politician, John F. Kennedy.

Scorn for the devious ways of statecraft and admiration for the clean, straight tracks of radical reform were major characteristics of history written by the "New Left." In Martin Duberman's significant anthology, *The Antislavery Vanguard*, Howard Zinn explained the "social roles" of the agitator and the politician. The latter, he wrote, is necessarily "a compromiser and a trimmer, who sets his sails by the prevailing breezes, and without the hard blowing of the radical reformer would either drift actionless or sail along with existing injustice." Lincoln, according to Zinn, was just such a trimmer—indeed, the "prototype of the political man in power." Duberman himself hardly concealed his contempt for the Republican program of merely restricting slavery, which he labeled "wishful thinking" and contrasted with the "tough-minded" realism of the abolitionists.[50]

New Left historians fully endorsed the total dedication of the abolitionists to the overthrow of slavery—a dedication which, in their view, was on a higher moral plane than concern for constitutional guarantees, preservation of the Union, or prevention of civil war. A relativist like Lincoln, who saw virtue in each of these competing values and sought to reconcile them, received little sympathy and much condescension from such writers, who were plainly irritated by his historical stature. They could not admire a man of limited and plural commitment who declared that slavery was wrong but supported enforcement of the Fugitive Slave Law, approved an amendment affirming the inviolability of the institution, and announced early in the war that saving the Union had a higher priority than settlement of the slavery question.

Moderate opponents of slavery, Duberman declared, were inhibited not only by their fear of the consequences of militancy but also by their assumption of the Negro's inherent inferiority.[51] The real focus of New Left interest was not slavery as an institution but the racial attitudes of white Americans. Here they found a detestable and almost universal consensus during the Civil War era. In his book *North of Slavery*, Leon Litwack demonstrated that the anti-slavery crusade was accompanied by subjection of the Northern Negro to increasing discrimination and legal disabilities. Thus racial prejudice was nationwide, and Abraham Lincoln, according to Litwack, was a consistently representative American in his racial attitudes.[52] Other writers joined in what became a veritable chorus of interpretation picturing the Republican party as basically anti-Negro and Lincoln as a typical white supremacist.[53] The curious effect of mixing intensely moralistic hindsight with historical judgment was, in this instance, to make a reactionary of a man whom 60 percent of the voting public had considered too radical and whose very election to the presidency had precipitated a counterrevolution and civil war.

Far from being new, the New Left concept of collective national guilt for the enslavement and degradation of the black race was eloquently set forth a century earlier by Abraham Lincoln. The Civil War, he reflected, must be God's punishment upon the whole nation, North as well as South, for the sin of human slavery. And the punishment would be altogether righteous even if it continued until "all the wealth piled by the bondman's two hundred and fifty years of unrequited toil" had been swept away, and until "every drop of blood drawn with the lash" had been paid for by "another drawn with the sword."[54] But along with this stern vision of God working through history, Lincoln retained his faith in law as the best instrument of justice, in democracy as the best form of government, and in the capacity of man to improve, as well as endure, an always imperfect world.

CHAPTER 15

The Anti-Lincoln Tradition

"All the world," wrote James G. Randall, "is familiar with Lincoln the emancipator, the author of the Gettysburg address, the timeless spokesman of democracy. Few of us are acquainted with Lincoln the baboon, the imbecile, the wet rag, the Kentucky mule. Yet these are typical examples of the names heaped upon him in those cruel days when high office brought him less of glory than of insult and abuse."[1] The anti-Lincoln strain in American thought, persisting from Civil War times to the present, is a healthy reminder that no single point of view has monopoly rights in the interpretation of the past. Furthermore, from the dissenting voices of his enemies one can learn a good deal about Lincoln and about the America that has continued to shape his image in the light of its own needs. This essay was presented as an address at the annual meeting of the Abraham Lincoln Association on February 12, 1982, and was published later that year in Volume 4 of the *Papers* of that organization.

Herbert Hoover, campaigning for reelection in the midst of the Great Depression, took special care to associate himself with Abraham Lincoln, but then so did his opponent, Franklin D. Roosevelt, who had remarked a few years earlier, "I think it is time for us Democrats to claim Lincoln as one of our own."[2] Late in the campaign, both men spoke in Springfield, and both paid ceremonial visits to the Lincoln tomb. By the 1930's, "getting right with Lincoln" in this manner had become an almost universal custom among public figures. Not only Republicans and Democrats, but also Communists, Socialists, and Prohibitionists, business executives and labor leaders, black Americans and members of the Ku Klux Klan—all seemed to want him on their side.[3]

Yet, here and there, a few voices of dissent could always be heard. In 1932, an old Virginia gentleman named Lyon Gardiner Tyler, son of President John Tyler, continued his long personal war upon the heroic image of Lincoln. "I think he was a bad man," Tyler wrote, "a man who forced the country into an unnecessary war, and conducted it with great inhumanity."[4] Tyler was the most prominent spokesman of his time for an anti-Lincoln tradition, attenuated but persistent, that had its sturdy roots in the years of the Civil War. An examination of that tradition may cast some light upon Lincoln's place in the national consciousness—a place that is apparently secure but never precisely the same from one year to the next.

There were three principal sources of hostility to Lincoln during the Civil War: first, the enemy—that is, the people of the Confederacy and a sizable part of the population in the Southern border states; second, the political opposition—that is, primarily the Democratic party in the North and the border states, but including a good many conservative Whigs as well; third, the antislavery radicals, including elements both within and outside the Republican party. One might also designate as a fourth category the hostile critics watching and commenting on the war from Europe—most notably, a substantial portion of the English press.

The Southern image of Lincoln began as a mere sectional stereotype, and Southern hostility to his presidential candidacy was largely impersonal. Secession, although undertaken in response to the outcome of the election of 1860, had nothing to do with the particular qualities and qualifications of the man elected. It was the "Black Republican party" that Southerners hated and feared, whoever might happen to be the party's official leader. But when the secession crisis erupted into civil war, Southerners laid the blame squarely on Lincoln. In the years of bloody struggle and withering hope that followed, they came increasingly to view him as the principal author of all the woe that had descended upon them. Of course Jefferson Davis at the same time became a detested figure in the North, but with a significant difference. Davis, leading a rebellion, symbolized treason in the mold of Benedict Arnold, while Lincoln's role, in Southern eyes, was that of a military conqueror—a ruthless Attila bent upon the destruction of a superior civilization. In fact, the Confederate image of Abraham Lincoln in the 1860's bears a striking resemblance to the American image of Adolf Hitler in the 1940's.

The Southern indictment of Lincoln usually began with the assertion that he had made war unavoidable by opposing sectional compromise and then forcing the issue at Fort Sumter. After the first major battle of the war at Bull Run (or Manassas) in July 1861, the Richmond *Enquirer* blamed him for all the deaths on both sides. "Of these men Abraham Lincoln is the murderer," it declared. "We charge their blood upon him. . . . May the Heavens, which have rebuked his madness thus far, still battle his demon designs."[5]

Confederates called Lincoln a "tyrant," a "fiend," and a "monster" for making war on civilians through the blockade, for authorizing the destruction of private property, for setting the likes of Ben Butler and William T. Sherman upon the Southern population, for suppressing civil liberties, for cruelly refusing to exchange prisoners, and, most of all, for emancipation, which they viewed as an incitement of slaves to rebellion and wholesale murder. In speeches, sermons, and songs, in books, magazines, newspapers, pamphlets, and broadsides, they also portrayed him as a simpleton, a buffoon, a drunkard, a libertine, a physical coward, and a pornographic storyteller.[6]

Hatred of Lincoln sometimes crystallized into threats against his life. For instance, soon after the firing on Fort Sumter, he received from Mississippi a newspaper clipping in which a reward of $100,000 was offered for his "miserable traitorous head."[7] Spontaneous rejoicing at his death, though perhaps more the exception than the rule in the Confederacy, was nevertheless widespread. To a Georgia woman overcome with bewilderment and grief at Lee's surrender, the assassination came as "one sweet drop among so much that is painful."[8] A Texas newspaper declared, "The world is happily rid of a monster that disgraced the form of humanity."[9]

Such intensity of feeling was by no means confined to the rebellious South. The Civil War divided Northern and border state Democrats into three factions: those who supported both the war and the Lincoln administration, thereby in effect changing their political allegiance; those who supported the war but opposed the administration, thus playing the classic role of "loyal opposition"; and those who opposed both the war and the administration, in some cases to the verge of treason. The latter two groups became the war and peace wings of the wartime Democratic party. Differing in their basic attitudes toward the conflict itself, they could nevertheless agree in denouncing Lincoln for misuse of presidential power and subversion of the Constitution.[10] They charged the administration with repressing civil liberties, with subverting the rights and powers of the states, and with transforming a war for defense of the Union into a revolutionary struggle for abolition and racial equality.

It was the progress toward emancipation that most infuriated Democratic and other conservative leaders. In their view, the same puritanical spirit of New England abolitionism that had disrupted the Union was dictating administration policy.[11] On January 1, 1863, the day of the final Emancipation Proclamation, Benjamin R. Curtis, former Supreme Court justice, said that Lincoln had been terrified and completely subdued by the antislavery radicals. "He is shattered, dazed and utterly foolish," Curtis wrote. "It would not surprise me if he were to destroy himself."[12] In 1864, that old Jacksonian Amos Kendall published a series of letters attacking the President. "Our federal Union," he declared, "is in more danger this day from Abraham Lincoln and the unprincipled and fanatical faction to whom he has surrendered himself, soul and body, than from all other causes combined."[13]

Of course the rankest abuse came from the copperheads, among whom none was more inventive in his vituperation than a Wisconsin editor, Marcus M. Pomeroy. Lincoln, he wrote, was "but the fungus from the corrupt womb of bigotry and fanaticism"—indeed, a "worse tyrant and more inhuman butcher than has existed since the days of Nero." As the election of 1864 approached, Pomeroy editorialized: "The man who votes for Lincoln now is a traitor and murderer. . . . And if he is elected to misgovern for another four years, we trust some bold hand will pierce his heart with dagger point for the public good."[14]

Among the antislavery radicals, in contrast, Lincoln seemed the embodiment of timorous, vacillating conservatism—too inhibited by constitutional qualms, too solicitous about border state feeling, too obliging to Democrats (especially in the appointment of generals), and much too cautious in his approach to emancipation. "He is," said a Maine critic, "a tall, lank, lean, homely, weak-kneed man, a poor, good-dispositioned horse that *must be led*! Kind to a fault, obliging to everybody, and, consequently, devillish short of square work."[15]

One must distinguish, of course, between the outright abolitionists and the radical free-soilers who made up the left wing of the Republican party. Once the war had begun, however, the two elements tended to merge in the sense that both were vehemently emancipationist. Yet within both groups there was considerable difference of opinion about the man in the White House. For instance, after indulging in much early abuse of Lincoln as "a dwarf in mind" and "a man of very small calibre" who was "nothing better than a wet rag," William Lloyd Garrison came around to urging the President's renomination and reelection in 1864. But his fellow abolitionist Wendell Phillips refused to do likewise and gave his support instead to the abortive candidacy of John C. Frémont.[16] Similarly, Charles Sumner, though often critical of Lincoln, maintained a delicate balance between friendship and opposition, whereas his senatorial colleague Benjamin F. Wade, labeling the President a "fool" and declaring that "no country was ever before cursed with such imbecility," led the radical attacks on Lincoln in Congress, opposed his renomination, and regarded his assassination as a political blessing.[17]

Lincoln's apparent conservatism on the slavery issue drew strong criticism from radicals as early as the fall of 1861. His revocation of Frémont's edict proclaiming emancipation in Missouri provoked a storm of recrimination that was renewed in May 1862 when he revoked a similar order issued by General David Hunter for South Carolina, Georgia, and Florida. In a letter to another senator, Wade sneered that nothing better could be expected from a man of Southern antecedents, and "poor white trash" at that.[18] Frederick Douglass, the leading black abolitionist, declared in his monthly magazine that Lincoln had become the "miserable tool of traitors and rebels," and had shown himself to be "a genuine representative of American prejudice and negro hatred."[19]

The Emancipation Proclamation won some antislavery radicals to Lincoln's side, but many others continued to regard him as such a poor excuse for a president that he ought to be replaced. His bitterest radical critic was the Maryland congressman Henry Winter Davis, co-author of the Wade-Davis manifesto, which charged the President with pursuing "personal ambition" and exercising "dictatorial usurpation," while at the same time promoting "anarchy."[20] When Lincoln was reelected, Davis wrote to Admiral Samuel F. DuPont, "We must for four years more rely on the forcing process of Congress to *wring* from that old fool what can be gotten for the nation." The people, in voting for Lincoln, he said, had held their stomachs and subordinated "disgust to the necessities of a crisis."[21]

Radical hostility to Lincoln cut closest to the bone because so much of it came from the inner circles of his own party and even from his cabinet in the person of Salmon P. Chase, whose file of incoming letters is a storehouse of unreproved attacks on the President. The fierceness of such infighting is perhaps less surprising than the vehemence and malice with which Lincoln was criticized by much of the British press. The articulate portion of the British public became emotionally involved in the American Civil War for both material and symbolic reasons. The war had a disruptive effect upon the British economy, geared as it was to cotton manufacture. But Britons also recognized the struggle from its beginning as a test of the viability of democracy, that new social force which the English ruling class feared, which the United States represented before the world, and which Lincoln in background and style virtually caricatured.

A number of conservative publications hastened to draw a lesson from the ordeal of the United States. "It is only by calamities so startling as this," said the *Quarterly Review*, "that men can be warned of the dangers with which democracy is surrounded."[22] *John Bull*, voice of the landed aristocracy, declared that Americans, after having talked so much about the virtues of their republic, were now finding it to be "a mere bubble or a piece of rotten timber, an abominable and worthless tyranny of the sovereign mob."[23] The principal British complaints against Lincoln were that he persisted unreasonably in waging a futile war of reconquest, and that in the process, he was fastening a dictatorship on the United States—all the while making bad jokes as he proceeded along his sanguinary course. Several months after the first battle of Bull Run, one London newspaper concluded that he was a "feeble, confused and little-minded mediocrity."[24] Another, as the election of 1864 drew near, called him a "foul-tongued and ribald punster" who was also the "most despicable tyrant of modern days." A Leeds editor at about the same time denounced him as "that concentrated quintescence [*sic*] of evil, that Nero in the most shrunken . . . form of idolatry, that flatulent and indecent jester."[25] The language of the London *Times* was scarcely more restrained. Condemning the Emancipation as an effort to incite murderous slave uprisings, it suggested that Lincoln might ultimately be classed "among that catalogue of monsters, the wholesale assassins and butchers of their kind."[26]

The *Times* viewed Lincoln's reelection in November 1864 as "an avowed step towards the foundation of a military despotism." The United States, it said, had "entered on that transition stage, so well known to the students of history, through which Republics pass on their way from democracy to tyranny."[27] Yet, less than half a year later, the same newspaper told its readers, "Abraham Lincoln was as little of a tyrant as any man who ever lived."[28] What had intervened, of course, was Appomattox and the assassination.

One of the great Lincoln mysteries is the relationship between the man's martyrdom and his historical stature. Few would agree with the judgment once tossed out by Harry Elmer Barnes that Booth's shot made all the difference between a hero and a "discredited politician."[29] But few would deny that the timing and manner of his death transformed the Lincoln image. The first sign of that transformation was the enormous outpouring of grief from the American people. It astonished men in public life and chastened some of them. Even Wendell Phillips concluded, just a few days after the assassination, "Lincoln had won such loving trust from the people that it was impossible to argue anything against him."[30]

The apotheosis of Lincoln thus began as soon as he died. Savior of the Union, liberator of a race, struck down on Good Friday in "the most impious murder done since Calvary," he was readily assimilated to the universal myths of the fallen hero and the dying god.[31] Many of his critics at home and abroad hastened to revise their estimates of his worth and to scramble, as it were, aboard the funeral train. There was Tom Taylor's famous recantation in *Punch*, for instance, and there was George Bancroft, who had earlier called the President "ignorant" and "incompetent," now delivering the principal funeral oration in New York City.[32] In England, the self-exiled abolitionist Moncure D. Conway had published a bitterly hostile article soon after Lincoln's reelection, declaring, "Never before in America has a President been . . . so detested by his own electors as Abraham Lincoln." Five months later, using some of the same material, he published another, much kinder piece in which he spoke of Lincoln's "quiet firmness," his eloquence and wit, his "fidelity to himself," and his freedom from "cant or narrowness."[33]

Republicans, radical and otherwise, soon learned what an asset they had in the dead Lincoln, and before long they had turned February 12 into a day for celebrating party loyalty. Northern Democrats, for the most part, acquiesced in and frequently participated in the enshrining of Lincoln. For example, Samuel S. Cox of Ohio had little good to say about the President during the war, but writing twenty years afterward he called Lincoln "the peer of the purest and greatest men of whom history leaves a record."[34]

Cox and other Democrats were able to identify with Lincoln by stressing his conservatism and his leniency toward the defeated Confederacy, thus dissociating him from the alleged excesses of Radical Reconstruction. Many Southerners came to terms with the Lincoln image along this same route. Even Jefferson Davis, while continuing to hold Lincoln responsible for starting the war, concluded that his death had been a great misfortune for the South.[35] Southerners could also take comfort from some of Lincoln's remarks about race that seemed compatible with the developing post-Reconstruction system of segregation. And for progressive advocates of a "New South," such as the Georgia newspaper editor Henry W. Grady, an appreciation of Lincoln was part of the sectional reconciliation that their aspirations required.[36]

But for Southerners who bitterly regretted the failure of the Confederacy and looked back with painful nostalgia to their lost antebellum world, Lincoln remained a villain, one whom the poet Paul Hamilton Hayne was still describing in 1871 as a "gawky, coarse, not over-cleanly, whisky-drinking, and whisky-smelling Blackguard."[37] Southerners devoted to the Lost Cause were the principal bearers of the anti-Lincoln tradition in the late nineteenth and early twentieth centuries. They found themselves losing ground, even in their own section, being regarded more and more as a cranky remnant of the past. Yet their case against Lincoln grew stronger, or so it seemed to them, as additional evidence emerged with the passing years.

To the end of the nineteenth century and beyond, knowledge about Lincoln was continually enriched by a flow of biographies and reminiscences from men who had known him with varying degrees of intimacy. Although the tone of this often dubious material was overwhelmingly laudatory, the personal revelations of some writers, particularly William H. Herndon and Ward H. Lamon, provided welcome ammunition for the dwindling but resolute corps of Lincoln-haters. Eagerly they seized upon assertions that Lincoln, among other things, had mocked at Christianity, sold liquor in his grocery, told off-color stories, treated women with disrespect, admitted to Herndon that his mother was probably illegitimate, and suggested that a finger and thumb were as good as a handkerchief.[38]

The anti-Lincoln tradition seems to have reached a low ebb during the decade from the great centennial celebration of 1909 to the close of the First World War, but then it made a comeback in the 1920's, a time when Lincoln studies in general were entering their most brilliant era. One feature of the revival was a crusade to get pro-Northern history books out of Southern schools. Supporting that cause, the United Confederate Veterans in 1922 unanimously adopted a report declaring that the Civil War "was deliberately and personally conceived and its inauguration made by Abraham Lincoln." Immediately, there were angry responses from the G.A.R. and the Dames of the Loyal Legion.[39]

The leader of the schoolbook crusade was Mildred Lewis Rutherford, historian-general of the Confederated Southern Memorial Association, who maintained that Southern children must be told the truth about Abraham Lincoln. Among the "truths" she herself purveyed in a series of pamphlets were these: that Lincoln was a slaveholder; that as a quartermaster in the Mexican War he tried to starve American soldiers; that he contributed $100 to the support of John Brown's raid on Harpers Ferry; that the Gettysburg Address was written by William H. Seward, and that Ulysses S. Grant, as commanding general of the Army, in 1867 imposed a forty-five-year censorship on all important newspapers, prohibiting any abuse of Lincoln.[40]

By this time, however, the more learned and distinguished Lyon Gardiner Tyler had placed himself at the head of the anti-Lincoln cult. Retiring in 1918 from the presidency of the College of William and Mary, he established *Tyler's Quarterly Historical and Genealogical Magazine* and edited it until his death on, of all days, February 12, 1935. Rare was the issue of the *Magazine* that did not contain some kind of attack upon what he regarded as an absurd and infamous myth. Tyler's Lincoln was ugly to look at, vulgar in his tastes, and filthy in his use of language. Often linked in honor with George Washington, he should, said Tyler, be compared instead to George III, except that the latter was a "kinder man." Tyler did not allow consistency to hamper his denunciations. On the one hand, Lincoln was the weakest, most vacillating, most incompetent president in American history—one who took four years to win a war that should have been won in two. On the other hand, Lincoln was a mighty, satanic force in history, who, by his "blind will" alone, demolished the old Union, shattered the Constitution, and destroyed one million lives and twenty billion dollars worth of property.[41]

Meanwhile, Lincoln biography in the 1920's, though still dominated by gifted amateurs like Carl Sandburg and Albert J. Beveridge, was being turned into professional channels. Two signals of the change were the conversion of the Lincoln Centennial Association into a research organization and the publication of James G. Randall's first book, *Constitutional Problems Under Lincoln*. Professionalization had the important effect of drawing Lincoln studies into the mainstream of American historiography, so that interpretation of Lincoln became virtually inseparable from interpretation of the Civil War.

Just at that time, as it happened, the theme of "revisionism" was about to become a major element in Civil War scholarship. To the revisionists, the war was an avoidable conflict—a tragedy brought on by the agitation of extremists and the blundering of politicians. Abolitionists and other antislavery radicals were the prime villains of the piece, while the heroes were those compromisers like Stephen A. Douglas and John J. Crittenden who struggled so valiantly to hold the Union together. The interpretation was plainly anti-Republican and thus, to a certain extent, anti-Lincoln. One can see its influence in a tendency toward harsher judgment of Lincoln's antebellum career, first by Beveridge, and later by historians like Richard Hofstadter, Donald W. Riddle, and Reinhard H. Luthin.[42]

An especially pungent expression of revisionism, one that also reflected the "debunking" vogue of the 1920's, was the poet Edgar Lee Masters's experiment in character assassination, *Lincoln the Man*. Masters's Lincoln, a cold-hearted, undersexed, intellectually lazy, cunning, devious, calculating, sophistical, unscrupulous, demagogic politician, forced war treacherously and illegally upon the South, waged it cruelly, and in the process, "crushed the principles of free government." The book has with good reason been called a "copperhead biography."[43]

Yet most revisionists, in spite of their anti-Republican perspective, were remarkably tender in their treatment of Lincoln. Indeed, one of the leading revisionists, James G. Randall, was also one of the great Lincoln biographers, and an admiring one. Randall managed this straddle by positioning Lincoln relatively close to the Douglas Democrats and as far as possible from the abolitionists and radical Republicans. Randall's well-known article "The Unpopular Mr. Lincoln" is devoted almost entirely to the abuse of Lincoln by the wartime radicals.[44] Thus revisionism, which obviously had much in common with the views expressed by Samuel S. Cox and other Northern Democrats during the Civil War, nevertheless tended, like Cox in the postwar period, to come to terms with the heroic image of Lincoln.

Soon, however, a more aggressive challenge to that image came from another quarter—that is, from what amounted to a revival of the radical wing of the anti-Lincoln tradition. The Old Left, including Socialists and Communists, had assimilated Lincoln to its ideals and aspirations. But the New Left and the black power militants of the 1960's found little in him to admire. Compared with a Wendell Phillips or a Charles Sumner, he seemed unheroic, opportunistic, and uninspired by deep moral commitment. Instead of the "Great Emancipator," suggested I. F. Stone, he might better be called the "Great Equivocator."[45] This "tragically flawed figure," wrote Lerone Bennett, Jr., a senior editor of *Ebony*, "shared the racial prejudices of most of his white contemporaries." On every issue related to blacks, he was "the very essence of the white supremacist with good intentions."[46] He came to emancipation reluctantly, under radical pressure, and, indeed, according to some cynics, may have "issued the Proclamation to forestall more forcible action by Congress."[47] That is, his real intention may have been to prevent effective emancipation.

In their use of evidence to support such judgments, radical writers were biased, selective, and often uncritical. Furthermore, they generally paid little attention to the limits of circumstance within which Lincoln had to work and the variety of considerations claiming his attention—such as the plain fact that proclaiming emancipation would have been a waste of time without military victory. But then the radicals of the 1960's were interested less in scholarly fairness than in making history serve the social causes to which they had committed themselves. And there was nothing new or corrupt in that point of view. The past is not an exclusive preserve of historians. It may legitimately be used to inspire social action. Lincoln himself did so, and Jefferson too, with spectacular success in the Declaration of Independence. The ethical problem arises when social polemics masquerade as historical scholarship, and that was sometimes the case in New Left evaluations of Lincoln.

Meanwhile, the Southern version of the anti-Lincoln tradition had continued to flourish. One finds expressions of it in private correspondence as well as in speeches and publications. For example, in the 1920's Hamilton J. Eckenrode of the University of Virginia wrote to Albert J. Beveridge, calling Lincoln "an unscrupulous politician of overmastering ambition," with "utter want of principle" and "indescribable hypocrisy." As for emancipation, "the chief result of the liberation of the negro race has been the political paralysis of half the country and the general weakening of the nation."[48]

In 1937, Charles W. Ramsdell, a native Texan teaching at the University of Texas, presented the classic statement of the already familiar thesis that Lincoln deliberately "maneuvered the Confederates into firing the first shot" at Fort Sumter so that they would receive the blame for starting a war that he himself wanted.[49] A book-length reiteration of the thesis in more intemperate language was published four years later by an Alabama attorney, John S. Tilley.[50]

In 1947, a few dozen Southerners who had gathered in Statuary Hall of the national capitol to celebrate the birthday of Jefferson Davis, found themselves listening to what a *Time* correspondent on the scene called "a historical Pickett's charge." It was delivered by the guest speaker, "sallow, hawk-nosed Dr. Charles C. Tansill, Texas-born history professor at . . . Georgetown University." Characterizing Lincoln as a "do-nothing" soldier, "invincible in peace and invisible in war," Tansill accused him of precipitating hostilities by tricking the Confederates into their attack on Sumter. The most prominent person in the audience, Representative John Rankin of Mississippi, left discreetly as soon as he could, muttering that the professor had gone "too far" and that it was time to "draw the mantle of charity over all that."[51]

In 1959, soon after *Brown v. Board of Education* had inaugurated the "Second Reconstruction," there appeared a book comparing Lincoln and Jefferson Davis written by Russell Hoover Quynn, the son of a Confederate veteran from Maryland. Quynn was almost apoplectic in his hatred for Lincoln (whom he called the country's first "dictator") and in his determination to defend that "civilized, beneficial, humane" arrangement that was mislabeled "slavery." "The real monument to the Great Emancipator," he wrote, "is the maiming of the United States Constitution . . . and the imposition upon the nation of a Negro race problem that progressively grows."[52]

Some years later, the neo-Confederate attack on Lincoln was carried forward by Ludwell H. Johnson of the College of William and Mary. Echoing and elaborating upon one of Lyon Gardiner Tyler's favorite arguments, Johnson maintained that the great mystery of the Civil War is not why the South lost, but rather, why the North, with its "enormous material and numerical superiority," took so long to win. His answer was the poor quality of Northern leadership and the intensely political composition of Northern society. Lincoln, according to Johnson, was essentially a politician and little more, a man for whom "political imperatives were moral imperatives," even when that meant blinking at corruption and incompetence. Lincoln's major aim, said Johnson, was a political one—to make the Republican party "a permanent majority in the nation"—and this political purpose impeded and tainted the conduct of the war.[53]

In an article comparing the Union and Confederate presidents, Johnson found Davis "clearly superior" to Lincoln as a war leader. He was more dignified, more decisive, and more willing to accept responsibility. He made wiser appointments, had a better strategic sense, maintained a stronger cabinet, handled his generals with greater skill, was more effective as a legislative manager, and kept his military policies free from the contamination of politics. Indeed, Davis, according to Johnson, was one of the most remarkable Americans of all time and has been denied his rightful place in history because he happened to be on the losing side. "Nothing succeeds like success," Johnson remarked more than once. The comparison between Lincoln and Davis would have turned out quite differently if the South had won its independence, he argued. "Suppose the French had not come to the rescue of the Patriots, and the British had crushed the American bid for independence? What would be George Washington's reputation?"[54] The answer one might give is that, in those circumstances, Washington would have been fortunate to come out with a reputation as high as that of Robert E. Lee (for Lee, rather than Davis, is the Civil War analogue of Washington the Revolutionary general). Johnson never confronted the interesting question of why defeat should have had a disastrous effect upon Davis's historical stature as a political leader but not upon Lee's stature as a military leader. Furthermore, Johnson's whole argument proves to be ultimately self-destructive. For if we accept all of his assertions at face value, then the greatest mystery of the Civil War is this: How could Jefferson Davis and his associates have been so stupid as to get involved in a war that, according to Johnson, they had not the slightest chance of winning—not even against an enemy that was governed and commanded, according to Johnson, with pitiful incompetence?

Fiercer than Johnson in his hostility to Lincoln was M. E. Bradford, a Texas-born, Vanderbilt-trained professor of English at the University of Dallas. Bradford's views reflected not only his Southern background but also his intellectual conservatism in the tradition of Russell Kirk, Willmoore Kendall, and Eric Voegelin. Kendall, for instance, had attacked Lincoln as a revolutionary who falsified history in order to make equality, rather than liberty, the fundamental national purpose.[55]

The Lincoln portrayed by Bradford in a series of articles was a demagogue, a "country hustler," a "self-made Caesar"—cold and calculating in his ambition, dishonest in his rhetoric, and unscrupulous in his use of power—a man who precipitated civil war, waged it inhumanely, spurned efforts to end it by negotiation, put political considerations ahead of the lives and welfare of his soldiers, and secured his own reelection by illegitimate military force. Unlike Johnson, whose depreciation of Lincoln's abilities and achievements had the effect of reducing his historical significance, Bradford saw a figure of towering influence who catastrophically changed the course of American history. Bradford's Lincoln was the prime agent of a "gnostic" revolution that imposed the reform imperatives of New England puritanism upon American politics, thereby bringing about destruction of the old Union of sovereign states and setting the nation on the road to totalitarianism. Lincoln, in short, is America's Cromwell. He created the imperial presidency and converted the national government into a "juggernaut," all the while "wrapping up his policy in the idiom of Holy Scripture, concealing within the Trojan Horse of his gasconade and moral superiority an agenda that would never have been approved if presented in any other form."[56] Bradford's rhetorical flair tended thus to outrun his concern for historical accuracy, but in the intensity of his conviction he was a worthy heir and custodian of the anti-Lincoln tradition.

As Bradford's counterpart on the radical side one may point to William Appleman Williams. The Lincoln portrayed by Williams was an "arrogant" man, "full of ruthless righteousness." He wanted to "reform everyone—America first and then the world." A "Houdini with words," he somehow managed to camouflage "the frightening—even appalling—things" he was actually saying. It was Lincoln's historic purpose and achievement, said Williams, to crush with imperialistic force the right of self-determination claimed by the South. In the process, he became the first "truly . . . Faustian figure" among American political leaders. That is, he made a pact with the Devil and came out the loser in the end. The bargain "began to go sour almost at once." The expected quick victory did not materialize. "The evil of empire proved a demon," and he found himself involved in "a ruthless war of annihilation." Consequently, "small wonder that he became increasingly prone to dreams about his death. It was the only way out."[57]

Still another important recruit to the anti-Lincoln tradition in the late twentieth century was the political scientist Dwight G. Anderson, whose psychohistorical study of Lincoln portrayed him as malevolent both in his personal motivation and in his influence on American history. Anderson's "demonic" Lincoln, "by acting on his motive of revenge against constitutional fathers for having preempted the field of glory," became the "very tyrant against whom Washington had warned in his Farewell Address, a tyrant who would preside over the destruction of the Constitution in order to gratify his own ambition." Furthermore, Lincoln served as the model for certain later presidents (notably, the two Roosevelts, Wilson, and Kennedy) in their respective quests for fame on the stage of international affairs. His political rhetoric provided the rationale for modern American expansionism, with its persistent effort to Americanize the whole planet. The menace of Lincoln's poisonous legacy did not begin to wane until a century after his death, when the young people of the Vietnam era declared themselves unwilling "to be cast as spear-carriers and supernumeraries in America's grand historical Passion Play."[58]

Such dark visions of Lincoln in recent literature are perhaps not so much products of historical research as by-products of contemporary history and reflections of the gnawing uneasiness with which many modern Americans view themselves and their cultural heritage. More often than not, the great events and major trends of our own era have tended to make Lincoln less satisfactory as a national hero. The civil rights revolution underscored the relative poverty of his thought about the problem of race and the inadequacy of his plans for the aftermath of emancipation. The Vietnam War and the Watergate affair dramatized the growth and menace of the so-called imperial presidency, which could be traced directly to his extraordinary use of executive power. The modern drift toward social pluralism, with its emphasis upon minority rights and its sanction of organized protest, bears little relation to the coercive majoritarianism with which he met the threat of secession. And the apocalyptic meaning of total war in our time casts a shadow of doubt across his willingness to accept war and wage it totally as an alternative to acquiescence in disunion. Furthermore, Lincoln's reputation has become more vulnerable as a result of what C. Vann Woodward calls "the fall of the American Adam"—that is, the substitution of a sense of guilt about the nation's past for an earlier sense of virtue and pride.[59]

Modern interpretation of Lincoln has been profoundly affected by the practice of history as a discipline, and by the progress of history as human experience. The expanding professionalization of Lincoln studies produced greater variety and sophistication in the assessment of his character, motives, conduct, and influence. The emerging portrait, a composite of scholarship, reveals a mixture of faults and virtues, mistakes and achievements. It has become a less coherent and less heroic portrait, but perhaps a more meaningful one in our unheroic, troubled age.

In spite of all adverse influences, Lincoln retains the admiration of most Americans and his place of preeminence in the national pantheon. Perhaps a kind of historical inertia holds him there now; perhaps the twenty-first century will view him much differently. But in the polls he still ranks first. One recent presidential poll merits special attention. Of 41 historians, 39 labeled him "great," one called him a "near great," none classified him as "average" or "below average," but one branded him a "failure."[60] Thus the anti-Lincoln tradition persists in lonely splendor, and the study of that tradition does tell us something, though far from everything, about Lincoln's unique hold upon the memory and imagination of his countrymen. In a word, he matters. He has never settled quietly into his historical niche. For anyone trying to understand America's past or shape its future, he is a force to be reckoned with—an ineluctable presence. In the words of an Englishwoman, Barbara Ward, "he is one of the very few of the world's leaders who stay alive."[61]

CHAPTER 16

The Deep Reading of Lincoln

Saul Bellow once reported having heard a new explanation of *Moby Dick*. The whale, a young acquaintance had told him, "is everybody's mother wallowing in her watery bed. Ahab has the Oedipus complex and wants to slay the hell out of her." That, said Bellow, was "deep reading."[1] Efforts at reading Abraham Lincoln in depth, though they began long ago, have only recently come to be a central feature of Lincoln literature. The following comment on those efforts began as an essay reviewing books by Charles B. Strozier and Dwight G. Anderson for the March 1983 issue of *Reviews in American History*, but I have extensively revised and enlarged the original text to consider work of various other writers.

The inner life of Abraham Lincoln, explored but occasionally and with indifferent success for more than a century, has become a subject of renewed interest with the rise of psychohistory as a specialized discipline. Although that discipline flourishes, it continues to be suspect among historians. Much of the difficulty arises from the incompatibility of its main working premise with the traditional rules of historical evidence. For if the primary sources of human motivation do lie hidden beneath the surface of consciousness, then the psychohistorian must use the documentary record as a mere base of operations from which to seek the implicit meaning of explicit behavior. His task, by its very nature, constantly draws him away from the realm of fact into the realm of inference. Occupational necessity accordingly tends to release his imagination from certain restraints of the historical method, and the result more often than not is a kind of writing described by Gordon S. Wood as "not quite fiction, but . . . not quite history either."[2]

For the chronic weakness of his evidence, the psychohistorian compensates with elaborate theory, most of it drawn thus far from psychoanalysis. But psychoanalytic theory, after nearly a century of luxuriant growth, remains largely unauthenticated and highly controversial. Its generalizations are essentially a body of speculative lore rather than scientific knowledge. Bold assertion, emphatic reiteration, clinical anecdotage, and a richly metaphorical terminology all contribute to masking the paucity of empirical verification. And there is, moreover, a tendency to logical circularity in psychoanalysis that makes much of it, like astrology, unscientifically immune to refutation. Even if one rejects the mordant suggestion of Nobel Laureate P. B. Medawar that psychoanalytic doctrine may be "the most stupendous intellectual confidence trick of the twentieth century,"[3] there can be no doubt that history written from the psychoanalytic point of view has been severely compromised by the numerous follies committed in its name.

Besides complaining of flimsy evidence and dubious theory, critics of psychohistory charge that it is too often reductionist, tending to ignore or underestimate social forces and situational imperatives; that it is mechanical and deterministic in the application of formulas (such as the Oedipus complex) to particular persons and incidents; that it anachronistically imposes modern psychological models upon past cultures, as though human nature were uniform and unchanging; that it makes excessive use of technical language in order to give mere assertion the ring of authority; and that it habitually converts biography into medical diagnosis, almost always with derogatory effects. Two additional problems are especially relevant to the study of public leaders. One is the question of how supposedly universal psychological experience (such as infantile traumas and identity crises) can be used to explain the extraordinary achievement of someone like Lincoln. The other is the methodological difficulty of demonstrating causal connections between such a person's private life and the public events in which he or she participates.

The complexity of the psychohistorian's task should be enough in itself to inspire humility, and the pressures of heavy criticism have undoubtedly encouraged many practitioners to be more thorough and sophisticated in their scholarship, more judicious and tentative in their generalizations. One can only admire, for instance, the good sense and breadth of vision in the little essay on method with which psychiatrist John E. Mack begins his biography of T. E. Lawrence.[4] Cross-disciplinary training (or self-education) is reducing the problem of lopsided expertness—the historian with too little knowledge of psychology and the psychologist with too little understanding of history. Nevertheless, amateurism in one respect or the other is still a characteristic of much psychohistorical writing.

Lincoln's earliest psychobiographer of a sort was doubly an amateur whose invaluable contributions as a historian were sometimes impaired by his pretensions to psychological insight. William H. Herndon first saw Lincoln in 1832, began to know him well in 1837, and became his law partner in 1844. The recollections that he recorded in the Herndon-Weik biography and in hundreds of letters written between 1865 and 1891 constitute a primary source for the entire twenty-four years of Lincoln's residence in Springfield—the period of his legal career and of his political rise from the state legislature to the presidency. Beyond that, however, much of the available information about Lincoln's childhood, youth, and early manhood comes from Herndon as a secondary source. Most notable is the large body of material that he collected in 1865 and 1866, consisting of interviews and exchanges of correspondence with persons who had known Lincoln long before. But in addition, he himself frequently recounted things that Lincoln had supposedly told him about his family and early life. For example, according to Herndon writing in 1870, Lincoln in 1852 had said that his mother, Nancy Hanks Lincoln, "was a bastard" and that the Hankses were generally "*lascivious, lecherous*, not to be trusted."[5]

The reliability of such recollective data is questionable in itself, and to it Herndon added a great deal of pseudo-scientific theorizing and uninhibited surmise. Believing that he had special intuitive powers as well as a learned familiarity with mental processes, he was sure that no one else had ever come so close to understanding the mind and character of his late partner. "I know Lincoln better than I know myself," he declared, and, on another occasion: "I knew the man so well that I think I could read his secrets and his ambitions."[6] As the years passed, Herndon tended to confuse what he remembered with what he had conjectured and with gossip that he had heard. His reminiscences as a whole, says David Donald, are filled with contradictions and amount to "a queer hodgepodge of fact and fancy."[7] Yet psychobiographers must depend heavily on Herndon for the information about Lincoln's childhood and youth that their theory requires. The result, a cynic might say, is interpretation arrived at by applying debatable methodology to dubious and ambiguous materials.

There were other early writers besides Herndon who gave at least passing attention to Lincoln's thought processes and emotional life,[8] but not until after the First World War did professional psychology—and especially psychoanalytic theory—begin to have some slight influence on Lincoln studies. Nathaniel W. Stephenson, in an avowed effort to portray the inner Lincoln, decorated his highly praised 1922 biography with a number of vaguely Freudian passages, but more typically he depended for insight upon intuitive perception and historical grasp.[9] At about the same time, L. Pierce Clark offered a practicing psychoanalyst's interpretation of Lincoln in an article that grew into a 570-page book. Clark stressed oedipal factors in explaining Lincoln's depressive tendencies and their shaping effect on his character. "It seems," he wrote, "that the benignant attitude Lincoln took toward the weak and downtrodden, shown, for instance, in his making the abolition of slavery the slogan for continuing the struggle of the Civil War, was prompted not a little by the more than filial devotion he must have felt for his mother."[10]

Clark's *Lincoln: A Psycho-Biography*, which appeared in 1933, was a curious blend of lushly sentimental narrative and technical psychoanalytic exposition, all written in the present tense. He had read widely but uncritically in the source materials, accepting wholeheartedly, for instance, the Ann Rutledge legend and Herndon's sour view of the Lincoln marriage. Repeating the story that Lincoln failed to appear for his wedding ceremony, Clark explained this and virtually all other Lincoln behavior as originating in a mother complex—more particularly in an infantile desire to "ingest" the one he loved and absorb her wholly into himself.

> He remains emotionally fixed upon that earlier pattern of longing to incorporate the loved object; there will arise from it in all his love-relationships the inclination, so typical of the depressive temperament, to introject the object within his own ego. . . . When he fails to receive from Mary Todd the answer to his craving for love, he establishes her symbolically within his own personality and seeks to settle the conflict within himself rather than to influence the situation in the outer world. . . . A person such as Lincoln not infrequently renounces the possible attainment of a life of perfect bliss in connubial union, and redirects his energies toward an uprearing of self-esteem and ambition more capable of realization.[11]

Though it won the praise of some social scientists, Clark's book was generally disparaged by historians and had no significant influence on subsequent Lincoln biography.[12]

In the same year, Milton H. Shutes published a "medical narrative" of Lincoln's life that included some discussion of his mental health. Shutes rejected "mother fixation" as the underlying cause of Lincoln's depressive tendencies, but he agreed with Clark that the ordeal of Willie Lincoln's death in 1862 had a curative effect, profoundly spiritual in nature. Lincoln, like many of the world's great men, was a psychoneurotic, Shutes declared. "That phase of his character went into the mosaic of his intensely interesting personality and was an indissoluble part of his greatness." Shutes also suggested in passing that Lincoln's "athletic-asthenic physique" indicated a schizoid personality.[13] For another medical man, William F. Peterson, writing ten years later, body structure as acted upon by climate was the very key to understanding Lincoln's psychic condition. Being emphatically a "linear" type of human being, he lacked physical reserves and responded much better to warm weather than to cold. Thus, said Peterson, he was at his best in the summer heat of the senatorial contest with Douglas, and his worst emotional crises occurred at times when the temperature had fallen well below normal.[14]

Psychiatrist Edward J. Kempf likewise regarded body structure as a determinant of personality, but the crucial element in Lincoln's case, he believed, was brain damage suffered at the age of nine from the kick of a horse. First in an article (1952) and then in a three-volume treatise (1965), Kempf argued that the head injury and Lincoln's lifelong adjustment to it shaped his personality and career. It was the root cause of his melancholy, for example, and of the indulgence in humor with which he sought to counteract depression.[15] Even though historians were somewhat more receptive to psychological interpretation by the 1960's, Kempf's thesis made little headway; for he compromised his credibility in a number of ways. Like Clark, he read sources uncritically, and too often he erected complex explanations upon pinheads of evidence. For instance, he used a dubious story about the slaughtering of a pet pig to explain Lincoln's alienation from his father, then went on to insist that the incident gave the boy an "unforgettable presentiment" of the tragedies lying ahead of him, and that as a consequence of this experience, "his heart became set upon fighting against dominating injustice wherever he met it."[16]

Plainly, Kempf's work constituted no advance over that of Clark a generation earlier. In 1965, it could still be said that the theories and methods of formal psychology, Freudian and otherwise, had made little impression on Lincoln scholarship. Nevertheless, some important deep reading of Lincoln was proceeding from other intellectual milieux. Most notably, Harry V. Jaffa in 1959 published *Crisis of the House Divided*, a masterful study of Lincoln's political ideas as they developed during the antebellum years. Jaffa, a political scientist, cited Aristotle at least a dozen times and never mentioned Freud. He was concerned, not with Lincoln's emotional depths, but rather with the depths of meaning in his words, and with how those words, addressed specifically to the sectional conflict over slavery, fitted into the great Western tradition of political philosophy.[17] For instance, when Jaffa spoke of a "tension in Lincoln's thought" between the principle of equality and the principle of government by consent, he was obviously talking about a logical, not a psychological tension.[18] Lincoln's thought was also probed in a nonpsychological way by several scholars studying his religious beliefs. With greater skill than had previously been brought to bear, they investigated such themes as Lincoln's conception of God and divine will, his increasing religiosity, his attitude toward death, and his theological explanation of the Civil War.[19]

Meanwhile, psychohistory was emerging as a professional subdiscipline. Among the landmarks in its early development were William L. Langer's presidential address to the American Historical Association in 1957, calling for the use of depth psychology in historical research, and, a year later, the publication of Erik H. Erikson's *Young Man Luther*, with its emphasis on "stages of growth" and "identity crises."[20] By the early 1970's there were enough persons interested to organize within the American Historical Association the "Group for the Use of Psychology in History," which later set about publishing the *Psychohistory Review*.[21] At the same time, a number of other historians not officially enrolled in the new movement were fitting psychological theory into their explanatory structures. One thinks especially of works by Richard Hofstadter on the Populists and the "paranoid style" in politics, by David Donald on the abolitionists and Charles Sumner, and by Stanley Elkins on slavery.[22]

Another growing influence on mid-twentieth-century historical writing was the methodological example of literary criticism, a discipline characteristically concerned with extracting the deepest meaning of a text and often seasoned with insights from depth psychology. Notable in this respect were writers of the "myth and symbol" school who constituted perhaps the most distinctive element in the burgeoning American studies movement. Beginning with Henry Nash Smith's *Virgin Land* in 1950, they provided an exciting new perspective on the American past by examining the elaborated connotative meanings of the images with which the mind orders reality—images such as "wilderness," "machine," "Yankee," and "progress."[23] To a considerable extent, this meant a search for the emotional content of ideas, a shift of attention from rational to nonrational motivation. Among major historical figures, it was Andrew Jackson who at first received the most attention from myth-and-symbol writers,[24] but plainly there was no reason why the same method should not be applied to the life of Lincoln.

The most influential interpretation of Lincoln by a literary critic came from Edmund Wilson in his volume of essays on Civil War literature titled *Patriotic Gore*.[25] Although not associated with the myth-and-symbol group, Wilson's primary purpose was to demonstrate the shaping of the Lincoln legend by Lincoln himself.[26] There was poetry, he declared, not only in Lincoln's writings but in the acting out of his life. "He created himself as a poetic figure, and he thus imposed himself on the nation."[27] Wilson's perceptions were arrived at intuitively—one might almost say imaginatively—but he made use of psychological terminology in what proved to be the essay's most memorable passage. He suggested that Lincoln, in his speech to the Young Men's Lyceum of Springfield, "projected himself into the role" of the towering genius who seizes dictatorial power—the danger against which he was ostensibly warning his audience.[28] With that one speculative leap, Wilson set a new fashion in the interpretation of Lincoln's character and career.

Thus there were several intellectual disciplines and movements out of which psychobiographical treatment of Lincoln began to emerge in the 1970's. The theoretical and methodological variety becomes plain enough if one examines two articles and three books that appeared between 1975 and 1982.

Gabor S. Boritt, a historian, consulted practicing psychiatrists in preparing a Freudian explanation of Lincoln's advocacy of Negro colonization. The question Boritt raised was why a man of such good practical sense should have so persistently recommended an unrealistic program that had already proved itself a total failure. My own belief is that Lincoln's support of colonization, however it may have originated, became during his presidential years a calculated, dissimulative strategy aimed primarily at the white mind rather than the black population—in other words, that he hoped for nothing more than a token emigration of blacks to relieve some of the racial fears engendered by the thought of emancipation. Boritt argues, however, that in advocating colonization Lincoln was to some extent fooling himself, subconsciously employing the defense mechanism of "avoidance" to cope with his own conflicted feelings about the racial consequences of the war. In technical terms: "Part of Lincoln's id, seeking the Lincolnian derivative pleasure of truth, came into conflict within the ego with the reality that colonization . . . was not possible. The conflict was mitigated through avoidance until his ego goal, emancipation, was achieved."[29] Whatever one may think of the psychoanalytic theory (and Boritt himself is diffident in his use of it), the article makes good common sense, at least as a partial explanation of Lincoln's behavior. Perhaps the best answer is that there was an unanalyzable mixture of calculation and self-deception in Lincoln's public attitude toward colonization.

Soon after Boritt's venture, Robert L. Randall published a brief psychohistorical commentary on the various personal crises in Lincoln's life. Both a psychologist and an ordained minister, Randall used no Freudian jargon, but his essay plainly reflected the influence of the post-Freudian "self psychology." There was a correspondence, Randall argued, between Lincoln's "own fears of personal self-dissolution" and the threat of civil dissolution facing the nation. His struggle for inner cohesiveness became linked with the struggle to preserve the Union. And this "fortuitous juncture of his emotional needs with the needs of a distressed country proved, in the long run, beneficial to both."[30]

The two most controversial studies of Lincoln in the psychohistorical vein were doctoral dissertations turned into books—George B. Forgie's *Patricide in the House Divided* (1979) and Dwight G. Anderson's *Abraham Lincoln: The Quest for Immortality* (1982).[31] Both Forgie (a historian) and Anderson (a political scientist) made use of Freudian theory while at the same time drawing upon a variety of other intellectual resources for inspiration and insight. Both depicted Lincoln as a man torn between his veneration of the nation's founders and his anger at their having preempted the pathways to glory. Both placed heavy emphasis upon Lincoln's Lyceum address and followed the lead of Edmund Wilson in his interpretation of the passage about the dangers of dictatorship. But there were also significant differences between their respective arguments.

According to the Forgie version, Lincoln repressed his resentment of the founding fathers and likewise repressed any subversive thoughts of playing the role of tyrant. Instead, he cast Stephen A. Douglas as the destructive genius and himself as the prospective savior of the nation. In generational terms, Douglas was the "bad son" engaging in patricidal rebellion who must be stalked and "killed." By thus inventing a villain and summoning up an illusive threat to the Republic, Lincoln, without consciously intending to do so, set the stage for disruption of the Union.[32]

According to Anderson, on the other hand, Lincoln consciously and deliberately put the nation on the road to disaster. Anderson's Lincoln was a man "hounded by a death anxiety" and therefore hungry for the immortality of historical renown. As a young man, inspired by his reading of Parson Weems, he tried to be a virtuous son of the founding fathers. He sought fame in the manner enjoined by Washington, honoring the Constitution and following a conventional path toward political distinction. But then, says Anderson, he met failure in Congress and humiliation in his pursuit of greatness, whereupon a radical change came over him. "Denied the opportunity of 'building up,' this ambitious genius 'would set boldly to the task of pulling down.'" Now driven by rage, self-hatred, and a desire for vengeance, as well as by ambition, he turned away from the Constitution and the example of Washington, boldly determined to play the part of revolutionary leader and tyrant. This new, demonic Lincoln of the 1850's, whose avowed principles were but creatures of his ambition, found in the slavery issue a means of escaping the confines of political obscurity. The "malignant passions" within him, kept under control until his election to the presidency, were at last released in the Fort Sumter crisis, when he maneuvered the South into striking the first blow of the conflict. Quickly seizing "virtually dictatorial powers," he set about founding a new nation and supplanting Washington as the country's symbolic father. He also began to erect a civil religion with himself as God's appointed savior of the Union. This assumption of the role of Christ, even to the ultimate sacrifice on Good Friday, 1865, was "his greatest gesture of cosmic defiance."[33]

Thus, in the Anderson portrayal of Lincoln there was a studied virulence that one does not find in Forgie's writing. Both books are nevertheless works of considerable imaginative power, executed with considerable literary skill. Their common weakness is that psychohistorical explanation, often stated with emphatic assurance, runs far beyond the kind of evidence that will satisfy most historians. Both Forgie and Anderson were, in a sense, straining to discover the mythic meaning of Lincoln's career, but in the process they may have contributed to the manufacture of myth—that is, to the creation of still another legendary Lincoln.

As late as 1982, in *The Abraham Lincoln Encyclopedia*, Mark E. Neely, Jr., declared that all psychobiographies of Lincoln to date have been "unmitigated disasters." He saw reason for hope, however, in an article by Charles B. Strozier, a professional historian who had studied at the Chicago Institute of Psychoanalysis and was the editor of the *Psychohistory Review*.[34] Strozier, as it happened, was by then in the final stages of publishing a complete book on the interplay of Lincoln's private emotional life and his public career. Entitled *Lincoln's Quest for Union*, it consisted of nine essays devoted largely to the pre-presidential years. One chapter, the longest, was a splendidly sensitive study of Mary Todd Lincoln. There was also an ambitious effort to explain the crisis mentality of antebellum America, which did little more than dress up some familiar ideas in clinical terminology. The other seven essays were more directly about Lincoln—his childhood on the frontier; the sexual perplexities of early manhood; his relations with his father and with the memory of the founding fathers; the changing patterns of his marriage and family life; the practice of law as a search for order and a process of intellectual growth; his trial-and-error formulation of a political rhetoric to suit the slavery controversy; and, in a closing sketch of the inner man, his melancholy, humor, empathy, creativity, and guilt.[35]

In his preface, Strozier declared that he had made eclectic use of psychoanalytic theory from Freud onward. At the same time, he acknowledged the particularly strong influence of his teacher, Heinz Kohut, a leading figure in the study of narcissistic disorders and in the development of the school of thought known as "self psychology." Strozier was most effective, I think, when he wore his special training lightly—that is, when historical data were illumined with psychological insight but not pressed into psychoanalytic molds. A notable example was his fresh, perceptive, and generally nontechnical treatment of Lincoln's friendship with Joshua F. Speed, the young merchant from Kentucky with whom he lived and shared a bed in Springfield for nearly four years. During that same period, Lincoln met and courted Mary Todd, only to draw back from marriage at almost the last moment. Strozier argued convincingly that "such close male contact during the years of Lincoln's greatest heterosexual tension heightened the difficulty he found in securing intimacy with a woman." Surely, as Strozier suggested, there must have been more than coincidence in the fact that Lincoln broke off his engagement to Mary on the very same day that Speed sold his mercantile partnership, preparatory to moving back to Kentucky.[36]

The affair of the turkey, however, is something else again. One might think that Freud's famous mistake involving a vulture would have made psychohistorians wary of birds in general, but Strozier did not hesitate to analyze what he called a "curious story" parenthetically included in the autobiographical sketch that Lincoln wrote in 1860 after his nomination for the presidency: "(A few days before the completion of his eighth year, in the absence of his father, a flock of wild turkeys approached the new log-cabin, and A. with a rifle gun standing inside, shot through a crack, and killed one of them. He has never since pulled a trigger on any larger game.)"

Lincoln followed this anecdote with a sentence telling of his mother's death and his father's remarriage. "Such a juxtaposition of memories," Strozier wrote, "suggests an association between the wild turkey and his dead mother. Both are helpless and both die." Lincoln's "deep remorse" at having killed the turkey made it "impossible" for him thereafter to fire at any larger game. But it was a remorse displaced from his mother onto the bird, a guilt originating in "renounced infantile sexual longings." The meaning of this "dreamlike" story, Strozier maintained, was that Lincoln wished his father away because he wanted to possess his mother. He therefore appropriated the magical power of his father's gun, only to find it "more deadly than anticipated." The result was the death not only of the turkey but of his mother as well. She died as punishment for his forbidden love.[37]

This wild turkey hypothesis was not wholly Strozier's invention. It had already been put forward, for example, by Fawn M. Brodie and Michael Paul Rogin.[38] But Strozier gave fuller oedipal meaning to a structure of inference that rested entirely upon a misreading of the passage in question. First of all, a parenthesis is usually associated with the *preceding* set of words as an elaboration or qualification. Therefore, to quote parenthetic material without also quoting what appears immediately before it is likely to be deceptive. In the autobiography, Lincoln told of his family's move from Kentucky to an "unbroken forest" in Indiana. Then he talked about his experience with the two prime instruments for conquering the wilderness. An axe, he said, was "put into his hands at once," and he used it almost constantly until his twenty-third year. About the other instrument he was wryly self-depreciative: "At this place A. took an early start as a hunter, which was never much improved afterwards." That sentence (not quoted by Strozier) would have been rather cryptic if left to stand by itself. So he added the turkey story in parentheses as an explanation.[39]

The point is surely plain enough. Lincoln became a skilled axeman but was no great shakes with a rifle—indeed, he never thereafter "pulled a trigger on any larger game." In viewing the latter statement as an expression of "remorse," Strozier mistakenly injected modern sensitivities into a cruder frontier culture.[40] Besides, if Lincoln felt guilty about killing the turkey (instead of bursting with pride like any normal frontier boy), why did he not give up shooting at *turkeys*? What would have been so contrite and humane about solemnly refusing ever to fire at a bear or a deer while continuing (as he apparently did) to hunt turkeys, raccoons, and other smaller creatures?[41] No, Lincoln was talking about a lack of prowess, a lack of interest, and perhaps also a scarcity of opportunity, but *not* about a stricken conscience, when he said that he never afterward pulled a trigger on larger game. At any rate, the turkey story was neither "odd" nor "dreamlike" but in fact integral to Lincoln's brief discussion of pioneering in Indiana. When he turned next in his autobiography to telling of his mother's death, he did so for the very good reason that it was the next major event in his life after the move from Kentucky. In short, the sequence from dead turkey to dead mother can be fully explained as a narrator's conventional observance of chronology. The "juxtaposition" supposedly dictated by oedipal anxiety is entirely gratuitous.

Furthermore, it should not be forgotten that the autobiographical summary was prepared with deliberation and care for use in a campaign biography. Before turning the turkey story into an unconscious effusion of oedipal guilt, one ought to consider the possibility that Lincoln had a conscious purpose in telling it. That is, the distinction between rifle and axe as cultural symbols may have seemed very important to a man whose persona as a presidential candidate was just then in the making. Like Andrew Jackson, Lincoln stood to profit politically from association with the American West, but only if it were the more or less civilized West of pioneer farmers and not the wilder, even savage West of the raw frontier. As John William Ward has pointed out, "Friendly portrayals pictured Jackson at his plow and stressed the fact that he worked his farm himself. Adverse comments attempted to push Jackson out beyond the pale of civilization into the chaotic regions of unorganized nature."[42] So Lincoln had good reason to identify himself with the farmer's axe and dissociate himself from the hunter's rifle.

Nowhere else in the Strozier book does psychoanalytic formula so patently conjure evidence, but the tension between the author's two disciplines is frequently visible. For example, after having conceded that it was risky to use recollective material, he went ahead and did so extensively and unguardedly, even treating as authentic such Lincolnian apocrypha as the "Chronicles of Reuben."[43] And on the question of whether Lincoln really retired from politics during the years 1849–54, Strozier was pulled in opposite directions by historical facts and psychological theory.[44]

Strozier's title referred to his perception of Lincoln as a man who sought "inner coherence" and found it in the public struggle over slavery, ultimately shaping his "heroic image to fit a nation longing for unity and greatness." But this theme appeared only now and then in the text and was wrapped up in a mere two-page conclusion.[45] *Lincoln's Quest for Union* is in fact a book devoted primarily to the application of a method, rather than to the pursuit of a thesis. Perhaps in part for that reason, reviewers have been disposed to regard it as the best work yet published combining history and psychology in the study of Lincoln. Strozier was considerably more successful, however, in demonstrating the heuristic value of psychohistorical investigation than in dispelling doubts about the reliability of psychohistorical judgment.

There remains, first of all, the problem of theory—not only the dubiousness of psychoanalytic theory as a historical tool but the broader question of whether any historical scholarship can be sound if it is engineered to fit preselected theory. There remains also the problem of evidence. Strozier's book only reinforces the impression that psychobiographical interpretation, by its very nature, too often depends on questionable data and too often overburdens even sound data with the weight of elaborated inference.

It is a curious paradox that if an author puts imagined words into the mouth of a historical figure, his writing will surely be called fiction, whereas if he attributes thoughts (even subconscious thoughts) to the same figure, his writing may well be classified as nonfiction. The deep reading of Lincoln from Herndon to Strozier sometimes seems more imaginative than any fiction into which he has been introduced. Essentially, deep reading is conjecture—often learned and technical and emphatically stated, but conjecture nonetheless. Sound historical interpretation cannot be founded on conjecture but may be enriched by its hum of implication. That Lincoln suffered from oedipal guilt associated with his mother's death, that he projected himself into the role of a dictator—these are possibilities to be borne speculatively in mind as one struggles to construct the truc story of his life out of better-verified material. Psychohistorical possibility is in a sense the inner wilderness of history, a twilight region with treacherous footing that nevertheless invites adventurous exploration because of the profound truths it is rumored to conceal—and probably does.

CHAPTER 17

The Fictional Lincoln

The pages of the following essay that deal with Gore Vidal's *Lincoln* were part of my contribution to a panel discussion on recent Lincoln biography during a conference held at Gettysburg College in September 1984. From that specific beginning, my interest expanded to embrace the broader theme of this essay. I soon found myself exploring a fascinating and relatively unfamiliar realm of Lincoln literature that lies on the border between history and imagination. A shorter version of this essay appeared in the Spring 1986 issue of the *Stanford Magazine*.

It was John Stafford, more than anyone else, who turned Abraham Lincoln into a vigorous opponent of slavery. Stafford, a Massachusetts editor with strong abolitionist convictions, moved his family to Illinois in 1850 and settled near Springfield in the little community of Bakerstown. As pioneers the Staffords had a hard time of it, but from the beginning they were aided and encouraged by Lincoln. On the day of their arrival, he pulled their wagon out of the mudhole into which it had sunk. After that, he stopped by regularly while riding the lawyers' circuit, sometimes staying overnight, often bringing food or some other gift, and usually lending a hand with the chores. Indeed, he spent Christmas of 1850 with the Staffords (Mary Lincoln and the children having gone to Kentucky for a visit), and he dressed up as Santa Claus in a buffalo robe and red flannel shirt, with a well-filled gunnysack slung over his shoulder. Frequently, the two men fell into argument about the problem of slavery. Lincoln resisted Stafford's radicalism and questioned the wisdom of his establishing an abolitionist newspaper in Bakerstown. "I hope I'll live to see slavery abolished," he said, "but by ballots, not bullets." Eventually, however, Lincoln was won over to a more activist point of view. Two events that helped change his mind were the passage of the Kansas-Nebraska Act in 1854 and the vandalizing of Stafford's newspaper shop at about the same time.

This relationship between Lincoln and John Stafford is an episode unknown to historians for the simple reason that it never happened. The Stafford family and the Stafford newspaper never existed. Neither did Bakerstown, Illinois. They were all the creations of Katharine Holland Brown, who many years ago put them together with Lincoln into her novel *The Father* and won a literary prize of $25,000.[1] The book is just one of the titles in a substantial body of literature—most of it remembered dimly if at all. Before Gore Vidal there were Irving Bacheller, Bernie Babcock, Mary Raymond Shipman Andrews, Honoré Willsie Morrow, Bruce Lancaster, and many others. The Lincoln of historical scholarship has an interesting counterpart in the Lincoln of historical fiction.

Although one might say that it all began with certain propagandistic Confederate dramas such as *The Royal Ape* and *King Linkum the First*,[2] the introduction of Lincoln into American prose fiction is usually dated from the publication of Edward Eggleston's *The Graysons* in 1887. Eggleston was the already famous author of *The Hoosier Schoolmaster* and other novels about frontier life that combined realistic detail with a sentimental outlook. In *The Graysons*, Lincoln appears about halfway through the book as a young lawyer who defends Tom Grayson against a charge of murder and wins his acquittal by using an almanac to destroy the credibility of a key witness. Eggleston obviously based this part of his plot on Lincoln's defense of Duff Armstrong in 1858 but moved the event back to the 1830's.[3] In Joseph Kirkland's *The McVeys*, which came out the following year, a more mature Lincoln makes a brief appearance riding the judicial circuit during the 1850's.[4] Bret Harte's *Clarence*, a Civil War novel published in 1895, introduces President Lincoln near the end of the book. The hero, a Union general unjustly removed from his command, goes to the White House and pleads his case. Lincoln, after a full discussion, restores him to active duty, promotes him to major general, and reunites him with the woman he loves—all in the space of a few pages.[5] In 1900, Joel Chandler Harris, famous for his "Uncle Remus" stories, published a story of novelette length titled "The Kidnapping of President Lincoln." The would-be kidnappers, two Georgians, manage to become acquainted with Lincoln and even get him into a carriage. He has proved so likable, however, that they find themselves unwilling to carry out the plot.[6] These, then, were the pioneers—Eggleston, Kirkland, Harte, and Harris—but the fictional Lincoln is for the most part a twentieth-century creation.

In 1901, a young St. Louis novelist named Winston Churchill offered the first important fictional treatment of Lincoln as a heroic national figure. *The Crisis* is a "hearts-divided" story of love and conflict in Civil War Missouri. Stephen Brice, a recent arrival from New England, meets Lincoln during the summer of 1858 and hears the great debate with Douglas at Freeport. Deeply moved by the experience, he becomes a Republican leader in St. Louis and later a Union officer, serving with Sherman in the Georgia campaign. The circumstances thus frown on his half-concealed love for Virginia Carvel, a spirited Southern belle, who is attracted to Brice even while trying to despise him for his Yankee birth and antislavery sympathies. After many trials and adventures, the two young people are drawn to Washington at the end of the war and there are brought together in Lincoln's presence. Now Virginia comes to feel the force of character that inspired Brice and to see the "ineffable sadness" of this victorious President. She and Stephen, having at last declared their love for each other, are married on what proves to be the day of Lincoln's death. They mourn him as a friend lost and as a martyr who "gave his life for his country even as Christ gave his for the world."[7]

The Crisis is a historical novel in the classic mode of Sir Walter Scott. Its principal characters and happenings are imaginary but intermingled with real historical figures and events that provide background and sometimes agency for the developing plot. General Frémont, Frank Blair, the seizure of Camp Jackson, Sherman's march from Atlanta to the sea—these are all, in a sense, part of the author's historical scenery. But Lincoln, though he makes only two appearances in the novel, plays a more crucial role. On the first occasion, he gives motivation to the hero's life, and on the second, he helps bring hero and heroine together in love's embrace.

The Lincoln of fiction is commonly just such an animator and disposer and comforter and rescuer. Again and again we find him defending some innocent person accused of murder, pardoning a condemned soldier, or smoothing the course of true love.[8] Even as a young man, in Bernie Babcock's *The Soul of Ann Rutledge*, he goes about putting things right. He attends a sick mother, feeds her baby, and provides it with a badly needed blanket. He deals forcefully with a bully and punishes a child-beater, whose little victim says that God came to help "with the longest legs on earth" and calling himself Abe Lincoln. When Ann Rutledge falls ill and dies in his arms, it is scarcely surprising that this paragon should exclaim, "My God—why hast Thou forsaken me!"[9]

Thus the fictional Lincoln is often a blend not only of historical fact and literary invention but of folklore and myth—especially the folklore of the American West and the myth of the dying god. Babcock presents Lincoln as a young frontiersman of such tremendous strength that he once strangled a cougar, yet smart enough to win a spelling contest and discuss theology.[10] Bret Harte's Lincoln has deep-set eyes "abstracted with the vague prescience of the prophet and the martyr."[11] Virginia Carvel sees in those eyes "the sorrow of a heavy cross borne meekly" and the "pain of a crown of thorns" worn for a world that does not understand.[12] Churchill's treatment of the Freeport debate is especially interesting in the way it mixes history and fiction with political legend—the legend that Lincoln, against the pleading of his advisers, chose a strategy at Freeport that would surely mean defeat in the Senate race but would keep Douglas out of the White House and thereby save the country. This display of self-sacrificial patriotism is what makes Stephen Brice realize the greatness of the man he expected to patronize but has come instead "to worship."[13]

Fictional writing about Lincoln during the early decades of the twentieth century was generally in the classic mode of *The Crisis*, but with variations in the portrayal of his character and in the degree of his importance to the story line. For instance, Upton Sinclair introduced Lincoln more or less gratuitously into one of his first novels, *Manassas*, and depicted him as a crude backwoods jokester struggling ineptly, at the outbreak of the war, to act like a national leader.[14] In Thomas Dixon's *The Clansman*, on the other hand, a much loftier Lincoln dominates the early chapters as the "Great Heart" who is determined that the defeated South shall be treated generously. Before his assassination, he pardons the hero, a young Confederate colonel condemned to die as a guerrilla, and he rejects the vindictive reconstruction plans set forth by Austin Stoneman, the radical who controls Congress. This novel celebrating the Ku Klux Klan, which was translated by D. W. Griffith into his great film *Birth of a Nation*, presents the image of Lincoln as a Southerner at heart, especially in his views on race. "I can conceive of no greater calamity," he tells Stoneman, "than the assimilation of the Negro into our social and political life as our equal. A mulatto citizenship would be too dear a price to pay even for emancipation."[15]

Dixon later returned to the same theme in another novel, *The Southerner*, which he subtitled *A Romance of the Real Lincoln*. This effusion of melodrama interlarded with passages of unreliable history is a story of two brothers divided by the Civil War. John Vaughan remains loyal to the Union while his younger brother Ned joins the Confederate army. Both are in love with Betty Winter, the daughter of a fiercely abolitionist senator who is the President's worst political enemy. Betty nevertheless becomes a special friend of the Lincolns and spends a good deal of time at the White House. Ned slips into Washington as a spy. Trying to see Betty, he is captured and condemned to die. Betty summons his mother from the family home in Missouri and together they plead for his life. Lincoln offers a pardon if he will take the oath of loyalty to the United States. Ned replies that he cannot forswear his allegiance to the Confederacy. Lincoln expresses regret and admiration. "You're a brave man, Ned Vaughan," he says, ". . . the kind that makes this Nation great and worth saving whole!" Shortly before the hour set for his execution, Ned, with Betty's help, escapes from prison and returns to his regiment.

Meanwhile, John Vaughan has been serving on McClellan's staff. He idolizes the General and shares his low opinion of Lincoln. The removal of McClellan from command after the battle of Antietam fills John with hatred for the "bungler" in the White House. Just before the battle of Gettysburg, Lincoln offers to support McClellan for the presidency in the coming election if he will guarantee to save the Union. McClellan rejects the proposal. During a fierce engagement later in the war, the two brothers meet in personal combat, not recognizing each other until John has received a sword thrust and responded with a shot from his pistol. The mortally wounded Ned has time for just a few heroic words before he dies. John, now beside himself with grief and anger, is further enraged by the news that his father has been arrested in Missouri for speaking against the war. Once recovered from his wound, he sets out for Washington, determined to assassinate Lincoln, whom he blames for all his troubles and for the continuation of "this carnival of murder." His resolve collapses, however, when Lincoln tells him about the offer to McClellan and how it was received. Remorsefully, he confesses the intent of his visit. The President, instead of having him arrested, rejoices that he has turned a murderer into a friend and immediately sends him off on a dangerous secret mission to Richmond and Atlanta. After more exciting adventures, John returns safely to Washington and Betty's arms. The war comes to an end at last, and Lincoln turns his thoughts to the two great tasks remaining. He must "heal the bitterness of the war and remove the negro race from physical contact with the white." Radical theorists in Congress are demanding that the freed slaves should have the right to vote and intermarry with white persons, but they will be able to pass such measures only "over the dead body of Abraham Lincoln." The book ends with the great crime in Ford's Theatre.[16]

The Southerner, with its fast pace and gaudy plot, is a historical novel that has much of the appeal of a good trashy thriller. Entertainment was ostensibly Dixon's primary purpose, but this one-time Baptist minister also had a strong urge to instruct. His portrait of Lincoln was part of a sustained effort by certain Southern writers to assimilate the Great Emancipator to the social values of the South. Not inappropriately, *The Southerner* appeared in 1913, inaugural year of the first Southern president since Andrew Johnson. Woodrow Wilson, who lent his endorsement to *The Birth of a Nation*, bestowed a major ambassadorship upon Thomas Nelson Page, the Southern writer perhaps most responsible for the legend of the antebellum South as a splendidly feudal society in the Walter Scott tradition. Into his last novel, *The Red Riders*, Page introduced the Lincoln of war's end. The hero, a South Carolina youth, learns of the Booth conspiracy and tries in vain to save the life of the President. Later, in a manner reminiscent of Dixon's *The Clansman*, he helps form the "Red Shirts" to redeem the South from the tyranny of Radical Reconstruction.[17]

Although Dixon's novelized propaganda was particularly blatant and egregious, fictional writing about Lincoln has often carried some sort of message, stated or implied. Frequently, for example, one finds celebration of American democracy as it developed on the frontier. Thus, Irving Bacheller's *A Man for the Ages*, which takes place largely in the raw village of New Salem, is subtitled *A Story of the Builders of Democracy*, and Lincoln is called "the strongest, longest thread" in the democratic fabric.[18] Bruce Lancaster's fine novel *For Us the Living* is essentially about pioneering communities in Indiana and Illinois, with the story enlivened but not significantly altered by the fact that one of the pioneers is the youthful Lincoln, living and talking as one of the common people whom he will one day come to symbolize.[19] Similarly, the protagonist of Harold Sinclair's *American Years* is not Lincoln or any other single character, but rather a whole community—the imaginary town of Everton, Illinois, built by American enterprise from empty prairie to a thriving railroad center in the three decades preceding the Civil War.[20]

Lincoln's six-year residence in New Salem lends itself especially well to literary treatment because it has dramatic unity, because of the pioneering theme, and because that was the time of his maturation and emergence from the restrictive background of the frontier. Still a rather aimless young man at the beginning of those six years, the New Salem Lincoln injected purpose into his life and found in himself a capacity for leadership. He entered upon a double career in law and politics, won election to the state legislature, had a brief turn of military service, and, at the end of the period, moved on to test the more abundant opportunities of Springfield. He may also have had a tragic experience with love and death.

As history, the Ann Rutledge affair remains a possibility at best, neither proved nor disproved by the sketchy and contradictory evidence. Few writers of fiction can resist its appeal, however, and so in literature the legend has a firmer status. Robert E. Sherwood, for instance, exploited the theme fully in his Pulitzer Prize–winning play, *Abe Lincoln in Illinois*, even while acknowledging in his supplementary notes that little is really known about the relationship between Lincoln and Ann.[21] In E. P. Conkle's *Prologue to Glory*, staged at about the same time and rated one of the ten best plays of the year by Burns Mantle, Ann's death is the climax of the drama and a turning point in Lincoln's life. At first devastated and ready to forget all his ambition, he comes around to thinking, "I reckon I ort to try and live th' way *she'd* want me to." He then renews his determination to go to Springfield and become a lawyer.[22]

Although the most elaborate version of the romance was Bernie

Babcock's *The Soul of Ann Rutledge*, the subject also figured prominently in Irving Bacheller's *A Man for the Ages*. Bacheller, like Conkle, pictured Ann's illness and death as having a transforming effect on Lincoln. "I saw Abe when he came out of the tavern that day," says one of the novel's main characters. "He was not the Abe we had all known. He was different. There were new lines in his face. . . . He had passed out of his young manhood. When I spoke to him, he answered with that gentle dignity now so familiar to all who know him. From that hour he was Abraham Lincoln."[23] Sherwood Anderson, in a fictional biography of Lincoln that he never finished, likewise made much of the Ann Rutledge theme. He even embraced the extravagant notion that Ann was the only woman Lincoln ever really loved.[24] But perhaps the most unusual treatment of the legend was that of Harold Winsor Gammans in his play *Spirit of Ann Rutledge*. After an opening act set in New Salem, Ann's spirit shows up at the White House on inauguration day, 1861, and proceeds to give Lincoln guidance throughout his presidency. By the time of the Gettysburg Address, he is a wholehearted convert to spiritualism. "The dead, indeed, are the living," he declares. "It is the spirits of the blessed dead that lead us on and on. Little I know, but Ann has come to me and she has taught me . . . she will direct me till death shall call me." When the call comes at Ford's Theatre in April of 1865, Ann is there, looking "young and fair and shining and clothed as if in living flame from off God's altar," ready, presumably, to claim him for all eternity.[25]

To be sure, not all fiction set in New Salem exploits the Ann Rutledge legend. Ann appears as just a minor character in Bruce Lancaster's *For Us the Living* and in *Steamboat on the River* by Darwin Teilhet. The latter is a pleasantly romanticized version of a real event in New Salem history—the journey in 1832 of the steamboat *Talisman* from Cincinnati to the vicinity of Springfield via the Ohio, Mississippi, Illinois, and Sangamon rivers. For a brief, euphoric interval, the achievement seemed to demonstrate the commercial navigability of the Sangamon, but such hopes soon faded. With a love story, plenty of adventure, and a young hero who is befriended by Lincoln, the Teilhet book fits the classic pattern of historical novels.[26]

In fiction about the mature Lincoln of the 1850's and 1860's, the celebration of democracy, though by no means absent, is subordinated to the problem of nationhood. Plot and characters frequently serve to particularize the conflict of loyalties in the sectional struggle. Both Winston Churchill and Thomas Dixon, as we have seen, relied heavily on the theme of the personal divisiveness of the Civil War. So did Bernie Babcock in *The Soul of Abe Lincoln* and Irving Bacheller in *Father Abraham*. Babcock's heroine is a Mississippi girl in love with a Unionist Virginian and separated from him until the very day of Lincoln's death.[27] Bacheller's hero and heroine are kept apart by her Southern mother throughout the war and find each other just in time to be together at Ford's Theatre on that historic evening in April 1865.[28]

Ben Ames Williams took advantage of the historical doubt about Nancy Hanks Lincoln's legitimacy to offer an interesting variation on the theme of familial division. His gigantic novel *House Divided* follows the tragic fortunes of an upper-class Virginia family through the ordeal of the Civil War. Devoted to the Confederacy, they all hate "that monster in the White House" as the chief cause of their suffering, but there comes a day when one of them discovers conclusive proof that Abraham Lincoln is their father's grandson. The knowledge of this relationship affects members of the family in various ways. Tony Currain rides his horse to death, then turns to the bottle and gaming table for comfort. His brother Faunt, in even wilder rage, sets the old family home aflame room by room, "smashing every movable thing into kindling to feed the waxing fires." But the response of Cinda, their sister, is more complex. She feels angry and ashamed, but also curious and just a little proud. The knowledge causes her to view the war somewhat differently, makes her less certain about the righteousness of the Southern cause. Then, when her youngest son is badly wounded and captured, she goes to Washington hoping to bring him home and has an interview with Lincoln in the process. That experience leaves her more confused than ever; for, as she tells about it afterward, the "strange, sad, tender man" gave her the pass she needed and made her feel "warm" and "safe" in his presence. Yet, with one son dead and two crippled, Cinda continues to feel some of the old hatred. In the midst of final defeat, she rejoices at the news of Lincoln's assassination, but acknowledges that she may not mean it.[29]

Of course, the fictional Lincoln can be found in other literary forms besides the historical novel. There are many Lincoln short stories, for instance. Some have been published separately as little books; others have appeared in various magazines (usually in the month of February). Thus, Ida M. Tarbell, remembered as one of the major Lincoln biographers, also wrote some short pieces in which a fictional Springfield druggist reminisces about his old friend.[30] The distinguished historian and novelist Paul Horgan published two Lincoln stories in the 1950's, one of them about a child befriended, the other about an imploring mother and a military pardon.[31] The well-known man of letters Christopher Morley wrote "Lincoln's Doctor's Dog" as a literary stunt, exploiting the old publishing-house joke that books about pets, medicine, and the Great Emancipator were always successful.[32] In a special category is L. E. Chittenden's *Lincoln and the Sleeping Sentinel*, offered as a true account, but actually an extravagant reworking of the best-known folk story about Lincoln's executive clemency.[33]

A story that Carl Sandburg especially liked was Richard Henry Little's *Better Angels*. Told in Negro dialect by a Southern mammy, it has a familiar plot. The mother and sweetheart of a condemned soldier plead for his life with the help of the old mammy; Lincoln remains adamant until he learns that the girl's name is Ann; then he signs the pardon papers with tears rolling down his cheeks. "An' we goes away an' Ah look back an' see him still a-sittin' in de chair in de moonlight wid his haid in his han's an' he stovepipe hat a-fallen on de groun'."[34]

The most popular of all Lincoln short stories may be one published back in 1906. *The Perfect Tribute*, by Mary Raymond Shipman Andrews, is about the Gettysburg Address and the alleged silence with which it was received by the attending crowd. Lincoln, walking alone in Washington the next day, muses that "it must have been pretty poor stuff." He visits a prison hospital, and there a badly wounded Confederate soldier, without recognizing the man to whom he is speaking, praises the address as "one of the great speeches of history." The reverent silence at its close, he declares, was "the most perfect tribute that has ever been paid by any people to any orator." The young Confederate dies holding the hand of a saddened and yet heartened President.[35] In two other stories by Andrews, Lincoln walks twenty miles to defend a youth charged with murder and, as President, persuades a senator to adopt a boy orphaned by the war.[36]

Honoré Willsie Morrow, who deserves special attention in any study of Lincoln fiction, entered the field with two short stories before undertaking a full-length novel. During the First World War, when she was editor-in-chief of the *Delineator*, Morrow wrote *Benefits Forgot*, a tale of Lincoln's kindness to a mother seeking word of her son in the army. She followed that eight years later with *The Lost Speech of Abraham Lincoln*, a romance about the formation of the Illinois Republican party in 1856.[37] By then she had published a number of novels and was ready to launch a major Lincoln project. Between 1927 and 1931 she published a trilogy about Lincoln in the presidency.

The first book, *Forever Free*, in some respects fits the classic pattern of historical fiction. That is, the main plot and the central character are imaginary—indeed, excessively so. Miss Ford, a tall Virginia beauty who lives in Washington but also owns a plantation with many slaves, worms her way into the White House as Mary Lincoln's social secretary in order to spy for the Confederacy. Before the novel ends, she has corrupted the patriotism of General McClellan and declared her love for the President. She masterminds an attempt to kidnap Lincoln before he can issue the Emancipation Proclamation. She tries to shoot Mary, is imprisoned, escapes and reenters the White House in disguise, but is killed by one of the servants. Yet if all such melodramatic features were removed, there would still be a book to read—a book about family life in the presidency, about cabinet members and congressmen, about the Peninsular campaign and the problem of McClellan and the progress toward emancipation.[38]

Apparently realizing that the sensational aspects of *Forever Free* had detracted from its more serious qualities, Morrow changed her literary strategy. In the two companion volumes, she drew her main plot and principal characters almost entirely from history, confining invention for the most part to dialogue and the occasional rearrangement of events. *With Malice Toward None* is primarily about Lincoln's curiously ambiguous relationship with Charles Sumner and their disagreement over reconstruction policies.[39] A reviewer noted that it did not "quite classify as either history or fiction."[40] *The Last Full Measure* concentrates on the final months of the Civil War, with attention shifting back and forth between the occupants of the White House and the members of Booth's conspiracy. "Except for conversations and thought processes I tried not to step outside of fact," Morrow declared in an afterword. "I used no fictitious characters. I needed to improvise surprisingly few situations. History itself provided the art and the unalterable movement. I believe that the novel gives a picture more accurate in its effect than many of the so-called histories of Lincoln's last days."[41] Thus she subordinated fiction to fact and seemingly elevated historical purpose above literary purpose, while at the same time offering the method of the novelist as an alternative to the method of the historian in the quest for historical truth.

In earlier fiction, Lincoln had sometimes been a major character playing a functional role in the plot, but *With Malice Toward None* and *The Last Full Measure* were the first novels centering upon him as the protagonist and taking their plot lines entirely from history. The two books were therefore markedly different from the old-fashioned historical novel typified by Churchill's *The Crisis*. They belong more appropriately in the category of "fictionized [or "fictionalized"] biography." This term does not refer to fiction set in a context of history or to fiction palmed off as history, but rather to history presented in fictional form and elaborated by fictional devices. A case in point is the joint production of a book titled *Lincoln's Other Mary*. R. Gerald McMurtry, a college teacher and Lincoln specialist, did a thorough job of research on Lincoln's halfhearted courtship of Mary Owens. But then, presumably in order to secure a wider readership, he turned his notes over to Olive Carruthers for working up into a fictional version. Her novel was published in 1946, with a 35-page appendix by McMurtry giving all the relevant historical data.[42]

The "undisputed king" of fictionalized biography in the United States has been Irving Stone, whose subjects include Vincent Van Gogh, Jessie Benton Frémont, Michelangelo, Sigmund Freud, and Charles Darwin.[43] In 1954, Stone published *Love Is Eternal*, a well-crafted, sentimental account of the Lincoln marriage from Mary's point of view. His narrative followed the record of actual events more or less faithfully, but not always critically. For instance, it contained the already discredited story that Lincoln humiliated Mary by failing to show up for their wedding on January 1, 1841.[44] At least half the text is literary invention—especially of dialogue and of Mary's unspoken thoughts. Yet Stone claims that his "biographical novels," as he calls them, are "based 98 percent on documentary evidence."[45] He obviously can mean nothing more than that the invented material is inspired by, and intended to be compatible with, the documentary record.

Stone, in trying to bring historical figures to life by putting words into their mouths, was working much like a dramatist. Correspondingly, most of the plays written about Lincoln for stage, screen, radio, and television have been akin to fictionalized biography—that is, centering on Lincoln himself and dealing with real historical events. Among the most memorable productions have been the plays by John Drinkwater, Robert E. Sherwood, and E. P. Conkle; D. W. Griffith's motion picture starring Walter Huston; Henry Fonda's film portrayal of the young Lincoln; Herbert Mitgang's widely played monodrama; and Hal Holbrook's television presentation of the "Sandburg Lincoln."[46] But what may be the best of all Lincoln dramas is relatively little known. Mark Van Doren's *The Last Days of Lincoln*, though splendid as literature and as history, has never been seen in a major theatrical production.[47]

There is nothing new about mixing fiction and nonfiction in a single literary creation—witness, for instance, Daniel Defoe's *A Journal of the Plague Year*, or, for that matter, the historical plays of Shakespeare. Nevertheless, the fictionalized biographies of Irving Stone may be viewed as part of a modern trend exemplified also in William Styron's *The Confessions of Nat Turner*, Alex Haley's *Roots*, Truman Capote's *In Cold Blood*, and Norman Mailer's *The Armies of the Night*.[48] A common characteristic of all these works is their blending of fact and fiction so skillfully that the very distinction loses some of its meaning and becomes difficult to apply in critical discourse. Such is likewise the case with Gore Vidal's immensely popular excursion into the Lincoln field.

Vidal had combined historical fact with literary invention in a number of earlier books, including *Burr* and *1876*, but his *Lincoln* comes closer to the category of fictionalized biography. Subtitled *A Novel*, it is nevertheless almost entirely about real persons whose depicted words and actions were drawn largely, says Vidal, from the historical record. While using the techniques and exercising the freedom of a novelist, he obviously intended the work to have historical as well as literary merit. For that reason, he submitted it before publication to the scrutiny of a leading Civil War historian, David Herbert Donald.[49]

Owing to such duality of method and purpose, the fictionalized biography as a genre poses a difficult problem for critics with respect to criteria of evaluation. Is historical soundness a matter of central importance, or should a book calling itself a novel be judged simply as a literary creation? Predictably, both the *New York Times Book Review* and the *New York Review of Books* assigned Vidal's *Lincoln* to literary reviewers, neither of whom was an expert on Lincoln and his era. In the *Times*, author and critic Joyce Carol Oates brushed aside the question of historical accuracy. "Surely," she wrote with fetching innocence, "the history cannot be faulted, as it comes with the imprimatur of one of our most eminent Lincoln scholars." Oates saw the book as one in which the author had subordinated the role of novelist to the role of "historian-biographer," thereby producing "not so much an imaginative reconstruction of an era as an intelligent, lucid, and highly informative transcript of it."[50] In the *New York Review*, Harold Bloom of Yale ventured the categorical statement that no biographer and no other novelist "has had the precision of imagination to show us a plausible and human Lincoln." Vidal, he declared "does just that, and more: he gives us the tragedy of American political history, with its most authentic tragic hero at the center."[51]

Here, then, we have literary critics classifying and praising Vidal's *Lincoln* as history, while formal criticism by professional historians has been relatively scarce. One of the principal objections of the latter to any such work is that it tends to confuse readers about what actually happened. For example, Oates speaks of the "shrewd judgment" made by Stephen A. Douglas that Lincoln as a young man "had already fantasized dictatorial powers." She quotes Douglas as reminding Lincoln in 1861 of words that he had uttered in 1838: "You said that the founders of the republic had got all the glory that there was and that those who come after can never be anything except mere holders of office, and that this was not enough to satisfy 'the family of the lion, or the tribe of the eagle.'" What Oates failed to realize was that Vidal invented these remarks of Douglas in order to introduce passages from the most notable speech of Lincoln's younger years. She mistook fiction for historical fact.[52]

The difficulty of separating history from fiction in the book is compounded by a certain amount of factual error and other unreliable information. When Vidal has Lincoln say, "I was in New Orleans once" (instead of twice); when he declares that the Taylor administration offered Lincoln "no government appointment other than the secretaryship of the Oregon territory" (ignoring the governorship of Oregon, also offered); when he has Douglas winning reelection "decisively" (instead of narrowly) in 1858; and when he speaks of Robert E. Lee as "the rebel commander" in June 1861 (a year too early)—in each of these instances, it seems fair to assume that he has simply committed an error.[53] But when he makes Elihu B. Washburne one of Lincoln's frequent companions on the judicial circuit; when he pictures Mary Lincoln as having once been in love with Lyman Trumbull; when he portrays Lincoln as a thoroughgoing racist, "unshaken in his belief that the colored race was inferior to the white," has he likewise fallen into error, or is he engaging in literary invention?[54] Another question to be asked is whether Vidal's prerogatives as a novelist include the right to retail dubious testimony (such as Herndon's maggoty speculation that Lincoln contracted syphilis and infected his family with it), and the right to perpetuate outmoded interpretations (such as the notion that Lincoln in 1858 deliberately adopted a strategy calculated to lose the senatorial contest with Douglas in order to win the presidency two years later).[55]

Although one also finds "much good history" in Vidal's *Lincoln*, as Donald has asserted,[56] the mixing of fact, fiction, and error produced a work seductively unreliable as biography. Still, for all its faults, the book is no doubt the most important novel written about Lincoln to date. For one thing, it concentrates on the few presidential years in which Lincoln played a major historical role. For another, it goes beyond any other work of fiction in dramatizing the political behavior of that inveterately and intensely political man. According to Joseph Blotner, Lincoln has been a dominant influence on the genre of the American political novel, not as a character but rather as the model from which many protagonists have been drawn.[57] Vidal's book is the first political novel of any consequence making Lincoln himself the central figure.

Vidal, despite his general cynicism about American politics, treats Lincoln with more respect than he accorded Jefferson, for example, in his earlier novel *Burr*. He admires Lincoln's political skill but seems puzzled by what lies behind it. He circles Lincoln quizzically, viewing him from different angles, but seldom trying to get inside the man in the same way that he puts himself inside the minds of John Hay, Mary Lincoln, and several other characters.[58] His Lincoln remains something of an enigma throughout the book, and is perhaps all the more believable as a consequence. What Vidal provides most effectively is not an analysis of character but a delineation of leadership—leadership as it was manifested in the relations between Lincoln and the circle of persons most intimately associated with his presidential career.

Authors of fictionalized biography like Vidal and Stone usually strive for historical credibility, keeping the narrative close to what really happened or at least to what might have happened. There is another kind of imaginative writing, however, that deliberately falsifies the past as a way of speculating on what might have been—call it counterhistorical fiction. What if the South had won the Civil War, for instance? Both England's Winston Churchill and the novelist MacKinlay Kantor experimented with fantasies on that subject. In Kantor's novelette, first published by *Look* magazine in 1960, a smashing Confederate victory at Gettysburg and the capture of Washington bring the conflict swiftly to an end. Lincoln resigns from the presidency of the diminished United States and languishes for some months in a Richmond prison. After his release, he returns to Illinois and resumes the practice of law. On April 14, 1865, while attending a theater in Chicago, he is shot to death by an actor still consumed with hatred for the wartime President.[59]

But the speculative question most often asked about Lincoln is: What if he had not been assassinated? How would his continuance in office until 1869 have affected the course of American history and his own place in that history? Many historians have pondered the question, and it has inspired at least two pieces of fiction that portray Lincoln as a failure at the task of reconstruction. In Milton Waldman's "If Booth Had Missed Lincoln," the President is hounded to his death by the triumphant radicals, dying from the effects of a stroke halfway through his second term.[60] The Lincoln in Oscar Lewis's little book *The Lost Years* does manage to complete his term, but as a defeated and unpopular man.[61]

The assassination, as the most sensational event in Lincoln's life, figures prominently in Lincoln fiction from Churchill's *The Crisis* to Vidal's *Lincoln*. Adding to the fascination of the affair is the melodramatic, perversely appealing character of the assassin. Indeed, beginning with a potboiler dashed off in 1865 by the dime novelist Ned Buntline, there has come to be a shelf of fiction centering on John Wilkes Booth and his historic act of murder.[62] Take, for a frothy example, *The Lincoln Diddle*, by Barbara and Dwight Steward. In this offbeat mystery novel, the white-haired protagonist (none other than Edgar Allan Poe, redivivus and incognito) discovers the assassination plot and warns the President. Lincoln knows, however, that he is fatally ill. He therefore contrives to make things easy for Booth, thus virtually committing suicide in the hope that his death will unite the country.[63] Extravagant plotting of this sort is not uncommon in assassination literature. But even the wildest fiction scarcely seems much wilder than some writing on the subject that is offered as historical fact.[64]

Undoubtedly the image of Lincoln in the American consciousness has been shaped in no small part by writers of fiction. (And that, by the way, includes writers of juvenile fiction; for there is a whole library of children's literature about Lincoln—novels, short stories, plays, and fictionalized biographies—that may have affected the image as much as all the adult literature on the subject.)[65] Fictionalizers of Lincoln have tended to stereotype and sentimentalize the man. Too many of them have been prone to accept folklore as history and to follow discredited interpretations. Usually untrained as historians, they often get their facts wrong and, what is worse, their generalizations. For example, in John Jakes's popular novel *North and South*, two characters are talking about the Fort Sumter crisis. One of them asks whether there is any solution to the problem, and the other replies: "Lincoln and some others have proposed one. End slavery but compensate the South for the loss. Compensate the South if it takes every last ounce of gold in the treasury. It isn't ideal, perhaps, or morally clean, but at least it might avoid armed conflict." One has difficulty visualizing the range and depth of misunderstanding that would inspire such a passage attributing such talk to Lincoln or anyone else in the early months of 1861. This is more than just factual inaccuracy; it is a failure of historical grasp.[66]

Thus, whatever may be said of it as literature and entertainment, fictionalized history is likely to be dubious history. Yet if it disseminates error, it also nourishes interest on a broad front. The best fictional portraits of Lincoln, however defective they may be, have a vitality that stimulates remembrance. It may be that what we need most from written history is not accurate knowledge of the past but rather a capacity for incorporating the richness of the past into our own lives. If so, the use of fictional techniques to vivify history may have some place, even in the work of historians. Besides, fiction and nonfiction are arbitrary categories. On the one hand, most fiction is written about the real world; that is why so many first novels are quasi-autobiographies. On the other hand, there is a fictional element in all historical narrative, and even in analytical writing there is a point beyond which inference takes on the quality of fiction. Neither the historical Lincoln nor the fictional Lincoln is the totally "real" Lincoln. Both are constructs of factual materials shaped and cemented with imagination.

CHAPTER 18

The Minor Affair: An Adventure in Forgery and Detection

Ann Rutledge, often called Lincoln's "first love," belongs in that special category of historical figures who have died without any notion of the fame lying ahead. By the early decades of the twentieth century, however, she was about as well known as any woman in American history. Indeed, the tragic romance of young Ann and Abe had become one of the great national legends. Skeptics might point to the flimsiness of the evidence, but the general public accepted the story as historical fact, and so did the leading Lincoln biographers of the day—some, to be sure, with more circumspection than others. Then suddenly out of nowhere in the late 1920's, there appeared a woman named Wilma Frances Minor with a collection of documents that seemed to provide full corroboration of the Lincoln-Rutledge romance. But eventually it proved instead to be the most famous of all Lincoln forgeries. Somehow the legend was never quite the same afterward.

The Minor affair first aroused my interest as a graduate student, and some thirty years later I made it the subject of my R. Gerald McMurtry Lecture, delivered at Fort Wayne, Indiana, in 1979. Source materials available by that time in several institutions were richly supplemented when I was permitted, through the courtesy of Edward A. Weeks, to examine the correspondence files of the *Atlantic Monthly* relating to the affair. The Louis A. Warren Lincoln Library and Museum published the lecture as a pamphlet in 1979, and a slightly shorter version, titled "Lincoln's Lost Love Letters," appeared in the February–March 1981 issue of *American Heritage*. What follows is the pamphlet version, considerably revised and extended.

The 1920's, so well remembered as the age of jazz, flappers, speakeasies, and Coolidge prosperity, were also the heyday of the old-fashioned detective story—meaning the kind of popular fiction in which an amateur sleuth or private investigator solves a puzzling crime (usually a murder) and exposes the guilty person in a dramatic conclusion that fully satisfies the reader only if it takes him by surprise. It was during the 1920's that Sherlock Holmes made his last authentic appearance in print and that Hercule Poirot, Lord Peter Wimsey, Philo Vance, Ellery Queen, and others arrived on the scene to take his place.[1]

One and all, they were heroes notable for their powers of mind. The essential theme of the classic detective story is intellect brought to bear on mystery. Holmes acknowledged having chosen his profession because of a craving for "mental exaltation," and according to Dr. Watson, he was "the most perfect reasoning and observing machine that the world has seen." For Poirot, likewise, detection consisted principally of ratiocination—the exercise of those "little grey cells" inside his egg-shaped head. "The power of the human brain," he told his friend Hastings, "is almost limitless." Lord Peter and Philo Vance virtually parodied each other as dilettante intellectuals, foppish in manner but with minds like steel traps. Vance in particular was not only insufferably erudite but also interminably precise in demonstrating the logic of detection. At one point in *The Greene Murder Case* (1928), he presented ninety-eight statements of fact which, if arranged in the right order, would lead to the name of the murderer. The detective story in such hands was becoming a stylized contest between author and reader, with certain rules of fair play understood. Ellery Queen, in his early novels, made the contest explicit. Just before each denouement, he interrupted his narrative with a formal "challenge to the reader," declaring that all the information needed to solve the mystery had now been provided.

Whether viewed as entertainment or as mental exercise, detective fiction was popular among academics, journalists, and other intellectuals, some of whom made their own contributions to the literature. For instance, the Philo Vance books were written by a professional art critic. The Lord Peter Wimsey novels were the work of a woman who took first-class honors in medieval literature at Oxford and published translations and studies of Dante. When British mystery writers founded the Detection Club in 1928, they elected as its first president the inimitable G. K. Chesterton—poet, critic, novelist, and creator of Father Brown. And the man calling himself Nicholas Blake, who began to publish highly literate detective stories in the next decade, was actually Cecil Day Lewis, one of England's leading poets and subsequently Poet Laureate. As for addicted readers of crime fiction, the long list of well-known names includes Woodrow Wilson, Oliver Wendell Holmes, W. Somerset Maugham, W. H. Auden, and Jacques Barzun.

It is not surprising, then, that even the elegant *Atlantic Monthly*, though unwilling to publish detective fiction, should have taken some notice of its mounting popularity—especially among intellectuals. The *Atlantic* for April 1929 carried an article titled "The Professor and the Detective," in which the author, Marjorie Nicolson of Smith College, argued that scholars and detectives were very much alike. "After all," she wrote, "what essential difference is there between the technique of the detective tracking his quarry . . . and that of the historian tracking his fact, the philosopher his idea, down the ages?" Thus the professor reading a mystery novel was not indulging in escape but rather "carrying over to another medium the fun of the chase, the ardor of the pursuit, which makes his life a long and eager and active quest."[2]

At that very time, as it happened, the *Atlantic* was involved in a real-life mystery of its own—not murder, to be sure, but forgery, which is the scholarly equivalent of murder. The editor and his staff, together with various professional experts, private detectives, and amateur sleuths from New England to California, were all caught up in the excitement of a case that frequently made newspaper headlines. At issue was the authenticity of certain documents recently published by the *Atlantic*—documents that ostensibly confirmed, once and for all, the shadowy, tragic romance between Abraham Lincoln and Ann Rutledge.

According to the full-blown legend, Ann Rutledge was Lincoln's first and only true love, forever closest to his heart. Her death in 1835 filled him with youthful despair verging on madness and drove him into the political career that made him ready, when the time came, to save the American nation. Thus, in the poem by Edgar Lee Masters, she lays claim to a place in history, exclaiming: "Bloom forever, O Republic, / From the dust of my bosom!" In the 1920's, this luxuriantly sentimental story, although it had won public credence and acceptance in some degree by most Lincoln scholars, rested entirely on reminiscences gathered after Lincoln's death by his law partner, William H. Herndon. It had no basis in contemporary records, no documentary existence as a historical event.[3] Such was the status of the Ann Rutledge legend in late June or early July 1928, when the *Atlantic Monthly* received its first letter from Wilma Frances Minor of San Diego, California.

Miss Minor reported that she had just finished writing the "true love story" of Abraham Lincoln and Ann Rutledge, basing it upon their original letters to each other and related manuscript materials, all of which had been handed down in her mother's family. The question was, would such a book be eligible for the nonfiction prize of $5,000 offered biennially by the Atlantic Monthly Press? "Harper's," she confided, "have been very anxious to get it and have sent several long telegrams and were just wonderful, but I know a prize book gets such wide acclaim and the material is worthy of the best."[4]

The letter caused a stir in the sedate *Atlantic* offices on Arlington Street, across from the Boston Public Garden. Edward A. Weeks, then newly in charge of book publication, read it first and headed straight for a conference with the *Atlantic*'s editor and owner, Ellery Sedgwick. Both men were somewhat skeptical but at the same time eager to learn more about the possibly precious documents in Miss Minor's possession. She was immediately informed by telegram that her book would be a welcome entry in the prize contest. Sedgwick himself took over the subsequent correspondence.[5]

Ellery Sedgwick was a short, heavyset man of fifty-six years with strong features and a forceful manner. One of his fellow editors said that he looked like a prosperous merchant but sounded like a professor of English. Descended from old Massachusetts stock, educated at Groton and Harvard, married to a Cabot, he embodied New England's genteel tradition on its cosmopolitan and liberal side. In his twenty years as editor, he had raised the *Atlantic Monthly* to a new level of prestige by making it, more than ever before, a magazine of affairs as well as literature, thereby broadening without diluting its candidly elitist appeal. The *Atlantic*'s principal function was, as he put it, "to inoculate the few who influence the many."[6] Nearly every issue of the magazine somehow reflected Sedgwick's enormous range of interest and his lively curiosity about the human condition in its countless variations. He was, above all, a journalist, with a keen eye for news material and a willingness to take editorial risks. An editor, Sedgwick declared, should have an open mind, always steering closer to credulity than to skepticism. In any encounter with improbability, he should "put on the brakes gently but let the motor run."[7]

Negotiations with Wilma Frances Minor proceeded briskly during the summer and early fall of 1928. She mailed her manuscript of 227 typewritten pages to the *Atlantic*, enclosing photostats of some of the documents. Sedgwick decided that he and his staff must see what kind of person they were dealing with. Miss Minor was accordingly invited to visit Boston as the *Atlantic*'s guest. She happily agreed, telling him that he was "just darling to be so considerate," and adding that her "gifted mother" would make the journey too at her own expense.[8]

It was early September when Miss Minor arrived, accompanied not only by her mother, Mrs. Cora DeBoyer, but also by her half-sister, a twelve-year-old named Clover. They stopped briefly in New York, where a representative of the *Atlantic* met their train, lodged them at the Commodore Hotel, and provided tickets to one of the season's hit plays, "The Front Page." In Boston, where they were put up at the Ritz, the entertainment included a tour of Concord. Edward Weeks remembers that the three of them seemed completely uninterested in literary history but "stowed away a big tea at the Concord Inn." The mother, according to Weeks, was tall and beady-eyed, with hair suspiciously black for her age. She reminded him somehow of a fortune-teller. Wilma, on the other hand, proved to be a handsome woman with a curvaceous figure, seductive gray-green eyes, and an appealingly ingenuous manner. She and Sedgwick took to each other at once. "Isn't it strange," he wrote to her some days later, "that sometimes one feels as though they have known a person a long time, although their hours together may have been very brief?"[9]

Miss Minor's personal charm only heightened the enthusiasm with which Sedgwick contemplated the manuscript treasure that she was offering the *Atlantic*. There were ten letters written by Lincoln, including three to Ann Rutledge and four to John Calhoun, a local Democratic politician who appointed Lincoln deputy surveyor of Sangamon County in 1833. There were four letters from the pen of Ann Rutledge, including two to Lincoln. (Nothing written by Ann had ever previously been discovered.) There were several pages from the diary of Matilda ("Mat") Cameron, Ann's cousin and bosom friend. There was a memorandum about Lincoln written in 1848 by Calhoun's daughter Sally. There were four books bearing Lincoln's signature and annotations. And there were letters verifying the provenance of the collection, which had passed through a number of hands to Wilma's great-uncle, Frederick W. Hirth of Emporia, Kansas, and then to her mother, Mrs. DeBoyer.[10]

The collection, if authentic, did more than confirm the betrothal of Lincoln and Ann Rutledge. It also reinforced the larger legend that she was the primary inspiration of his career. Here is Lincoln writing to Calhoun in 1848, some thirteen years after Ann's death and during the sixth year of his marriage to Mary Todd: "Like a ray of sun-shine and as brief—she flooded my life, and at times like today when I traverse past paths I see this picture before me—fever burning the light from her dear eyes, urging me to *fight* for the right. . . . I have *kept faith*. Sometimes I feel that in Heaven she is pleading for my furtherance."[11]

In conferences extending over several days, it was decided that Miss Minor's story of "Lincoln the Lover" should be remodeled into a three-part series for the *Atlantic*, then expanded into a book. She would receive $500 for each of the articles and an advance of $1,000 on the book, with another $4,000 to be paid on publication. There was also discussion of converting the story into a play and motion picture. These arrangements were contingent, of course, upon proof of the collection's authenticity, and Miss Minor agreed that it must be submitted to appropriate tests. Soon after her return home, she sent all of the original manuscripts to Boston by express. She also informed a delighted Sedgwick that he was to have his choice of one of the Lincoln letters.[12]

The continuing flow of correspondence between San Diego and Boston reveals much of what is known about Wilma Frances Minor. Besides writing frequently to Sedgwick, she exchanged cordial letters with Teresa Fitzpatrick, the short, energetic woman who presided over the *Atlantic*'s circulation department. Miss Fitzpatrick signed herself "Affectionately yours." Wilma addressed her as "Dear little friend" and declared: "I feel I can come to you with problems and joys as I would to a much loved sister."[13]

In what may have been an overstatement aimed at arousing sympathy, Wilma later declared that she had had "a desperately hard and bitter life."[14] Of her earlier history there are but few traces, and she herself was reticent about certain details—refusing, for instance, to give her date of birth, and withholding the fact that she was married until it could no longer be concealed. Born in Los Angeles and sent to a convent school, she had apparently lived in various parts of the country, including Florida and Kansas. She had been an actress in a touring company, and there are indications that she had tried her hand at dress designing and at writing scenarios for motion pictures.[15]

More recently, however, she had become a part-time reporter and columnist for the San Diego *Union*. Her column, "Sidelights on Life," usually appeared in the Sunday women's section and featured a profile of a local writer, artist, or other minor celebrity. Among her subjects in 1928 were Mrs. J. C. Hawkesworth, an eighty-six-year-old painter whose eyes were "round and merry and bright with the light of many dreams"; Der Ling, a visiting Manchu princess; Mrs. Francis M. Hinkle, author of "Wild Ginger," a narrative poem about army life in Honolulu; Elizabeth Beachley, author of *Hip Shot Forest*, a book "so full of fresh air and high zest of living that it plays on jaded senses pleasantly like the muted strings of a violin"; and Belle Willey Gue, author of a drama in blank verse titled *Washington the Statesman*, a work of "exquisite beauty," which in addition had "all the sustained interest of a high class, thrilling novel." It was Ellen Beach Yaw who inspired the highest praise, however. "Against the odds of ill-health, a dependent family, and lacking influence," Wilma wrote, "this dauntless young soul, nevertheless, forged a brilliant career . . . and is today one of the foremost singers on the concert stage."[16]

That was how Wilma Frances Minor also saw herself—as a dauntless young soul struggling against formidable odds to win recognition in her chosen career. Romance suffused her outlook. "I read fairy tales and believed them long past the age of most children," she recalled.[17] But in maturity it was to the American myth of success that she clung most tenaciously. Several years of interviewing successful people and writing about them had sharpened her own hunger for success. All the more keenly, perhaps, because of her desultory, marginal life, she yearned to be somebody important. Wilma's model of a successful woman was the English novelist Marie Corelli, whose melodramatic plots and overblown style made her, for nearly thirty years, a laughingstock among critics and the best-selling writer in the world.[18] According to Wilma, Corelli had addressed her in correspondence as "My dear protégé" and had encouraged her ambition to become known as "the American Corelli." The exchange of letters had presumably taken place shortly before Marie Corelli's death in 1924.[19]

In her Lincoln manuscript, Wilma tried very hard to write like Corelli. For example, this is how she said that it was getting dark: "Night, like a black sinewy panther, crawled cautiously through the unbending straight directness of the saplings on the river bank." And this is her picture of Lincoln leaving New Salem: "Thus he rides with bent head and eyes full of pathetic suffering out of his garden of Gethsemane toward Springfield. . . . Here we will leave him thorn-torn and scarred." For the *Atlantic*, such prose would never do, and so Sedgwick's assistant, Theodore Morrison, in the process of shaping the manuscript into three installments, virtually rewrote it sentence by sentence.[20]

Meanwhile, Sedgwick had taken up the task of verifying the authenticity of the Minor documents. Early in September, he consulted the Reverend William E. Barton, a vigorous, self-important man of sixty-seven years who regarded himself (not without some justification) as the foremost living authority on Lincoln. Although his books tended to be superficial, discursive, and tediously detailed, Barton had few peers as a historical detective. "He is such a blood-hound after the facts," said one reviewer.[21] Visiting Sedgwick's office, Barton looked briefly at the Minor photostats but reserved judgment until he could see the original documents. He left Boston before the originals arrived from California, however, and never did get a chance to inspect them. Barton found the pedigree of the collection "remarkably consistent and satisfactory." But the collection itself, he warned Sedgwick, was suspiciously high in its yield of important historical data and suspiciously pat in its accord with popular tradition. In short, it seemed too good to be true. Sedgwick, however, was already bracing himself against negative evaluations. "I want the material fairly judged," he wrote Barton on September 10. "I think the tendency of 'experts' would be to cast discredit on the possibility of finding important new material."[22]

Sedgwick also showed the photostats to Worthington Chauncey Ford, the peppery seventy-year-old editor of the Massachusetts Historical Society, who had recently prepared Albert J. Beveridge's unfinished biography of Lincoln for posthumous publication. Ford without hesitation pronounced the collection spurious. The letters supposedly written by Lincoln, he said, bore no resemblance to Lincoln's handwriting. Sedgwick's response was to mark Ford down as biased and consult him no more. Thus Ford, like Barton, never saw the original documents.[23]

The originals arrived from Miss Minor in several shipments, beginning on September 21, and they swept away any remaining doubts that Sedgwick may have had. To Barton, who was teaching the autumn semester at Vanderbilt University, he subsequently wrote: "There are so many documents in the complete collection and their source is so varied and their evidence so interlocking that a hoax is not, I think, within the realm of possibility. . . . I am sure we should have your blessing on our venture were you here."[24]

With Barton not available, Sedgwick sought the help of Ida M. Tarbell, the famous muckraking journalist, business historian, and Lincoln biographer. Miss Tarbell, whose writings on Lincoln dated back to the 1890's, entertained a deep affection for the Ann Rutledge legend, although she had toned the story down somewhat in her most recent book.[25] Sedgwick called on her in New York, and they spent at least several hours going over the documents. Immediately afterward he wrote: "She feels not only the same confidence that I do, but is joyful because the contention in which she has always believed seems now proved to the hilt." In a telegram and a letter, both dated October 19, Miss Tarbell expressed reservations on a few specific points but came down firmly on the positive side. "My faith is strong," she declared, "that you have an amazing set of true Lincoln documents—the most extraordinary that have come to us in many, many years."[26] The decisive influence of her endorsement is revealed in the minutes of an *Atlantic* staff meeting held on October 19: "As Miss Tarbell's comments, after the study of the new Lincoln material, were favorable, Mr. Sedgwick feels justified in going ahead with the magazine articles and with the book."

Certain other developments also affected Sedgwick's decision. A well-known commercial chemist, after examining some of the Minor documents, reported that their paper was appropriately of rag content, with no sign of telltale wood pulp, and that the appearance of the ink was consistent with its supposed age. In addition, the *Atlantic* received letters from several persons who had known Frederick Hirth and remembered hearing him mention Lincoln letters in his possession. And Sedgwick's confidence was further reinforced when Herbert Putnam of the Library of Congress expressed a willingness to arrange a public exhibition of the collection.[27]

Still, Sedgwick acted with extraordinary haste in making the decision in favor of publication just four weeks after the original documents began to arrive. During that time, the originals had been shown to only one Lincoln scholar, and only part of the collection had been subjected to chemical analysis. He had not sought the advice of any handwriting experts or manuscript dealers. Furthermore, he was deliberately ignoring the doubts expressed by Barton and the negative verdict so emphatically rendered by Ford.

Why did this veteran editor choose to forgo additional precautions and rush the Minor articles into print? For one thing, his emotional commitment to the project had warped his judgment. But in addition, as a good businessman, he wanted to use the series for promotion of subscription sales during the holiday season. The *Atlantic* accordingly launched an extensive advertising program to announce the forthcoming publication. "At last," it declared, "after nearly a century during which their existence was always suspected and hoped for, appear the priceless documents which lift the veil shrouding the love affair between Abraham Lincoln and young Ann Rutledge. . . . This feature alone, the first printing of these documents, will make an *Atlantic* subscription for the coming year a lifelong keepsake—and incidentally a most appropriate Christmas remembrance."[28]

Meanwhile, Dr. Barton was making a trip to California, and on November 12, by prior arrangement, he met Miss Minor for an hour in the Los Angeles train station. Each found the other charming. Barton welcomed her to the fellowship of Lincoln writers and said nothing about the doubts he had expressed to Sedgwick. He also invited her to visit him at his summer home in Massachusetts. Wilma, in turn, told him how much she had relied upon his books and presented him inscribed photostats of some of her Lincoln letters. A lonely man since the death of his wife three years earlier, Barton scribbled an affectionate note to Wilma soon after boarding the eastbound Sunset Limited. "What a lively little adventure we had," he exclaimed. "It was very pleasant to meet you as the train pulled in this morning and to have an hour's visit and to learn all the interesting news you had to tell me! And you are going to write me ever so many love-letters and I shall inlay them in your book later. And when you are in Boston in the summer you are to call me up at Foxboro, only 25 miles out, and come and sleep under my pines and see my Lincoln material and swim in my little lake. Tell your mother I made love to you and hope to do it again. And write me very soon and often."[29]

In spite of this foolishness, Barton was no fool where Lincoln documents were concerned. It appears that on the trip back to Nashville, he made a careful study of the photostats given him by Miss Minor and concluded that the letters were spurious. Yet in writing to Sedgwick on November 15, he continued to balance his misgivings with a cordial hope that the collection would prove to be authentic.[30]

The latter part of November was a time of golden fulfillment for Wilma Frances Minor. She began to receive speaking invitations. The San Diego branch of the League of American Penwomen elected her to membership and honored her at a meeting. Collectors and dealers began to inquire about sale of the Lincoln documents. They would command a "vast sum" at public auction, said one New York firm. Sedgwick agreed to act as her exclusive agent in such matters, and she told him that he was "perfectly adorable" to do so. Then, on November 26, she received the December *Atlantic* with the first installment of "Lincoln the Lover." The layout was attractive, for the magazine had waived its rule against illustrations and printed facsimiles of several documents. Wilma promptly telegraphed Sedgwick: "Just read the December *Atlantic*. I am thrilled over the splendid arrangement of my material and your fine editorial touch. Your added features make it perfect. A thousand thanks for everything. You are a darling."[31]

The first storm signal came from Worthington Ford. He prepared a press release denouncing the Minor documents and sent a copy to Sedgwick, who offered to publish it in the *Atlantic* as a letter to the editor. Ford refused, wanting to make his views public without delay. "Have you gone insane or have I?" he demanded. "You are putting over one of the crudest forgeries I have known." Sedgwick replied that such impetuous behavior did not become a "sober historian."[32]

Ford's continuing hostility was offset by the recruitment of Carl

Sandburg to the ranks of believers. The Illinois poet, whose *Abraham Lincoln: The Prairie Years* had appeared in 1926, visited Sedgwick's home as a Thanksgiving guest and spent several hours poring over the Minor documents. "These new Lincoln letters," he declared, "seem entirely authentic—and preciously and wonderfully co-ordinate and chime with all else known of Lincoln."[33]

By this time, however, other voices were speaking from Illinois—most notably, Paul M. Angle, secretary of the Lincoln Centennial Association in Springfield, and Oliver R. Barrett, a Chicago attorney who was also the country's leading private collector of Lincoln manuscripts. The twenty-eight-year-old Angle, with much help and guidance from the Centennial Association's president, Logan Hay, had already established himself as an authority in the Lincoln field. He was bright, ambitious, and, as he put it, "keen for a fight."[34] He detested both pretense and pretentiousness. In the words of Earl Schenck Miers, he had a mind that could not "be budged one inch beyond its own scrupulous standards."[35] A year earlier, Angle had published an article casting doubt on the Ann Rutledge legend.[36] Now he became the first critic to say publicly that the Lincoln letters in the *Atlantic* were forgeries. His statement appeared in the *Illinois State Journal* and a few other newspapers on November 27, but its distribution elsewhere was temporarily held up by the Associated Press for fear of a libel suit. Angle also printed his charges in a special bulletin of the Centennial Association and sent a copy to Sedgwick. "It's the biggest thing that ever happened to me," he exulted in a letter to his parents. "One doesn't get a chance very often to put the magazine of the country in the frying pan and cook it brown."[37]

Barrett likewise drafted a statement for the press. The Minor letters, he declared, were not Lincoln's, either in their handwriting or in their composition. Then he added, in what proved to be a remarkably appropriate simile: "Coming as it does, the 'message' from Lincoln produced by the *Atlantic* is very much like the messages drawn from the spirit world by the intervention of 'mediums.'"[38]

Ford's pronouncement, released on November 30, was printed in the New York *Times* on December 2, and the statements of Angle and Barrett appeared the following day. The chorus of criticism had meanwhile been swelled by various scholars, collectors, and handwriting experts—including Georgia L. Osborne, secretary of the Illinois State Historical Society; Louis A. Warren, director of the Lincoln Historical Research Foundation in Fort Wayne, Indiana; and William H. Townsend, an authority on Lincoln's Kentucky background.[39]

The case for forgery rested first of all on the assertion that the handwriting of the two Lincoln letters reproduced in the December *Atlantic* bore no resemblance to authenticated Lincoln letters of the same period. "A novice would have no difficulty distinguishing the difference," said one well-known collector.[40] At the same time, there was a suspicious similarity between the Lincoln letters and the handwriting in a memorandum attributed to Sally Calhoun. Both Warren and Barrett insisted that all three documents had been written by the same person.[41] The Lincoln letters also contained several factual discrepancies, such as locating Mary Lincoln in Washington at a time when she was almost certainly in Kentucky.[42] Furthermore, the punctuation, phrasing, and content of the letters were in many ways uncharacteristic. A New York *Times* editorial some weeks later said that the collection revealed a "slobbering, inflated and illiterate Lincoln."[43]

Sedgwick replied that critics ought to defer final judgment until the entire series had been publicly exhibited. He named Barton, Tarbell, Putnam, and Sandburg as persons who believed the collection to be authentic.[44] Sandburg provided welcome reinforcement on December 4 in an effusive article published under his by-line in the New York *World*. Its headline read: "Lincoln Letters Called Authentic." Their discovery, Sandburg declared, was "a curious and amazing—we might almost say miraculous" event. Hitherto, the betrothal of "young Abe Lincoln and sweet Ann Rutledge" had lacked details.

Now out of the dusk and dust of nearly a hundred years of hiding have come old fading pieces of paper that testify to this beloved lyric and tragic folk tale of the American people. They appear, these evidences, not merely to corroborate the main parts of the folk tale. They carry it farther at all essential points. They give its events new shadings, deeper and more luminous tintings. And it may be said . . . that more than one man has had tears come to his eyes on looking over and scrutinizing closely the strange, sweet tell-tale things that come out of these vestiges. . . . While this is a case where no one can prove the documents to be absolutely authentic any one who tries to impeach them and throw them out of the record will have difficulties and end in disaster. They have come to stay in the Lincoln record.[45]

Just one day later, however, Sandburg was in full retreat, bowing to the superior authority of Barrett and Angle (whom he called "formidable sleuths") and acknowledging that the *Atlantic* documents were probably a hoax. He went on to explain rather lamely: "When I scrutinize original source material of this kind I let my emotions have full play. I try to do my hard-boiled analyzing later." Miss Tarbell too began to retreat, denying somewhat untruthfully that she had ever vouched for the authenticity of the documents. And Herbert Putnam protested that he had never "formed, much less ventured, any opinion whatever in the matter."[46]

For Barton, the situation had become highly embarrassing. He could no longer hope to preserve both his warm relationship with Miss Minor and his reputation as a Lincoln scholar. On December 5, he wrote a note to the *Atlantic* declaring that the Lincoln letters were forgeries, and he said the same thing in an interview with a Boston *Herald* reporter on December 9. "I confess I am not happy," he sighed, "when I think what Miss Minor is likely to say when she learns that I have deserted her." Not until December 11 did Barton work up enough courage for a letter to California, but then he wrote with stern frankness and sent a copy to Sedgwick. "I have come to the conviction," he said, "that the letters which you are sending to the *Atlantic* . . . are not genuine. And, my dear, I am afraid you know it. I could omit this last sentence, but it is right that I should be utterly honest with you. I am very sorry, very sorry."[47]

This communication reached Boston first and caused an uproar in the *Atlantic*'s offices. Sedgwick, in acknowledging it, used the phrase "defamation of character." Miss Fitzpatrick telegraphed Wilma, warning her of what Barton's letter contained and urging her to seek legal advice. Wilma received the "dastardly document" on December 17 and immediately fired off an indignant letter, the first of several in which she demanded a retraction, threatened a lawsuit, and reminded Barton of his calling. His "brutal" letter, she said, was "unworthy a gentleman" and had given her "the greatest shock" of her life. "What sort of Christianity do you follow," she asked, "that makes you use such methods to undermine a sincere and stainless charactered girl?" Did he not remember "the history of the men who once crucified a Man because he presented something they were not familiar with—therefore called it fraudulent?" Eventually, in desperation, she showed her claws to their full length by writing:

And then there is the very amorous effusion that you dashed off to me after our meeting. I think you will remember it as the one you wrote on the train. I am strongly advised to give it to the Associated Press, and if you persist in this public tirade that is utterly lacking in real foundation, I must in turn be forced to humiliate you by broadcasting that letter, and if your mind serves you well you will remember that each passage when viewed by a coldly critical, dispassionate world will brand the Reverend Barton as a silly old sheik.

Barton refused to be intimidated, however, and Wilma made no move to carry out either of her threats.[48]

By mid-December it was plain that Sedgwick had no support whatever among Lincoln scholars and other experts. Yet he clung stubbornly to his faith in the authenticity of the Minor documents. "We must remember," he wrote bravely to Wilma, "that the greater the excitement now, the greater will be the triumph of the book if we can compel the acquiescence of leading critics." Wilma echoed his determination in her own peculiar literary style. "Let us gird our armor and fight our way through to victory," she replied.[49] Sandburg's defection especially incensed her. "A man cannot," she wrote, "come out and make a statement during his period of honest convictions, and then, from some pressure brought to bear, change his forceful statements to *fall in line* as a sheep to its Bell Weather [*sic*]."[50]

On about December 10, proof sheets of the second installment of "Lincoln the Lover" came off the press, and a set of them, obtained from Sandburg, circulated quietly among Barrett, Angle, and Ford. At Angle's suggestion, the three men prepared a joint statement for release as soon as the January issue appeared. The Boston *Herald* and the New York *Times* printed it on December 23.[51]

The second installment, titled "The Courtship," was richly documented. It contained one or more letters from Lincoln to Ann Rutledge, from Ann to Lincoln, from Ann to her cousin Mat Cameron, and from Lincoln to John Calhoun, together with excerpts from Mat's diary and passages from the memorandum of Sally Calhoun. When the three sharpshooters opened fire, these documents proved to be pitifully vulnerable. The Cameron family Bible indicated that Matilda (Mat) Cameron never existed. The same was probably true of Sally Calhoun. Mat's diary, supposedly written in the early 1830's, mentioned Martha Calhoun, who was not born until 1843. Mat wrote twice of the "boat from Springfield" as though speaking of a regular service, but the Sangamon was only rarely navigable by boats of any considerable size, and besides, Springfield was six miles from the river. Ann at one point mentioned Spencer's copybook, which did not appear in print until thirteen years after her death. Lincoln, writing to John Calhoun at a time when both men were publicly employed as surveyors, referred to a controversy over "Section 40," but in the land survey system, sections were numbered no higher than 36. And, in the same letter, Lincoln spoke of a family as leaving "for some place in Kansas"—this at a time when the region was not called Kansas and was not yet open to white settlement.[52]

It was a devastating attack, and Sedgwick may have been tempted to follow the advice given him earlier in the month by the Librarian of Brown University: "Better eat your peck of dirt now before it becomes a bushel."[53] Instead, he publicly reaffirmed his confidence in the Minor collection, insisting that "noted experts" had studied the material and pronounced it authentic. But at the same time, his letters to California sounded weary and discouraged. "Our own efforts seem to have come up against a stone wall," he admitted. "It is useless to disguise the fact that we are confronting very serious evidence."[54] Wilma responded by continuing to play the undaunted heroine. "Situation gives no cause for alarm," she telegraphed on December 26, and, in a letter the next day, she declared: "The objectionists die hard, they are now jumping at and clinging to, flimsy straws, but the more they bark the more optimistic I become." On January 2, she issued a lengthy defense which appeared in a number of newspapers across the country. Most of it, however, was an elaboration of the history of the collection. She said little in direct response to the Angle-Barrett-Ford attack.[55]

Early in January, an exhausted Sedgwick set out for Arizona to get a little rest and spend some time with his invalid son. He did not intend to visit Miss Minor in San Diego, but a rush of events soon altered his plans. Certain members of the *Atlantic* staff were already beginning to take matters into their own hands. Nelson J. Peabody, the magazine's business manager, quietly hired the J. B. Armstrong Detective Agency in Los Angeles to investigate Wilma Frances Minor. And Teresa Fitzpatrick arranged for an examination of the Minor collection by William E. Hingston, a well-known handwriting expert, who reported back that the documents were forgeries.[56]

Before receiving the Hingston report, Miss Fitzpatrick had telegraphed Wilma, urging her to announce initiation of a lawsuit against Barton. The handwritten reply, dated January 2, 1929, came from Cora DeBoyer, who said that her daughter's health could not stand such an ordeal. "She is a very high strung and super-sensitive girl who does not seem to understand how to cope with the rebuffs of this crass world," Mrs. DeBoyer explained. "I think it best that we do not complicate things for her by an added burden." But the members of the *Atlantic* staff were less interested in the content of the letter than in its script. There, they agreed in an exciting moment of revelation, was the hand that had forged the Minor collection! Telephoning Peabody, then in Chicago on magazine business, they found that he had reached the same conclusion from information supplied by the detective agency.[57]

Meanwhile, Angle and Hay were conducting their own investigation, having enlisted the help of an army captain in Kansas and one of Hay's former law partners in California. Information dug up by the captain about Wilma and her mother as onetime residents of Emporia led Angle and Hay to believe that one or the other of the women had fabricated the documents.[58] They came to that conclusion at about the same time that the *Atlantic* staff was reading Mrs. DeBoyer's letter and fixing upon her as the forger.

At this point, Angle took an important step. Through an intermediary, he suggested that the *Atlantic* and its chief critics work together toward a solution. Sedgwick, consulted by telegram, gladly agreed. Peabody accordingly conferred with Angle in Springfield and then headed west to join Sedgwick in a showdown with Wilma and her mother.[59] By this time, a good deal of information about the two women had been gathered, and it did not inspire confidence in their reliability. Both had given false information on wedding licenses, for instance. Wilma was actually in her early forties, some ten years older than she pretended to be. She had been married twice and seemed unsure of the name of her father. Cora DeBoyer, according to the detective reports, had had at least five marriages and some interim cohabitation besides. In Emporia, Kansas, Cora's home town, both she and her daughter were remembered as a little too bold and pleasure-loving to be entirely respectable. One person who knew them well said that Cora was a very clever woman, much more capable than Wilma of planning and executing such a forgery.[60]

The confrontation took place at a hotel in Los Angeles on the weekend of January 19–20. Sedgwick revealed to Wilma and her mother what had been learned about their background and then accused Mrs. DeBoyer of fabricating the collection. The two women, though frightened by the investigation of their past, emphatically denied his charge and could not be coaxed or driven into a confession. At last it was agreed to issue a joint statement withdrawing the Minor series from further publication—that is, canceling plans to expand the articles into a book. Sedgwick for the first time acknowledged publicly that the documents lacked authenticity. He promised to continue his search for the truth and make a "full presentation" at the "earliest possible moment."[61]

The ordeal, according to both Wilma and her ex-husband, left Mrs. DeBoyer a "physical wreck," whose death, if it occurred, would be Sedgwick's responsibility.[62] The person Wilma had come to fear most, however, was not Sedgwick but Angle, and with characteristic impetuosity she tried to neutralize him. Before returning home to San Diego from the Los Angeles showdown, she sent off a wire, saying: "Your sincere investigation has caused me to withdraw Lincoln documents. I submitted them in good faith and hope you will continue research from originals which I shall submit to you." She followed that with a long letter urging Angle to visit her so that they could discuss the collection at length. "You will find in me," she wrote, "a person not actuated by any petty motives and with no ideas about big money. I have gold fish, a flower garden, a dear husband whose health is bad & who is my constant care, and a mother, God bless her, who is simply prosterated [*sic*] over this argument . . . I fear she will not recover."[63] Surprised and puzzled by these communications, Angle concluded that they had been arranged by Sedgwick in order to placate him and prevent a rupture of their newly formed alliance.[64]

Traveling by train back to Boston, Sedgwick stopped off in Chicago for a conference with Barrett and Angle. By then, the final installment of "Lincoln the Lover" was out in the February *Atlantic*. If Angle, Barrett, and Ford had not agreed to refrain from public comment on it,[65] they could have pointed to further indications of literary fraud. For instance, it was now quite obvious that some of the documentary material had been drawn from Barton's life of Lincoln, published in 1925, and the derivation became especially apparent in one sentence of Mat Cameron's diary that read: "Father opines he ruther go to Fulton Co Iway sted of Missouri—as lokatin land is ezier ther." Here the forger had made a bad slip; for Iowa, unlike Illinois, never had a Fulton County. The mistake apparently came from misreading a footnote in Barton, namely: "After the failure of New Salem, Cameron and his family moved to Fulton County, Illinois, and thence to Iowa."[66]

Along with this last, virtually repudiated installment in the February issue, there appeared something more incendiary. Sarcastically presented in the Contributors' Column was the jubilant letter from Angle to his parents—the one in which he had spoken of putting the magazine into a frying pan and cooking it brown. The letter had been brought to Sedgwick's attention after it appeared in a local newspaper, and the decision to print it had been made several weeks before Angle and the *Atlantic* staff reached their agreement to work together. Publication of the letter, which gave the impression that he was interested primarily in self-advertisement, embarrassed Angle so much that he submitted his resignation as secretary of the Lincoln Centennial Association. To his relief, it was not accepted.[67]

The atmosphere was consequently less than cordial when Sedgwick met Angle, Barrett, and several other Illinoisans at the Union League Club in Chicago on January 26. He had arrived bearing the original documents and still more than half disposed to defend them as genuine, but after a full day of discussion he accepted defeat. Then, as Angle tells it,

> The upshot of the whole matter was that Sedgwick (prompted, I suspect, by Barrett) asked me to write a refutation of the whole series for publication in the Atlantic as soon as possible. I answered that I was afraid it would be extremely embarrassing to the Atlantic to print an article over my signature, since in the columns of that magazine I did not bear a very handsome reputation. (That may have been unwise, but I couldn't resist the temptation.) He came back with an apology, I made one too, and we agreed to dismiss the incident. So I'm to write the criticism.[68]

In thirteen days of hard work, Angle finished an article that effectively summarized the evidence against the authenticity of the Minor collection. Appearing in the April issue (along with Marjorie Nicolson's essay on scholarship and detection), it remained the last authoritative word on the subject for nearly half a century and came to be regarded as a classic exercise in historical method. But Angle, while emphatically labeling the collection spurious, was vague and cautious in the one paragraph that he devoted to the question of "who fabricated it?" He spoke only of what the documents revealed about the "sort of person the forger was" and ventured no hint of the strong suspicion that Wilma and her mother were the culprits. Legal considerations no doubt encouraged such reticence.[69]

In the meantime, a reproachful Miss Minor had been bombarding the *Atlantic* with demands for the return of her original documents. "Telegram after telegram and letter after letter . . . fail to get a definite reply as to the why and wherefore of withholding my personal property from me," she wrote. The documents, however, were now regarded as legal evidence of fraud, and Sedgwick refused to comply.[70] In California, the investigations of the Armstrong Detective Agency continued, with Armstrong himself working to the point of exhaustion on the case.[71] Then, in April, another piece of the puzzle fell into place.

The new information came from James B. A. Ashe, head of a publishing company in San Diego. Early in 1928, he declared, Miss Minor had come into his office a number of times, usually to arrange interviews with his authors. She never mentioned an interest in Lincoln until she interviewed Scott Greene, a son of one of Lincoln's New Salem friends, who was spending the winter in San Diego. Then she reported in great excitement that Greene had letters of Lincoln and Ann Rutledge in his possession, and that she hoped to buy them from him. Later, after several more visits with Greene, she told Ashe that she had gotten all she wanted from the old man. It was Ashe who first suggested that her manuscript be submitted to the *Atlantic*. Assuming all along that she had obtained the documents from Greene, he was astonished to read the story of how they had been handed down in her own family.[72]

On the same day that Ashe first communicated with the *Atlantic* about his suspicions, the Harvard *Crimson* published a long article purporting to show by handwriting analysis that all the documents reproduced in the Minor series were the work of Wilma Frances Minor herself.[73] Peabody decided that the time had come for another confrontation and ordered Armstrong to San Diego. On April 3, accordingly, the detective interviewed Wilma and her mother in his hotel suite, with two agents listening from the adjoining room by means of a dictagraph. After he summarized the imposing evidence against the Lincoln documents, the two women acknowledged that they had somehow been "deceived" but denied any complicity in the forgery. Upon the advice of an attorney hastily brought in by Cora DeBoyer's husband, the women also refused to sign the legal release that Armstrong laid before them. This time, Mrs. DeBoyer proved to be hardier than her daughter. "The old woman is the hard nut of the two," Armstrong reported. "She is a hard boiled old hen, who does not know what the word truth means. The other one was very badly disrupted and plainly showed the ordeal she had been through." Indeed, at one point in the interview, Wilma seemed "about ready to pass out."[74]

By this time, two somewhat different strategies had taken shape in the *Atlantic* offices on Arlington Street. Peabody and the company's lawyers were interested primarily in getting legal releases, recovering the $1,000 advance, and closing the entire affair as quickly as possible. Members of the editorial staff, on the other hand, wanted to learn the whole truth about the forgery and report it to the magazine's readers, just as Sedgwick had promised. In pursuit of the truth, Weeks traveled to Springfield, Illinois, for a visit with Scott Greene at the end of April. What he learned there strengthened the suspicion, first awakened by James Ashe, that the forgeries had been inspired by Miss Minor's interview with Greene in February 1928.[75]

The assembled evidence now seemed overwhelming, and it added up, not only to a solution of the mystery, but also to a story with a lively plot and some interesting characters, eminently suitable for publication in the *Atlantic*. The writing of the story was assigned to Sedgwick's young assistant, Theodore Morrison, who would later distinguish himself as a novelist and a professor of English at Harvard. During May he turned out an article of twenty-two typewritten pages—offered, as he put it, so that the *Atlantic*'s readers could "share in the fascination of the chase." Morrison opened his account with a flat accusation: "On a day not far from February 12, 1928, two women in San Diego, California, began to prepare an elaborate series of books, diaries, and letters. . . ." He closed with the suggestion that it was time "to season Miss Minor's passage across the footlights with laughter." The article never appeared in print, however. On May 27, Sedgwick announced to a staff meeting that the *Atlantic*'s lawyers had decided against any further publication on the subject.[76]

About a month later, Teresa Fitzpatrick traveled to California and succeeded where both Sedgwick and Armstrong had failed. That is, she persuaded Wilma to make and sign a statement that amounted to a weird confession. Dated July 3, 1929, it read in part:

> I went to see Scott Greene and got his story and went home to Mama and said to her, Mama at last our faith of a lifetime has led to something. It has been given us for a divine purpose. On another plane those people (Lincoln and Ann and those other people) must exist. We have talked to many others, our family and close friends, and I said to Mama, Don't you think I have earned the right to be the channel to tell that real story to the world? Mama said, I don't know darling, we can try. Mama had always been the medium through whom the spirits had spoken. . . .
>
> On the next opportunity a few days later I asked through my Mother, who at that time was in a trance, the guide—I believe it was my uncle who came, if I might have the divine privilege of being the instrument through whom the real story might come to the world. He answered he would find out and let me know the next week. The next week when Mother came again she went into her trance and the guide said he had asked the people (Lincoln, Ann, etc.) and they said they would give the story to me, provided I was willing to tie myself down to months and months of systematic labor. I agreed. I then began to prepare a series of questions. I would write out the questions. I would hand them to my Mother then in the trance; the spirit would come, whoever it might be, and fill out the answers. For instance, I would ask the ages of the two when Ann and Abe first met, and in the blank left under the question which was typewritten on a large sheet, the guide would answer through my Mother. . . .
>
> Every word in Matilda Cameron's Diary is verbatim as given by the guide. Every word written through my Mother as the medium. All this continued for a long period, but we had to stop for three or four weeks as my Mother was threatened with blindness. By this time I went to her home frequently. She would phone me that a "message come through last night," and I would go to see her, and she would give me the message she had received in her handwriting. . . .
>
> I asked where I would get the paper to write this on, the guide answered (oftentimes it would be Marie Corelli) that I could get it from old books and gave me a list of books that Lincoln used at that period of his life. I went to old bookshops and had no difficulty in picking them up. Then the guide told me for my continuity that I must look up written books for well known facts which were available to everyone. . . . Mr. Ashe told me about

> the Atlantic Contest and although I had offered it to Harpers, I wrote to the Atlantic offering it as original Lincoln letters. I would die on the gallows that the spirits of Ann and Abe were speaking through my Mother to me, so that my gifts as a writer combined with her gifts as a medium could hand in something worthwhile to the world.[77]

Thus from supernatural sources Wilma had received the text of her documents, together with instruction in how to go about fabricating them. And thus Oliver Barrett had proved to be amazingly accurate in his remark that the Minor letters were "like messages drawn from the spirit world by the intervention of 'mediums.'"

Even with this document in his possession, Sedgwick made no move to publicize what the *Atlantic* had learned about the forgery. He was advised and pestered to do so, especially by William E. Barton, who lectured him repeatedly on his duties as an editor. "Why not tell the truth," Barton urged, "and if it brings you a libel suit, accept it as under the circumstances perhaps no more than you deserve, and something you owe to the public."[78] But Sedgwick stubbornly maintained his silence, motivated not only by legal considerations but also by weariness and mortification. He wanted to hear no more about Wilma Frances Minor and her Lincoln collection. After Angle's critique, the *Atlantic* never printed another word on the subject. Wilma herself disappeared quietly from public view. Sedgwick, when he came to write his autobiography titled *The Happy Profession* (1946), discussed Lincoln at some length but said nothing about the Minor affair. A few years later, Teresa Fitzpatrick arranged to tell the story in the *Saturday Review of Literature*, but she gave up the project at the request of Edward Weeks, who had succeeded Sedgwick as editor of the *Atlantic*. "I am not sensitive about the subject, but others are," Weeks said, "and for the time being it is probably the right and friendly thing for us both to draw the curtain."[79]

The curtain remained drawn until long after Sedgwick's death in 1960 at the age of eighty-eight. At last, in 1973, Weeks published an autobiography of his early career, and he included an account of the Minor affair, together with the full text of Wilma's confession.[80] Of course that confession provided only a partial solution of the mystery. It left unanswered certain questions that are now probably forever unanswerable, such as who did the actual forging and how many persons were involved in the plot.

As for the Ann Rutledge legend, it has declined in credibility since the 1920's.[81] A recent biography of Lincoln suggests that there was nothing more than a "platonic" friendship between young Abe and Ann.[82] It is unlikely that we shall ever know for sure. Yet perhaps somewhere in a battered trunk pushed into the darkest recesses of an old attic there are documents—authentic documents—waiting to tell us the whole truth. And perhaps on the day they are discovered we shall receive a wistful message from Wilma Frances Minor, using Ellery Sedgwick as her guide.

CHAPTER 19

The Words of Lincoln

Most of Lincoln's prose is "strictly functional," I wrote many years ago. "To read it is to see him in action, pursuing practical results, rather than ultimate truth."[1] Some of his words nevertheless seem destined to survive even longer than the memory of his specific role in American history. Precisely what Lincoln did say, however, and what he meant by what he said, is in many instances still a matter of dispute. The following essay on the problems of text and context is a revised version of a paper presented at a Brown University symposium on Lincoln in June 1984 and published in John L. Thomas, ed., *Abraham Lincoln and the American Political Tradition* (Amherst, Mass., 1986).

'Tis a kind of good deed to say well; and yet words are no deeds." So declares Shakespeare's Henry VIII to Cardinal Wolsey. The same distinction is made in several old adages. "Deeds are fruits, words are but leaves," says one. "Words are but the shadows of actions," says another. Yet the difference between word and deed has become increasingly blurred in the modern age when so many combinations of words (such as "You're under arrest") constitute acts, and so many physical acts (such as certain kinds of terrorism) are essentially statements. Among modern public leaders especially, important action is nearly always verbal. In the words of a Jefferson, a Napoleon, or a Churchill one finds not only the record but the substance of his principal deeds, as well as the clearest traces of his character.

To study Abraham Lincoln, then, we must examine his words, and not only the words that he wrote but also those that he uttered, insofar as they are known. There, of course, one encounters difficulty; for spoken words in the days before the phonograph were literally breaths instantly dissolved in the air. Though sometimes captured by note taking when the occasion called for it, they were more often reconstituted through memory—memory exercised over lengths of time varying from a few hours to half a century. Historical sources of this kind have a curiously mixed status; for they are not regarded as canonical but are nevertheless used extensively by biographers. More specifically, utterances of Lincoln not written out in his own hand or recorded in contemporary newspaper reports are generally excluded from the *Collected Works*.[2] Yet much of our impression of the man's character and style is based upon spoken words attributed to him in diaries, contemporary letters, and reminiscent writings.

Take, for instance, the countless putative examples of Lincoln's wit and humor that have appeared in print. They derive almost entirely from oral tradition and are therefore almost entirely uncanonical. Paul M. Zall, in his book *Abe Lincoln Laughing*, presents 325 items carefully selected from a much larger mass of material, including representative apocrypha, together with the stories that Lincoln "most likely told."[3] Of the 325, only 16 (about 5 percent) appear also in the *Collected Works*, and only 3 (less than 1 percent) exist in Lincoln's own handwriting.

But let us pursue this subject into the mainstream of Lincoln literature as represented by Stephen B. Oates's prime biography, *With Malice Toward None*. Choosing at random the chapter on the five-month period between the election of 1860 and the firing on Fort Sumter, I counted some forty Lincoln quotations, ranging in length from several words to a dozen lines.[4] Three-quarters of them are spoken words, either taken down at the time or recollected later. Fewer than half of the forty items are drawn from the *Collected Works*. They include a series of excerpts from letters written to various Republican leaders enjoining them to resist compromise, and also a long string of quotations from the speeches Lincoln made on his journey to Washington.

The chapter is titled "My Troubles Have Just Begun," and it opens with the following sentence: "'Well, boys,' he told newsmen the day after his election, 'your troubles are over now, mine have just begun.'" Oates cites as his source Charles M. Segal's book *Conversations with Lincoln*, where the quotation reads: "Well, boys, your troubles are over now, *but* mine have just begun."[5] Segal, in turn, cites an article by Samuel R. Weed, a St. Louis newspaperman. Written in 1882 ("apparently," Segal tells us, "from detailed notes made at the time"), the article remained unpublished until the New York *Times* printed it in 1932. The *Times* version of the quotation runs: "Well, boys, your troubles are over now, but mine have just *commenced*." Nothing whatever is said about the article's having been based on notes taken in 1860, and we are left wondering where Segal got the notion that it was.[6] The purpose here is not to demonstrate that Oates should have titled his chapter "My Troubles Have Just Commenced." It is rather to suggest that if both Oates and Segal could modify a twelve-word quotation in the process of copying it from text, we may with good reason suspect much greater slippage between what Lincoln allegedly said in 1860 and what Weed allegedly remembered in 1882. Even if one assumes the honesty of this unknown man and overlooks the lack of corroborating evidence that he ever spent any time in Lincoln's company, there remains the problem of what Daniel Aaron calls "the treachery of recollection."[7] The Weed article is, in short, dubious source material, especially as a source of direct quotation.

The chapter contains several other direct quotations of Lincoln taken from recollective writings,[8] including one about a curious mystical experience. Some weeks after his election to the presidency, Oates tells us, Lincoln lay down to rest on a sofa in his chamber.

> He glanced across the room at a looking glass on the bureau and saw himself reflected at almost full length. But his face had two separate and distinct images. Startled, he got up and approached the glass, but the illusion vanished. He lay back down, and the double image reappeared, clearer than before. Now one face was flushed with life, the other deathly pale. A chill passed through him. Later he told Mary about it and she became very upset. She interpreted the vision to mean that he would live through his first administration, but would die in his second. Lincoln tried to put it out of his mind, but "the thing would come up once in a while and give me a little pang, as though something uncomfortable had happened."[9]

Oates cites two authorities for this passage, *Washington in Lincoln's Time* (1895) by Noah Brooks and the *Recollections of Abraham Lincoln* (1911) by Ward Hill Lamon. It is the Brooks memoir upon which Oates principally relies and from which he extracts the direct quotation attributed to Lincoln. Brooks, in fact, published much the same account in *Harper's Monthly* for July 1865, just eight months or so after the incident had been related to him, he said, by Lincoln. Lamon's contribution lends support to the Brooks version while differing from it in certain details, but the independence of his testimony is open to question. However, the main features of the story are also corroborated by the artist Francis Carpenter in his book *Six Months in the White House*, published in 1866. Carpenter mentions the recent Brooks article in a footnote and states that he did not read it until after his own account was written. That, if true, makes them independent witnesses to Lincoln's narration of the incident. Taking them all together, the effect of the Brooks, Lamon, and Carpenter recollections is partly corroboration and partly contradiction.[10]

According to Brooks, Lincoln talked about the double-image incident at the time of his reelection in 1864, saying that it had occurred at the time of his election in 1860. According to Carpenter, Lincoln talked about the incident at the time of his renomination in 1864, saying that it had occurred at the time of his nomination in 1860. According to Lamon, who splits the difference between the other two, Lincoln spoke of the incident at the time of his renomination in 1864, saying that it had occurred at the time of his election in 1860. It is Brooks alone who credits Mrs. Lincoln with the prophetic interpretation of the experience as signifying that her husband would not survive his second presidential term. Lamon asserts that Lincoln himself conceived the idea. Carpenter declares that Lincoln, in telling him the story, attached no such gloomy significance to it. As for the quotation that Oates draws from the Brooks memoir ("the thing would come up once in a while and give me a little pang, as though something uncomfortable had happened"),[11] it is more or less contradicted by Carpenter, who quotes Lincoln as saying that the phenomenon ceased to trouble him after he decided that it was the result of some natural principle of refraction or optics. Furthermore, the passage in question is part of a 300-word paragraph that Brooks ventured to enclose in quotation marks, while claiming only that he was giving Lincoln's "own words, as nearly as they could then be recalled" eight months after he had heard them. Thus the phrasing of the quotation is probably a Lincoln-Brooks mixture at best.

It would be difficult to find a better illustration of how recollective writings can be at once valuable and dubious as primary historical sources. Here, the direct quotation in question is suspect; the dates are confused; Lincoln's feelings about his curious illusion are in doubt; and Mary Lincoln's spooky prescience is not easy to swallow. Nevertheless, we are left with strong evidence that Lincoln did see the double image in 1860, that the incident made a considerable impression on his mind, that he spoke of it perhaps more than once in 1864, and that at least some part of the substance of his account can be summarized with some confidence. This information, though not given the canonical seal of inclusion in the *Collected Works*, is nevertheless an item likely to be useful in the study of Lincoln's intellectual and emotional life.

Further on in the chapter, Oates describes a meeting on April 4, 1861, between Lincoln and John B. Baldwin, a Virginia Unionist. Lincoln wanted the Virginia state convention, then sitting, to adjourn. "But Baldwin," Oates tells us, "insisted that Lincoln must pull out of Sumter first, warning that if he didn't and if a shot were fired, then . . . Virginia would secede in forty-eight hours." Lincoln remained firm, however. "'Sir,' he said of Baldwin's demand, 'that is impossible.'"[12] Oates's authority for this account is the record of Baldwin's testimony before the Joint Committee on Reconstruction in 1866.[13] But when one reads the entire passage, it becomes apparent that Lincoln's alleged response, "Sir, that is impossible," was allegedly addressed, not to the demand for evacuation of Fort Sumter, as Oates asserts, but rather to Baldwin's warning that otherwise Virginia would secede. In other words, Baldwin in 1866 was portraying the Lincoln of 1861 as a man who stubbornly and obtusely refused to believe that hostilities at Sumter would drive Virginia out of the Union. As a historical source, this testimony has all the weaknesses of other recollective material, and it also inspires doubt because it was so patently self-serving.

There are also quotations in the Oates chapter drawn from the diary of Orville H. Browning, from a contemporary memorandum of John G. Nicolay, and from a contemporary political letter to Simon Cameron.[14] This kind of recollective material inspires considerable confidence because such a short time elapsed between the event and the recording of it. Of course the value of such evidence still depends upon the competence, objectivity, and plain honesty of the witness. And sometimes there can be confusion about whose words, precisely, are being reproduced. For example, Oates quotes Lincoln as saying to Browning in February 1861 that only "the surrender of everything worth preserving" would satisfy the South. But what Browning recorded in his diary was this: "He agreed with me no concession by the free States short of a surrender of every thing worth preserving, and contending for would satisfy the South." Thus the words and the thought actually came from Browning, and Lincoln merely acquiesced in them.[15]

Likewise relatively credible are those quotations in the chapter that come from contemporary newspaper articles written by reporters after talking with Lincoln.[16] For the lapse of time between hearing and recording was brief, and in each instance there is the possibility that notes were taken on the spot. Indeed, contemporary newspaper sources have been considered reliable enough for inclusion in the *Collected Works*, although such inclusion has generally been limited to reports of public speeches.

Oates was on the solidest ground, of course, in the numerous quotations he drew from the *Collected Works*. Yet even within those canonical covers there are different levels of credibility—newspaper summaries of speeches, for instance, not having the same status as autograph letters signed. Although the ten volumes of the *Collected Works* constitute a splendid editorial achievement, they do contain a few questionable patches. One conspicuous example is the letter that Lincoln supposedly wrote to General James S. Wadsworth early in 1864. This document has come to be regarded as at least partly spurious; for its provenance is unsatisfactory, and it does not ring true with respect to Lincoln's attitude toward racial equality at that date.[17] In contrast, there is a much fainter breath of doubt associated with the famous letter of condolence to Mrs. Lydia Bixby. Since the original letter was lost, and its words survived only as they were printed in a Boston newspaper, there is no way of verifying or disproving some dubious gossip that attributes the authorship to John Hay. Nevertheless, there seems to be general agreement among scholars in the field that the words of the Bixby letter are characteristically and peculiarly Lincoln's.[18]

For one other interesting example of a questionable patch in the *Collected Works*, let us examine a portion of Lincoln's famous House Divided speech:

> [Para. 1] Either the *opponents* of slavery, will arrest the further spread of it, and place it where the public mind shall rest in the belief that it is in

course of ultimate extinction; or its *advocates* will push it forward, till it shall become alike lawful in *all* the States, *old* as well as *new—North* as well as *South*.

[Para. 2] Have we no *tendency* to the latter condition?

[Para. 3] Let any one who doubts, carefully contemplate that now almost complete legal combination—piece of *machinery* so to speak—compounded of the Nebraska doctrine, and the Dred Scott decision. Let him consider not only *what work* the machinery is adapted to do, and *how well* adapted; but also, let him study the *history* of its construction, and trace, if he can, or rather *fail*, if he can, to trace the evidences of design, and concert of action, among its chief bosses, from the beginning.

[Para. 4] But, so far, *Congress* only, had acted; and an *indorsement* by the people, *real* or apparent, was indispensable, to *save* the point already gained, and give chance for more.

[Para. 5] The new year of 1854 found slavery excluded from more than half the States by State Constitutions, and from most of the national territory by Congressional prohibition.

[Para. 6] Four days later, commenced the struggle, which ended in repealing that Congressional prohibition.

[Para. 7] This opened all the national territory to slavery; and was the first point gained.

[Para. 8] This necessity had not been overlooked; but had been provided for, as well as might be, in the notable argument of "*squatter sovereignty*."[19]

There is something wrong in the above passage, and I confess that it had to be pointed out to me by a Lincoln scholar with a keener eye than mine—namely, George B. Forgie. Paragraph 4 is plainly a non sequitur, and so is paragraph 8. The lapses of logic disappear, however, and everything is made right if one simply picks up paragraph 4 and inserts it between paragraph 7 and paragraph 8. The error of transposition is incorporated in three books of selected Lincoln writings that were derived from the *Collected Works*—one edited by the late T. Harry Williams (1957), one by me (1964), and one by Richard N. Current (1967).[20] The error also appears in Paul M. Angle's edition of the Lincoln-Douglas debates titled *Created Equal* (1958).[21] Yet Robert W. Johannsen's edition of the debates (1965) has the text in the right order, and so does the Nicolay and Hay *Complete Works* (1894).[22] In the latter two works, moreover, the paragraphs are generally longer, and the profuse italicization of the *Collected Works* is missing.

There are, in fact, two original sources of the House Divided address. Roy P. Basler and the other editors of the *Collected Works* used the version published in the *Illinois State Journal* on June 18, 1858, two days after Lincoln's delivery of the speech. Paul M. Angle did likewise. This text was presumably set from Lincoln's own manuscript copy. If we can believe the recollective testimony of journalist Horace White, both he and Lincoln read proof of the speech in the *Journal* office.[23] Yet, if so, neither discovered the transposition of paragraphs. That the error was not present in the manuscript becomes clear when we examine the other original source, namely, a "phonographic"—that is, a stenographic—report of the speech, taken down as the words fell from Lincoln's lips, and printed in the Chicago *Tribune* on June 19. There, the sentences are in their logical order, italics are absent, and the paragraphing is different, having been arbitrarily determined by the stenographer. It was the *Tribune* version that Lincoln put into his scrapbook and later provided for inclusion with the Lincoln-Douglas debates when they were published as a book in 1860.[24] That was the text followed by Nicolay and Hay in the 1890's, by Arthur Brooks Lapsley in his 1905 edition of Lincoln's writings,[25] and by Robert Johannsen in the 1960's.

Thus, two somewhat different versions of the House Divided speech have been perpetuated, emanating from different sources, and proceeding down through the years like two columns of soldiers marching along separate but parallel roads. One source is a slightly garbled copy of the words Lincoln *wrote*. The other is a stenographic record, no doubt less than perfect, of the words he *spoke*. Clearly, the best version would be one making intelligent use of both sources. I can find only one scholar who employed such strategy, and that, ironically, was Roy P. Basler—not in the *Collected Works*, but in an earlier book, *Abraham Lincoln: His Speeches and Writings*. There Basler followed the text of the *Illinois State Journal*, with "a few emendations" taken from the Chicago *Tribune* version. His most important change was to correct the error of the transposed paragraphs—a correction that he failed to make as chief editor of the *Collected Works*.[26]

Errors in the *Collected Works* are so few and far between that a biographer who quoted Lincoln only from its pages would have secure footing indeed, but his work would be impoverished as a consequence. He could not, for example, repeat Lincoln's comparison of Horace Greeley to an old shoe, "so rotten that nothing can be done with him"; or his comparison of Salmon P. Chase to a blue-bottle fly, laying eggs in "every rotten spot" it could find; or his comparison of a dwindling army on the march to a "shovelfull of fleas pitched from one place to another."[27] And a biographer so fastidious would likewise have to omit such gems as Lincoln's reported comment in pardoning a certain condemned soldier: "If a man had more than one life, I think a little hanging would not hurt this one"; and his response to a pestering favor-seeker, as remembered by John Hay: "Now, my man, go away! I cannot attend to all these details. I could as easily bail out the Potomac with a spoon."[28] The *Collected Works*, after all, comprises not only the *writings* of Lincoln but also many of his utterances as recorded by newspaper reporters. Outside the *Collected Works*, in addition, there is a great accumulation of spoken words attributed to Lincoln that cannot be ignored. Yet as examination of a single chapter in one major Lincoln study has demonstrated, to use this rich resource is to walk on treacherous ground.

What we need, and may never have, is a systematic, critically evaluative compilation of all the utterances, whether quoted or merely summarized, that have been attributed to Lincoln in contemporary and recollective primary sources. Until some such authoritative treasury of his spoken words is provided, several cautionary rules respecting the use of such material may be in order.

First, it should be recognized that many a quotation has a provenance too weak and/or a substance too dubious to be incorporated in serious historical writing.

Second, much recollected utterance, and especially the lengthy remark recalled over a long span of time, should probably be treated as, at best, *indirect* rather than *direct* quotation.

Third, insofar as the pace of the narrative or argument will allow it, the reader should be given some measure of a quotation's authenticity.

And finally, the interpretative weight placed upon a quotation should be compatible with the quality of its authentication.

Maximum accuracy in quoting Lincoln is not merely a pedantic ideal. It becomes increasingly a necessity as ever more ponderous burdens of discovered meaning are laid upon his words by psychoanalytic scholars and other deep readers of historical texts. Charles B. Strozier, in his psychohistorical study of Lincoln, builds an elaborate structure of Freudian diagnosis upon two sentences that Lincoln wrote about shooting a wild turkey.[29] Whatever one may think of his interpretation, it rests on the unimpeachable foundation of a handwritten Lincoln document.[30] Elsewhere in the book, while analyzing Lincoln's periodic bouts of depression, Strozier makes the flat assertion that "political defeat could devastate Lincoln." But the proof he offers consists almost entirely of the following statement:

> There is some evidence that in 1858 Lincoln was distraught at the loss to Douglas. On the evening of the defeat he said to his friend Henry C. Whitney that his life had been "an abject and lamentable failure." Whitney reported: "I never saw any man so radically and thoroughly depressed, so completely steeped in the bitter waters of hopeless despair."[31]

Here is what Whitney actually wrote, however:

> On January 5th, 1859, the day of Douglas' last election to the U.S. Senate by the legislature—I was alone with Mr. Lincoln from 2 o'clock P.M. till bed-time—and I feel authorized to say that no man in the State was so gloomy, dejected and dispirited, and no man so surely and heartily deemed his life to have been an abject and lamentable failure, as he then considered his to have been. I never saw any man so radically and thoroughly depressed, so completely steeped in the bitter waters of hopeless despair.[32]

Plainly, Whitney does not assert that *Lincoln* called his life "an abject and lamentable failure." The words and the thought are Whitney's, not Lincoln's. They are part of a description of Lincoln's mood on a particular day in 1859, as Whitney supposedly remembered it more than thirty years later. Furthermore, Whitney's reputation for honest recollection is a tainted one, and, as Strozier acknowledges in a footnote, there is countervailing testimony that Lincoln took the senatorial defeat in stride.[33] Whitney's account is therefore a weak peg upon which to hang a significant conclusion about Lincoln's temperament.

To illustrate minutely the importance that precise quotation can assume, let me return to the House Divided speech and one of its most famous sentences: "I believe this government cannot endure, permanently half *slave* and half *free*." In the *Illinois State Journal*'s version (and therefore in the *Collected Works*), there is a comma after the word "endure," presumably put there deliberately by Lincoln. In the Chicago *Tribune*'s version and others derived from it, that comma is omitted. The omission has the effect of linking "endure" with "permanently," thereby causing Lincoln to say little more than that the nation cannot go on forever divided between freedom and slavery—a rather weak prediction of crisis at some future time. But with the comma inserted, "permanently" is separated from "endure" and associated with the second half of the sentence. The shade of meaning changes as a consequence. The Union, Lincoln is saying, cannot survive as a nation permanently divided into free and slave sections. And since each section is already committed to the permanency of its condition with respect to slavery, this means that the crisis is already at hand. Thus the comma tends to radicalize the sentence. Was that Lincoln's intention? Or was the comma, instead, nothing more than eccentric punctuation—or perhaps just an error introduced by the printer? Whenever he quoted the sentence in later correspondence, Lincoln omitted the comma, and he repeatedly explained the House Divided passage in moderate tones. But these facts are not as conclusive as they might seem, for the paragraphing confirms that he was quoting from the commaless Chicago *Tribune* version, which he had put into his scrapbook, and as a presidential candidate he needed to dissociate himself from the radical implications of the speech.[34]

Testing the historical value of attributed spoken words is a more complex and inconclusive enterprise than testing the value of written words. With documents, the problem of authenticity is largely a physical matter (paper, ink, handwriting, etc.) that can be dealt with separately from the problem of the credibility of testimony, whereas with attributed words, the problem of authenticity is itself largely a matter of credibility. For example, if A writes to B saying, "C tried to bribe me yesterday," the authenticity of the quotation depends upon the genuineness of the letter as an artifact, while its credibility as historical evidence depends upon A's reliability as a witness, considering the circumstances in which he wrote. But if A writes in a memoir, "Just before the election, B telephoned and said, 'C has just tried to bribe me,'" the authenticity of the quotation depends upon A's reliability as a recollective witness of the utterance, while its credibility depends upon B's reliability as a witness of the event. Reliability will vary, not only from person to person but also from situation to situation. For instance, one finds it relatively easy to believe Herndon when he tells us that Lincoln said to him in 1861, "Give our clients to understand that the election of a President makes no change in the firm of Lincoln and Herndon." But I for one become more suspicious when he recalls telling his partner in 1858, after hearing a preview reading of the House Divided address, "Lincoln, deliver that speech as read and it will make you President."[35]

There is no simple formula for judging the authenticity of recollected utterances. One looks first for independent corroboration but rarely finds it. The elapse of time between the utterance and the recording of it is always significant, though never conclusive. Certainly the kind of record in which the quotation appears, as well as the relationship of the quoter to the person quoted, must be carefully weighed. But every recollection of spoken words is a separate problem in historical method.[36] In each instance, the historian must call upon his professional experience, his knowledge of the particular historical context, and his common sense to make a judgment of probability—not only about the authenticity of the quotation, but also about how close it comes to being a verbatim report as distinguished from a mere paraphrase.

Of course, the historian studies words in a search for meanings. To know as fully and accurately as possible what Lincoln really said is the firmest foundation upon which to build an understanding of what he and his life meant. But accurate quotation of a person's words is only a beginning. It does not ensure their satisfactory interpretation.

Consider, for instance, the exclamatory comment that Lincoln jotted down sometime during or soon after his debates with Douglas: "Negro equality! Fudge!! How long, in the government of a God, great enough to make and maintain this Universe, shall there continue knaves to vend, and fools to gulp, so low a piece of demagougeism [*sic*] as this."[37] LaWanda Cox, in her book *Lincoln and Black Freedom*, says that this passage "can be read as scorn for his opponent's appeal to prejudice, and scorn for those who applauded that appeal."[38] But such a reading misjudges the direction of Lincoln's anger. "Fudge," after all, means "nonsense," and Lincoln was talking, not about the repulsiveness of racial prejudice, but rather about the absurdity and dishonesty of the charge that he, and Republicans generally, favored racial equality. Denying the charge again and again during the senatorial campaign, he bitterly resented the "demagougeism" that forced him to do so.

Consider also the meaning that has been read into those paragraphs of the young Lincoln's Lyceum speech in which he discussed the possible emergence of an American usurper driven by a hunger for renown. "Is it unreasonable . . . to expect," he asked, "that some man possessed of the loftiest genius, coupled with ambition sufficient to push it to its utmost stretch, will at some time, spring up among us?"[39] Edmund Wilson seems to have been the first writer to suggest that in this passage Lincoln projected himself into the demonic role he was so eloquently describing. Subsequently, there have been several elaborations of the same theme, the effect of which is to make the nation's tragic destiny in the mid-nineteenth century a mere extension of Lincoln's towering ambition and relentless will.[40]

It is no doubt true that anyone seeking to explain the feelings of a historical figure must establish a bond of empathy, however synthetic and temporary the bond may be. But aside from such normal literary identification with one's subject of the moment, the lifetime record of Lincoln's words and behavior lends little support to Wilson's conjecture and the line of interpretation associated with it. On the contrary, much of that record points in the opposite direction. Perhaps the greatest weakness of the interpretation is that it endows Lincoln with far more control over the course of events and over his own fate than common sense will accept or the facts warrant. But in addition, it ignores two usurpative models that Lincoln may have had in mind. One was Andrew Jackson, whom Whigs had so recently been calling violator of the Constitution and would-be tyrant. The other, more likely to be thought of as a "towering genius," was Napoleon Bonaparte, dead only seventeen years at the time of the Lyceum speech.[41]

As a third and final example of how words can be misinterpreted, let us consider a passage from Dwight G. Anderson's psychohistorical study of Lincoln. "During an 1857 speech at Springfield, discussing the Declaration of Independence," Anderson writes, "he [Lincoln] seemed to have lost his train of thought momentarily, digressing into what was for him a rare non sequitur. Noting that the framers of the Declaration would scarcely recognize their work in recent times, he suddenly changed the subject." Anderson then proceeds to quote Lincoln's most elaborate experiment in metaphor, which runs as follows:

> All the powers of earth seem rapidly combining against him. . . . They have him in his prison house; they have searched his person, and left no prying instrument with him. One after another they have closed the heavy iron doors upon him, and now they have him, as it were, bolted in with a lock of

a hundred keys, which can never be unlocked without the concurrence of every key; the keys in the hands of a hundred different men, and they scattered to a hundred different and distant places; and they stand musing as to what invention, in all the dominions of mind and matter, can be produced to make the impossibility of his escape more complete than it is.

"It is clear from the larger context of the speech," says Anderson, "that Lincoln's reference here was to the Negro slave; but it is also clear that he too felt himself to be equally imprisoned in a life of political obscurity." And especially so because at that very moment, "eastern Republicans were preparing to support Douglas for reelection to the Senate."

In this textual analysis there is nothing right except the year and place. Anyone who reads the passage in question will soon discover that its subject was not the Declaration of Independence but rather the Dred Scott decision, and more specifically, Chief Justice Taney's implication that the lot of the black race had improved since the Revolution. Lincoln's extended metaphor, far from being a digression or a non sequitur, served as the climax of his rebuttal to Taney. The assertion that Lincoln was at the same time describing his own condition of "imprisonment" is preposterous. It is also more or less incompatible with the one sentence that Anderson omitted from his quotation, namely: "Mammon is after him; ambition follows, and philosophy follows, and the Theology of the day is fast joining the cry." As for Douglas, he received no Republican support until he began his revolt against the Lecompton constitution in December 1857. That was six months *after* Lincoln's Springfield speech.[42]

Sound interpretation of any historical text begins with an effort to determine the author's intended meaning. That includes paying attention to context and circumstance, keeping a sharp eye out for irony and other kinds of indirection, discriminating between denotative and connotative meanings, and coming to terms with the fact that intentions may be overt, or deliberately concealed, or at work only beneath the surface of consciousness.

The complexity that sometimes encumbers a search for intent can be illustrated with Lincoln's famous letter to Horace Greeley, in which he declared:

My paramount object in this struggle *is* to save the Union, and is *not* either to save or destroy slavery. If I could save the Union without freeing *any* slave I would do it, and if I could save it by freeing *all* the slaves I would do it; and if I could save it by freeing some and leaving others alone I would also do that.[43]

By itself, this pronouncement bears some resemblance to Stephen A. Douglas's notorious assertion during the Lecompton controversy that he did not care whether slavery was "voted down or voted up" in Kansas.[44] But the letter will be misunderstood if it is read as a straightforward statement of Lincoln's political and ethical priorities, with the Union counting for everything and slavery, nothing. Lincoln's ostensible neutralism about slavery was misleading—and intentionally so. He had, in fact, already committed himself to emancipation, had drafted a proclamation, and was using the exchange with Greeley "to prepare the people for what was coming."[45] Preservation of the Union and abolition of slavery were already bound together as twin purposes of the Civil War. Saving the Union had become more than an end in itself. It was also the indispensable means of achieving emancipation. But Lincoln, for reasons of political strategy, had to put it the other way around, viewing emancipation as a means, and very likely a necessary means, of saving the Union. Still there is more to be said. To this perception of cool calculation and dissembled purpose in the Greeley letter one should add some understanding of the deeper uncertainties with which Lincoln contemplated the relation of the war to emancipation, and of emancipation to the future of the nation.

Along with the *intended* meaning of Lincoln's words, one must consider their *effective* meaning—that is, what they were *understood* to mean by his primary and his secondary audiences, and also what *consequences* they may have produced. There is a Thomas Nast cartoon that dramatizes how differently the North and South understood the First Inaugural. It presents two Abraham Lincolns, one dressed as a prince of peace, the other armed as a god of war.[46] More difficult for the modern mind to comprehend is how the Emancipation Proclamation, perhaps the greatest document of social reform in American history, could have been understood, not only in the Confederacy but by the London *Times*, as a barbarous effort to incite servile rebellion.[47] To seek the *consequential* meaning of words is to treat them as actions and thus pursue one's study into the realm of historical causation. Lincoln's famous interrogation of Douglas at Freeport is a good example of an utterance whose meaning has come to consist almost entirely in the consequences attributed to it. Likewise, his letters opposing compromise in the secession winter of 1860–61 have little meaning apart from the formidable question of whether they were enough to make the difference between reconciliation and disunion.

Besides their intended meanings and effective meanings within a definite historical context, some of Lincoln's words have acquired *transcendent* meaning as contributions to the permanent literary treasure of the nation. Just why his prose at its best is so splendid, so memorable, has been pondered by all sorts of critics. Edmund Wilson is one of those who emphasize the leanness and muscular strength of Lincoln's style, compared with the more ornate oratorical fashion of the day.[48] Yet, in his more formal pieces especially, Lincoln employed some of the structures and rhetorical devices of eighteenth-century expository writing. In the Gettysburg Address, for example, one scholar finds "two antitheses, five cases of anaphora, eight instances of balanced phrases and clauses, thirteen alliterations."[49] Several critics stress the richness and vigor of Lincoln's imagery, drawn as it was from everyday American experience and culture.[50] Jacques Barzun speaks of his gift of rhythm, "developed to a supreme degree," and of an extraordinary capacity for verbal discipline. "Lincoln," he says, "acquired his power by exacting obedience from words."[51]

Lincoln's literary skill is most readily observable in those instances when he took someone else's prose and molded it to his own use. The first sentence of the House Divided speech, for instance, was a simpler, crisper version of the rhetorical flourish with which Daniel Webster began his "Second Reply to Hayne."[52] And the familiar opening words of the Gettysburg Address may have been derived from a speech delivered on July 4, 1861, by Galusha A. Grow in assuming office as Speaker of the House of Representatives.[53]

Perhaps the best example, however, is Lincoln's plea for reconciliation in the final paragraph of the First Inaugural—a paragraph drafted originally by his secretary of state, William H. Seward. Let us look first at just the short opening sentence. Seward wrote: "I close." Lincoln changed it to: "I am loth to close." The improvement in cadence is obvious enough, but the addition of three words also makes the sentence throb with connotative meanings and emotive force. It expresses an almost elegiac reluctance to break off discussion of the crisis—a sense of remnant opportunities slipping away, of a cherished world about to be lost. Then Lincoln went on to make the moving appeal that was the first oratorical summit of his presidency: "Though passion may have strained, it must not break our bonds of affection. The mystic chords of memory, stretching from every battlefield, and patriot grave, to every living heart and hearthstone, all over this broad land, will yet swell the chorus of the Union, when again touched, as surely they will be, by the better angels of our nature."[54]

Here was an occasion calling for eloquence; here was an ear keenly tuned to the music of the English language; here were intellectual grasp and moral urgency; here was great emotional power under firm artistic control. Here, in short, was the mastery that we associate with genius.

Reference Matter

Notes

Preface

1. Relevant article-length writings not included in this book are: "The Nomination of Lincoln in 1858," *Abraham Lincoln Quarterly*, 6 (1950–51): 24–36; "The Judd-Wentworth Feud," *Journal of the Illinois State Historical Society*, 45 (1952): 197–211; "The Historical Significance of the Lincoln-Douglas Debates," *Wisconsin Magazine of History*, 42 (1959): 193–99; "The Origins and Purpose of Lincoln's 'House-Divided' Speech," *Mississippi Valley Historical Review*, 46 (1960): 615–43; "Lincoln, Douglas, and the Freeport Question," *American Historical Review*, 66 (1961): 599–617; "Disunion and Reunion," in John Higham, ed., *The Reconstruction of American History* (London, 1962), pp. 98–118; "Comment," in George Harmon Knoles, ed., *The Crisis of the Union, 1860–1861* (Baton Rouge, La., 1965), pp. 21–29; "Roger B. Taney and the Sectional Crisis, *Journal of Southern History*, 43 (1977): 555–66; "The Missouri Controversy and the Sources of Southern Separatism," *Southern Review*, 14 (1978): 653–67; *The Federal Government and Slavery* (Claremont, Calif., 1984); "Race and Slavery in the American Constitutional System," *this Constitution*, no. 4 (Fall, 1984): 31–37.

Chapter 1

1. *Sangamo Journal* (Springfield, Ill.), June 4, 1846.
2. Lincoln was in Lexington, en route to Washington, on Nov. 13, 1846, when he no doubt heard Clay deliver a speech denouncing the war.
3. Roy P. Basler, Marion Dolores Pratt, and Lloyd A. Dunlap, eds., *The Collected Works of Abraham Lincoln* (9 vols.; New Brunswick, N.J., 1953–55), 1: 420–22, 431–42; *Congressional Globe*, 30 Cong., 1 sess., p. 95.
4. G. S. Borit[t], "A Matter of Political Suicide? Lincoln's Opposition to the Mexican War," *Journal of the Illinois State Historical Society*, 67 (1974): 79–100; Mark E. Neely, Jr., "Lincoln and the Mexican War: An Argument by Analogy," *Civil War History*, 24 (1978): 5–24.
5. Basler et al., *Collected Works*, 3: 6, 56, 168, 319–20.
6. *Ibid.*, 2: 527; 3: 16–17, 182–83; 4: 66; 6: 302; Roy P. Basler, ed., *The Collected Works of Abraham Lincoln: Supplement, 1832–1865* (Westport, Conn., 1974), p. 59.

7. New York *Times*, Feb. 17, 1962, pp. 1, 8. The Chicago *Tribune* of the same date (p. 4) carried a slightly different account and quoted Kennedy as follows: "I think it was unjustified. It was not a very bright spot in our history. Not one to be very proud of."

8. For mid-nineteenth-century American attitudes toward the war, see Robert W. Johannsen, *To the Halls of the Montezumas: The War with Mexico in the American Imagination* (New York, 1985).

9. Otis A. Singletary, *The Mexican War* (Chicago, 1960), p. 5.

10. New York *Times*, March 5, 1947, pp. 1, 4; Sept. 14, 1947, p. 24.

11. This literature is surveyed in Homer Campbell Chaney, Jr., "The Mexican–United States War As Seen by Mexican Intellectuals, 1846–1956," Ph.D. diss., Stanford University, 1959. For mid-nineteenth-century Mexican attitudes, see Gene M. Brack, *Mexico Views Manifest Destiny, 1821–1846: An Essay on the Origins of the Mexican War* (Albuquerque, N.Mex., 1975).

12. Justo Sierra, *The Political Evolution of the Mexican People*, trans. Charles Ramsdell, (Austin, Tex., 1969), p. 233.

13. Alfonso Teja Zabre, *Historia de Mexico: Una moderna interpretación* (3d ed.; Mexico City, 1951), p. 331. At the centennial ceremonies in 1947, the minister of education declared that the Niños' sacrifice had transformed "the brutal defeat by force of arms into a triumph of national conscience" (New York *Times*, Sept. 14, 1947, p. 24).

14. Chaney, "Mexican–United States War," pp. 145–56, 233–36.

15. Sierra, *Mexican People*, pp. 235–36.

16. William Jay, *A Review of the Causes and Consequences of the Mexican War* (Boston, 1849); James Ford Rhodes, *History of the United States from the Compromise of 1850*, 1 (New York, 1892): 75–89. See also James Schouler, *History of the United States of America*, 4 (New York, 1889): 440–42, 525–26, 530; Horatio O. Ladd, *History of the War with Mexico* (New York, 1883); Goldwin Smith, *The United States: An Outline of Political History* (New York, 1893), pp. 210–12; Henry William Elson, *History of the United States of America* (New York, 1904), p. 529. A brief historiographical summary is given in Peter T. Harstad and Richard W. Resh, "The Causes of the Mexican War: A Note on Changing Interpretations," *Arizona and the West*, 6 (1964): 289–302. A general guide to writings on the background and causes of the war is Norman E. Tutorow, *The Mexican-American War: An Annotated Bibliography* (Westport, Conn., 1981), pp. 222–24. For the earliest efforts at writing the history of the war, see Johannsen, *Halls of the Montezumas*, pp. 228–57.

17. Chauncey W. Boucher, "In Re That Aggressive Slavocracy," *Mississippi Valley Historical Review*, 8 (1921–22): 30

18. Notably John S. Jenkins, *History of the War Between the United States and Mexico* (Auburn, N.Y., 1848); John S. Jenkins, *James Knox Polk and a History of His Administration* (Auburn, N.Y., 1850); N.C. Brooks, *A Complete History of the Mexican War: Its Causes, Conduct, and Consequences* (Philadelphia, Pa., 1849).

19. Charles H. Owen, *The Justice of the Mexican War* (New York,

1908); Robert McNutt McElroy, *The Winning of the Far West* (New York, 1914), pp. v–vi. In a textbook that was to run through many editions, David Saville Muzzey, *An American History* (Boston, 1911), pp. 347–48, declared that the Mexican War was itself "eminently just," but that the annexation of Texas had been a "wicked extension of the slavery area."

20. Justin H. Smith, *The War with Mexico* (2 vols.; New York, 1919), 1: 82–155.

21. Glyndon G. Van Deusen, *The Jacksonian Era, 1828–1848* (New York, 1959), p. 226. For an excellent example of the modern historiographical trend, which divides responsibility for the war between Mexico and the United States but stresses American expansionism, see Ray Allen Billington, *Westward Expansion* (3d ed.; New York, 1967), pp. 574–80. See also William H. Goetzmann, *When the Eagle Screamed: The Romantic Horizon in American Diplomacy, 1800–1860* (New York, 1966).

22. Chaney, "Mexican–United States War," pp. 217, 267–68; Diego Garcia Loya, *Mosaic of Mexican History* (Mexico City, 1958), p. 219. National and Southern expansionism are combined in Luis G. Zorrilla's interpretation, *Historia de las relaciones entre Mexico y los Estados Unidos de America* (2 vols.; Mexico City, 1965), 1:156.

23. George P. Garrison, *Westward Extension, 1841–1850* (New York, 1906); Willis Fletcher Johnson, *A Century of Expansion* (New York, 1903); Jesse S. Reeves, *American Diplomacy Under Tyler and Polk* (Baltimore, Md., 1907), pp. 58–59. See also Edwin E. Sparks, *The Expansion of the American People* (Chicago, 1900); Edmund J. Carpenter, *The American Advance* (New York, 1903); H. Addington Bruce, *The Romance of American Expansion* (New York, 1909).

24. Ray Allen Billington, *The Far Western Frontier, 1830–1860* (New York, 1956), p. 144. The psychology of expansionism is studied extensively in Frederick Merk, *Manifest Destiny and Mission in American History: A Reinterpretation* (New York, 1963).

25. Edward Channing, *A History of the United States*, 5 (New York, 1921): 550.

26. Richard R. Stenberg, "The Failure of Polk's Mexican War Intrigue of 1845," *Pacific Historical Review*, 4 (1935): 39–68; Glenn W. Price, *Origins of the War with Mexico: The Polk-Stockton Intrigue* (Austin, Tex., 1967).

27. Norman A. Graebner, *Empire on the Pacific* (New York, 1955), pp. 226–28. For a critique of Graebner's thesis, see Shomer S. Zwelling, *Expansion and Imperialism* (Chicago, 1970).

28. Charles Sellers, *James K. Polk: Continentalist, 1843–1846* (Princeton, N.J., 1966), p. 232.

29. Walton Bean, *California: An Interpretative History* (New York, 1968), pp. 87–88. This statement remains intact on p. 68 of the fourth edition, co-authored by James J. Rawls and published in 1983.

30. Alfonso Trueba, *California: Tierra Perdida* (2 vols.; Mexico City, 1956–58), 2: 143–69.

31. There might have been some other kind of forcible intervention,

such as sponsorship of a California revolt against Mexico, but that strategy probably would have led to war. Norman A. Graebner, in "The Mexican War: A Study in Causation," *Pacific Historical Review*, 49 (1980): 425, declares, "There simply was no way that the United States could acquire California peacefully."

32. Ephraim Douglass Adams, *British Interests and Activities in Texas, 1838–1846* (Baltimore, Md., 1910), pp. 234–64.

33. For a discussion of Polk's freedom of choice and an alternative policy that he might have followed, see David M. Pletcher's definitive work, *The Diplomacy of Annexation: Texas, Oregon and the Mexican War* (Columbia, Mo., 1973), pp. 607–11.

Chapter 2

1. R. Kent Newmyer, *The Supreme Court Under Marshall and Taney* (New York, 1968), p. 141. See also Stanley I. Kutler, *Judicial Power and Reconstruction Politics* (Chicago, 1968), p. 9; Wallace Mendelson, "Dred Scott's Case—Reconsidered," *Minnesota Law Review*, 38 (1953–54): 23.

2. Charles Warren, *The Supreme Court in United States History* (rev. ed., 2 vols.; Boston, 1932), 2: 330. See also Albert J. Beveridge, *Abraham Lincoln, 1809–1858* (2 vols.; Boston, 1928), 2: 418–19.

3. For a more extensive discussion of this point, see Don E. Fehrenbacher, *Prelude to Greatness: Lincoln in the 1850's* (Stanford, Calif., 1962), pp. 131, 133–34, 190. See also Robert W. Johannsen, *Stephen A. Douglas* (New York, 1973), pp. 568–70, 670.

4. Galena *Daily Advertiser*, July 26, 1856. The article was then reprinted in the *Advertiser*'s weekly edition, the *North-Western Gazette*, on July 29, and this is the source cited in Roy P. Basler, Marion Dolores Pratt, and Lloyd A. Dunlap, eds., *The Collected Works of Abraham Lincoln* (9 vols.; New Brunswick, N.J., 1953–55), 2: 353–55. The *Advertiser* had carried a much briefer article about the speech on July 25.

5. For instance, the diary of John Hay provides a number of familiar quotations, such as Lincoln's insistence that every soldier must somehow contribute to the battle effort: "Those not skinning can hold a leg." Tyler Dennett, *Lincoln and the Civil War in the Diary and Letters of John Hay* (New York, 1939), p. 179.

6. One notable example of a nonautograph document is the House Divided speech; another is the famous letter of condolence to Mrs. Lydia Bixby. For further discussion of both, see pp. 275–76 and 279–80 in this book.

7. Basler et al., *Collected Works*, 2: 349–53, 361–66.

8. *Ibid*., pp. 344–49, 359, 366–73, 375–80.

9. *Ibid*., 4: 67.

10. The reporter, in introducing his five paragraphs of reproduction, claimed only that Lincoln "spoke something as follows," but he then offset this caution by enclosing what followed in quotation marks.

11. Basler et al., *Collected Works*, 2: 353, 364–66, 372–73, 377.

12. Phelps had previously served on the supreme court of Vermont, and this experience may have made him more amenable to a judicial settlement. He had been a member of the special committee that reported the Clayton compromise; see Charles M. Wiltse, *John C. Calhoun: Sectionalist, 1840–1850* (Indianapolis, Ind., 1951), pp. 349–53. In 1850, Phelps served on the Committee of Thirteen, which reported the famous "Omnibus bill."

13. *Congressional Globe*, 31 Cong., 1 sess., Appendix, pp. 91–97. Quotations from pp. 95–96.

14. Italics added.

15. In *Marbury v. Madison*, John Marshall had emphatically asserted the power of the Supreme Court to declare a federal law unconstitutional, but the decision itself was no test of judicial power. It invalidated an unimportant section of a statute that would have extended the Court's original jurisdiction, and was thus a self-denying decision. For a brief, cogent comparison of the Marbury and Dred Scott cases, see Harry V. Jaffa, *Crisis of the House Divided: An Interpretation of the Issues in the Lincoln-Douglas Debates* (Garden City, N.Y., 1959), pp. 285–86.

16. Basler et al., *Collected Works*, 1: 112.

17. The charge that Taney's invalidation of the Missouri Compromise was obiter dictum no longer carries the conviction it once did. See Don E. Fehrenbacher, *The Dred Scott Case: Its Significance in American Law and Politics* (New York, 1978), pp. 322–34; Frederick S. Allis, Jr., "The Dred Scott Labyrinth," in H. Stuart Hughes, ed., *Teachers of History: Essays in Honor of Laurence Bradford Packard* (Ithaca, N.Y., 1954), pp. 341–68.

18. Basler et al., *Collected Works*, 2: 387–88.

19. *Ibid.*, pp. 400–403. For additional discussion of Lincoln's attitude toward judicial review, see pp. 124–26 in this book. See also Gary J. Jacobsohn, "Abraham Lincoln 'on this question of judicial authority': The Theory of Constitutional Aspiration," *Western Political Quarterly*, 36 (1983): 52–70. Jacobsohn argues that Lincoln's rejection of the Dred Scott decision was based on a belief that the Constitution must be interpreted in such a way as to advance the natural rights principles of the Declaration of Independence. This is the theory of "constitutional aspiration." The argument is no doubt valid with respect to Lincoln's view of ultimate purposes, but it underestimates, I think, the degree of his readiness to acquiesce, for the time being, in legal actions and arrangements detrimental to natural rights—*if* they had been legitimated by judicial reiteration, legislative acceptance, and a suitable measure of public sanction. His attitude toward the fugitive-slave laws is a case in point.

20. For other Lincoln citations of Jefferson on the subject, see Basler et al., *Collected Works*, 2: 516–17, 552; 3: 28, 80, 232.

21. *Ibid.*, 4: 268.

22. For example, in 1862, Lincoln signed an act abolishing slavery in the territories, and his attorney general, Edward Bates, issued an opinion virtually setting aside Taney's ruling that Negroes were ineligible for United States citizenship.

23. Basler et al., *Collected Works*, 1: 170–71.

Chapter 3

1. Charles Francis Adams, [Jr.,] *Charles Francis Adams* (Boston, 1900), pp. 144–46. In an excellent essay, Mark E. Neely, Jr., has demonstrated that the change of subject was less abrupt than it seems because of a political connection between the Chicago post office appointment and the British mission. See *Lincoln Lore*, no. 1667 (Jan. 1977).

2. In the 1850's, more than 80 percent of all federal civilian employees were in the Post Office Department. And the money paid to independent contractors for transportation of the mail was about double the amount paid as salaries to postmasters and postal clerks. U.S. Bureau of the Census, *Historical Statistics of the United States, Colonial Times to 1957* (Washington, D.C., 1960), p. 710; *Senate Executive Documents*, 36 Cong., 1 sess., 3 (Serial 1025), 1388–89.

3. Dorothy Ganfield Fowler, *The Cabinet Politician: The Postmasters General, 1829–1909* (New York, 1943), pp. 89–90.

4. *Register of Officers and Agents, Civil, Military, and Naval, in the Service of the United States on the Thirtieth September, 1861* (Washington, D.C., 1862), pp. 354–79.

5. Isaac R. Diller to Stephen A. Douglas, Dec. 15, 1854, Stephen A. Douglas Papers, University of Chicago.

6. D. J. Connely to Douglas, Feb. 14, 1859, Douglas Papers.

7. Decatur *Gazette*, quoted in the Chicago *Press and Tribune*, Nov. 24, 1859; Bloomington *Pantagraph*, Dec. 6, 1859.

8. F. C. Wing to Lyman Trumbull, Feb. 8, 1856, Lyman Trumbull Papers, Manuscript Division, Library of Congress.

9. W. L. Walker to Joseph Chandler, Feb. 21, 1859, Douglas Papers.

10. Chicago *Democratic-Press*, Feb. 9, 1858.

11. F. Priest to Douglas, Jan. 26, 1860, Douglas Papers.

12. Chicago *Democratic-Press*, Aug. 18, 1856.

13. *Ibid*., Oct. 24, 1856; Herman Kreismann to Trumbull, Aug. 9, 1856, Trumbull Papers.

14. George W. Gray to Douglas, May 26, 1858, Douglas Papers.

15. J. P. Heiss to Douglas, July 15, 23, 1858; James Spencer to Douglas, July 15, 1858; O. J. Wise to Douglas, Sept. 27, 1858, Douglas Papers.

16. *United States Statutes at Large*, 1: 238 (Act of Feb. 20, 1792); 4: 110–11 (Act of Mar. 3, 1825); 5: 738 (Act of Mar. 3, 1845); 9: 588 (Act of Mar. 3, 1851); Culver H. Smith, *The Press, Politics and Patronage: The American Government's Use of Newspapers, 1789–1875* (Athens, Ga., 1977), pp. 6–8.

17. Chicago *Journal*, Apr. 13, 1854; Aurora *Beacon*, Sept. 28, 1855. The second citation is from the collection of source materials gathered by Arthur Charles Cole and deposited in the University of Illinois Library, Urbana—hereafter cited as Cole's Notes.

18. Chicago *Democratic-Press*, Sept. 15, 1854.

19. *Ibid*., Oct. 5, 1854.

20. Enclosed in letter of Truman Huling to Douglas, May 14, 1858, Douglas Papers. For newspaper complaints about postal service, see Chicago *Democrat* (weekly), Sept. 16, 1854; Chicago *Herald*, Mar. 17, 1859; Canton *Register* (weekly), July 3, 1860, Cole's Notes.

21. May 25, 1855.

22. Charles H. Ray to Trumbull, Feb. 25, 1861, and Joseph Medill to Trumbull, Mar. 4, 1861, Trumbull Papers.

23. The list of postmasters in the *Register of Officers and Agents* for 1855, 1857, 1859, and 1861 was compared with the listing of editors and publishers in Franklin William Scott, *Newspapers and Periodicals of Illinois, 1814–1879* (Springfield, Ill., 1910).

24. Sept. 16, 1854.

25. T. C. Wetmore to Douglas, Feb. 27, 1856; D. Hoffbine to Douglas, Mar. 4, 1856; A. M. Herrington to Douglas, Dec. 18, 1857, Douglas Papers.

26. Oct. 9, 1858.

27. Chicago *Times*, Mar. 9, 21, 1858; George Gillaspey to Douglas, July 6, 1858, Douglas Papers; Roy Franklin Nichols, *The Disruption of American Democracy* (New York, 1948), p. 212.

28. A Freeport correspondent informed Douglas that the only Democrat in the city supporting the President had set out for Washington "to effect a *coup de grace* in relation to the P.O. here." F. W. L. Bradley to Douglas, Dec. 30, 1857, Douglas Papers.

29. *Rock River Democrat* (Rockford), Dec. 29, 1857, Cole's Notes.

30. "Having the controll of the press and P. office is *all* that gives them [the Buchanan supporters] in Princeton any influence," wrote D. G. Salisbury to Douglas, Mar. 5, 1858, Douglas Papers.

31. Chicago *Democratic-Press*, Mar. 13, 1858; Peter Sweat to Douglas, Feb. 8, 1858; C. Ballance to Douglas, Feb. 11, 1858; J. B. Taylor to Douglas, Mar. 20, 1858, Douglas Papers.

32. T. Huling to Douglas, Apr. 29, May 31, 1858; J. W. Caldwell to Douglas, May 1, 1858, Douglas Papers.

33. See, for example, Chicago *Democratic-Press*, Mar. 21, 1854, Jan. 5, 1855; Chicago *Democrat*, Nov. 17, 1855; Canton *Register*, Feb. 7, 1858, Cole's Notes.

34. Chicago *Democratic-Press*, Apr. 19, 1854, Feb. 2, 1856.

35. *Ibid.*, Feb. 2, 1856; Canton *Register*, Feb. 7, 1858, Cole's Notes; Greenville *Advocate*, Dec. 30, 1858; Chicago *Press and Tribune*, Mar. 25, 1859; David Seem to Douglas, May 21, 1860, Douglas Papers.

36. Nov. 17, 1856.

37. Fowler, *Cabinet Politician*, p. 106.

38. Dorothy Ganfield Fowler, *Unmailable: Congress and the Post Office* (Athens, Ga., 1977), pp. 45–51; J. G. Randall, *Constitutional Problems Under Lincoln* (rev. ed.; Urbana, Ill., 1951), pp. 500–502.

39. Herman V. Ames, "Proposed Amendments to the Constitution, 1789–1889," American Historical Association *Annual Report, 1896*, 2: 141–42.

Chapter 4

1. John Wentworth to his sister Lydia, Nov. 9, 1836, in the John Wentworth Papers, Chicago Historical Society, gives a vivid account of the latter part of the trip. For a fuller account of Wentworth's career, see Don E. Fehrenbacher, *Chicago Giant: A Biography of "Long John" Wentworth* (Madison, Wis., 1957).

2. Chicago *American*, Dec. 17, 1836; Wentworth to Horatio Hill, Jan. 9, Feb. 5, 16, 1837, printed in Chicago *Times*, June 21, 1874.

3. *Illinois State Register* (Springfield), May 12, June 30, Aug. 4, 1843; Elijah Middlebrook Haines, "John Wentworth's First Election to Congress," unpublished manuscript in Chicago Historical Society; Theodore Calvin Pease, *Illinois Election Returns, 1818–1848* (Springfield, Ill., 1923), p. 138.

4. *Congressional Globe*, 28 Cong., 1 sess., Appendix, pp. 55–58. Quotation from p. 55.

5. Pease, *Election Returns*, pp. 145, 156. Wentworth was also elected in 1848, 1852, and 1864, for a total of six terms in the House of Representatives.

6. *Congressional Globe*, 29 Cong., 1 sess., pp. 1217–18.

7. *Weekly Chicago Democrat*, Oct. 7, 1854.

8. *Ibid.*, June 7, 1856.

9. *Ibid.*, Aug. 23, 1856.

10. Chicago *Tribune*, Mar. 2, 1857; W. A. Brown to Lyman Trumbull, Feb. 28, 1857, Trumbull Papers, Manuscript Division, Library of Congress.

11. Roy P. Basler, Marion Dolores Pratt, and Lloyd A. Dunlap, eds., *The Collected Works of Abraham Lincoln* (9 vols.; New Brunswick, N.J., 1953–55), 2: 390.

12. Bessie Louise Pierce, *A History of Chicago*. Vol. 2, *From Town to City, 1848–1871* (New York, 1940), p. 223.

13. Chicago *Tribune*, Sept. 22, 1857; Feb. 26, 1858; Chicago *Press and Tribune*, June 15, July 6, 1859; Chicago *Democrat*, July 15, 1859.

14. Chicago *Tribune*, June 20, 22, 1857.

15. Chicago *Democratic-Press*, Apr. 21, 1857; Chicago *Tribune*, Apr. 21, 1857.

16. Boston *Journal*, quoted in Clinton, Ill., *Central Transcript*, Sept. 3, 1857.

17. Chicago *Tribune*, Nov. 23, 25, 1857.

18. Lincoln to Henry C. Whitney, Dec. 18, 1857, in Basler et al., *Collected Works*, 2: 429.

19. Chicago *Times*, May 19, June 2, 8, 1858; *Illinois State Register*, June 4, 1858.

20. Chicago *Tribune*, May 25, 1858.

21. *Ibid.*, Apr. 21, 1858; Chicago *Journal*, Apr. 24, May 20, 1858; Jesse K. Dubois to Trumbull, Apr. 8, 1858, Trumbull Papers; John H. Bryant to Lincoln, Apr. 19, 1858, Robert Todd Lincoln Collection, Manuscript Division, Library of Congress.

22. *Illinois State Journal* (Springfield), June 17, 1858.

23. Lincoln to Trumbull, June 23, 1858, Basler et al., *Collected Works*, 2: 472.

24. *Weekly Chicago Democrat*, Oct. 2, 1858.

25. *Ibid.*, Nov. 20, 1858; David Davis, quoting Wentworth, in a letter to Lincoln, Jan. 1, 1859 (misdated 1858), Robert Todd Lincoln Collection.

26. *Weekly Chicago Democrat*, Nov. 20, 1858.

27. *Ibid.*, Nov. 12, 26, 1859; Judd to Lincoln, Dec. 1, 1859, Robert Todd Lincoln Collection; Judd to Trumbull, Dec. 1, 1859, Trumbull Papers.

28. Walter Wright to Trumbull, Dec. 20, 1859, Trumbull Papers.

29. N. Niles to Lincoln, Dec. 16, 1859, Robert Todd Lincoln Collection.

30. Lincoln to Messrs. Dole, Hubbard, and Brown, Dec. 14, 1859, in Basler et al., *Collected Works*, 3: 507–8.

31. Wentworth to Lincoln, Dec. 21, 1859, Robert Todd Lincoln Collection.

32. The disclaimer is quoted in David Davis to Lincoln, Feb. 21, 1860, Robert Todd Lincoln Collection. Lincoln's letters to Wentworth are not extant. For a fuller account of the affair, see Don E. Fehrenbacher, "The Judd-Wentworth Feud," in *Journal of the Illinois State Historical Society*, 45 (1952): 197–211.

33. Wentworth to Lincoln, Feb. 19, 1860, Robert Todd Lincoln Collection; Chicago *Press and Tribune*, Feb. 18, 20, 1860.

34. Chicago *Press and Tribune*, Mar. 2, 3, 5, 1860; *Weekly Chicago Democrat*, Mar. 10, 17, 1860; Judd to Lincoln, Feb. 21, 1860, Robert Todd Lincoln Collection.

35. Wentworth to Lincoln, Apr. 21, 1860; Davis to Lincoln, Apr. 23, 1860, Robert Todd Lincoln Collection.

36. Henry C. Whitney, *Life on the Circuit with Lincoln* (Caldwell, Id., 1940), pp. 152–53; Tyler Dennett, ed., *Lincoln and the Civil War in the Diaries and Letters of John Hay* (New York, 1939), pp. 28–29.

37. Davis to Lincoln, May 5, 1860, Robert Todd Lincoln Collection; Pierce, *Chicago*, 2: 241.

38. H. Kreismann to Elihu B. Washburne, May 13, 1860, Washburne Papers, Manuscript Division, Library of Congress; William Jayne to Trumbull, May 13, 1860; Horace White to Trumbull, May 14, 1860, Trumbull Papers; Judd to Lincoln, May 25, 1860, Robert Todd Lincoln Collection.

39. Kreismann to Washburne, May 15, 1860, Washburne Papers; Mark Delahay to Lincoln, May 15, 1860, Robert Todd Lincoln Collection; *Weekly Chicago Democrat*, May 19, 1860; William E. Baringer, *Lincoln's Rise to Power* (Boston, 1937), p. 235.

40. Chicago *Democrat*, Oct. 30, 1860.

41. Greenville *Advocate*, Aug. 16, 1860.

42. *Weekly Chicago Democrat*, Nov. 17, 1860; Feb. 9, 1861.

Chapter 5

1. More recent scholarship has doubly stressed and clearly demonstrated the extent to which the ground was prepared for the party revolution of

1854 by local struggles in many states over prohibition, nativism, and other ethnocultural issues. See, for example, Ronald P. Formisano, *The Birth of Mass Political Parties: Michigan, 1827–1861* (Princeton, N.J., 1971), pp. 217–38.

2. Such as in the writings of Henry Wilson, Hermann E. Von Holst, and especially James Ford Rhodes. See Thomas J. Pressly, *Americans Interpret Their Civil War* (Princeton, N.J., 1954), pp. 38–40, 47–48, 138–47.

3. Charles A. and Mary R. Beard, *The Rise of American Civilization* (2 vols.; New York, 1927), 2: 53–54; see Pressly, *Americans Interpret Their Civil War*, pp. 238–62.

4. John R. Commons, "Horace Greeley and the Working Class Origins of the Republican Party," *Political Science Quarterly*, 24 (1909): 488.

5. Wilfred E. Binkley, *American Political Parties: Their Natural History* (New York, 1943), p. 213.

6. Reinhold H. Luthin, *The First Lincoln Campaign* (Cambridge, Mass., 1944), pp. 220–21.

7. Michael F. Holt, *The Political Crisis of the 1850s* (New York, 1978), p. 189; Larry Gara, "Slavery and the Slave Power: A Crucial Distinction," *Civil War History*, 15 (1969): 5–18.

8. For a more extensive discussion of the ethnocultural interpretation, see Chapter 7 below.

9. Richard H. Sewell, *Ballots for Freedom: Antislavery Politics in the United States, 1837–1860* (New York, 1976), p. 292. See also Eric Foner, *Free Soil, Free Labor, Free Men: The Ideology of the Republican Party Before the Civil War* (New York, 1970), pp. 304, 311; Kenneth M. Stampp, *The Imperiled Union: Essays on the Background of the Civil War* (New York, 1980), pp. 118–19.

10. Arthur M. Schlesinger, Jr., Fred L. Israel, and William P. Hansen, eds., *History of American Presidential Elections, 1789–1968* (4 vols.; New York, 1971), 2: 902–5.

11. In an autobiographical sketch written after his nomination for president in 1860, Lincoln declared that passage of the Kansas-Nebraska Act "aroused him as he had never been before." Roy P. Basler, Marion Dolores Pratt, and Lloyd A. Dunlap, eds., *The Collected Works of Abraham Lincoln* (9 vols.; New Brunswick, N.J., 1953–55), 4: 67.

12. Compare the election maps for 1854 and 1860 in Arthur Charles Cole, *The Era of the Civil War, 1848–1870* (Chicago, 1922), opposite pp. 132, 200.

13. Buchanan received 45.3 percent of the popular vote, Frémont 33.1 percent, and Fillmore 21.6 percent. See Roy F. Nichols and Philip S. Klein, "Election of 1856," in Schlesinger et al., *Presidential Elections*, 2: 1032.

14. Chicago *Tribune*, Feb. 5, 1856.

15. "It is the Pope of Rome . . . who says that Abraham Lincoln shall not be United States Senator," declared the Chicago *Democrat* on June 5, 1858, as the famous campaign of that year got under way, and on December 4, when the election was over, the paper added, "The triumph of Douglas is as

much a triumph over Protestantism as it is over free labor." See also the Chicago *Press and Tribune*, Aug. 10, 1860, and the *Bureau County Republican* (Princeton, Ill.), Aug. 16, 1860, which asked: "Is Douglas a Catholic? If he is a Catholic, he owes allegiance to a foreign despotic power, and if elected President will not be the President of the people, but an instrument of evil in the hands of the Pope of Rome." If Douglas became a Catholic, he did so only on his deathbed, and even that is doubtful. Compare the account in George Fort Milton, *The Eve of Conflict: Stephen A. Douglas and the Needless War* (Boston, 1934), p. 568, with that in Robert W. Johannsen, *Stephen A. Douglas* (New York, 1973), p. 872.

16. Basler et al., *Collected Works*, 3: 460–61, 486–87, 501, 547–50; 4: 49.

17. Albert J. Beveridge, *Abraham Lincoln, 1809–1858* (2 vols.; Boston, 1928), 2: 453–54.

18. New York *Tribune*, Dec. 17, 21, 23, 1857; Mar. 3, May 4, 11, 27, 1858; Horace Greeley, *Recollections of a Busy Life* (New York, 1868), pp. 357–58; Jeter Allen Isely, *Horace Greeley and the Republican Party, 1853–1861* (Princeton, N.J., 1947), pp. 238–48.

19. Springfield (Mass.) *Republican*, Apr. 30, 1858.

20. *Congressional Globe*, 35 Cong., 1 sess., p. 521.

21. *Illinois State Journal* (Springfield), June 17, 1858.

22. John H. Bryant to Lincoln, Apr. 19, 1858, Robert Todd Lincoln Collection, Manuscript Division, Library of Congress; Chicago *Tribune*, Apr. 21, 1858; Lincoln to Ozias M. Hatch, Mar. 24, 1858, in Roy P. Basler, ed., *The Collected Works of Abraham Lincoln: Supplement, 1832–1865* (Westport, Conn., 1974), p. 29.

23. Basler et al., *Collected Works*, 3: 345.

24. *Ibid*., pp. 233, 369, 405.

25. *Ibid*., p. 369.

26. *Ibid*., pp. 522–35.

27. *Congressional Globe*, 36 Cong., 1 sess., pp. 910–17.

28. Schlesinger et al., *Presidential Elections*, 2: 1124–27.

29. *The First Three Republican National Conventions* (Minneapolis, Minn., 1892), pp. 133–37, 140–42; William E. Baringer, *Lincoln's Rise to Power* (Boston, 1937), pp. 259–62.

30. William B. Hesseltine, ed., *Three Against Lincoln: Murat Halstead Reports the Caucuses of 1860* (Baton Rouge, La., 1960), p. 159.

31. William B. Hesseltine, *Lincoln and the War Governors* (New York, 1948), p. 57.

32. Isely, *Horace Greeley and the Republican Party*, p. 283.

33. Luthin, *First Lincoln Campaign*, pp. 140–42, 154–57; Willard L. King, *Lincoln's Manager, David Davis* (Cambridge, Mass., 1960), pp. 136–38, 140–41.

34. *First Three Republican Conventions*, pp. 148–55; Hesseltine, ed., *Three Against Lincoln*, pp. 166–73.

35. Hesseltine, ed., *Three Against Lincoln*, p. 174.

Chapter 6

1. V. O. Key, Jr., "A Theory of Critical Elections," *Journal of Politics*, 17 (1955): 3–18.

2. The Whig ticket carried eight Southern and seven Northern states; the Democratic ticket, precisely the reverse. Arthur M. Schlesinger, Fred L. Israel, and William P. Hansen, eds., *History of American Presidential Elections, 1789–1968* (4 vols.; New York, 1971), 2: 918.

3. Taylor's determined opposition to the compromise package in 1850 might have been enough to provoke a secession movement. On the danger of disunion in 1850, see David M. Potter, *The Impending Crisis, 1848–1861* (New York, 1976), pp. 96, 122–30.

4. Roger B. Taney to J. Mason Campbell, Oct. 19, 1860, Benjamin C. Howard Papers, Maryland Historical Society. On the slave-revolt fear of 1860, see Ollinger Crenshaw, *The Slave States in the Presidential Election of 1860* (Baltimore, Md., 1945), pp. 89–107; Wendell G. Addington, "Slave Insurrections in Texas," *Journal of Negro History*, 35 (1950): 408–34.

5. Harvey Wish, "The Slave Insurrection Panic of 1856," *Journal of Southern History*, 5 (1939): 206–22.

6. The *Literary Digest*, which had forecast the results of the four preceding presidential elections with remarkable accuracy, predicted a Landon victory by 370 to 161.

7. For discussion of the narrowness of Lincoln's victory, see G. S. Boritt, "Was Lincoln a Vulnerable Candidate in 1860?" *Civil War History*, 27 (1981): 46–48. As the principal thesis of his article, Boritt maintains that the Democrats missed a good opportunity when they failed to combat the "Honest Abe" image by presenting Lincoln as "'Tricky Old Abe,' the friend of stock jobbers, swindling bankers, and tax-dodging railroad barons." But in my opinion, the evidence that he presents does not bear the weight of his argument. One suspects that if Lincoln had indeed been vulnerable to such strategy, a few Democrats, at least, would have been smart enough to realize it and act accordingly.

8. Crenshaw, *Slave States*, p. 211.

9. Out of 33 votes in a House election, Republicans were sure of only 15, but there was reason to believe that some Northern Democratic congressmen would vote for Lincoln if Douglas was not in the contest. One remote Southern hope was that no candidate would be able to get a majority in the House, whereupon the duties of the presidency would devolve upon the new vice president chosen by the Senate. That would almost certainly be the candidate of the Southern Democrats, Joseph Lane of Oregon (running mate of John C. Breckinridge). See Crenshaw, *Slave States*, pp. 61–73; Roy Franklin Nichols, *The Disruption of American Democracy* (New York, 1948), pp. 338–39.

10. Boritt ("Was Lincoln a Vulnerable Candidate?" p. 46) argues persuasively that New York was another state very insecure for the Republicans.

11. George Fort Milton, *The Eve of Conflict: Stephen A. Douglas and the Needless War* (Boston, 1934), p. 496.

12. In the eleven states that eventually constituted the Confederacy, Lincoln received only about 2,000 votes, all in Virginia. Schlesinger et al., *Presidential Elections*, 2: 1152.

13. I have since dealt with this battle over the Lecompton constitution in *The Dred Scott Case: Its Significance in American Law and Politics* (New York, 1978), pp. 458–70, and in *The South and Three Sectional Crises* (Baton Rouge, La., 1980), pp. 53–56. See also Nichols, *Disruption of American Democracy*, pp. 153–76, and Potter, *Impending Crisis*, pp. 297–327.

Chapter 7

1. Edward Eggleston, "The New History," American Historical Association *Annual Report, 1900*, 1: 37–47.

2. Reviewing Karl Lamprecht's *Deutsche Geschichte* in 1898, Earle Wilbur Dow used the phrase "the new history," declaring that it took into account "all the activities of man as a social being" and entailed describing the human past "from the point of view of rational evolution," *American Historical Review*, 3 (1897–98): 448. Buckle's call for a "science of history" is in the first chapter of his *History of Civilization in England*, published in 1857. Spencer's prescription for usable history is in his essay "What Knowledge Is of Most Worth?" which first appeared in the *Westminster Review*, July 1859, and was reprinted the next year as the first chapter of his *Education: Intellectual, Moral, and Physical.* On Voltaire's view of history, see his preface to the *Essai sur les Moeurs et l'esprit des Nations* and his article on history in the *Encyclopédie*, where he declares: "On exige des historiens modernes plus de détails, des faits plus constatés, des dates précises, des autorités, plus d'attention aux usages, aux lois, aux moeurs, au commerce, à la finance, à l'agriculture, à la population" (8: 225).

3. James Harvey Robinson, *The New History: Essays Illustrating the Modern Historical Outlook* (New York, 1912); James Harvey Robinson, "The Conception and Methods of History," in Howard J. Rogers, ed., *Congress of Arts and Science, Universal Exposition, St. Louis, 1904* (Boston, 1906), 2: 40–51, especially p. 51; James Harvey Robinson, "The New History," in *American Philosophical Society Proceedings*, 50 (1911): 179–90, especially p. 187.

4. See especially Harry Elmer Barnes, *The New History and the Social Studies* (New York, 1925), pp. 3–39; Harry Elmer Barnes, *The History of Western Civilization* (2 vols.; New York, 1935), 1: v–ix.

5. See Richard Jensen, "History and the Political Scientist," in Seymour Martin Lipset, ed., *Politics and the Social Sciences* (New York, 1969), pp. 1–28.

6. "I speak of the historian as having contacts with the social sciences rather than as being a social scientist"—Richard Hofstadter, "History and

the Social Sciences," in Fritz Stern, ed., *The Varieties of History* (Cleveland, Ohio, 1956), p. 360.

7. Social Science Research Council, *Theory and Practice in Historical Study: A Report of the Committee on Historiography* (New York, 1946), Bull. 54, p. 138. Italics added.

8. *Ibid*., pp. 55–102, 134–35, 139–40.

9. Thomas C. Cochran, "'The Presidential Synthesis' in American History," *American Historical Review*, 53 (1948): 748.

10. Social Science Research Council, *The Social Sciences in Historical Study: A Report of the Committee on Historiography* (New York, 1954), Bull. 64, p. 13.

11. Richard D. Challener and Maurice Lee, Jr., "History and the Social Sciences: The Problem of Communications," *American Historical Review*, 61 (1956): 334.

12. Hofstadter, "History and the Social Sciences," p. 364.

13. *Social Sciences in Historical Study*, pp. 150–51.

14. Edward N. Saveth, "Scientific History," in Donald Sheehan and Harold C. Syrett, eds., *Essays in American Historiography: Papers Presented in Honor of Allan Nevins* (New York, 1960), p. 16.

15. V. O. Key, Jr., "A Theory of Critical Elections," *Journal of Politics*, 17 (1955): 3–18; Alfred H. Conrad and John R. Meyer, "The Economics of Slavery in the Ante Bellum South," *Journal of Political Economy*, 66 (1958): 95–130; Merle Curti, *The Making of an American Community: A Case Study of Democracy in a Frontier Community* (Stanford, Calif., 1959); Lee Benson, "Research Problems in American Political Historiography," in Mirra Komarovsky, ed., *Common Frontiers of the Social Sciences* (Glencoe, Ill., 1957), pp. 113–83, 418–21; Lee Benson, *The Concept of Jacksonian Democracy: New York as a Test Case* (Princeton, N.J., 1961); Robert William Fogel, *The Union Pacific Railroad: A Case in Premature Enterprise* (Baltimore, Md., 1960).

16. Carl Bridenbaugh, "The Great Mutation," *American Historical Review*, 68 (1963): 326; Robert William Fogel, "Scientific History and Traditional History," in L. Jonathan Cohen et al., eds., *Logic, Methodology and Philosophy of Science, 6: Proceedings of the Sixth International Congress of Logic, Methodology and Philosophy of Science, Hannover, 1979* (Amsterdam, 1982), p. 49. This essay has been reprinted with a response by G. R. Elton, in *Which Road to the Past? Two Views of History* (New Haven, Conn., 1983).

17. Lee Benson predicted in 1966 that within two decades "a significant proportion of American historians will have accepted Buckle's two basic propositions: (1) past human behavior can be studied scientifically; (2) the main business of historians is to participate in the overall scholarly enterprise of discovering and developing general laws of human behavior." Quoted from "Quantification, Scientific History, and Scholarly Innovation," in Benson, *Toward the Scientific Study of History: Selected Essays* (Philadelphia, Pa., 1972), p. 99. See also Robert William Fogel, "The Limits of Quantitative Methods in History," *American Historical Review*, 80

(1975): 329–50; Samuel P. Hays, *American Political History as Social Analysis* (Knoxville, Tenn., 1980); Allan G. Bogue, "Quantification in the 1980s," in Theodore K. Rabb and Robert I. Rotberg, eds., *The New History: The 1980s and Beyond* (Princeton, N.J., 1982), pp. 137–75; J. Morgan Kousser, "Quantitative Social-Scientific History," in Michael Kammen, ed., *The Past Before Us: Contemporary Historical Writing in the United States* (Ithaca, N.Y., 1980), pp. 433–56; J. Morgan Kousser, "History QUASSHed: Quantitative Social Scientific History in Perspective," *American Behavioral Scientist*, 23 (1980): 885–904.

18. Allan G. Bogue, "The New Political History in the 1970s," in Kammen, *The Past Before Us*, p. 232.

19. Ronald P. Formisano, *The Birth of Mass Political Parties: Michigan, 1827–1861* (Princeton, N.J., 1971), pp. 102–3, 110, 138, 160–64; Paul Kleppner, *The Cross of Culture: A Social Analysis of Midwestern Politics, 1850–1900* (New York, 1970), pp. 69–91; Paul Kleppner, *The Third Electoral System, 1853–1892: Parties, Voters, and Political Cultures* (Chapel Hill, N.C., 1979), pp. 143–97; Paul Kleppner, "Partisanship and Ethnoreligious Conflict: The Third Electoral System, 1853–1892," in Paul Kleppner et al., *The Evolution of American Electoral Systems* (Westport, Conn., 1981), pp. 134–36; Formisano used the terms "evangelicals" and "nonevangelicals." Kleppner first spoke of "pietists versus ritualists," but later of "pietists" and "antipietists," with the latter divided into "ritualists" and "salvationists." This subcategorization enabled him to finesse the problem of the statistically troublesome Methodists. Richard J. Jensen preferred the terms "pietists" and "ritualists"—see note 40 below.

20. See especially J. Morgan Kousser, "The 'New Political History': A Methodological Critique," *Reviews in American History*, 4 (1975): 1–14; Richard B. Latner and Peter Levine, "Perspectives on Antebellum Pietistic Politics," *ibid*., pp. 15–24.

21. Hays, *American Political History*, pp. 115–16, 293.

22. Frederick Jackson Turner, "The Significance of the Frontier in American History," in American Historical Association *Annual Report, 1893*, p. 217.

23. Charles A. and Mary R. Beard, *The Rise of American Civilization* (2 vols.; New York, 1927), 2: 36–40, 53–54.

24. Benson, *Scientific Study of History*, p. 191.

25. Cochran, "Presidential Synthesis," p. 759.

26. Joel H. Silbey, "The Civil War Synthesis in American Political History," *Civil War History*, 10 (1964): 130–40.

27. Joel H. Silbey, "The Surge of Republican Power: Partisan Antipathy, American Social Conflict, and the Coming of the Civil War," in Stephen E. Maizlish and John J. Kushma, eds., *Essays on American Antebellum Politics, 1840–1860* (College Station, Tex., 1982), p. 201.

28. *Ibid*., pp. 203–7.

29. The essay is in Benson, *Scientific Study of History*. See especially pp. 316n, 323, 326, 331. Benson was not the first historian to link the coming of the Civil War with the Jackson presidency. Charles M. Wiltse, in *John C.*

Calhoun: Nullifier, 1829–1839 (Indianapolis, Ind., 1949), p. 172, declared: "If any single date can be fixed as that on which a given event was predetermined, the Civil War became inevitable on December 10, 1832." That was the date of Jackson's proclamation to the people of South Carolina in response to the ordinance of nullification.

30. One of the main reasons for the establishment of the unitary executive was that the members of the Convention had George Washington clearly in mind when they designed the office. Thus Alexander's line of reasoning could lead to the conclusion that Washington, just by existing in 1787, contributed significantly to the disruption of the Union seventy-four years later.

31. The essay, an expanded version of Alexander's presidential address to the Southern Historical Association, appeared in the *Journal of Southern History*, 47 (1981): 3–32.

32. Joel H. Silbey, *The Shrine of Party: Congressional Voting Behavior, 1841–1852* (Pittsburgh, Pa., 1967); Thomas B. Alexander, *Sectional Stress and Party Strength: A Study of Roll-Call Voting Patterns in the United States House of Representatives, 1836–1860* (Nashville, Tenn., 1967). See the reviews of Silbey by David Donald in *Political Science Quarterly*, 83 (1968): 455–56, and by Frank Otto Gatell in *Journal of American History*, 54 (1967–68): 402–3; and the reviews of both books by Charles B. Dew in *Wisconsin Magazine of History*, 52 (1968–69): 182–84, and by Richard P. McCormick in *Journal of Southern History*, 33 (1967): 568–69, and in *Journal of American History*, 54 (1967–68): 893–94.

33. Silbey, *Shrine of Party*, p. 145. Silbey quotes Wolff, but Wolff's conclusion was that "both party and sectional influences played a major role in determining the voting behavior of Senators on the issue." Gerald W. Wolff, "Party and Section: The Senate and the Kansas-Nebraska Bill," *Civil War History*, 18 (1972): 293–311, quotation on p. 307.

34. Silbey, *Shrine of Party*, pp. 109–14, 189–200. In calculating percentages, I have corrected one error. According to Table 8.6 on p. 112, there were 25 "pro-compromise" (scale-type 0–3) senators, 19 of them Southerners, but a count of such senators on the list of scale positions, pp. 189–200, indicates 30 classified as "pro-compromise," 24 of them Southerners. This latter count is confirmed by examination of the Guttman scale on the compromise issue as it appears in Silbey's Ph.D. dissertation, "Congressional Voting Behavior and the Southern-Western Alliance, 1841–1852," University of Iowa, 1963, pp. 520–21.

35. On July 31, 1850, for instance, those five senators not only voted three times for indefinite postponement of the "Omnibus Bill," but also joined wholeheartedly in the strategy of destroying the measure by striking out most of its provisions. See *Congressional Globe*, 31 Cong., 1 sess., Appendix, pp. 1479–83.

36. David M. Potter, *The Impending Crisis, 1848–1861* (New York, 1976), p. 90; Don E. Fehrenbacher, *The Dred Scott Case: Its Significance in American Law and Politics* (New York, 1978), pp. 162–63.

37. Silbey, "Congressional Voting Behavior," pp. 521, 527–28." The ten

Senate roll calls scaled by Silbey were associated with the abortive "Omnibus Bill" rather than with the actual passage of the compromise measures, and in at least half of them, Silbey's designation of a vote as "pro-compromise" or "anti-compromise" appears to have been wholly arbitrary. More striking is the fact that of the thirteen House roll calls scaled, eleven dealt with the Texas question and none dealt with California. Yet a vote for the Texas bill or for one of the territorial bills was in itself a pro-Southern vote; it became a vote for compromise only if it was accompanied by a vote for the admission of California.

38. Walter Dean Burnham, "Theory and Voting Research," in his *The Current Crisis in American Politics* (New York, 1982), pp. 80, 84–86 (an essay first published in the *American Political Science Review*, 68 [1974]: 1002–23). Compare with Burnham's explanation in 1967 in "Party Systems and the Political Process," in William Nisbet Chambers and Walter Dean Burnham, eds., *The American Party Systems: Stages of Political Development* (New York, 1967), pp. 288, 294–95.

39. See, for example, Michael Fitzgibbon Holt, *Forging a Majority: The Formation of the Republican Party in Pittsburgh, 1848–1860* (New Haven, Conn., 1969), pp. 145–46, 307–8; Formisano, *Birth of Mass Political Parties*, pp. 217–18, 235, 252–53.

40. Richard J. Jensen, *Grass Roots Politics: Parties, Issues, and Voters, 1854–1983* (Westport, Conn., 1983), pp. 5, 7. See also Richard J. Jensen, *The Winning of the Midwest: Social and Political Conflict, 1888–1896* (Chicago, 1971), pp. 62–69.

41. Burnham, "Theory and Voting Research," p. 80.

42. For critiques of the ethnocultural thesis, see James E. Wright, "The Ethnocultural Model of Voting: A Behavioral and Historical Critique," *American Behavioral Scientist*, 16 (1972–73): 653–74; Richard L. McCormick, "Ethno-Cultural Interpretations of Nineteenth-Century American Voting Behavior," *Political Science Quarterly*, 89 (1974): 351–77; Eric Foner, *Politics and Ideology in the Age of the Civil War* (New York, 1980), pp. 16–19; and the articles cited in note 20 above. Kleppner and Formisano class Methodists with anti-pietists. Jensen puts them with the pietists, as historians of American religion are generally disposed to do.

43. Michael F. Holt, *The Political Crisis of the 1850s* (New York, 1978).

44. See, for example, the essays by George H. Daniels, Robert P. Swierenga, Paul J. Kleppner, and James M. Berquist in Frederick C. Luebke, ed., *Ethnic Voters and the Election of Lincoln* (Lincoln, Neb., 1971).

45. One such beginning is Dale Baum, *The Civil War Party System: The Case of Massachusetts, 1848–1876* (Chapel Hill, N.C., 1984), pp. 24–54, where it is demonstrated that Massachusetts Know-Nothings contributed little to Lincoln's victory in 1860. A forthcoming book by William E. Gienapp promises to shed much new light on the emergence and triumph of the Republican party.

46. Seymour Martin Lipset, *Political Man: The Social Bases of Politics* (2d ed.; Baltimore, Md., 1981), pp. 372–84.

47. Peyton McCrary, Clark Miller, and Dale Baum, "Class and Party in

the Secession Crisis: Voting Behavior in the Deep South, 1856–1861," *Journal of Interdisciplinary History*, 8 (1978): 429–57. For Georgia, see Michael P. Johnson, *Toward a Patriarchal Republic: The Secession of Georgia* (Baton Rouge, La., 1977), pp. 63–78, 206–10.

48. Silbey, "Surge of Republican Power," quotations from pp. 227, 229.

49. *Ibid*., p. 213n.

50. McCrary, Miller, and Baum, "Class and Party in the Secession Crisis," pp. 444–45.

51. Richmond *Enquirer*, quoted in Avery Craven, *The Coming of the Civil War* (New York, 1942), p. 300. For an ambitious, eccentric, and unpersuasive effort to quantify the causes of the Civil War—one in which it is calculated, for instance, that "northern preferences to eliminate slavery were more than twenty times as strong as those to preserve the Union"—see Gerald Gunderson, "The Origin of the American Civil War," *Journal of Economic History*, 34 (1974): 915–45, quotation from p. 944.

52. Silbey, "Surge of Republican Power," p. 204, misrepresents me as dismissing the new political history with the words "often synthetic and modish . . . reflecting the latest fashions in behavioral science theory and terminology but adding little to the substance of explanation." Anyone taking the trouble to read this passage in *The South and Three Sectional Crises* (Baton Rouge, La., 1980), p. 3, will discover that I was referring, not to the methods and achievements of the new political history, but rather to the trendy overuse, by historians in general, of certain concepts picked up from other disciplines, and that I was talking particularly about the concept of "modernization." It may be worth adding that my cautionary words echoed similar sentiments expressed even more emphatically by one of the leading new political historians, Ronald P. Formisano, in his essay "Toward a Reorientation of Jacksonian Politics: A Review of the Literature, 1959–1975," *Journal of American History*, 63 (1976): 64–65.

53. For a different view on this point, see J. Morgan Kousser, "The Revivalism of Narrative: A Response to Recent Criticisms of Quantitative History," *Social Science History*, 8 (1984): 133–49.

54. Kleppner, *Third Electoral System*, p. xx.

Chapter 8

1. Benjamin P. Thomas, *Abraham Lincoln, a Biography* (New York, 1952); Stephen B. Oates, *With Malice Toward None: The Life of Abraham Lincoln* (New York, 1977).

2. See text, pp. 153–56.

3. Richard Henry Stoddard, *Abraham Lincoln: An Horatian Ode,* cited in Roy P. Basler, *The Lincoln Legend: A Study in Changing Conceptions* (Boston, 1935), p. 234.

4. Basler, *The Lincoln Legend*, pp. 264–65.

5. David Donald, *Lincoln's Herndon* (New York, 1948), p. 305; Richard N. Current, *The Lincoln Nobody Knows* (New York, 1963), pp. 11–13.

6. John T. Morse, Jr., *Abraham Lincoln* (2 vols.; Boston, 1893), 2: 356.

7. See Chapter 15 for development of this theme.
8. David Donald, *Lincoln Reconsidered* (2d ed.; New York, 1969), p. 16.
9. Michael Davis, *The Image of Lincoln in the South* (Knoxville, Tenn., 1971), p. 159.
10. *Ibid.*, p. 138.
11. Jefferson Davis, *The Rise and Fall of the Confederate Government* (2 vols.; New York, 1881), 2: 683.
12. Thomas Dixon, Jr., *The Clansman: An Historical Romance of the Ku Klux Klan* (New York, 1905), p. 47; Davis, *Image of Lincoln*, pp. 147–52.
13. Leon F. Litwack, *North of Slavery: The Negro in the Free States, 1790–1860* (Chicago, 1961), p. 276.
14. Fawn M. Brodie, "Who Defends the Abolitionist?" in Martin Duberman, ed., *The Antislavery Vanguard: New Essays on the Abolitionists* (Princeton, N.J., 1965), pp. 63–64.
15. Current, *Lincoln Nobody Knows*, p. 236.
16. Howard Zinn, "Abolitionists, Freedom-Riders, and the Tactics of Agitation," in Duberman, *Antislavery Vanguard*, pp. 438–39.
17. Martin Duberman, "The Northern Response to Slavery," in *Antislavery Vanguard*, pp. 396, 402.
18. Lerone Bennett, Jr., "Was Abe Lincoln a White Supremacist?" *Ebony*, 23 (February 1968): 37.
19. *Ibid.*, pp. 37–38, 40.
20. Richard Claxton Gregory, *No More Lies: The Myth and the Reality of American History* (New York, 1971), p. 182.
21. Bennett, "Lincoln a White Supremacist?" p. 36.
22. Davis, *Image of Lincoln*, p. 156: "There is something sadly ironic in seeing black extremists and Ku Kluxers clasping hands over the grave of the Great Emancipator's reputation."
23. Robert Penn Warren, *Who Speaks for the Negro?* (New York, 1965), p. 262.
24. Roy P. Basler, Marion Dolores Pratt, and Lloyd A. Dunlap, eds., *The Collected Works of Abraham Lincoln* (9 vols.; New Brunswick, N.J., 1953–55), 3: 145–46.
25. Arthur Zilversmit, ed., *Lincoln on Black and White* (Belmont, Calif., 1971).
26. See Michael Banton, "The Concept of Racism," in Sami Zubaida, ed., *Race and Racialism* (London, 1970), pp. 17–34.
27. David M. Reimers, ed., *Racism in the United States: An American Dilemma?* (New York, 1972), p. 5.
28. Banton, "Concept of Racism," p. 18.
29. Forrest G. Wood, *Black Scare: The Racist Response to Emancipation and Reconstruction* (Berkeley, Calif., 1970), p. 15.
30. George M. Fredrickson, *The Black Image in the White Mind: The Debate on Afro-American Character and Destiny, 1817–1914* (New York, 1971), p. 2.

31. Margaret Nicholson, *A Dictionary of American-English Usage* (New York, 1958), p. 469.

32. Fredrickson, *Black Image*, p. 101.

33. Bennett, "Lincoln a White Supremacist?" p. 36.

34. Benjamin Quarles, *Lincoln and the Negro* (New York, 1962), pp. 16–18.

35. Basler et al., *Collected Works*, 1: 260.

36. George M. Fredrickson, "A Man But Not a Brother: Abraham Lincoln and Racial Equality," *Journal of Southern History*, 41 (1975): 44.

37. George Sinkler, *The Racial Attitudes of American Presidents from Abraham Lincoln to Theodore Roosevelt* (Garden City, N.Y., 1971), p. 75.

38. Fredrickson, "A Man But Not a Brother," p. 58.

39. See Banton, "Concept of Racism," pp. 22–24, for the "inductivist explanation of racism," which, he says, "is chiefly found in the writings of American sociologists. They are acquainted with racism in its modern forms and work backwards, viewing earlier statements about race from a modern standpoint instead of setting them in the intellectual context of the time in which they were made."

40. For example, although he carefully qualifies his stated conclusions, this is the effect of Eugene H. Berwanger's *The Frontier Against Slavery: Western Anti-Negro Prejudice and the Slavery Extension Controversy* (Urbana, Ill., 1967).

41. See Larry Gara, "Slavery and the Slave Power: A Crucial Distinction," *Civil War History*, 15 (1969): 5–18.

42. "Our republican robe is soiled, and trailed in the dust," said Lincoln in 1854. In the same speech, he called slavery a "monstrous injustice," and then added, "I hate it because it deprives our republican example of its just influence in the world." Basler et al., *Collected Works*, 2: 255, 276. Duberman, "Northern Response to Slavery," pp. 399–401, points to nationalism as one reason for opposition to abolitionism; but it should also be emphasized that national pride fortified the antislavery movement.

43. Basler et al., *Collected Works*, 3: 9–10, 29, 80, 95, 112–13, 146, 216, 280, 300–304, 470.

44. *Ibid.*, 2: 255–56.

45. *Ibid.*, 2: 391.

46. *Ibid.*, 2: 405, 408; 3: 16, 88, 249.

47. *Ibid.*, 3: 399.

48. The principal exceptions are the Peoria speech of Oct. 16, 1854, and the statement to the delegation of Negroes on Aug. 4, 1862.

49. Fredrickson, "A Man But Not a Brother," pp. 40–44. But for an argument belittling Clay's influence on Lincoln, see Marvin R. Cain, "Lincoln's Views on Slavery and the Negro: A Suggestion," *Historian*, 26 (1964): 502–20.

50. Basler et al., *Collected Works*, 3: 16; 4: 156; 5: 372–73.

51. Allen Thorndike Rice, ed., *Reminiscences of Abraham Lincoln by Distinguished Men of His Time* (New York, 1886), p. 193.

52. J. G. Randall and Richard N. Current, *Lincoln the President: Last Full Measure* (New York, 1955), pp. 317–18.

53. Quarles, *Lincoln and the Negro*, p. 204.

54. See especially his comment on a statement by Chief Justice Roger B. Taney implying that the Negro's status had improved since the framing of the Constitution, Basler et al., *Collected Works*, 2: 403–4.

55. See the discussion of factors discouraging abolitionism in Duberman, "Northern Response to Slavery," pp. 398–401.

56. Lord Charnwood, *Abraham Lincoln* (New York, 1916), p. 452.

57. Julius Lester, *Look Out, Whitey! Black Power's Gon' Get Your Mama!* (New York, 1968), p. 58.

58. For a good statement of Lincoln's strategy, see Hans L. Trefousse, *The Radical Republicans, Lincoln's Vanguard for Racial Justice* (New York, 1969), p. 182.

59. Basler et al., *Collected Works*, 5: 388–89.

60. Thomas, *Abraham Lincoln*, p. 342. For further discussion of the Greeley letter, see text, pp. 283–84.

61. Speech at Cooper Institute, Feb. 1863, quoted in Zilversmit, *Lincoln on Black and White*, p. 133.

62. Basler et al., *Collected Works*, 5: 372.

63. Quarles, *Lincoln and the Negro*, pp. 108–23, 191–94.

64. Basler et al., *Collected Works*, 2: 255.

65. Benjamin F. Butler, *Butler's Book* (Boston, 1892), pp. 903–8. The credibility of Butler's statement has been pretty well destroyed by Mark E. Neely, Jr., in his "Abraham Lincoln and Black Colonization: Benjamin Butler's Spurious Testimony," *Civil War History*, 25 (1979): 76–83.

66. Eric Foner, *Free Soil, Free Labor, Free Men: The Ideology of the Republican Party Before the Civil War* (New York, 1970), p. 271. See also Harry V. Jaffa, *Crisis of the House Divided: An Interpretation of the Issues in the Lincoln-Douglas Debates* (Garden City, N.Y., 1959), p. 61.

67. Basler et al., *Collected Works*, 5: 534–35. See also Lincoln's letter to John A. Andrew, Feb. 18, 1864, in *ibid.*, 7: 191. Lincoln's argument bears some resemblance to the doctrine of "diffusion," which Southerners had used earlier in the century to justify the expansion of slavery.

68. See William B. Hesseltine, *Lincoln's Plan of Reconstruction* (Tuscaloosa, Ala., 1960); Ludwell H. Johnson, "Lincoln and Equal Rights: The Authenticity of the Wadsworth Letter," *Journal of Southern History*, 32 (1966): 83–87; Harold M. Hyman, "Lincoln and Equal Rights for Negroes: The Irrelevancy of the 'Wadsworth Letter,'" *Civil War History*, 12 (1966): 258–66; Ludwell H. Johnson, "Lincoln and Equal Rights: A Reply," *Civil War History*, 13 (1967): 66–73; Herman Belz, *Reconstructing the Union: Theory and Policy During the Civil War* (Ithaca, N.Y., 1969); Peyton McCrary, *Abraham Lincoln and Reconstruction: The Louisiana Experiment* (Princeton, N.J., 1978); Stephen B. Oates, "Toward a New Birth of Freedom: Abraham Lincoln and Reconstruction, 1854–1865," *Lincoln Herald*, 82 (1980): 287–96; LaWanda Cox, *Lincoln and Black*

Freedom, a Study in Presidential Leadership (Columbia, S.C., 1981). See also text, pp. 153–56, 171–72.

69. *The Works of Charles Sumner* (15 vols.; Boston, 1870–83), 6: 152.

70. Basler et al., *Collected Works*, 3: 146.

71. *Life and Times of Frederick Douglass, Written by Himself* (New York, 1962, reprint of 1892 edition), p. 485.

Chapter 9

1. Clinton Rossiter, ed., *The Federalist Papers* (New York: Mentor edition, 1961), pp. 290–93 (no. 45), 309–10 (no. 48), 322 (no. 51), 414 (no. 68), 443 (no. 73), 464–66 (no. 78).

2. Carl N. Degler, *Out of Our Past: The Forces That Shaped Modern America* (New York, 1959), p. 200.

3. Roy P. Basler, Marion Dolores Pratt, and Lloyd A. Dunlap, eds., *The Collected Works of Abraham Lincoln* (9 vols.; New Brunswick, N.J., 1953–55), 4: 196, 434.

4. Alexander H. Stephens, *A Constitutional View of the Late War Between the States: Its Causes, Character, Conduct and Results . . .* (2 vols.; Philadelphia and Chicago, 1868–70), 1: 12; William B. Hesseltine, *Lincoln's Plan of Reconstruction* (Tuscaloosa, Ala., 1960), pp. 36–37, 141.

5. "Law Address of Ex-Senator James R. Doolittle, Delivered Before the Union College of Law at Chicago, June 6th, 1879," *Journal of the Illinois State Historical Society*, 19 (Apr.–July 1926): 82–83.

6. Basler et al., *Collected Works*, 3: 146.

7. Philip S. Paludan, *A Covenant with Death: The Constitution, Law, and Equality in the Civil War Era* (Urbana, Ill., 1975), p. 15. See also Harold M. Hyman, *A More Perfect Union: The Impact of the Civil War and Reconstruction on the Constitution* (New York, 1973), p. 447.

8. Clinton Rossiter, *The American Presidency* (New York, 1956), p. 74. For further discussion of the dictatorship theme, see text, Chapter 10. The most thorough treatment of the subject is by Herman Belz in his McMurtry Lecture, *Lincoln and the Constitution: The Dictatorship Question Reconsidered* (Fort Wayne, Ind., 1984).

9. David Donald, *Lincoln Reconsidered* (2d ed.; New York, 1961), pp. 187–208. See also G. S. Boritt, *Lincoln and the Economics of the American Dream* (Memphis, Tenn., 1978), pp. 195–97.

10. Basler et al., *Collected Works*, 4: 214.

11. *Ibid.*, 4: 430; 7: 281.

12. Andrew A. Lipscomb and Albert Ellery Bergh, eds., *The Writings of Thomas Jefferson* (20 vols.; Washington, 1903), 12: 418, 183. See also Arthur M. Schlesinger, Jr., *The Imperial Presidency* (Boston, 1973), pp. 23–25.

13. Carl B. Swisher, *The Taney Period* (New York, 1974), pp. 844–50.

14. Rocco J. Tresolini, *Justice and the Supreme Court* (Philadelphia, Pa., 1963), p. 16.

15. Frank Otto Gatell, ed., "Roger B. Taney, the Bank of Maryland

Rioters, and a Whiff of Grapeshot," *Maryland Historical Magazine*, 59 (1964): 263.

16. Bernard Schwartz, *The Reins of Power: A Constitutional History of the United States* (New York, 1963), p. 94.

17. Robert H. Jackson, *The Supreme Court in the American System of Government* (Cambridge, Mass., 1955), p. 76. And see text, pp. 134–36.

18. Basler et al., *Collected Works*, 1: 112; 4: 264.

19. *Ibid.*, 2: 495. See text, p. 21, for Lincoln's discussion of judicial review in his First Inaugural.

20. *Ibid.*, 8: 100.

21. *Ibid.*, 8: 52.

22. *Ibid.*, 4: 267.

23. Bertrand Russell, "The Future of Democracy," *New Republic*, 90 (May 1937): 381.

Chapter 10

1. Roy P. Basler, Marion Dolores Pratt, and Lloyd A. Dunlap, eds., *The Collected Works of Abraham Lincoln* (9 vols.; New Brunswick, N.J., 1953–55), 7: 301–2.

2. Richard Bardolph, "Malice Toward One: Lincoln in the North Carolina Press," *Lincoln Herald*, 53 (1951–52): 39, 43–44; Michael Davis, *The Image of Lincoln in the South* (Knoxville, Tenn., 1971), pp. 82–84.

3. Basler et al., *Collected Works*, 4: 432.

4. Benjamin R. Curtis, *Executive Power* (Boston, 1862).

5. Horatio Seymour's message to the New York legislature, reported in the New York *Times*, Jan. 8, 1863.

6. London *Times*, Oct. 7, 1862.

7. Basler et al., *Collected Works*, 6: 261n.

8. Lord Bryce, *The American Commonwealth* (2d ed., 2 vols.; London, 1890), 1: 51, 61, 289.

9. James Ford Rhodes, *History of the United States from the Compromise of 1850* (7 vols.; New York, 1893–1906), 3: 441, 442.

10. Samuel Eliot Morison, *The Oxford History of the United States, 1783–1917* (2 vols.; London, 1927), 2: 254.

11. Arthur M. Schlesinger, Jr., *The Imperial Presidency* (Boston, 1973); see pp. 58–64 for his treatment of Lincoln.

12. Basler et al., *Collected Works*, 6: 266.

13. Alvy L. King, *Louis T. Wigfall, Southern Fire-Eater* (Baton Rouge, La., 1970), pp. 110–14.

14. Bruce Catton, *The Coming Fury* (Garden City, N.Y., 1961), pp. 226–29, 236.

15. Don E. Fehrenbacher, "Roger B. Taney and the Sectional Crisis," *Journal of Southern History*, 43 (1977): 560.

16. Of the 1,080 army officers on active duty at the beginning of the Civil War, 313 resigned to join the Confederate forces. Mark Mayo Boatner III, *The Civil War Dictionary* (New York, 1959), p. 495.

17. *Ex parte Merryman*, 17 Federal Cases 144 (no. 9487).

18. Allan Nevins, *The War for the Union* (4 vols.; New York, 1959–71), 1: 81–83; Dean Sprague, *Freedom Under Lincoln* (Boston, 1965), pp. 6–7, 11–12.

19. Basler et al., *Collected Works*, 4: 344, 347.

20. *Ibid.*, 4: 364–65, 419; 5: 436–37; 6: 451–52.

21. *Congressional Globe*, 37 Cong., 2 sess., pp. 90–91, 98. Trumbull offered a resolution of inquiry concerning arbitrary arrests, but denied that he was criticizing the President.

22. *Trial of Abraham Lincoln by the Great Statesmen of the Republic: A Council of the Past on the Tyranny of the Present* (New York, 1863), pp. 28–29.

23. Basler et al., *Collected Works*, 7: 281.

24. *Ibid.*, 5: 53.

25. Mortimer J. Adler, *The Idea of Freedom: A Dialectical Examination of the Conceptions of Freedom* (2 vols., Garden City, N.Y., 1958–61), 1: 87.

26. James Gouinlock, ed., *The Moral Writings of John Dewey* (New York, 1976), pp. 191, 195.

27. Basler et al., *Collected Works*, 7: 512.

28. George Birkbeck Hill and L. F. Powell, eds., *Boswell's Life of Johnson* (rev. ed., 6 vols.; Oxford, 1934–50), 4: 12.

29. Edmund Burke, "A Letter to John Farr and John Harris, Esqurs., Sheriffs of the City of Bristol, on the Affairs of America, 1777," in *The Works of the Right Honourable Edmund Burke* (8 vols.; London, 1887–1902), 2: 30. It should be added, however, that Burke, in this instance, was explaining his opposition to an act for partial suspension in America of the privilege of the writ of habeas corpus.

30. Basler et al., *Collected Works*, 8: 100.

31. *Ibid.*, 6: 300–306.

32. *Ibid.*, 4: 430.

33. *Ibid.*, 6: 267.

34. John Stuart Mill, *Considerations on Representative Government* (London, 1861), p. 52.

35. Basler et al., *Collected Works*, 8: 152.

36. *Ibid.*, 7: 505, 528.

37. *Ibid.*, 4: 440.

38. John Emerich Edward Dalberg-Acton, First Baron Acton, *The History of Freedom and Other Essays* (London, 1909), p. 4.

39. John Stuart Mill, *On Liberty* (London, 1926), pp. 10–13, 30–31.

40. Basler et al., *Collected Works*, 4: 256–57.

Chapter 11

1. Edwin M. Stanton to John S. Phelps, July 19, 1862, *The War of the Rebellion: A Compilation of the Official Records of the Union and Confederate Armies* (128 vols.; Washington, D.C., 1880–1901), series 3, vol. 2, p.

233; vol. 3, p. 474 (hereafter cited as *Official Records*); Thomas S. Staples, *Reconstruction in Arkansas, 1862–1874* (New York, 1923), pp. 9–11. Phelps apparently continued to hold his seat in Congress throughout the greater part of his tenure as military governor of Arkansas, in spite of the constitutional provision (Article I, Section 6) forbidding it. See *Congressional Globe*, 38 Cong., 1 sess., pp. 3410–11.

2. Roy P. Basler, Marion Dolores Pratt, and Lloyd A. Dunlap, eds., *The Collected Works of Abraham Lincoln* (9 vols.; New Brunswick, N.J., 1953–55), 7: 53–56.

3. See text, pp. 161–62.

4. Gen. Stephen A. Hurlbut to Gen. Ulysses S. Grant, Aug. 1, 1863; Gen. Frederick W. Steele to Gen. John M. Schofield, Sept. 12, 1863, *Official Records*, series 1, vol. 22, part 2, pp. 424–25; part 1, pp. 474–77; Kenneth P. Williams, *Lincoln Finds a General: A Military Study of the Civil War* (5 vols.; New York, 1959), 5: 108–17; Leo E. Huff, "The Union Expedition Against Little Rock, August-September, 1863," *Arkansas Historical Quarterly*, 22 (1963): 224–37; Thomas A. Belser, Jr., "Military Operations in Missouri and Arkansas, 1861–1865," Ph.D. diss., Vanderbilt University, 1958, pp. 579–84; John M. Harrell, "Arkansas," in Clement A. Evans, ed., *Confederate Military History* (12 vols.; Atlanta, Ga., 1899), 10: 207–22.

5. Williams, *Lincoln Finds a General*, 5: 113.

6. There is a manuscript biography by Catherine B. Steele in the Steele Papers at Stanford. Steele's career is summarized by Thomas M. Spaulding in Allan Johnson and Dumas Malone, eds., *Dictionary of American Biography* (New York, 1937), 17: 555–56.

7. Catherine B. Steele manuscript, p. 7 of chapter titled "The General Commanding," Steele Papers.

8. Albert Castel, *General Sterling Price and the Civil War in the West* (Baton Rouge, La., 1968), p. 154.

9. To a delegation of Arkansas leaders visiting him in January 1864, Lincoln explained that out of past experience he had decided not to appoint a separate military governor, but rather to minimize cause for dissension by entrusting Steele with both the military and civil administration of the state. Basler et al., *Collected Works*, 7: 144.

10. Sherman to Steele, Oct. 24, 1863, *Official Records*, series 1, vol. 22, part 2, pp. 673–74; Steele to Sherman, Nov. 9, 1863, Steele Papers.

11. Fishback, a Virginian, had become acquainted with Lincoln during several years' residence in Illinois, making such a favorable impression that he had been hired in the spring of 1858 to do some legal research on land titles for the firm of Lincoln and Herndon. William M. Fishback to Lincoln, May 17, 1858; Fishback to C. M. Smith, Dec. 1, 1858, Robert Todd Lincoln Collection, Manuscript Division, Library of Congress; Lincoln to Samuel C. Davis and Company, Nov. 17, 1858; Lincoln to Fishback, Dec. 19, 1858, in Basler et al., *Collected Works*, 3: 338, 346.

12. Little Rock *National Democrat*, Mar. 26, 1864, with a quotation from the *Unconditional Union* of Mar. 25. Fishback at about the same time was spreading the word that Meador had acted as a pimp for the officers of

of Steele's staff, citing Steele as his authority. Fishback to Steele, May 3, 1864, Steele Papers.

13. Staples, *Reconstruction in Arkansas*, pp. 15–34; Ruth Caroline Cowen, "Reorganization of Federal Arkansas, 1862–65," *Arkansas Historical Quarterly*, 18 (1959): 39–45.

14. Lincoln to Steele, Jan. 20, 1864, in Basler et al., *Collected Works*, 7: 141–42.

15. Lincoln to Steele, Jan. 27, 30, 1864; to Isaac Murphy, Feb. 8, 1864; to John M. Thayer, Feb. 15, 1864; to Fishback, Feb. 17, 1864, in *ibid.*, 7: 154–55, 161, 173, 185, 189.

16. Lincoln to Fishback and to Murphy, Mar. 12, 1864, in *ibid.*, 7: 239, 240.

17. John B. Steele to Frederick W. Steele, Jan. 14, 1864, Steele Papers.

18. Little Rock *National Democrat*, Mar. 5, 1864. Steele's address of Feb. 29 to the people of Arkansas, praising the work of the convention, is in *Official Records*, series 1, vol. 34, part 2, p. 484.

19. *Personal Memoirs of U. S. Grant* (2 vols.; New York, 1886), 2: 139–40.

20. The idea of sending Steele south to the Red River came under discussion soon after his occupation of Little Rock. See Schofield to Banks, Nov. 19, 1863, *Official Records*, series 1, vol. 22, part 2, pp. 710–11. The most important monograph on the whole subject is Ludwell H. Johnson, *Red River Campaign: Politics and Cotton in the Civil War* (Baltimore, Md., 1958).

21. Steele to Banks, Feb. 5, 28, 1864, *Official Records*, series 1, vol. 34, part 2, pp. 246–47, 448–49.

22. Sherman to Steele, Mar. 4, 1864, *ibid.*, pp. 496–97.

23. Steele to Banks, Feb. 28, Mar. 7, 1864, *ibid.*, pp. 448–49, 518–19.

24. Sherman to Steele, Mar. 6, 1864, *ibid.*, p. 516. To Banks, Sherman declared: "The civil election is as nothing compared with the fruits of military success," Mar. 4 endorsement on letter from Steele to Banks, Feb. 28, 1864, *ibid.*, p. 449. Sherman also expressed dissatisfaction with Steele's assertion that he would have no more than 7,000 infantry available for a movement in force to the support of Banks.

25. Staples, *Reconstruction in Arkansas*, pp. 39–42.

26. Steele to Lincoln, Mar. 18, 1864, Robert Todd Lincoln Collection.

27. New York *Times*, Mar. 21, 1864.

28. Steele to Banks and Steele to Sherman, Mar. 10, 1864, *Official Records*, series 1, vol. 34, part 2, pp. 542, 547.

29. Steele to Halleck, Mar. 12, 1864, *ibid.*, p. 576.

30. Grant to Steele, Mar. 14, 15, 1864, *ibid.*, pp. 603, 616.

31. Sherman to Steele, Mar. 20, 1864, *ibid.*, p. 668.

32. Johnson, *Red River Campaign*, p. 171.

33. Sherman somewhat unrealistically maintained that Steele could requisition horses, mules, forage, and most of his provisions from the countryside along his line of march. Sherman to Steele, Mar. 4, 1864, *Official Records*, series 1, vol. 34, part 2, pp. 496–97; to Steele, Mar. 20, 1864, Steele Papers.

34. Johnson, *Red River Campaign*, pp. 171–80; Castel, *Sterling Price*, pp. 174–76; Belser, "Military Operations," pp. 652–53.

35. Clarence C. Buel and Robert U. Johnson, eds., *Battles and Leaders of the Civil War* (4 vols.; New York, 1887), 4: 372–73; Castel, *Sterling Price*, pp. 176–79; Joseph Howard Parks, *General Edmund Kirby Smith, C.S.A.* (Baton Rouge, La., 1954), pp. 397–98; Johnson, *Red River Campaign*, pp. 184–94; Belser, "Military Operations," pp. 654, 656, 657–68; Sherman to Halleck, May 6, 1864, *Official Records*, series 1, vol. 34, part 3, p. 479.

36. Belser, "Military Operations," pp. 668–78; Castel, *Sterling Price*, pp. 179–83; Johnson, *Red River Campaign*, pp. 194–202. For Steele's own account of the retreat from Camden, see *Official Records*, series 1, vol. 34, part 1, pp. 667–71.

37. Grant to Halleck, Mar. 28, 1864, *Official Records*, series 1, vol. 33, pp. 752–53; Sherman to Grant and to Steele, Apr. 7, 1864, *ibid*., vol. 34, part 3, pp. 76–77.

38. Halleck to Canby, May 7, 1864, *ibid*., p. 491.

39. Castel, *Sterling Price*, pp. 203–4; Belser, "Military Operations," pp. 691–96. Steele defended his performance in a letter to his brother, who transmitted the pertinent passages to the President. See John B. Steele to Lincoln, Nov. 22, 1864, Robert Todd Lincoln Collection.

40. Grant to Halleck, Nov. 25, 1864; General Orders No. 71, Headquarters Military Division of West Mississippi, Nov. 25, 1864, *Official Records*, series 1, vol. 41, part 4, pp. 672–73, 674. Grant recommended the removal but left the decision to Canby. He had concluded that Steele, though "a first-class commander of troops in battle," was "not . . . quite equal to the efficient command of a department."

41. John Steele to Frederick Steele, May 14, 1864, Steele Papers. G. L. Miller of Little Rock wrote to Steele on Mar. 30, 1864: "Your character and policy alike attest to your conservatism. As a conservative, you are known to all, recognized by the whole country, and praised by all but Radicals," *ibid*.

42. Steele to Isaac Murphy, Jan. 21, 1864, *ibid*.; Chicago *Times* of Nov. 19, quoted in Little Rock *National Democrat*, Dec. 5, 1863; Chicago *Tribune*, Jan. 9, 1864. Kirby-Smith, writing to Jefferson Davis on Jan. 20, 1864, spoke of Steele's "conciliatory policy" as potentially dangerous to the Confederate cause, *Official Records*, series 1, vol. 34, part 2, p. 896.

43. Murphy to Lincoln, May 27, July 23, 1864, Robert Todd Lincoln Collection; to Lincoln, June 29, 1864, *Official Records*, series 3, vol. 4, p. 463.

44. Horace Greeley, *The American Conflict: A History of the Great Rebellion in the United States of America, 1860–65* (2 vols.; Hartford, Conn., 1866–67), 2: 555–56.

45. Halleck to Sherman, Apr. 8, 1864, *Official Records*, series 1, vol. 32, part 3, p. 289.

46. The St. Louis *Missouri Democrat* of Dec. 7, for example, approved Steele's removal, calling him "conservative"; quoted in the Little Rock *National Democrat*, Dec. 17, 1864. The latter paper declared that the radical

party in Arkansas was "the refuge of former secessionists and rebels who try to gloss their former treason with thick radical varnish." The Chicago *Tribune*, Sept. 16, 1864, had published a dispatch from St. Louis declaring that Steele's removal "would benefit the whole country."

47. For one thing, Lincoln sent no political instructions of any kind to Steele's successor, General Joseph J. Reynolds.

48. LaWanda Cox, *Lincoln and Black Freedom: A Study in Presidential Leadership* (Columbia, S.C., 1981).

49. *Ibid.*, pp. 59, 77–80; Lincoln to Banks, Aug. 5, 1863, in Basler et al., *Collected Works*, 6: 365.

50. Lincoln to Hahn, Mar. 13, 1864, in Basler et al., *Collected Works*, 7: 243.

51. Cox, *Lincoln and Black Freedom*, pp. 99–100; Peyton McCrary, *Abraham Lincoln and Reconstruction: The Louisiana Experiment* (Princeton, N.J., 1978), pp. 253–65.

52. Basler et al., *Collected Works*, 8: 403; Cox, *Lincoln and Black Freedom*, p. 112.

53. In Jan. 1864, Lincoln did endorse the plans of certain Arkansas plantation owners to contract for the labor of their former slaves. Basler et al., *Collected Works*, 7: 145–47.

54. Francis Newton Thorpe, ed., *The Federal and State Constitutions, Colonial Charters, and Other Organic Laws of the States, Territories, and Colonies Now or Heretofore Forming the United States of America* (7 vols.; Washington, D.C., 1909), pp. 290, 291–92, 296, 302. Compare with the provisions of the Louisiana constitution, pp. 1433, 1446. The provision for one-year indenture was identical to a passage in the Illinois constitution of 1818, p. 980. Lincoln, it should be noted, approved the admission of Nevada to statehood in 1864 with a constitution limiting suffrage to whites.

55. See McCrary, *Lincoln and Reconstruction*, pp. xi, 4, 355; Cox, *Lincoln and Black Freedom*, pp. 23, 43, 142, and the underlying argument of pp. 46–139.

56. Ludwell H. Johnson, "Lincoln and Equal Rights: A Reply," *Civil War History*, 13 (1967): 71. See also George M. Fredrickson, "A Man But Not a Brother: Abraham Lincoln and Racial Equality," *Journal of Southern History*, 41 (1975): 57.

57. Basler et al., *Collected Works*, 8: 404–5.

58. See, for instance, McCrary, *Lincoln and Reconstruction*, pp. 186, 210, 348; Cox, *Lincoln and Black Freedom*, pp. 69–72; Joseph G. Dawson III, *Army Generals and Reconstruction: Louisiana, 1862–77* (Baton Rouge, La., 1982), pp. 12–19; J. G. Randall and Richard N. Current, *Lincoln the President: Last Full Measure* (New York, 1955), pp. 15–17.

59. Benjamin Quarles, *Lincoln and the Negro* (New York, 1962), p. 227.

60. In the summer of 1864 and again early in 1865, Congress refused to seat the senators and representatives elected by Louisiana and Arkansas. Lincoln's former associate, William Fishback, was one of those denied a senatorship. Congressional reconstruction, as embodied in the Wade-Davis

bill, was pocket-vetoed by Lincoln in July 1864, and efforts to pass a revised version failed in the early months of 1865.

61. In December 1864, Lincoln expressed his opposition on political grounds to the general enfranchisement of blacks as proposed in a revised version of the Wade-Davis bill. See Herman Belz, *Reconstructing the Union: Theory and Policy During the Civil War* (Ithaca, N.Y., 1969), pp. 252–53; Michael Les Benedict, *A Compromise of Principle: Congressional Republicans and Reconstruction, 1863–1869* (New York, 1974), pp. 90–91.

Chapter 12

1. Roy P. Basler, Marion Dolores Pratt, and Lloyd A. Dunlap, eds., *The Collected Works of Abraham Lincoln* (9 vols.; New Brunswick, N.J., 1953–55), 6: 392–93. Hackett presumed further on the acquaintanceship by applying for a diplomatic post; see David Chambers Mearns, *Largely Lincoln* (New York, 1961), pp. 131–33.

2. New York *Herald*, Sept. 17, 1863. The *Herald*'s comment is reproduced in its entirety in Roy P. Basler, *A Touchstone for Greatness: Essays, Addresses, and Occasional Pieces About Abraham Lincoln* (Westport, Conn., 1973), pp. 209–11.

3. Basler et al., *Collected Works*, 6: 558–59.

4. Earl Schenck Miers, William E. Baringer, and C. Percy Powell, eds., *Lincoln Day by Day: A Chronology, 1809–1865* (3 vols.; Washington, 1960), 3: 227–28; Tyler Dennett, ed., *Lincoln and the Civil War in the Diaries and Letters of John Hay* (New York, 1939), pp. 138–39.

5. Francis B. Carpenter, *Six Months at the White House with Abraham Lincoln* (New York, 1866), p. 52. John Hay, remembering his secretarial years in the White House, said that Lincoln "read Shakespere more than all other writers together," and that "where only one or two were present he was fond of reading aloud. He passed many of the summer evenings in this way when occupying his cottage at the Soldiers' Home. He would there read Shakespere for hours with a single secretary for audience." *Addresses of John Hay* (New York, 1906), pp. 334–35.

6. Carpenter, *Six Months*, p. 49. Lincoln nevertheless had strong feelings about how certain lines should be read. See, for example, Dennett, *Lincoln and the Civil War*, pp. 138–39.

7. Basler, *Touchstone*, pp. 206–27, offers the most comprehensive study of "Lincoln and Shakespeare." On p. 226, he asks: "To what extent then, one wonders, may Lincoln have adapted himself, consciously or subconsciously, to the spirit of Shakespearean tragedy in the role he sought to play in American history?"

8. Rebecca West, *The Court and the Castle* (New Haven, Conn., 1957), pp. 43, 81–82.

9. "The Perpetuation of Our Political Institutions," given before the Young Men's Lyceum of Springfield, Ill., on Jan. 27, 1838, Basler et al., *Collected Works*, 1: 113–14.

10. Edmund Wilson, *Patriotic Gore: Studies in the Literature of the American Civil War* (New York, 1962), pp. 106–8, 129.

11. Lincoln thought that actors did not take Richard seriously enough; see Carpenter, *Six Months*, pp. 51–52. He saw Edwin Booth as Richard III on Feb. 19, 1864; *Lincoln Day by Day*, 3: 241.

12. Richard E. Neustadt, *Presidential Power: The Politics of Leadership* (New York, 1960), p. 161.

13. Richard Hofstadter, *The American Political Tradition and the Men Who Made It* (New York, 1948), p. 134.

14. John Hay said that Lincoln "never tired of 'Richard II,'" *Addresses*, p. 334.

15. Marquis de Chambrun, "Personal Recollections of Mr. Lincoln," *Scribner's Magazine*, 13 (1893): 34–35.

16. Carpenter, *Six Months*, p. 50. For a similar judgment of the soliloquy, see George Lyman Kittredge's introduction to his edition of *Hamlet* (Boston, 1939), pp. xviii–xx.

17. George Lyman Kittredge, *Shakespere: An Address* . . . (Cambridge, Mass., 1916), p. 37. See also Eleanor Prosser, *Hamlet and Revenge* (2d ed.; Stanford, Calif., 1971), pp. 185–87.

18. Basler et al., *Collected Works*, 5: 403–4.

19. Memorandum of Edward Bates, quoted in *ibid*., 5: 486.

20. Quoted words are from Kenneth M. Stampp, *The Era of Reconstruction, 1865–1877* (New York, 1965), pp. 36–37. See also Hofstadter, *American Political Tradition*, p. 133; J. G. Randall and Richard N. Current, *Lincoln the President: Last Full Measure* (New York, 1955), 4: 376; Charles W. Ramsdell, "Lincoln and Fort Sumter," *Journal of Southern History*, 3 (1937): 288; David M. Potter, *Lincoln and His Party in the Secession Crisis* (New Haven, Conn., 1942), p. 375.

21. Basler et al., *Collected Works*, 7: 282.

22. *Ibid*., 5: 537.

23. *Ibid*., 8: 332–33.

24. Chambrun, "Personal Recollections," p. 32.

25. On Lincoln's tragic vision, see Henry Alonzo Myers, *Tragedy: A View of Life* (Ithaca, N.Y., 1956), pp. 161–66.

Chapter 13

1. Of this poem by William Knox, Lincoln once said: "I would give all I am worth, and go in debt, to be able to write so fine a piece." He quoted six verses from the poem to conclude his eulogy of Zachary Taylor in 1850. Roy P. Basler, Marion Dolores Pratt, and Lloyd A. Dunlap, *The Collected Works of Abraham Lincoln* (9 vols.; New Brunswick, N.J., 1953–55), 1: 378; 2: 90; Mark E. Neely, Jr., *The Abraham Lincoln Encyclopedia* (New York, 1982), p. 240.

2. Basler et al., 1: 368.

3. Howard K. Beale, ed., *The Diary of Gideon Welles* (3 vols.; New

York, 1960), 2: 282–83. The words "towards an indefinite shore" were added later to the diary entry.

4. Robert V. Bruce, *Lincoln and the Riddle of Death* (Fort Wayne, Ind., 1981), pp. 1–24. Quotations are from p. 23.

5. Dwight G. Anderson, *Abraham Lincoln: The Quest for Immortality* (New York, 1982), pp. 7, 12, 16, 61, 79–81, 92, 95, 99, 120, 161–66. For further discussion of the Anderson book, see text Chapters 15, 16, and 19.

6. Thomas Reed Turner, *Beware the People Weeping: Public Opinion and the Assassination of Abraham Lincoln* (Baton Rouge, La., 1982).

7. David Balsiger and Charles E. Sellier, Jr., *The Lincoln Conspiracy* (Los Angeles, Calif., 1977). Issued also as a motion picture with the same title.

8. G. J. A. O'Toole, *The Cosgrove Report: Being the Private Inquiry of a Pinkerton Detective into the Death of President Lincoln* (New York, 1979); John K. Lattimer, *Kennedy and Lincoln: Medical and Ballistic Comparisons of Their Assassinations* (New York, 1980); William Hanchett, *The Lincoln Murder Conspiracies* (Urbana, Ill., 1983).

9. Chicago *Tribune*, Apr. 14, 1978, sec. 4, p. 10; *Time*, May 22, 1978, p. 83.

10. James D. Richardson, ed., *A Compilation of the Messages and Papers of the Presidents, 1789–1897* (10 vols.; Washington, D.C., 1896–1900), 6: 307–8.

11. Otto Eisenschiml, *Why Was Lincoln Murdered?* (Boston, 1937); William Hanchett, "The Eisenschiml Thesis," *Civil War History*, 25 (1979): 197–217; Hanchett, *Lincoln Murder Conspiracies*, pp. 158–213.

12. For discussion of the new evidence, see Robert H. Fowler, "Was Stanton Behind Lincoln's Murder?" *Civil War Times*, 3 (Aug. 1961): 4–23; Turner, *Beware the People Weeping*, pp. 5–8; and Hanchett, *Lincoln Murder Conspiracies*, pp. 214–17, 225–26, 230.

13. For the implication of Seward, see Vaughan Shelton, *Mask for Treason: The Lincoln Murder Trial* (Harrisburg, Pa., 1965), pp. 433–39. For the survival of Booth, see Los Angeles *Times*, May 22, 1977, part 4, p. 8; Balsiger and Sellier, *Lincoln Conspiracy*, p. 297.

14. Balsiger and Sellier, *Lincoln Conspiracy*, pp. 5–6, 26–71. For a critique of the book and motion picture, see William C. Davis, "Caveat Emptor," and "'The Lincoln Conspiracy'—Hoax?" in *Civil War Times Illustrated*, Aug. 1977, pp. 33–37, and Nov. 1977, pp. 47–49.

15. Basler et al., *Collected Works*, 3: 279.

16. T. Harry Williams, *Lincoln and the Radicals* (Madison, Wis., 1941), p. 384.

17. Oscar Lewis, *The Lost Years: A Biographical Fantasy* (New York, 1951).

18. Kenneth M. Stampp and Leon F. Litwack, eds., *Reconstruction: An Anthology of Revisionist Writings* (Baton Rouge, La., 1969), p. 23.

19. Lerone Bennett, Jr., "Was Abe Lincoln a White Supremacist?" *Ebony*, Feb. 1968, p. 42.

20. LaWanda Cox, *Lincoln and Black Freedom: A Study in Presidential Leadership* (Columbia, S.C., 1981), p. 151. Peyton McCrary, *Abraham Lincoln and Reconstruction: The Louisiana Experiment* (Princeton, N.J., 1978), p. 12, declares: "Although it is impossible to know precisely what shape Lincoln's postwar policy would have taken, it is almost inconceivable that he would have followed the strategy pursued by Johnson."

21. Stephen B. Oates, "Toward a New Birth of Freedom: Abraham Lincoln and Reconstruction," *Lincoln Herald*, 82 (1980): 294.

22. Don E. Fehrenbacher, "Lincoln and Reconstruction," *Illinois History*, 16 (1962–63): 100; also Fehrenbacher, ed., *Abraham Lincoln: A Documentary Portrait Through His Speeches and Writings* (New York, 1964), p. xxviii.

23. Harry Ammon, *James Monroe: The Quest for National Identity* (New York, 1971), pp. 543–44; Charles Francis Adams, ed., *Memoirs of John Quincy Adams* (12 vols.; Philadelphia, Pa., 1874–77), 7: 81.

24. Leonard D. White, *The Jeffersonians: A Study in Administrative History, 1801–1829* (New York, 1951), pp. 72–74; *Memoirs of John Quincy Adams*, 7: 209–13, 216, 239, 244–45, 248–49, 282–83, 285, 287–88, 289, 378.

25. James F. Kirkham, Sheldon G. Levy, and William J. Crotty, *Assassination and Political Violence: A Report to the National Commission on the Causes and Prevention of Violence* (New York, 1970), pp. 16–24.

26. Killed: James A. Garfield, William McKinley, John F. Kennedy, and Robert F. Kennedy. Wounded: Theodore Roosevelt and Ronald Reagan. Unhurt: Franklin D. Roosevelt, Harry S Truman, and Gerald R. Ford (twice), but others were killed in the attacks on Roosevelt and Truman. This summary does not include the strange case of Samuel Byck, who, in the last year of the Nixon administration, tried to hijack a plane at the Baltimore-Washington airport with the intent of crashing it into the White House. See James W. Clarke, *American Assassins: The Darker Side of Politics* (Princeton, N.J., 1982), pp. 128–42.

27. Kirkham et al., *Assassination*, p. 78; William J. Crotty, ed., *Assassinations and the Political Order* (New York, 1971), pp. 10–11.

28. Clarke, *American Assassins*, p. 39.

29. Charles Francis Adams, *Richard Henry Dana: A Biography* (3d ed., 2 vols.; Boston, 1891), 2: 264–65.

30. New York *Herald*, Apr. 17, 1865. The author was Charles G. Halpine. See William Hanchett, *Irish: Charles G. Halpine in Civil War America* (Syracuse, N.Y., 1970), pp. 134–35.

Chapter 14

1. The lectures were published as pamphlets in 1948 and 1968, respectively, by the Clarendon Press at Oxford. Potter's lecture was reprinted in his *The South and the Sectional Conflict* (Baton Rouge, La., 1968).

2. New York *Times*, Feb. 13, 1932, pp. 1, 8; Nov. 5, 1932, p. 9; Oct. 13, 1948, p. 18; Jan. 10, 1961, p. 20; Feb. 13, 1968, p. 1; *Memoirs by Harry S.*

Truman, Volume Two: Years of Trial and Hope (Garden City, N.Y., 1956), pp. 443–44; Robert J. Donovan, *Tumultuous Years: The Presidency of Harry S. Truman, 1949–1953* (New York, 1982), pp. 121, 354; David Donald, *Lincoln Reconsidered: Essays on the Civil War Era* (2d ed.; New York, 1961), pp. 13–17.

3. John G. Nicolay and John Hay, *Abraham Lincoln: A History* (10 vols.; New York, 1890). On Lincoln biographers generally, down to the mid-1940's, see Benjamin P. Thomas, *Portrait for Posterity: Lincoln and His Biographers* (New Brunswick, N.J., 1947).

4. William H. Herndon and Jesse W. Weik, *Herndon's Lincoln: The True Story of a Great Life* (3 vols.; Chicago, 1889); David Donald, *Lincoln's Herndon* (New York, 1948), p. 169.

5. Donald, *Lincoln's Herndon*, p. 368.

6. Some of the most important works of this kind were Francis B. Carpenter, *Six Months at the White House with Abraham Lincoln: The Story of a Picture* (New York, 1866); Elizabeth Keckley, *Behind the Scenes* (New York, 1868); Ward Hill Lamon, *The Life of Abraham Lincoln, from His Birth to His Inauguration as President* (Boston, 1872), a ghost-written book that made use of Herndon's materials and in some respects anticipated his biographical purposes; Ward Hill Lamon, *Recollections of Abraham Lincoln, 1847–1865* (Chicago, 1895), pieced together by Lamon's daughter after his death; Isaac N. Arnold, *The Life of Abraham Lincoln* (Chicago, 1885); Allen Thorndike Rice, *Reminiscences of Abraham Lincoln by Distinguished Men of His Time* (New York, 1886); Alexander K. McClure, *Abraham Lincoln and Men of War-Times* (Philadelphia, Pa., 1892); Henry C. Whitney, *Life on the Circuit with Lincoln* (Boston, 1892); Noah Brooks, *Washington in Lincoln's Time* (New York, 1895). Of course there was also much material on Lincoln in the memoirs and autobiographies of his contemporaries, such as those of Horace Greeley (1868); Ulysses S. Grant (1885–86); Hugh McCulloch (1888); Benjamin F. Butler, (1892); John Sherman (1895); John M. Palmer (1901); and Carl Schurz (1907–8).

7. See Carl Sandburg, *Abraham Lincoln: The Prairie Years* (2 vols.; New York, 1926), 2: 26–28; Albert J. Beveridge, *Abraham Lincoln, 1809–1858* (2 vols.; Boston, 1928), 2: 372–79; Arthur Brooks Lapsley, ed., *The Writings of Abraham Lincoln* (8 vols.; New York, 1905), 2: 247–75. Whitney and his reconstruction of the Bloomington speech are critically examined in Paul M. Angle's edition of Henry C. Whitney, *Life on the Circuit with Lincoln* (Caldwell, Id., 1940). Elwell Crissey, *Lincoln's Lost Speech: The Pivot of His Career* (New York, 1967), is extravagant in his estimate of the importance of the speech but judicious and thorough in his treatment of the Whitney reconstruction.

8. Ida M. Tarbell, *The Life of Abraham Lincoln* (2 vols.; New York, 1900).

9. David M. Potter, *The Lincoln Theme and American National Historiography: An Inaugural Lecture Delivered Before the University of Oxford on 19 November 1947* (Oxford, 1948), p. 17.

10. Lord Charnwood (Godfrey Rathbone Benson), *Abraham Lincoln* (New York, 1917).

11. Charles Willis Thompson, reviewing William E. Barton's *The Lineage of Lincoln* in the *New York Times Book Review*, May 12, 1929, p. 5.

12. William E. Barton, *The Paternity of Abraham Lincoln* (New York, 1920). "One of those rare books that deserve to be called definitive," says Paul M. Angle, *A Shelf of Lincoln Books* (New Brunswick, N.J., 1946), p. 66.

13. William E. Barton, *The Life of Abraham Lincoln* (2 vols.; Indianapolis, Ind., 1925), 1: 58–63.

14. Thomas, *Portrait for Posterity*, p. 242.

15. Sandburg, *Lincoln: Prairie Years*; Carl Sandburg, *Abraham Lincoln: The War Years* (New York, 1939). The fact that Sandburg's six volumes are wholly without documentation also limits their usefulness to scholars.

16. Beveridge, *Lincoln*, 1: 134.

17. William E. Barton, "A Noble Fragment: Beveridge's Life of Lincoln," *Mississippi Valley Historical Review*, 15 (1928–29): 498. By contrast, it took Sandburg only about 600 pages to reach the Lincoln-Douglas debates.

18. The *Atlantic Monthly* affair is the subject of text Chapter 18.

19. Thomas, *Portrait for Posterity*, pp. 267–74; Mark E. Neely, Jr., *Lincoln Lore*, no. 1697 (July 1979), pp. 1–3. Among the important works written by executive secretaries of the Association were the following: Paul M. Angle, *"Here I Have Lived": A History of Lincoln's Springfield, 1821–1865* (Springfield, Ill., 1935); Benjamin P. Thomas, *Lincoln's New Salem* (Springfield, Ill., 1934); Harry E. Pratt, *The Personal Finances of Abraham Lincoln* (Springfield, Ill., 1943); and William E. Baringer, *A House Dividing: Lincoln as President Elect* (Springfield, Ill., 1945). The Association, having exhausted its funds on the *Collected Works*, was dissolved in 1952, then subsequently revived in more attenuated form. The role of the Association has been more or less absorbed by the Illinois State Historical Library, but in some respects its successor is the Louis A. Warren Lincoln Library and Museum in Fort Wayne, Indiana, publisher of *Lincoln Lore*.

20. Nathaniel Wright Stephenson, *Lincoln: An Account of His Personal Life, Especially of Its Springs of Action as Revealed and Deepened by the Ordeal of War* (Indianapolis, Ind., 1922).

21. James G. Randall, *Constitutional Problems Under Lincoln* (New York, 1926).

22. The two biographies by academics are Reinhard H. Luthin, *The Real Abraham Lincoln* (Englewood Cliffs, N.J., 1960), and Stephen B. Oates, *With Malice Toward None: The Life of Abraham Lincoln* (New York, 1977).

23. Roy P. Basler, *The Lincoln Legend: A Study in Changing Conceptions* (Boston, 1935); William E. Baringer, *Lincoln's Rise to Power* (Boston, 1937).

24. T. Harry Williams, *Lincoln and the Radicals* (Madison, Wis., 1941).

25. David M. Potter, *Lincoln and His Party in the Secession Crisis* (New Haven, Conn., 1942). Louis A. Warren, one of the keepers of the Lincoln

flame, regarded the Potter book as the work of a "debunker." See *Lincoln Lore*, no. 712 (Nov. 30, 1942).

26. Harry J. Carman and Reinhard H. Luthin, *Lincoln and the Patronage* (New York, 1943).

27. J. G. Randall, *Lincoln the President: Springfield to Gettysburg* (2 vols.; New York, 1946). Randall devoted about three-quarters of his first volume to the pre-presidential years.

28. William B. Hesseltine, *Lincoln and the War Governors* (New York, 1948).

29. Kenneth M. Stampp, *And the War Came: The North and the Secession Crisis, 1860–1861* (Baton Rouge, La., 1950).

30. T. Harry Williams, *Lincoln and His Generals* (New York, 1952).

31. Allan Nevins, *Ordeal of the Union* (2 vols.; New York, 1947); Allan Nevins, *The Emergence of Lincoln* (2 vols.; New York, 1950); Bruce Catton, *Mr. Lincoln's Army* (Garden City, N.Y., 1951); Bruce Catton, *Glory Road: The Bloody Route from Fredericksburg to Gettysburg* (Garden City, N.Y., 1952); Bruce Catton, *A Stillness at Appomattox* (Garden City, N.Y., 1953).

32. For the history of the Robert Todd Lincoln Collection, see David C. Mearns, *The Lincoln Papers* (2 vols.; Garden City, N.Y., 1948), 1: 1–136.

33. Benjamin P. Thomas, *Abraham Lincoln: A Biography* (New York, 1952).

34. J. G. Randall, *Lincoln the President: Midstream* (New York, 1952); J. G. Randall and Richard N. Current, *Lincoln the President: Last Full Measure* (New York, 1955).

35. Some leading examples of these first-generation "primitives" are the following: Horace Greeley, *The American Conflict* (2 vols.; Hartford, Conn., 1864–66); Edward A. Pollard, *The Lost Cause* (New York, 1866); Henry Wilson, *History of the Rise and Fall of the Slave Power in America* (3 vols.; Boston, 1872–77); Jefferson Davis, *The Rise and Fall of the Confederate Government* (2 vols.; New York, 1881); John A. Logan, *The Great Conspiracy* (New York, 1886). On the earlier Civil War historiography, see Howard K. Beale, "What Historians Have Said About the Causes of the Civil War," Social Science Research Council Bull. 54, *Theory and Practice in Historical Study* (New York, 1946), pp. 53–102; Thomas J. Pressly, *Americans Interpret Their Civil War* (Princeton, N.J., 1954).

36. Woodrow Wilson, *Division and Reunion, 1829–1889* (New York, 1893); James Ford Rhodes, *History of the United States from the Compromise of 1850* (7 vols.; New York, 1893–1906); John W. Burgess, *The Middle Period, 1817–1858* (New York, 1897); John W. Burgess, *The Civil War and the Constitution, 1859–1865* (2 vols.; New York, 1901); John W. Burgess, *Reconstruction and the Constitution, 1866–1876* (New York, 1902); Pressly, *Americans Interpret Their Civil War*, pp. 121–92.

37. Charles W. Ramsdell, "Lincoln and Fort Sumter," *Journal of Southern History*, 3 (1937): 259–88; Pressly, *Americans Interpret Their Civil War*, pp. 231–53. See also text Chapter 15.

38. Charles A. and Mary R. Beard, *The Rise of American Civilization* (2

vols.; New York, 1927); Vernon Louis Parrington, *Main Currents in American Thought* (3 vols.; New York, 1927–30); Beale, "Causes of the Civil War," pp. 69–73; Pressly, *Americans Interpret Their Civil War*, pp. 195–228.

39. Pressly, *Americans Interpret Their Civil War*, pp. 257–92; Beale, "Causes of the Civil War," pp. 83–85; David M. Potter, *The South and the Sectional Conflict* (Baton Rouge, La., 1968), pp. 92–99; Kenneth M. Stampp, *The Imperiled Union* (New York, 1980), pp. 199–223. Among Avery Craven's most influential books were *The Coming of the Civil War* (New York, 1942) and *The Repressible Conflict, 1830–1861* (Baton Rouge, La., 1939).

40. Randall, *Lincoln: Springfield to Gettysburg*, 1: 105–9, 123–25, 342–50; 2: 204–5; J. G. Randall, *Lincoln and the South* (Baton Rouge, La., 1946), pp. 38–39, 47–48, 111; J. G. Randall, *Lincoln the Liberal Statesman* (New York, 1947), pp. 22, 88–117.

41. Richard Hofstadter, *The American Political Tradition and the Men Who Made It* (New York, 1948), pp. 94, 112.

42. Donald W. Riddle, *Congressman Abraham Lincoln* (Urbana, Ill., 1957), p. 249.

43. Luthin, *Real Lincoln*, p. 242.

44. Arthur M. Schlesinger, Jr., "The Causes of the Civil War: A Note on Historical Sentimentalism," *Partisan Review*, 16 (1949): pp. 978, 981; Potter, *South and Sectional Conflict*, pp. 99–100.

45. Harry V. Jaffa, *Crisis of the House Divided: An Interpretation of the Issues in the Lincoln-Douglas Debates* (Garden City, N.Y., 1959).

46. Don E. Fehrenbacher, *Prelude to Greatness: Lincoln in the 1850's* (Stanford, Calif., 1962).

47. Stampp, *And the War Came*; Kenneth M. Stampp, "Lincoln and the Strategy of Defense in the Crisis of 1861," *Journal of Southern History*, 11 (1945): 297–323; Pressly, *Americans Interpret Their Civil War*, pp. 288–91.

48. Kenneth M. Stampp, *The Peculiar Institution: Slavery in the Ante-Bellum South* (New York, 1956).

49. Kenneth M. Stampp, *The Era of Reconstruction, 1865–1877* (New York, 1965), p. 215.

50. Martin Duberman, *The Antislavery Vanguard: New Essays on the Abolitionists* (Princeton, N.J., 1965), pp. 396–98, 402, 437–41.

51. *Ibid*., p. 401.

52. Leon F. Litwack, *North of Slavery: The Negro in the Free States, 1790–1860* (Chicago, 1961), pp. 276–79.

53. See the works by Bennett, Gregory, Sinkler, Berwanger, and Lester cited in Chapter 8, notes 18, 20, 37, 40, 57; also Melvin Steinfeld, *Our Racist Presidents: From Washington to Nixon* (San Ramon, Calif., 1972), pp. 95–96; Robert F. Durden, "Ambiguities in the Antislavery Crusade of the Republican Party," in Duberman, *Antislavery Vanguard*, pp. 362–94; V. Jacque Voegeli, *Free But Not Equal: The Midwest and the Negro During the Civil War* (Chicago, 1967), pp. 176–82; Forrest G. Wood, *Black Scare:*

The Racist Response to Emancipation and Reconstruction (Berkeley, Calif., 1968), pp. 13–15, 31–32, 154–55; Charles Crowe, ed., *The Age of Civil War and Reconstruction, 1830–1900* (Homewood, Ill., 1966), pp. 239–40.

54. Roy P. Basler, Marion Dolores Pratt, and Lloyd A. Dunlap, eds., *The Collected Works of Abraham Lincoln* (9 vols.; New Brunswick, N.J., 1953–55), 8: 333.

Chapter 15

1. J. G. Randall, *Lincoln the Liberal Statesman* (New York, 1947), p. 65.

2. Alfred Haworth Jones, *Roosevelt's Image Brokers: Poets, Playwrights, and the Use of the Lincoln Symbol* (Port Washington, N.Y., 1974), p. 65.

3. New York *Times*, Oct. 22, 1932, p. 11; Nov. 5, 1932, p. 9. See also David Donald, "Getting Right with Lincoln," in his *Lincoln Reconsidered* (2d ed.; New York, 1961), pp. 3–18.

4. Lyon G. Tyler, "The South and Secession," *Tyler's Quarterly Historical and Genealogical Magazine*, 13 (1931–32): 212.

5. Richmond *Enquirer*, July 25, 1861.

6. Michael Davis, *The Image of Lincoln in the South* (Knoxville, Tenn., 1971), pp. 62–104; Richard Bardolph, "Malice Toward One: Lincoln in the North Carolina Press," *Lincoln Herald*, 53 (Winter, 1952): 34–45.

7. Clipping enclosed in Edmund James McGarn and William Fairchild to Lincoln, Apr. 20, 1861, Robert Todd Lincoln Collection, Manuscript Division, Library of Congress.

8. Robert Manson Myers, ed., *The Children of Pride: A True Story of Georgia and the Civil War* (New Haven, Conn., 1972), p. 1268.

9. *Texas Republican* (Marshall), quoted in Ralph W. Steen, "Texas Newspapers and Lincoln," *Southwestern Historical Quarterly*, 51 (1947–48): 201. See also Martin Abbot, "Southern Reaction to Lincoln's Assassination," *Abraham Lincoln Quarterly*, 7 (1952): 111–27.

10. See Joel H. Silbey, *A Respectable Minority: The Democratic Party in the Civil War Era, 1860–1868* (New York, 1977).

11. *Ibid.*, pp. 74–77.

12. Curtis to William Whitwell Greenough, Jan. 1, 1863, Benjamin Robbins Curtis Papers, Manuscript Division, Library of Congress.

13. Amos Kendall, *Letters Exposing the Mismanagement of Public Affairs by Abraham Lincoln* (Washington, D.C., 1864), p. 45–46.

14. Frank Klement, "A Small-Town Editor Criticizes Lincoln: A Study in Editorial Abuse," *Lincoln Herald*, 54 (Summer, 1952): 30, 32.

15. Sylvanus Cobb to Robert Bonner, Aug. 5, 1864, Illinois State Historical Library. Cobb wrote potboiler fiction for Bonner's New York *Ledger.*

16. Walter M. Merrill, ed., *The Letters of William Lloyd Garrison* (6 vols.; Cambridge, Mass., 1971–81); 5: 37, 47, 112, 220–34; James M

McPherson, *The Struggle for Equality: Abolitionists and the Negro in the Civil War and Reconstruction* (Princeton, N.J., 1964), pp. 260–86; Ralph Korngold, *Two Friends of Man: The Story of William Lloyd Garrison and Wendell Phillips* (Boston, 1950), pp. 325–26.

17. David Donald, *Charles Sumner and the Rights of Man* (New York, 1970), pp. 162–69, 173–74, 178–79, 185–91, 205–9, 212–15. Wade to Mrs. Wade, Oct. 25, 1861, Benjamin F. Wade Papers, Manuscript Division, Library of Congress; Hans L. Trefousse, *The Radical Republicans: Lincoln's Vanguard for Racial Justice* (New York, 1969), pp. 177–80, 184, 221–22, 246, 255–56, 293; Hans L. Trefousse, *Benjamin Franklin Wade: Radical Republican from Ohio* (New York, 1963), pp. 204–5, 218–32.

18. Trefousse, *Radical Republicans*, p. 177.

19. *Douglass' Monthly* (Rochester, N.Y.), Aug. 1862, pp. 694, 707.

20. The manifesto was first published in the New York *Tribune*, Aug. 5, 1864.

21. Gerald S. Henig, *Henry Winter Davis, Antebellum and Civil War Congressman from Maryland* (New York, 1973), p. 224; John D. Hayes, ed., *Samuel Francis DuPont: A Selection from His Civil War Letters* (3 vols.; Ithaca, N.Y., 1969), 3: 413n.

22. *Quarterly Review*, 110 (July 1861): 258–59.

23. *John Bull*, Sept. 14, 1861, quoted in Ephraim Douglass Adams, *Great Britain and the American Civil War* (2 vols.; London, 1925), 1: 179–80.

24. *Morning Chronicle*, Nov. 28, 1861, quoted in John Bach McMaster, *A History of the People of the United States During Lincoln's Administration* (New York, 1927), p. 146.

25. London *Evening Standard* and Leeds *Intelligencer*, quoted in Robert Bloom, "As the British Press Saw Lincoln," *Topic 9: A Journal of the Liberal Arts*, 5 (Spring, 1965): 48.

26. London *Times*, Oct. 21, 1862.

27. *Ibid.*, Nov. 22, 1864.

28. *Ibid.*, Apr. 29, 1865.

29. New York *Times*, Feb. 9, 1932, p. 14. In Gamaliel Bradford's *The Haunted Biographer: Dialogues of the Dead* (Seattle, Wash., 1927), p. 19, Lincoln says to John Wilkes Booth: "The smoke of your pistol blew a halo round me, I confess."

30. Phillips to Elizabeth Cady Stanton, Apr. 23, 1865, Ida Husted Harper Collection, Huntington Library.

31. Roy P. Basler, *The Lincoln Legend: A Study in Changing Conceptions* (Boston, 1935), pp. 4–6.

32. *Punch, or the London Charivari*, 48 (May 6, 1865): 182–84; Bancroft to Francis Lieber, Oct. 29, 1862, Lieber Papers, Huntington Library.

33. "President Lincoln," *Fraser's Magazine*, 71 (Jan. 1865): 1–21; "Personal Recollections of President Lincoln," *Fortnightly Review*, 1 (May 1865): 56–65. Only the second article was signed by Conway.

34. Samuel S. Cox, *Union-Disunion-Reunion: Three Decades of Federal Legislation, 1855 to 1885 . . .* (Providence, R.I., 1885), p. 345.

35. Jefferson Davis, *The Rise and Fall of the Confederate Government* (2 vols.; New York, 1881), 2: 683.

36. Davis, *Image of Lincoln*, pp. 146–47, 159–60.

37. Basler, *Lincoln Legend*, p. 57.

38. *Tyler's Quarterly*, 2 (1920–21): 213, 221n; 8 (1926–27): 147–48; 15 (1933–34): 24–25; Charles L. C. Minor, *The Real Lincoln, from the Testimony of His Contemporaries* (Richmond, Va., 1904), pp. 25–28; Mildred Lewis Rutherford, *The South Must Have Her Rightful Place in History* (Athens, Ga., 1923), pp. 26–27.

39. New York *Times*, June 22, 1922, p. 1, June 23, p. 16, June 24, p. 7, June 26, p. 17.

40. Mildred Lewis Rutherford, "Contrasted Lives of Jefferson Davis and Abraham Lincoln . . . ," in *Miss Rutherford's Historical Notes*, 3 (March 1927): 3; 6 (June 1927): 5–6; Rutherford, *South Must Have Her Rightful Place*, p. 30.

41. *Tyler's Quarterly*, 5 (1923–24): 220; 6 (1924–25): 152; 7 (1925–26): 7–8; 8 (1926–27): 72, 146; 14 (1932–33): 230–33.

42. Albert J. Beveridge, *Abraham Lincoln, 1809–1858* (2 vols.; Boston, 1928); Richard Hofstadter, *The American Political Tradition and the Men Who Made It* (New York, 1948), pp. 92–134; Donald W. Riddle, *Congressman Abraham Lincoln* (Urbana, Ill., 1957); Reinhard H. Luthin, *The Real Abraham Lincoln* (Englewood Cliffs, N.J., 1960).

43. Edgar Lee Masters, *Lincoln the Man* (New York, 1931), pp. 42, 85–86, 115, 139–40, 145, 252, 273–74, 355, 391, 404, 427–28, 494.

44. The essay was first published in the *Abraham Lincoln Quarterly*, 2 (1942–43): 255–80, and reprinted in Randall, *Lincoln the Liberal Statesman*, pp. 65–87.

45. *New York Review of Books*, June 20, 1968, p. 34.

46. Lerone Bennett, Jr., "Was Abe Lincoln a White Supremacist?" *Ebony*, 23 (Feb. 1968): 36–37. Bennett's essay has been discussed in text Chapter 8. A later work treating Lincoln in the same vein is Vincent Harding, *There Is a River: The Black Struggle for Freedom in America* (New York, 1981), especially pp. 223, 236.

47. Bennett, "Lincoln a White Supremacist?" p. 40; Charles Crowe, ed., *The Age of Civil War and Reconstruction, 1830–1900* (Homewood, Ill., 1966), p. 240.

48. Eckenrode to Beveridge, Nov. 1, 1926; Apr. 6, 1927, Albert J. Beveridge Papers, Manuscript Division, Library of Congress.

49. Charles W. Ramsdell, "Lincoln and Fort Sumter," *Journal of Southern History*, 3 (1937): 259–88, especially p. 285.

50. John Shipley Tilley, *Lincoln Takes Command* (Chapel Hill, N.C., 1941).

51. *Time*, 49 (June 16, 1947): 29.

52. Russell Hoover Quynn, *The Constitutions of Abraham Lincoln and Jefferson Davis: A Historical and Biographical Study in Contrasts* (New York, 1959), pp. 153, 164.

53. Ludwell H. Johnson, "Civil War Military History: A Few Revisions

in Need of Revising," *Civil War History*, 17 (1971): 115–30; Ludwell H. Johnson, *Division and Reunion, America, 1848–1877* (New York, 1978), p. 83; Ludwell H. Johnson, "Jefferson Davis and Abraham Lincoln as War Presidents: Nothing Succeeds Like Success," *Civil War History*, 27 (1981): 49–63, especially pp. 57–58.

54. Johnson, "Jefferson Davis and Abraham Lincoln," p. 51.

55. Willmoore Kendall, "Equality: Commitment or Ideal?" *Phalanx*, 1 (1967): 95–103.

56. M. E. Bradford, "The Lincoln Legacy: A Long View," *Modern Age*, 24 (1980): 355–63, especially p. 362; M. E. Bradford, "Dividing the House: The Gnosticism of Lincoln's Political Rhetoric," *ibid*., pp. 10–24, especially pp. 11, 15, 16, 19, 20–21; M. E. Bradford, *A Better Guide Than Reason: Studies in the American Revolution* (LaSalle, Ill., 1979), pp. 42–46, 56 (where Bradford compares Lincoln to Adolf Hitler), 187–92, 215.

57. William Appleman Williams, *America Confronts a Revolutionary World: 1776–1976* (New York, 1976), pp. 90–91, 105–19; William Appleman Williams, *Empire as a Way of Life: An Essay on the Causes and Character of America's Present Predicament Along With a Few Thoughts About an Alternative* (New York, 1980), pp. 90–93.

58. Dwight G. Anderson, *Abraham Lincoln: The Quest for Immortality* (New York, 1982), pp. 5, 7, 81, 99, 120–21, 159, 162, 166–68, 192, 193, 209–25. George B. Forgie, *Patricide in the House Divided: A Psychological Interpretation of Lincoln and His Age* (New York, 1979), likewise finds tragic consequences in the psychology of Lincoln's leadership, but he does not impeach Lincoln's conscious purposes. For discussion of the Anderson and Forgie books as psychohistorical studies, see text, pp. 221–23. For other discussion of the Anderson book, see text, pp. 282–83.

59. C. Vann Woodward, "The Fall of the American Adam," *American Academy of Arts and Sciences Bulletin*, 35 (Nov. 1981): 26–34.

60. David L. Porter to the author, Jan. 15, 1982; Chicago *Tribune*, Jan. 10, 1982, sec. 9, pp. 9–18. See also Robert K. Murray and Tim H. Blessing, "The Presidential Performance Study: A Progress Report," *Journal of American History*, 70 (1983–84): 535–55.

61. Barbara Ward, "That All Should Have an Equal Chance," *New York Times Magazine*, Feb. 12, 1956, p. 15.

Chapter 16

1. Saul Bellow, "Deep Readers of the World, Beware," *New York Times Book Review*, Feb. 15, 1959, pp. 1, 34.

2. Gordon S. Wood, "Histrionics and Hysteria in the American Revolution," *Reviews in American History*, 9 (1981): 476.

3. P. B. Medawar, "Victims of Psychiatry," *New York Review of Books*, Jan. 23, 1975, p. 17.

4. John E. Mack, *A Prince of Our Disorder: The Life of T. E. Lawrence* (Boston, 1976), pp. xvii–xxviii.

5. Emmanuel Hertz, ed., *The Hidden Lincoln, from the Letters and Papers of William H. Herndon* (New York, 1938), pp. 52, 59, 63.

6. Hertz, *Hidden Lincoln*, p. 64; David Donald, *Lincoln's Herndon* (New York, 1948), p. 306.

7. Donald, *Lincoln's Herndon*, pp. 301–2.

8. Such writing tended to be descriptive and anecdotal. See, for instance, a chapter in Henry C. Whitney, *Life on the Circuit with Lincoln* (Boston, 1892), titled "His Mental and Moral Characteristics."

9. Nathaniel Wright Stephenson, *Lincoln: An Account of His Personal Life, Especially of Its Springs of Action as Revealed and Deepened by the Ordeal of War* (Indianapolis, Ind., 1922). See, for example, the comment on "Stephenson's excursions into psychoanalysis" in Paul M. Angle, *A Shelf of Lincoln Books: A Critical, Selective Bibliography of Lincolniana* (New Brunswick, N.J., 1946), p. 45.

10. L. Pierce Clark, "Unconscious Motives Underlying the Personalities of Great Statesmen and Their Relation to Epoch-Making Events: A Psychologic Study of Abraham Lincoln," in Norman Kiell, ed., *Psychological Studies of Famous Americans: The Civil War Era* (New York, 1964), p. 105. The article was originally presented as a paper before the New York Psychiatric Society in 1919 and published in the *Psychoanalytic Review*, 8 (1921): 1–21.

11. L. Pierce Clark, *Lincoln: A Psycho-Biography* (New York, 1933), pp. 27–31, 55–79.

12. Compare the favorable review by Harold D. Lasswell in *American Journal of Sociology*, 39 (1933–34): 541–42, with the hostile reviews by Henry Steele Commager in *New York Herald Tribune Books*, Feb. 12, 1933, p. 1, and by Nathaniel W. Stephenson in *American Historical Review*, 39 (1933–34): 180. Stephenson labeled the book "treatise pure and simple, with Lincoln as a peg to hang dogmas upon."

13. Milton H. Shutes, *Lincoln and the Doctors: A Medical Narrative of the Life of Abraham Lincoln* (New York, 1933), pp. 36–39.

14. William F. Petersen, *Lincoln-Douglas: The Weather as Destiny* (Springfield, Ill., 1943).

15. Edward J. Kempf, "Abraham Lincoln's Organic and Emotional Neurosis," in Kiell, *Psychological Studies*, pp. 67–87, originally published in the American Medical Association's *Archives of Neurology and Psychiatry*, 67 (1952): 419–33; Edward J. Kempf, *Abraham Lincoln's Philosophy of Common Sense: An Analytical Biography of a Great Mind* (3 vols.; New York, 1965), 1: xvii–xix, 9–10, 58–59, 134–35, 233–35, 384.

16. Kempf, *Lincoln's Philosophy*, 1: 41–45. One historian who did find Kempf persuasive was Bell Irvin Wiley. See his Harmsworth Inaugural Lecture at Oxford University, *Lincoln and Lee* (Oxford, 1966), pp. 9–10.

17. Harry V. Jaffa, *Crisis of the House Divided: An Interpretation of the Lincoln-Douglas Debates* (Garden City, N.Y., 1959). Another reading in depth by a political scientist was Glen E. Thurow's *Abraham Lincoln and American Political Religion* (Albany, N.Y., 1976).

18. Jaffa, *House Divided*, p. 269.

19. William J. Wolf, *The Almost Chosen People: A Study of the Religion of Abraham Lincoln* (Garden City, N.Y., 1959); Elton Trueblood, *Abraham Lincoln: Theologian of American Anguish* (New York, 1973); Robert V. Bruce, *Lincoln and the Riddle of Death* (Fort Wayne, Ind., 1981); David Hein, "Abraham Lincoln's Theological Outlook," in Kenneth W. Thompson, ed., *Essays on Lincoln's Faith and Politics* (Lanham, Md., 1983), pp. 103–205.

20. William L. Langer, "The Next Assignment," *American Historical Review*, 63 (1957–58): 283–304; Erik H. Erikson, *Young Man Luther: A Study in Psychoanalysis and History* (New York, 1958). For a sampling of the extensive comment on the Erikson book, see Roger A. Johnson, ed., *Psychohistory and Religion: The Case of* YOUNG MAN LUTHER (Philadelphia, Pa., 1977).

21. Robert J. Brugger, ed., *Our Selves / Our Past: Psychological Approaches to American History* (Baltimore, Md., 1981), p. 5.

22. Richard Hofstadter, *The Age of Reform: From Bryan to FDR* (New York, 1955); Richard Hofstadter, *The Paranoid Style in American Politics and Other Essays* (New York, 1965); David Donald, "Toward a Reconsideration of the Abolitionists," in his *Lincoln Reconsidered: Essays on the Civil War Era* (New York, 1956), pp. 19–36; David Donald, *Charles Sumner and the Coming of the Civil War* (New York, 1960); Stanley M. Elkins, *Slavery: A Problem in American Institutional and Intellectual Life* (Chicago, 1959).

23. Henry Nash Smith, *Virgin Land: The American West as Symbol and Myth* (Cambridge, Mass., 1950); R. W. B. Lewis, *The American Adam: Innocence, Tragedy and Tradition in the Nineteenth Century* (Chicago, 1955); William R. Taylor, *Cavalier and Yankee: The Old South and American National Character* (New York, 1961); Leo Marx, *The Machine in the Garden: Technology and the Pastoral Ideal in America* (New York, 1964).

24. John William Ward, *Andrew Jackson: Symbol for an Age* (New York, 1955); Marvin Meyers, *The Jacksonian Persuasion: Politics and Belief* (Stanford, Calif., 1957).

25. Edmund Wilson, "Abraham Lincoln," in his *Patriotic Gore: Studies in the Literature of the American Civil War* (New York, 1962), pp. 99–130. An earlier and considerably different version of the essay was published in the *New Yorker*, Mar. 14, 1953, as a review of the *Collected Works*, and reprinted in Edmund Wilson, *Eight Essays* (Garden City, N.Y., 1954), pp. 181–202, with the title "Abraham Lincoln: The Union as Religious Mysticism."

26. Richard Hofstadter had previously suggested the same thing with the title "Abraham Lincoln and the Self-Made Myth," in his *The American Political Tradition and the Men Who Made It* (New York, 1948), pp. 92–134. In its substance, however, the essay did not really pursue the theme of the title.

27. Wilson, *Patriotic Gore*, p. 123.

28. *Ibid*., pp. 107–8.

29. G. S. Boritt, "The Voyage to the Colony of Linconia: The Sixteenth President, Black Colonization, and the Defense Mechanism of Avoidance," *The Historian*, 37 (1975): 619–32. The quotation is from p. 631n.

30. Robert L. Randall, "Lincoln's Crises: A Psycho-Historical Interpretation," *Lincoln Herald*, 79 (1977): 116–21.

31. Forgie's dissertation, "Fathers Past and Child Nation: The Romantic Imagination and the Origins of the American Civil War," was written under my supervision at Stanford University and completed in 1971. The other members of the supervisory committee were David M. Potter (until his death in 1970), Carl N. Degler, and Peter Stansky. Anderson's dissertation, "The Quest for Immortality: Abraham Lincoln and the Founding of Political Authority in America," was written under the supervision of Norman Jacobson at the University of California, Berkeley, and completed in 1972. The other members of the supervisory committee were Michael Paul Rogin and Henry Nash Smith.

32. George B. Forgie, *Patricide in the House Divided: A Psychological Interpretation of Lincoln and His Age* (New York, 1979), pp. 55–87, 247–93.

33. Dwight G. Anderson, *Abraham Lincoln: The Quest for Immortality* (New York, 1982), especially pp. 5–8, 79–81, 92, 95–96, 99–100, 108–21, 130–32, 159, 162, 166–68, 248–49.

34. Mark E. Neely, Jr., *The Abraham Lincoln Encyclopedia* (New York, 1982), p. 248.

35. Charles B. Strozier, *Lincoln's Quest for Union: Public and Private Meanings* (New York, 1982).

36. *Ibid.*, pp. 41–49.

37. *Ibid.*, pp. 25–26.

38. Fawn M. Brodie, "Hidden Presidents," *Harper's Magazine*, 254 (April 1977): 71; Michael Paul Rogin, "The King's Two Bodies: Abraham Lincoln, Richard Nixon, and Presidential Self-Sacrifice," *Massachusetts Review*, 20 (1979): 573. "It is almost," Rogin mused, "as if he [Lincoln] were denying that he shot his mother from within the crack in her body." That observation would seem to fall well within the Bellow definition of "deep reading." Strozier, *Lincoln's Quest for Union*, p. 239, revealed that the turkey hypothesis was first suggested to him by the author of an undergraduate thesis completed at Harvard University in 1966.

39. Roy P. Basler, Marion Dolores Pratt, and Lloyd A. Dunlap, eds., *The Collected Works of Abraham Lincoln* (9 vols.; 1953–55), 4: 62.

40. Other writers have jumped to the same conclusion. See, for example, Louis A. Warren, *Lincoln's Youth, Indiana Years, Seven to Twenty-one, 1816–1830* (Indianapolis, Ind., 1959), pp. 36–37. As Strozier concedes, the testimony on Lincoln's attitude toward animals is mixed. Certainly there was little squeamishness in the young man who helped sew shut the eyes of some thirty hogs as an experiment in droving. Recounting this incident in the same autobiographical sketch, Lincoln called it "ludicrous," not cruel. Strozier, *Lincoln's Quest for Union*, p. 27; Basler et al., *Collected Works*, 4: 63–64.

41. Strozier, *Lincoln's Quest for Union*, p. 27, notes testimony that Lincoln did go hunting from time to time. See also Emanuel Hertz, *The Hidden Lincoln, from the Letters and Papers of William H. Herndon* (New York, 1938), pp. 279, 281, 355.

42. Ward, *Andrew Jackson*, p. 44.

43. Strozier, *Lincoln's Quest for Union*, pp. xvi–xvii, 44.

44. *Ibid*., compare p. 115 with p. 209.

45. *Ibid*., pp. 40–41, 181, 232–33.

Chapter 17

1. Katherine Holland Brown, *The Father* (New York, 1928). The novel received the John Day Prize from *Woman's Home Companion*, which published part of it serially. Brown was born in Alton, Illinois, near the scene of the novel, and made a career of writing for women's magazines. It should perhaps be noted that on Christmas Day, 1850, Lincoln and his wife were actually at home in Springfield, she having given birth to a son, William Wallace, just four days earlier. The "ballots" and "bullets" wordplay is authentically Lincoln's, but apparently belongs to a later period. See Roy P. Basler, Marion Dolores Pratt, and Lloyd A. Dunlap, eds., *The Collected Works of Abraham Lincoln* (9 vols.; New Brunswick, N.J., 1953–55), 2: 454; 4: 439; 6: 410.

2. Michael Davis, *The Image of Lincoln in the South* (Knoxville, Tenn., 1971), pp. 69–72.

3. Edward Eggleston, *The Graysons: A Story of Illinois* (New York, 1887). The principal work on Lincoln in literature is Roy P. Basler, *The Lincoln Legend: A Study in Changing Conceptions* (Boston, 1935).

4. Joseph Kirkland, *The McVeys* (Boston, 1888). Kirkland made the mistake of including Stephen A. Douglas among Lincoln's companions on the legal circuit in the 1850's.

5. Bret Harte, *Clarence* (Boston, 1895), pp. 263–69.

6. Joel Chandler Harris, *On the Wing of Occasions: Being the Authorised Version of Certain Curious Episodes of the Late Civil War, Including the Hitherto Suppressed Narrative of the Kidnapping of President Lincoln* (New York, 1900), pp. 123–243. Another early work was Mary Hartwell Catherwood's *Spanish Peggy: A Story of Young Illinois* (Chicago, 1899). This melodramatic short novel is about a little lame Spanish girl brought to New Salem by a Sac Indian who has adopted her. Lincoln plays a prominent part in foiling the villain, a New Orleans gambler who tries repeatedly to carry off Peggy and her small fortune in gold.

7. Winston Churchill, *The Crisis* (New York, 1901). More than a million copies were sold. The quoted words are from pp. 509 and 520.

8. In *The Father*, for instance, Lincoln defends John Stafford's future son-in-law in a murder trial. In *The Crisis*, he prevents the execution of Virginia Carvel's cousin. See also the works cited in notes 3, 15, 16, 27, 31, 33, 34, and 36.

9. Bernie Babcock, *The Soul of Ann Rutledge: Abraham Lincoln's Romance* (New York, 1919), pp. 95–96, 99, 124–27, 169, 196, 292–93.

10. *Ibid.*, pp. 144, 193.

11. Harte, *Clarence*, p. 230.

12. Churchill, *The Crisis*, p. 509.

13. *Ibid.*, pp. 144–46. On the Freeport legend, see Don E. Fehrenbacher, *Prelude to Greatness: Lincoln in the 1850's* (Stanford, Calif., 1962), pp. 122–28.

14. Upton Sinclair, *Manassas: A Novel of the War* (New York, 1904), pp. 321–22, 326–28, 362–69. It was two years later that Sinclair became famous with publication of *The Jungle*. The technique of *Manassas* was later more fully developed in his Lanny Budd novels.

15. Thomas Dixon, *The Clansman: An Historical Romance of the Ku Klux Klan* (New York, 1905), pp. 19–55. The quotation is from p. 46. *Birth of a Nation* was also based upon Dixon's earlier novel *The Leopard's Spots* (New York, 1902), written to demonstrate the inferiority of the Negro race. Lincoln does not appear in the book, which is about the Reconstruction era.

16. Thomas Dixon, *The Southerner: A Romance of the Real Lincoln* (New York, 1913), quotations from pp. 314, 501, 543. Dixon converted part of the novel into a play titled *A Man of the People* (New York, 1920).

17. Thomas Nelson Page, *The Red Riders* (New York, 1924), published posthumously. Page served as ambassador to Italy from 1913 to 1919. On Wilson's endorsement of *Birth of a Nation*, see Richard Schickel, *D. W. Griffith: An American Life* (New York, 1984), pp. 268–70, but cf. Arthur S. Link, *Wilson: The New Freedom* (Princeton, N.J., 1956), pp. 252–54.

18. Irving Bacheller, *A Man for the Ages: A Story of the Builders of Democracy* (Indianapolis, Ind., 1919); quotation from the second page of the prefatory letter.

19. Bruce Lancaster, *For Us the Living* (New York, 1940).

20. Harold Sinclair, *American Years* (New York, 1938).

21. Robert Emmet Sherwood, *Abe Lincoln in Illinois* (New York, 1939), pp. 40–62, 208–9).

22. E. P. Conkle, *Prologue to Glory*, in Willard Swire, ed., *Three Distinctive Plays About Abraham Lincoln* (New York, 1961), pp. 3–66; Burns Mantle, ed., *The Best Plays of 1937–38* (New York, 1938), pp. 233–61. This play was a production of the WPA Federal Theatre.

23. Bacheller, *A Man for the Ages*, p. 264. Among other fictionalized versions of the legend are Carrie Douglas Wright, *Lincoln's First Love: A True Story* (Chicago, 1901), and Eleanor Atkinson, *Lincoln's Love Story* (New York, 1909). Perhaps the most ambitious effort was Denton J. Snider's *Lincoln and Ann Rutledge: An Idyllic Epos of the Early North-West* (St. Louis, Mo., 1912), a narrative poem running to 350 pages, part of a 1500-page tetralogy.

24. Paul Rosenfeld, ed., *The Sherwood Anderson Reader* (Boston, 1947), pp. 545–53. See also David D. Anderson, "Sherwood Anderson's Use of the Lincoln Theme," *Lincoln Herald*, 64 (1962): 28–32.

25. Harold Winsor Gammans, *Spirit of Ann Rutledge* (New York, 1927). The play was first enacted by Gammans's high school pupils in Scranton, then was performed professionally in Schenectady, but somehow never made it to Broadway.

26. Darwin Teilhet, *Steamboat on the River* (New York, 1952).

27. Bernie Babcock, *The Soul of Abe Lincoln* (Philadelphia, Pa., 1923).

28. Irving Bacheller, *Father Abraham: A Tale of the Last Years of Lincoln* (Indianapolis, Ind., 1925).

29. Ben Ames Williams, *House Divided* (Boston, 1947). The quotations are from pp. 554, 767, 803.

30. Ida M. Tarbell, *Father Abraham* (New York, 1909), and *In Lincoln's Chair* (New York, 1920).

31. Paul Horgan, "My Father's Child," *Collier's*, Feb. 14, 1953, pp. 54, 56–57; "Doomsday and Mr. Lincoln," *Saturday Evening Post*, Apr. 18, 1959, pp. 23, 46, 50, 53–54.

32. Christopher Morley, "Lincoln's Doctor's Dog," *Saturday Review*, Feb. 12, 1955, pp. 9–10, 40–42. For an interesting "short short" Lincoln story, see Zachary Gold, "The Answer," *Collier's*, Feb. 17, 1945, pp. 16–17, about an old Negro who finds a scrap of paper in Lincoln's room at Gettysburg subtracting 1776 from 1863.

33. L. E. Chittenden, *Lincoln and the Sleeping Sentinel: The True Story* (New York, 1909), a reprinting of a chapter in Chittenden's *Recollections of President Lincoln and His Administration* (New York, 1891). The story, to be sure, had some basis in fact. Compare Basler, *Lincoln Legend*, pp. 127–29, with Waldo F. Glover, *Abraham Lincoln and the Sleeping Sentinel of Vermont* (Montpelier, Vt., 1936).

34. Richard Henry Little, *Better Angels* (New York, 1928). The story was first written for newspaper publication in 1909 and was rediscovered by Sandburg, who wrote an introduction to the small volume.

35. Mary Raymond Shipman Andrews, *The Perfect Tribute* (New York, 1906). Andrews retails the legend that Lincoln wrote the address on a scrap of paper during the short railroad trip from Washington to Gettysburg.

36. Mary Raymond Shipman Andrews, *The Counsel Assigned* (New York, 1912), and *Passing the Torch* (New York, 1924). See also Margarita Spalding Gerry, *The Toy Shop: A Romantic Story of Lincoln the Man* (New York, 1908), about the proprietor of a toy shop whose talk of his service with Napoleon helps Lincoln make an important military decision.

37. Honoré Willsie Morrow, *Benefits Forgot: A Story of Lincoln and Mother Love* (New York, 1917), and *The Lost Speech of Abraham Lincoln* (New York, 1925). *Benefits Forgot* is about a young medical officer who shamefully neglects his mother until Lincoln has him arrested and brought to Washington for a stern lecture on the subject. *The Lost Speech* has a silly plot in which Lincoln urges the heroine to give up the man she loves so that her father, who dislikes the man, will lend his indispensable support to the Republican movement. When she protests that he is asking too much, Lincoln reminds her that he had to give up Ann Rutledge. In a later short story, Morrow dealt with Mary Lincoln's depression after the death of their son

Willie: "Dearer Than All," *Good Housekeeping*, 98 (Feb. 1934): 34–37, 136, 138, 140–41, 143–44.

38. Honoré Willsie Morrow, *Forever Free: A Novel of Abraham Lincoln* (New York, 1927).

39. Honoré Willsie Morrow, *With Malice Toward None* (New York, 1928). In one notable departure from historical fact, Morrow moves Sumner's proposal of marriage to Alice Hooper from 1866 (when it actually occurred) back to 1864 and involves the Lincolns deeply in the romance. At the same time, Morrow was also writing *Mary Todd Lincoln: An Appreciation of the Wife of Abraham Lincoln* (New York, 1928), a rather curious mixture of literary invention and historical essay.

40. *New York Times Book Review*, July 29, 1928, p. 6.

41. Honoré Willsie Morrow, *The Last Full Measure* (New York, 1930); quotation from p. 340. In 1935, the trilogy was republished in one volume titled *Great Captain*.

42. Olive Carruthers, *Lincoln's Other Mary* (Chicago, 1946).

43. See Edwin McDowell, "Behind the Best Sellers," *New York Times Book Review*, Sept. 14, 1980, p. 42.

44. Irving Stone, *Love Is Eternal: A Novel About Mary Todd and Abraham Lincoln* (Garden City, N.Y., 1954), pp. 117–19. See also Ida M. Tarbell, *The Life of Abraham Lincoln* (4 vols.; New York, 1900), 1: 174–80; William E. Barton, *The Life of Abraham Lincoln* (2 vols.; Indianapolis, Ind., 1925), 1: 257–59; J. G. Randall, *Lincoln the President: Springfield to Gettysburg* (2 vols.; New York, 1945), 1: 52–57. An earlier, inferior effort in the same vein as the Stone novel was Anne Colver, *Mr. Lincoln's Wife* (New York, 1943).

45. McDowell, "Behind the Best Sellers."

46. John Drinkwater, *Abraham Lincoln: A Play* (Boston, 1919); Sherwood, *Abe Lincoln in Illinois* (also produced as a motion picture in 1940 with the same star, Raymond Massey); Conkle, *Prologue to Glory*; Herbert Mitgang, *Mister Lincoln: A Drama in Two Acts* (Carbondale, Ill., 1982). Griffith's *Abraham Lincoln* appeared in 1930, John Ford's *Young Mr. Lincoln* in 1939. The Sandburg Lincoln premiered in 1974. Also notable was Norman Corwin's *The Rivalry*, a dramatization of the Lincoln-Douglas debates. An extensive study of Lincoln in drama, concentrating on the work of Drinkwater, Sherwood, Conkle, Corwin, and Mark Van Doren, is Gary Robert Planck, "Abraham Lincoln as Dramatic Hero," M.S. thesis, University of Wisconsin, 1963.

47. Mark Van Doren, *The Last Days of Lincoln: A Play in Six Scenes* (New York, 1959). It should perhaps be noted that one of the first efforts at serious drama about Lincoln was Hiram D. Torrie's *The Tragedy of Abraham Lincoln* (Glasgow, 1876), written in Shakespearean blank verse, with a mixture of Elizabethan and American frontier language. Here is the beginning of a Lincoln soliloquy on p. 41:

> There gathered, oh my country, at thy birth,
> Such god-like relics of time's grandest wrecks,
> As fired by Freedom, fresh baptized in blood:

Tried by such hearts as only great minds moved:
Bless'd by Jehovah's unmistakened smile:
That thou dost seem to hold the germs of all,
Bound by a new world's throbbings to be free.

The play was reprinted in the *Magazine of History*, 10, extra no. 40 (1915): 7–89.

48. William Styron, *The Confessions of Nat Turner* (New York, 1967); Alex Haley, *Roots* (New York, 1976); Truman Capote, *In Cold Blood* (New York, 1966); Norman Mailer, *The Armies of the Night: History as a Novel and the Novel as History* (New York, 1968). Haley's book was offered as history, but, as Willie Lee Rose said in the *New York Review of Books*, Nov. 11, 1976, "There is as much fiction as fact in *Roots*." Among earlier works that anticipated the "nonfiction novel" were Ernest Hemingway, *Green Hills of Africa* (New York, 1935), and the John Dos Passos trilogy, *U.S.A.* (1930–36). See Mas'ud Zavarzadeh, *The Mythopoeic Reality: The Postwar American Nonfiction Novel* (Urbana, Ill., 1976); Barbara Foley, "From *U.S.A.* to *Ragtime*: Notes on the Forms of Consciousness in Modern Fiction," *American Literature*, 50 (1978–79): 85–105.

49. See Vidal's "Afterword" on p. 659 of *Lincoln: A Novel* (New York, 1984); also his "Afterword" on pp. 429–30 of *Burr: A Novel* (New York, 1973).

50. *New York Times Book Review*, June 3, 1984, pp. 1, 36–37.

51. *New York Review of Books*, July 19, 1984, pp. 5–6, 8.

52. The quotation is from p. 111 of Vidal, *Lincoln*. The reference is to Lincoln's address before the Young Men's Lyceum of Springfield, Jan. 27, 1838, in Basler et al., *Collected Works*, 1: 108–15.

53. Vidal, *Lincoln*, pp. 9, 11, 28, 186.

54. *Ibid*., pp. 10, 199, 356.

55. *Ibid*., pp. 67, 100, 290. See also Vidal's essay on Lincoln in his *The Second American Revolution, and Other Essays* (New York, 1982), p. 276.

56. Quoted on the jacket of the book.

57. Joseph Blotner, *The Modern American Political Novel, 1900–1960* (Austin, Tex., 1966), pp. 17, 18.

58. Perhaps the most ambitious literary effort at writing from within Lincoln's mind is a long passage in Richard Slotkin's *The Crater* (New York, 1980), pp. 21–33. It is a kind of reverie about his youth in Indiana and especially his first trip to New Orleans. Somehow, it sounds more like the contrivance of a modern novelist than like the thoughts of Abraham Lincoln.

59. Winston Churchill, "If Lee Had Not Won the Battle of Gettysburg," *Scribner's Magazine*, 88 (1930): 587–97; MacKinlay Kantor, "If the South Had Won the Civil War," in MacKinley Kantor, *Story Teller* (Garden City, N.Y., 1967), pp. 219–69. There was virtually nothing about Lincoln in the Churchill story.

60. Milton Waldman, "If Booth Had Missed Lincoln," *Scribner's Mag-*

azine, 88 (1930): 473–84. It was this *Scribner* series that inspired James Thurber's classic piece "If Grant Had Been Drinking at Appomattox."

61. Oscar Lewis, *The Lost Years: A Biographical Fantasy* (New York, 1951). For more discussion of the Lewis book, see text, pp. 170–71.

62. Ned Buntline [Edward Zane Carroll Judson], *The Parricides* (New York, 1865). See Constance Head, "John Wilkes Booth in American Fiction," *Lincoln Herald*, 82 (1980): 454–62.

63. Barbara and Dwight Steward, *The Lincoln Diddle* (New York, 1979). The best novel about the assassination is probably Philip Van Doren Stern's *The Man Who Killed Lincoln* (New York, 1939).

64. See text, p. 169.

65. See, for example, Genevieve Foster, *Abraham Lincoln: An Initial Biography* (New York, 1950); Wilma Pitchford Hays, *Abe Lincoln's Birthday* (New York, 1961); Janet Halliday Ervin, *More Than Halfway There* (Chicago, 1970); F.N. Monjo, *Me and Willie and Pa: The Story of Abraham Lincoln and His Son Tad* (New York, 1973); A. P. Sanford, *Lincoln Plays* (New York, 1933); and *Plays: The Drama Magazine for Young People*, especially Jan. and Feb. issues in the 1940's and 1950's.

66. John Jakes, *North and South* (New York, 1982), p. 615. As for using "every last ounce of gold in the treasury," all the gold in the country (of which the federal government held only a small amount) probably would not have been enough to pay for Virginia's slaves alone.

Chapter 18

1. Holmes in A. Conan Doyle, *The Case Book of Sherlock Holmes* (1927); Poirot in Agatha Christie, *The Mysterious Affair at Styles* (1920); Wimsey in Dorothy Sayers, *Whose Body?* (1923); Vance in S. S. Van Dine [Willard Huntington Wright], *The Benson Murder Case* (1926); and Ellery Queen in Ellery Queen [Frederic Dannay and Manfred B. Lee], *The Roman Shoe Mystery* (1929).

2. Marjorie Nicolson, "The Professor and the Detective," *Atlantic Monthly*, 143 (Apr. 1929): 492, 493. The essay is reprinted in Howard Haycraft, ed., *The Art of the Mystery Story: A Collection of Critical Essays* (New York, 1946), pp. 110–27.

3. One account of the romance that antedates Herndon's was not discovered until the 1940's. See note 81 below.

4. Wilma Frances Minor to Editor, *Atlantic Monthly*, June 27, 1928, *Atlantic Monthly* File on the Minor Collection, Boston, examined through the courtesy of Edward A. Weeks. Eugene F. Saxton of the Harper organization later complained that Miss Minor had broken an explicit written promise of "first offer magazine and book rights." Saxton to Minor, Nov. 12 (telegram), and to Ellery Sedgwick, Nov. 20, 1928, *Atlantic Monthly* File.

5. Edward Weeks, *My Green Age* (Boston, 1973), p. 251; unsigned copy of telegram to Minor, July 3, 1928, *Atlantic Monthly* File.

6. Frederick Lewis Allen, "Sedgwick and the Atlantic," *Outlook and Independent*, 150 (Dec. 26, 1928): 1406–8, 1417; Weeks, *My Green Age*, pp. 197, 204–5; Ellery Sedgwick, *The Happy Profession* (Boston, 1946), pp. 6, 297.

7. Sedgwick, *Happy Profession*, p. 253.

8. Minor to Sedgwick, Aug. 29, 1928, *Atlantic Monthly* File, which also contains Miss Minor's manuscript in the original version and in a revised version.

9. W. C. Giffing to Nelson J. Peabody, no date; Sedgwick to Minor, Sept. 17, 1928, *Atlantic Monthly* File; Weeks, *My Green Age*, pp. 251–52.

10. *Atlantic Monthly*, 143 (Feb. 1929): 284; San Diego *Union*, Jan. 3, 1929, pp. 1, 6.

11. Lincoln to Calhoun, May 19, 1848, original in *Atlantic Monthly* File; printed in *Atlantic Monthly*, 143 (Feb. 1929): 221.

12. Weeks, *My Green Age*, p. 252; *Atlantic Monthly*, 143 (Feb. 1929): 288d; Minor to Sedgwick, Sept. 16, Nov. 15, and to Teresa Fitzpatrick, Oct. 20, 1928; Sedgwick to Minor, Sept. 17, 21, Oct. 25, Nov. 9, 1928, *Atlantic Monthly* File.

13. Minor to Fitzpatrick, Oct. 20, Nov. 16, Dec. 17, 1928; Fitzpatrick to Minor, Nov. 1, Dec. 14, 1928, *Atlantic Monthly* File.

14. Minor to Paul M. Angle, Jan. 24, 1929, Paul M. Angle Papers on the Lincoln Forgeries, Chicago Historical Society.

15. Minor vita (undated, but probably written in Nov. 1928); Minor to Fitzpatrick, Nov. 16, 1928; Feb. 8, 1929; J. B. Armstrong to Peabody, May 19, 1929, *Atlantic Monthly* File. To Fitzpatrick, Minor explained that her mother had "an overweening desire" to cling to youth. "For that reason she would never give us her age nor tell me mine. . . . If my life depended upon it I could not even hazard a guess this minute as to my age."

16. San Diego *Union*, Jan. 29, 1928, sec. XS, p. 3; Feb. 5, 1928, sec. XS, p. 13; Feb. 26, 1928, p. 5; Apr. 15, 1928, sec. XS, p. 6; Nov 18, 1928, sec. XS, p. 3; Dec. 9, 1928, sec. XS, p. 6.

17. Minor vita, *Atlantic Monthly* File.

18. Brian Masters, *Now Barabbas Was a Rotter: The Extraordinary Life of Marie Corelli* (London, 1978), p. 3.

19. Minor to Sedgwick, Aug. 29, 1928, *Atlantic Monthly* File. In her vita, Wilma called herself "a protégé of Marie Corelli."

20. Minor revised manuscript; Sedgwick to Oliver Barrett, Dec. 12, 1928, *Atlantic Monthly* File.

21. Charles Willis Thompson, reviewing William Barton's *The Lineage of Lincoln, New York Times Book Review*, May 12, 1929, p. 5. Benjamin P. Thomas, *Portrait for Posterity: Lincoln and His Biographers* (New Brunswick, N.J., 1947), p. 242, called Barton "a great historical detective."

22. Barton to Sedgwick, Sept. 6, 11, 1928, *Atlantic Monthly* File; Barton to Paul M. Angle, Dec. 8, 1928; May 1, 1929; to Georgia L. Osborne, Dec. 3, 1928; Sedgwick to Barton, Sept. 10, 1928, William E. Barton Papers, University of Chicago.

23. New York *Times*, Dec. 2, 1928, part 2, pp. 1, 6. According to Weeks, *My Green Age*, p. 254, "Ford was written off as an unbeliever." To Paul M. Angle, Ford wrote, on Feb. 2, 1929: "He [Sedgwick] may not have confidence in my judgment. That is his right. But he did ask my opinion of the papers and he was discourteous in not allowing me to see the originals after committing me to the photostats" (Angle Papers).

24. Sedgwick to Minor, Sept. 21; to Barton, Nov. 6, 1928, *Atlantic Monthly* File.

25. Ida M. Tarbell, *In the Footsteps of the Lincolns* (New York, 1924), pp. 211–24.

26. Sedgwick to Minor, Oct. 11; to Norman Hapgood, Nov. 6; to Barton, Nov. 6, 1928, *Atlantic Monthly* File. Sedgwick saw Tarbell first on the afternoon of Oct. 9. Sedgwick to Tarbell, Oct. 8; Tarbell to Sedgwick (telegram and letter), Oct. 19, 1928, *Atlantic Monthly* File.

27. Edward A. Weeks memorandum to Sedgwick, Oct. 18, 1928; Sedgwick to Barton, Nov. 6, 19; to Minor, Oct. 11, 1928, *Atlantic Monthly* File; Putnam to Sedgwick, Dec. 4, 1928, copy in Angle Papers; *Atlantic Monthly*, 142 (Dec. 1928): 835, 836; *Atlantic Monthly*, 143 (Feb. 1929): 288b–c.

28. Weeks, *My Green Age*, p. 253; *Atlantic Monthly*, 142 (Dec. 1928): 86–87 (advertisements).

29. Minor to Barton (telegram), Nov. 6, 1928; Barton to Sedgwick, Nov. 15, 1928, Barton Papers; Barton to Minor (copy), Nov. 12, 1928, *Atlantic Monthly* File. This was Barton's only meeting with Wilma, but he asserted that she had written to him about the collection a year earlier—that is, late in 1927. Barton to William H. Townsend, Nov. 15, 1928, copy in Louis A. Warren Lincoln Library and Museum, Fort Wayne, Ind.; Barton to Georgia L. Osborne, Dec. 3, 1928, Barton Papers.

30. Barton to Sedgwick, Nov. 15, 1928; to Paul M. Angle, May 1, 1929, Barton Papers, which also contain the photostats with Barton's notation: "I do not believe these three alleged letters of Lincoln . . . are genuine." We have only Barton's word that he came to this conclusion on the train back from California.

31. San Diego *Union*, Nov. 18, 1928, sec. XS, p. 3; Marjorie Brown Wright to Angle, Nov. 28, 1928, Angle Papers; Sedgwick to Minor, Nov. 15; Minor to Sedgwick, Nov. 20, 23, 26; Anderson Galleries to Minor, Nov. 13, 1928, *Atlantic Monthly* File; Wilma Frances Minor, "Lincoln the Lover: The Setting—New Salem," *Atlantic Monthly*, 142 (Dec. 1928): 838–56, preceded by an account of "The Discovery," pp. 834–37.

32. Ford to Sedgwick, Nov. 27; Sedgwick to Ford, Nov. 28, 1928, *Atlantic Monthly* File.

33. Sedgwick to Barton, Nov. 30, 1928, Barton Papers; Sedgwick to Minor, Dec. 6; Sandburg to Sedgwick, dated Nov. 25, 1928, *Atlantic Monthly* File. It seems likely that Sandburg's letter was written on Nov. 29 and misdated, for the correspondence indicates that he did not see the documents until his Thanksgiving visit on Nov. 28–29.

34. Angle to Oliver R. Barrett, Dec. 4, 1928, Angle Papers. Logan Hay was a grandson of Lincoln's second law partner, Stephen T. Logan, and a first cousin of John Hay.

35. Miers in his foreword to Paul M. Angle, ed., *Abraham Lincoln: His Autobiographical Writings* (Kingsport, Tenn., 1947), p. vi. On Angle generally, see Irving Dilliard, "Paul M. Angle: Warm Recollections and Clear Impressions," *Journal of the Illinois State Historical Society*, 68 (Nov. 1975): 435–43.

36. "Lincoln's First Love?" *Lincoln Centennial Association Bulletin*, no. 9 (Dec. 1, 1927).

37. "Atlantic Monthly Lincoln Letters Spurious," *ibid*., special bulletin (Dec. 1, 1928); *Atlantic Monthly*, 143 (Feb. 1929): 283. The Philadelphia *Record* also carried the story on Nov. 27, its publisher being a friend of Logan Hay, president of the Centennial Association. J. David Stern to Hay, Nov. 28; Angle to Sedgwick, Dec. 4, 1928, Angle Papers.

38. New York *Times*, Dec. 3, 1928, p. 20. Barrett to Louis A. Warren, Dec. 1, 1928, Louis A. Warren Lincoln Library and Museum, Fort Wayne, Ind.

39. *Illinois State Register* (Springfield), Nov. 28, 1928, p. 2; Warren to Sedgwick, Nov. 27; to New York *Times*, to Angle, and to Hewitt Howland, Nov. 28; Townsend to Angle, Nov. 28, 30, 1928, Warren Lincoln Library. See the Philadelphia *Record*, Nov. 28, p. 2; Dec. 2, 1928, p. 19, for statements by Dr. A. S. W. Rosenbach and George J. C. Grasberger, experts on manuscripts and autographs.

40. Signed statement by Joseph Benjamin Oakleaf, Dec. 4, 1928, Angle Papers. The Librarian of Brown University, which had a large collection of Lincoln manuscripts, was equally emphatic: "It is not a question of seeing the originals. No photographic reproduction could ever have transformed a genuine Lincoln letter into what you show as a facsimile . . . I could tell across the room that that was not a Lincoln letter, just as I could tell a friend from a stranger." H. L. Koopman to Sedgwick, Dec. 3, 1928, *Atlantic Monthly* File.

41. Barrett to Warren, Dec. 1, 1928; Warren memorandum, "The Sarah Calhoun and Abraham Lincoln Facsimile Writings Appearing in the Atlantic Monthly for December," Warren Lincoln Library.

42. On this subject, see especially Angle, "Lincoln Letters Spurious," pp. 6–7.

43. New York *Times*, Jan. 23, 1929, p. 22.

44. *Ibid*., Dec. 2, part 2, p. 6. Boston *Herald*, Dec. 4, 1928, p. 21.

45. In the matter of tearfulness, a memorandum in the *Atlantic* file says that, during a staff meeting, "the Editor [Sedgwick] carried one of the letters to the window, the better to read it aloud, but emotion overcoming him could not continue."

46. New York *Times*, Dec. 5, 1928, p. 18; Boston *Herald*, Jan. 16, 1929, p. 10; Tarbell to Angle, Dec. 6; Putnam to Sedgwick (copy), Dec. 4, 1928, Angle Papers; Angle to Sandburg, Dec. 6, 1928, Carl Sandburg Pa-

pers, University of Illinois Library, Urbana, Ill. Material on the Minor affair in the Sandburg collection is curiously sparse.

47. Barton to the *Atlantic Monthly*, Dec. 5; to Sedgwick, Dec. 8; to Minor, Dec. 11, 1928, Barton Papers (copies) and *Atlantic Monthly* File. Boston *Herald*, Dec. 10, 1928, pp. 1, 2.

48. Sedgwick to Barton, Dec. 14; Minor to Barton, Dec. 17, 26, 1928; Jan. 10, 1929, Barton Papers; Fitzpatrick to Minor, Dec. 14; Minor to Fitzpatrick, Dec. 15, 17, 1928, *Atlantic Monthly* File. According to a rumor recorded by Angle, Bruce Barton, the advertising executive and well-known author, "had to pay through the nose" to recover his father's letters to Wilma. Angle to Paul Z. DuBois, Apr. 4, 1966, Angle Papers.

49. Sedgwick to Minor, Dec. 12; Minor to Sedgwick, Dec. 18, 1928, *Atlantic Monthly* File. One notes that a letter in the Minor collection has Lincoln writing, "we gird on our armor for the next fray"—language that sounds much more like Miss Minor than Mr. Lincoln. *Atlantic Monthly*, 142 (Dec. 1928): 842.

50. Minor to Sedgwick, Dec. 7, *Atlantic Monthly* File.

51. Angle to Ford, Dec. 14, [15]; to Barrett, Dec. 14, [15]; to Wright, Dec. [16]; Ford to Angle, Dec. 17, 18, Angle Papers.

52. Wilma Frances Minor, "Lincoln the Lover: The Courtship," *Atlantic Monthly*, 143 (Jan. 1929): 1–14; Boston *Herald*, Dec. 23, 1928. Barrett also observed that the orthography seemed to be right out of Artemus Ward and Petroleum V. Nasby. Both Ann and her cousin Mat Cameron misspell words such as "one," "once," "was," "give," "says," and "said," but they spell correctly words such as "literary," "diary," outlandish," "wonderful," "poetry," and "Missouri." Barrett to Sandburg, Dec. 12, 1928, Sandburg Papers.

53. H. L. Koopman to Sedgwick, Dec. 3, 1928, *Atlantic Monthly* File.

54. New York *Times*, Dec. 24, p. 5; Boston *Herald*, Dec. 24, p. 4, Dec. 30, p. 7, 1928; Sedgwick to Minor, Dec. 26, 27, 1928, *Atlantic Monthly* File.

55. Minor to Sedgwick, Dec. 25, 26 (telegram), 27, 1928, *Atlantic Monthly* File; San Diego *Union*, Jan. 3, pp. 1, 6; Emporia (Kans.) *Gazette*, Jan. 12, p. 5; Philadelphia *Record*, Jan. 14, 1929, p. 2.

56. Sedgwick to Fitzpatrick (telegram), Jan. 12; Fitzpatrick to Sedgwick, Jan. 17, and to Barton, Jan. 17, 1929, *Atlantic Monthly* File; Angle to Ford, Jan. 16; to Captain James P. Murphy, Jan. 16; to Fred H. Hand, Jan. 16, 1929, Angle Papers; Boston *Herald*, Jan. 12, 1929, pp. 1, 3.

57. Fitzpatrick to Minor (telegram), Dec. 31, 1928; to Sedgwick, Jan. 17, 1929; DeBoyer to Fitzpatrick, Jan. 2, 1929 (photostat), *Atlantic Monthly* File.

58. Angle to Captain James P. Murphy, Dec. 19, 26, 31, 1928; Jan. 2, 1929; to Fred H. Hand, Jan. 2, 1929; Murphy to Angle, Dec. 28, 29, 1928; Logan Hay to J. David Stern, Jan. 2, 1929, Angle Papers.

59. Angle to Ferris Greenslet, Jan. 10; to Peabody, January 17; Weeks to Angle (telegram), Jan. 12; Peabody to Angle, Jan. 16, 1929, Angle Papers.

60. Reports of J. B. Armstrong Detective Service, *Atlantic Monthly* File;

Murphy to Angle, Dec. 29, 1928; Angle to Murphy, Feb. 6; Angle to Ford, Jan. 28, 1929, Angle Papers. Wilma was born in 1886 or 1887. She married Frank Maurice Minor, an actor, in 1907, and they were divorced in 1924. Three years later, she married Ernst Eugene Akins, a Marine Corps clerk, giving her age as 28. Minor remained friendly with Wilma and especially with her mother, whom he greatly admired. Frank Minor to Sedgwick, Feb. 9, 1929, *Atlantic Monthly* File.

61. Minor to Sedgwick, Feb. 8; to Fitzpatrick, Feb. 8, 1929, *Atlantic Monthly* File; Angle to Ford, Jan. 28, 1929, Angle Papers; Boston *Herald*, Jan. 21, 1929, p. 1; New York *Times*, Jan. 22, 1929, p. 17.

62. Minor to Sedgwick, Feb. 8; Frank Maurice Minor to Sedgwick, Feb. 9, 1929, *Atlantic Monthly* File.

63. Minor to Angle, Jan. 20 (telegram), 21, Angle Papers.

64. Angle to Barrett, Jan. 23; to Ford, Jan. 23, 1929, Angle Papers.

65. Angle to Ford, Jan. 23, 1929 (telegram); Ford to Angle, Jan. 18, 1929, Angle Papers. Ford had just prepared, but now withheld and never published, a denunciatory "Open Letter to the Editor of the Atlantic Monthly." A copy is in the Angle Papers.

66. *Atlantic Monthly*, 143 (Feb. 1929): 220; William E. Barton, *The Life of Abraham Lincoln* (2 vols.; Indianapolis, Ind., 1925), 1: 158n; Angle to Sedgwick, Feb. 5; Sedgwick to Hand, Feb. 6, 1929, *Atlantic Monthly* File; Angle to Murphy, Feb. 6, 1929, Angle Papers.

67. *Atlantic Monthly*, 143 (Feb. 1929): 283; Angle to Board of Directors, Lincoln Centennial Association, Jan. 23; to Ford, Jan. 23, 28; John E. Angle (father of Paul) to Angle, Jan. 23, 1929, Angle Papers.

68. Angle to Ford, Jan. 28, 1929, Angle Papers.

69. Angle to Ford, Jan. 28; to Sedgwick, Feb. 8, 1929, Angle Papers; Weeks, *My Green Age*, p. 256; Paul M. Angle, "The Minor Collection: A Criticism," *Atlantic Monthly*, 143 (April 1929): 516–25, reprinted in Robin W. Winks, ed., *The Historian as Detective: Essays on Evidence* (New York, 1969), pp. 127–41; and in Paul M. Angle, *On a Variety of Subjects* (Chicago, 1974), pp. 1–16. Not everyone accepted the scholarly verdict on the Minor documents. The Illinois State Historical Library has a manuscript of 866 typewritten pages defending the collection and attacking Angle's critique: Josefa Thornton, "Lincoln and the Olden Times."

70. Minor to Sedgwick, Jan. 22, 23, Feb. 8, 9 (telegram), Mar. 12; to Fitzpatrick, Feb. 8; to Little, Brown & Co., Feb. 12, 1929; staff meeting minutes, May 27, 1929; Sedgwick memorandum, May 29, 1929, *Atlantic Monthly* File.

71. Armstrong himself said that he had been working twelve to sixteen hours a day on the case. In May, he suffered a ruptured artery and was hospitalized. Armstrong to Peabody, Apr. 13; Armstrong agency to Peabody, May 22, 1929, *Atlantic Monthly* File.

72. Armstrong agent report, Apr. 1, 1929; undated memorandum of Weeks; Ashe to Sedgwick (telegram), Mar. 28; Peabody to Ashe, Apr. 15, 1929, *Atlantic Monthly* File.

73. *Harvard Crimson* (Cambridge, Mass.), Mar. 28, 1929.

74. Peabody to Armstrong, Mar. 29 (telegram); Armstrong to Peabody, Apr. 13, 1929, *Atlantic Monthly* File. Armstrong's report of the meeting runs to more than twenty single-spaced typewritten pages.

75. Peabody to Armstrong, Feb. 26, Apr. 6 (letter and telegram), 1929; Peabody to Nelson Greene and vice versa (telegrams), Apr. 24, 1929; Weeks, undated memorandum of his interview with Scott Greene, *Atlantic Monthly* File; Weeks, *My Green Age*, pp. 256–57.

76. The manuscript is in the *Atlantic Monthly* File. To William A. Bahlke, Sedgwick or a member of his staff wrote on June 2, 1929: "There are . . . certain further facts which we should like to give our public, but our lawyer tells us that for the present we ought not to print them in the Atlantic."

77. There are several copies of this document in the *Atlantic Monthly* File, including one made by Teresa Fitzpatrick and signed by her as an "exact copy," but the original, bearing Wilma Frances Minor's signature and that of three witnesses, was presumably placed in the hands of the *Atlantic*'s legal advisers and has not come to light. Writing to Alfred R. McIntyre of Little, Brown & Co. on July 12, 1929, Sedgwick spoke of having "secured a signed and witnessed confession."

78. Barton to Sedgwick, May 6; to Theodore Morrison, May 11, 20, 21, 1929, *Atlantic Monthly* File.

79. Fitzpatrick to Weeks, Sept. 7, 1950; Feb. 21, 1952; Weeks to Fitzpatrick, Sept. 13, 1950, *ibid*.

80. Weeks, *My Green Age*, pp. 257–59.

81. In 1944, Jay Monaghan of the Illinois State Historical Library came across an 1862 newspaper article telling the story of Lincoln's tragic love affair. If nothing else, this proved that it had not been invented by Herndon. But the effect of the discovery was soon offset by the critiques of James G. Randall and David Donald, which classified the romance as folklore springing from dubious history. See Jay Monaghan, "New Light on the Lincoln-Rutledge Romance," *Abraham Lincoln Quarterly*, 3 (1944–45): 138–45; J. G. Randall, *Lincoln the President: Springfield to Gettysburg* (2 vols.; New York, 1945), 2: 321–42; David Donald, *Lincoln's Herndon* (New York, 1948), pp. 185–87, 353–54, 358.

82. Stephen B. Oates, *With Malice Toward None: The Life of Abraham Lincoln* (New York, 1977), p. 19.

Chapter 19

1. Don E. Fehrenbacher, ed., *Abraham Lincoln: A Documentary Portrait Through His Speeches and Writings* (New York, 1964), p. xxix.

2. Roy P. Basler, Marion Dolores Pratt, and Lloyd A. Dunlap, eds., *The Collected Works of Abraham Lincoln* (9 vols.; New Brunswick, N.J., 1953–55), 1: ix.

3. P. M. Zall, *Abe Lincoln Laughing: Humorous Anecdotes from Orig-*

inal Sources by and about Abraham Lincoln (Berkeley, Calif., 1982), p. 10. The most exhaustive study is Wayne Lee Garner, "Abraham Lincoln and the Uses of Humor," Ph.D. diss., University of Iowa, 1963.

4. Stephen B. Oates, *With Malice Toward None: The Life of Abraham Lincoln* (New York, 1977), pp. 195–227.

5. Charles M. Segal, ed., *Conversations with Lincoln* (New York, 1961), p. 38. Emphasis added.

6. *New York Times Magazine*, Feb. 14, 1932, pp. 8–9, 21. Emphasis added.

7. Daniel Aaron, "The Treachery of Recollection: The Inner and the Outer History," in Robert H. Bremner, ed., *Essays on History and Literature* (Columbus, Ohio, 1966), especially p. 19, where he writes: "How true, really, are the tales from the horse's mouth? Eyewitness accounts of a murder or accident, we are told, often contradict each other. How much more untrustworthy may be the recollections of people who have conscious or unconscious motives for selective remembering or forgetting, who are themselves parties to the events described, whose view of the past is blurred by ignorance, hostility, or sentimentality? . . . Written history concocted from such sources can become little more than hypotheses about what might have happened." Aaron is talking particularly about oral history, but his remarks are no less applicable to written reminiscence.

8. Oates quotes from works by Donn Piatt (pp. 197–98), Thurlow Weed (p. 200), William H. Herndon (pp. 201, 207), and Henry Villard (pp. 213–14).

9. Oates, *With Malice Toward None*, p. 196.

10. Noah Brooks, *Washington in Lincoln's Time* (New York, 1895; 2d ed. edited by Herbert Mitgang, New York, 1958), pp. 198–200; Noah Brooks, "Personal Recollections of Abraham Lincoln," *Harper's New Monthly Magazine*, 31 (July 1865): 224–25; Ward Hill Lamon, *Recollections of Abraham Lincoln, 1847–1865*, edited by Dorothy Lamon Taillard (Washington, D.C., 1911), pp. 112–13; F. B. Carpenter, *Six Months at the White House with Abraham Lincoln: The Story of a Picture* (New York, 1866), pp. 163–65.

11. In the quotation Oates departs slightly from his source, *Washington in Lincoln's Time*, which reads: "the thing would once in a while come up, and give me a little pang as if something uncomfortable had happened."

12. Oates, *With Malice Toward None*, pp. 224–25.

13. Oates cites Segal, *Conversations with Lincoln*, pp. 102–7. Segal's source was *Report of the Joint Committee on Reconstruction, House Reports*, 39 Cong., 1 sess. (serial 1273), no. 30, part 2, pp. 102–6. Under questioning, Baldwin acknowledged, "My literal memory is not good." But he insisted that his ability to recall the substance of what he had heard was "unusually good."

14. Oates, *With Malice Toward None*, pp. 201, 203, 207, 222. Oates cites the Browning diary and the Nicolay memorandum directly. The quotation from the letter to Cameron on p. 203 was taken from Reinhard H. Luthin, *The Real Abraham Lincoln* (Englewood Cliffs, N.J., 1960), p. 248.

15. Oates, *With Malice Toward None*, p. 207; Theodore Calvin Pease and James G. Randall, eds., *The Diary of Orville Hickman Browning* (2 vols.; Springfield, Ill., 1925–33), 1: 453.

16. Oates, *With Malice Toward None*, pp. 197, 198, with quotations from the New York *Tribune*, from Henry Villard's *Lincoln on the Eve* (a collection of dispatches to the New York *Herald*), and from the Philadelphia *Bulletin*, as copied in the New York *Times*, as reprinted in Segal, *Conversations with Lincoln.*

17. Basler et al., *Collected Works*, 7: 101–2; Ludwell H. Johnson, "Lincoln and Equal Rights: The Authenticity of the Wadsworth Letter," *Journal of Southern History*, 32 (1966): 83–87.

18. Basler et al., *Collected Works*, 8: 116–17; Roy P. Basler, "Who Wrote the 'Letter to Mrs. Bixby'?" in his *A Touchstone for Greatness: Essays, Addresses, and Occasional Pieces about Abraham Lincoln* (Westport, Conn., 1973), pp. 110–19.

19. Basler et al., *Collected Works*, 2: 461–62.

20. T. Harry Williams, ed., *Abraham Lincoln: Selected Speeches, Messages, and Letters* (New York, 1957), p. 76; Fehrenbacher, *Abraham Lincoln*, pp. 95–96; Richard N. Current, ed. *The Political Thought of Abraham Lincoln* (Indianapolis, Ind., 1967), pp. 95–96.

21. Paul M. Angle, ed., *Created Equal? The Complete Lincoln-Douglas Debates of 1858* (Chicago, 1958), p. 2.

22. Robert W. Johannsen, *The Lincoln-Douglas Debates of 1858* (New York, 1965), pp. 14–15; John G. Nicolay and John Hay, eds., *Abraham Lincoln, Complete Works: Comprising His Speeches, Letters, State Papers, and Miscellaneous Writings* (2 vols.; New York, 1894), 1: 240–41.

23. William H. Herndon and Jesse W. Weik, *Abraham Lincoln: The True Story of a Great Life* (2 vols.; New York, 1892), 2: 92. In this revised edition of their book, Herndon and Weik printed Horace White's recollection as follows: "I sat at a short distance from Mr. Lincoln when he delivered the "house-divided-against-itself" speech, on the 17th [*sic*] of June. This was delivered from manuscript, and was the only one I ever heard him deliver in that way. When it was concluded he put the manuscript in my hands and asked me to go to the *State Journal* office and read the proof of it. I think it had already been set in type. Before I had finished this task Mr. Lincoln himself came into the composing room of the *State Journal* and looked over the revised proofs. He said to me that he had taken a great deal of pains with this speech, and that he wanted it to go before the people just as he had prepared it."

24. *Political Debates Between Hon. Abraham Lincoln and Hon. Stephen A. Douglas, in the Celebrated Campaign of 1858, in Illinois* . . . (Columbus, Ohio, 1860).

25. Arthur Brooks Lapsley, *The Writings of Abraham Lincoln* (8 vols.; New York, 1905–6), 3: 2–3.

26. Roy P. Basler, *Abraham Lincoln: His Speeches and Writings* (Cleveland, Ohio, 1946), pp. 372–81. The transposing was done by one of the assistant editors of the *Collected Works* in the process of collating the *Journal*

and *Tribune* texts, but Basler, the chief editor, assumes the ultimate responsibility for failing to catch the error. Basler to the author, May 9, 1985.

27. Tyler Dennett, ed., *Lincoln and the Civil War in the Diaries and Letters of John Hay* (New York, 1939), pp. 53, 110; Howard K. Beale, ed., *Diary of Gideon Welles, Secretary of the Navy Under Lincoln and Johnson* (3 vols.; New York, 1960), 2: 112.

28. Carl Sandburg, *Abraham Lincoln: The War Years* (4 vols.; New York, 1939), 3: 523; John Hay, "Life in the White House in the Time of Lincoln," in *The Addresses of John Hay* (New York, 1907), pp. 324–25.

29. Charles B. Strozier, *Lincoln's Quest for Union: Public and Private Meanings* (New York, 1982), pp. 25–28.

30. Basler et al., *Collected Works*, 4: 62. For my critique of Strozier's wild turkey hypothesis, see text, pp. 224–26.

31. Strozier, *Lincoln's Quest for Union*, p. 209.

32. Henry C. Whitney, *Life on the Circuit with Lincoln* (Boston, 1892), pp. 27–28. Strozier cites a later edition, edited by Paul M. Angle (Caldwell, Id., 1940), p. 51.

33. Strozier, *Lincoln's Quest for Union*, p. 259. Angle's introduction to the 1940 edition of *Life on the Circuit* provides information about Whitney's occasionally disreputable role in Lincoln scholarship. Whitney's assertion that he found Lincoln in his office at 2:00 P.M. on Jan. 5, 1859, and spent the rest of the day alone with him, is open to question because records indicate that Lincoln had at least three cases in court on that day.

34. See Basler et al., *Collected Works*, 2: 512–14; 3: 305–6, 519–20; 4: 147. Basler, in *Abraham Lincoln: His Speeches and Writings*, p. 381, calls attention to the comma as an example of how the *State Journal* version of the speech reveals "the oral emphasis Lincoln gave to each sentence, phrase, and word."

35. Paul M. Angle, ed., *Herndon's Life of Lincoln* (Cleveland, Ohio, 1949), pp. 326, 390.

36. As an example, see John D. Milligan, "The Treatment of an Historical Source," *History and Theory*, 18 (1979): 177–96.

37. Basler et al., *Collected Works*, 3: 399.

38. LaWanda Cox, *Lincoln and Black Freedom: A Study in Presidential Leadership* (Columbia, S.C., 1981), pp. 21–22.

39. Basler et al., *Collected Works*, 1: 114.

40. Edmund Wilson, *Patriotic Gore: Studies in the Literature of the American Civil War* (New York, 1962), pp. 106–8; George B. Forgie, *Patricide in the House Divided: A Psychological Interpretation of Lincoln and His Age* (New York, 1979), pp. 61–63, 84–87, and *passim*; Dwight G. Anderson, *Abraham Lincoln: The Quest for Immortality* (New York, 1982), pp. 68–78 and *passim*; Strozier, *Lincoln's Quest for Union*, pp. 59–61; James Hurt, "All the Living and the Dead: Lincoln's Imagery," *American Literature*, 52 (1980–81): 364–68.

41. See Richard N. Current, "Lincoln After 175 Years: The Myth of the Jealous Son," *Papers of the Abraham Lincoln Association*, 6 (1984): 22. Some two years later, in his speech on the Subtreasury proposal, Lincoln re-

ferred to Democratic leaders as "oppressors," and to their party as the "evil spirit" reigning in Washington that constituted a threat to American liberties. Basler et al., *Collected Works*, 1: 178.

42. Anderson, *Abraham Lincoln*, pp. 118–19; Basler et al., *Collected Works*, 2: 404.

43. Basler et al., *Collected Works*, 5: 388–89.

44. *Congressional Globe*, 35 Cong., 1 sess., p. 18.

45. Benjamin P. Thomas, *Abraham Lincoln* (New York, 1952), p. 342. For other discussion of the Greeley letter, see text, p. 109.

46. Albert Shaw, *Abraham Lincoln: The Year of His Election* (New York, 1929), p. 269.

47. Michael Davis, *The Image of Lincoln in the South* (Knoxville, Tenn., 1971), pp. 82–83; London *Times*, Oct. 7, 21, 1862.

48. Wilson, *Patriotic Gore*, pp. 122, 639–41, 643–47.

49. Charles N. Smiley, "Lincoln and Gorgias," *Classical Journal*, 13 (1917–18): 125.

50. Hurt, "All the Living and the Dead"; Theodore C. Blegen, *Lincoln's Imagery: A Study in Word Power* (La Crosse, Wis., 1954).

51. Jacques Barzun, *Lincoln the Literary Genius* (Evanston, Ill., 1960), pp. 26, 36.

52. Webster: "When the mariner has been tossed, for many days, in thick weather, on an unknown sea, he naturally avails himself of the first pause in the storm, the earliest glance of the sun, to take his latitude, and ascertain how far the elements have driven him from his true course." Lincoln: "If we could first know *where* we are, and *whither* we are tending, we could then better judge *what* to do, and *how* to do it." *Register of Debates in Congress*, 21 Cong., 1 sess., p. 58; Basler et al., *Collected Works*, 2: 461. The similarity is pointed out in Albert J. Beveridge, *Abraham Lincoln, 1809–1858* (2 vols.; Boston, 1928), 2: 576–77n.

53. The *Congressional Globe*, 37 Cong., 1 sess., p. 4, quoted Grow as saying: "Fourscore years ago fifty-six bold merchants, farmers, lawyers, and mechanics, the representatives of a few feeble colonists, scattered along the Atlantic sea-board, met in convention to found a new empire, based on the inalienable rights of man." The number "fifty-six" makes it absolutely clear that Grow, like Lincoln at Gettysburg, was talking about the Declaration of Independence, which means that he should have said "fourscore and five years ago." Either his arithmetic was bad, or, more likely, the *Globe*'s stenographer got it wrong. Since Lincoln almost certainly read the report of the opening session of Congress, it is not at all unlikely that the passage caught his eye and was stored in his memory for later use.

54. Basler et al., *Collected Works*, 4: 261–62n, 271. For comparisons of the Seward and Lincoln versions of the paragraph, see Basler, *Touchstone for Greatness*, pp. 99–100; Herbert J. Edwards and John E. Hankins, *Lincoln the Writer: The Development of His Literary Style* (Orono, Me., 1962), pp. 65–66.

Acknowledgments

The following permissions for republication are gratefully acknowledged:

The Abraham Lincoln Association, Springfield, Illinois: "The Anti-Lincoln Tradition," in the Association's *Papers*, 4 (1982).

The American Philosophical Society: "The Election of 1860," in *Crucial American Elections* (1973).

The California Historical Society: "The Mexican War and the Conquest of California," in George H. Knoles, ed., *Essays and Assays: California History Reappraised* (1973).

Civil War History: "Lincoln and Judicial Supremacy: A Note on the Galena Speech of July 23, 1856," 16 (1970); and "Only His Stepchildren: Lincoln and the Negro," 20 (1974). Copyright © 1970 and 1974 by the Kent State University Press.

Journal of the Illinois State Historical Society: "The Post Office in Illinois Politics of the 1850's," 46 (1953); and "Lincoln and the Weight of Responsibility," 68 (1975).

The Lincoln Memorial Shrine, Redlands, California: *The Death of Lincoln* (1983).

The Louis A. Warren Lincoln Library and Museum, Fort Wayne, Indiana: *The Minor Affair: An Adventure in Forgery and Detection* (1979).

Oxford University Press: *The Changing Image of Lincoln in American Historiography* (1968).

Pacific Historical Review: "The New Political History and the Coming of the Civil War," 54 (1985). Copyright © 1985 by the Pacific Coast Branch of the American Historical Association.

The Pennsylvania State University Press: "Lincoln and the Paradoxes of Freedom," in Norman A. Graebner, ed., *Freedom in America: A 200-Year Perspective* (1977).

Reviews in American History: "In Quest of the Psychohistorical Lincoln," 11 (1983). Copyright © 1983 by The Johns Hopkins University Press.

Southern Illinois University Press: "Lincoln and the Constitution," in Cullom Davis et al., eds., *The Public and the Private Lincoln: Contemporary Perspectives* (1979). Copyright © 1979 by Sangamon State University.

The University of Illinois Press: "The Republican Decision at Chicago," in Norman A. Graebner, ed., *Politics and the Crisis of 1860* (1961), © 1961 by the Board of Trustees of the University of Illinois.

The University of Massachusetts Press: "The Words of Lincoln," in John L. Thomas, ed., *Abraham Lincoln and the American Political Tradition* (1986).

Wisconsin Magazine of History: "Lincoln and the Mayor of Chicago," 40 (1957). Copyright © 1957 by The State Historical Society of Wisconsin.

Index

Library of Congress Cataloging-in-Publication Data

Fehrenbacher, Don Edward, 1920–
Lincoln in text and context.

Bibliography: p.
Includes index.
1. Lincoln, Abraham, 1809–1865. 2. Presidents—United States—Biography. I. Title.
E457.8.F28 1987 973.7'092'4 [B] 86-14346
ISBN 0-8047-1329-4 (alk. paper)